HONOR ON THE LINE

HONOR ON THE LINE

The Fifth Down
and the
Spectacular 1940 College Football Season

Robert J. Scott
and
Myles A. Pocta

iUniverse, Inc.
Bloomington

Honor on the Line
The Fifth Down and the Spectacular 1940 College Football Season

iUniverse books may be ordered through booksellers or by contacting:

iUniverse
1663 Liberty Drive
Bloomington, IN 47403
www.iuniverse.com
1-800-Authors (1-800-288-4677)

ISBN: 978-1-4759-3208-9 (sc)
ISBN: 978-1-4759-3209-6 (e)
ISBN: 978-1-4759-3210-2 (dj)

Library of Congress Control Number: 2012910252

Printed in the United States of America

iUniverse rev. date: 8/20/2012

Cover art: Ben Hamrick

Soon fades the spell, soon comes the night;
Say will it not be then the same,
Whether we played the black or white,
Whether we lost or won the game?

--THOMAS MACAULEY, *Sermon in a Churchyard*

Contents

ACKNOWLEDGEMENTS

There are many people we wish to thank for their help in completing this book. Jim Richards, Bill Macali, Scott Cash, Tony South, and Joe Flanagan gave generously of their time and advice. Jim Ducibella's assistance was more than generous and his encouragement was critical. Glenn Altschuler and Jim Roberts were quick to respond when we asked for help, and their direction led us to new insights and a much better outcome. Gloria Bardeau Smith, Bruce Smith, Jr., Father Michael Martin, and Father William Cantwell kindly and graciously shared their memories. Our editor, Sofia Starnes, not only corrected our numerous mistakes patiently but also kept our belief in the project strong. The staff at the Virginia Beach Public Libraries was diligent, energetic, and unfailingly helpful. Finally, our wives, Rene' and Denise, offered their technical advice as well as their patience and understanding, without which none of this would have been possible.

We also thank our parents, Alan and Verna Pocta and Ed and Jeanette Scott, whose work ethic, integrity and passion provided a special example and inspiration for this book.

INTRODUCTION

What would it take, in the 21st Century, for a major college football team, ranked second in the nation and in the midst of the chase for the national championship, to consider forfeiting a game? What would it take for that team to surrender victory after the game was won, even though its victory had followed all accepted rules and practices? What would it take for that team to put an end to its long winning streak, its undefeated season, and any hopes for a national championship? Today major teams play in stadiums that cost more than a billion dollars. Some football coaches are paid over five million dollars annually. Assistant coaches sometimes earn more than college presidents. Winning college football is an industry unto itself. Millions of people tune in to watch each televised contest, all for the purpose of fulfilling the seemingly irresistible urge to single out one team as champion of the entire nation. Forfeit? Inconceivable.

On November 16, 1940, a legendary Cornell football team, among the best in the country, forfeited a victory and a possible national championship when it discovered a grievous error by the game official in awarding an extra down on the last and deciding play of the game. The victorious team was already on the train returning home. Thousands of alumni who had made the long trip to the game and sat through a cold snowy afternoon were rejoicing at gatherings all over town. Victory songs had risen and echoed for hours. The scores had been widely broadcast over the airwaves; reporters had already written the next day's newspaper accounts. It would have been so easy to let the disputed ending stand. Yet, the events of that afternoon, and over the following days, stand as a hallmark of integrity. They remind us anew why sports are important.

Nearly every day the sports sections brim with stories of human failure— cheating, lying, cover-ups, and worse. Modern society seems to embrace bad news, and the opportunities for tales of woe, even in sports, are abundant. But the world of sports has far more to offer. Its history over the years is rich in examples of human character laid bare and affirmed through competition. And what greater story could there be than one of victory, hard-earned, yielded in the name of fairness? We decided to investigate.

The ranks of those who remember the events of that day have thinned with the years, and memories have dimmed. But the newspapers and magazines of the era, reliable and unerring, tell a thrilling story. Among the ads for Stetson hats, Blackstone cigars, and Oldsmobiles with hydra-matic transmissions, we discovered an account far richer than we could have imagined. Not only was the Cornell team of 1940 a great team, it was also regarded by many as the best in the country, undefeated for more than two years. Its gesture rocked the football world. And the journals of the day reveal even more. If it is true that we are known by the company we keep, then the Cornell story benefits tremendously from its unfolding in the midst of the illustrious 1940 season. That same year, Tom Harmon of Michigan dominated college football as few players ever have; Clark Shaughnessy had the ingenuity and boldness to introduce the T-formation at Stanford and with it guide the greatest turnaround in college football history; and the Notre Dame legend came alive on the screen only to fizzle on the field. That year, too, Leonard Bates and Lou Montgomery were kept from competition because of the color of their skin. The discrimination against them launched a wave of rebellion that would reverberate through the civil rights movement of later years. And for one incomparable season, college players all over the country enjoyed their last gridiron fling before war overtook them—and took over their lives.

The Fifth Down—as the controversy would inevitably be called—was an event that sparked passionate discussions in the fall of 1940; decades later, it would evoke only occasional knowing nods; today, it is in danger of slipping altogether from our collective recollection. But it is important that this story not be relegated to that bin of dim and distant memories known as sports trivia; it is a testament to human character too important for that.

Today's fans may find it hard to believe that there was a time when Ivy League teams were powerful forces in the game, and television was not; when leather helmets were commonplace, and plays signaled in from the coach's box were not; when black players did not venture on the field, and 60-minute players never came off. We believe this story will convince them that there was a time, in the midst of turmoil, imminent war, and conflicting social mores, when honor ruled the day.

CHAPTER 1
THE CONTENDERS

Fire is the test of gold; adversity, of strong men.

--SENECA, *Moral Essays*

By the second week of September, while the warm days of summer dwindled to a last precious few, the leaves high on the hillsides of upstate New York had already begun to change colors. The fall of 1940, local residents later insisted, would be the most spectacular fall foliage season in many years. Already the crisp bite of autumn was in the night air, and the sumac and the goldenrod were staging their opening acts. First a random leaf would turn around the edges, then a lone tree would stand out from its neighbors still cloaked in their green summer hues. Soon the landscape would be awash in the vibrant russets of the oaks and the brilliant ochres of the poplars. On the campus of Cornell University in Ithaca, overlooking Lake Cayuga, the ivy-covered walls prepared for a scintillating fashion show, when they would soon take on a brilliant scarlet hue. The leaves, it seemed, could hardly wait to burst forth. The early colors, shimmering in the late summer breeze, were a harbinger of a spectacular autumn to come.

When Coach Carl Snavely greeted the Cornell football team for the first day of fall practice on September 11, about two weeks before the rest of the student body arrived on campus for classes, he had every reason for optimism. Since his arrival in 1936, Snavely had presided over a resurgence of Cornell football that had lifted it from a winless season in 1935 under his predecessor, Gil Dobie, to a spot among the national elite by 1938, a year in which Cornell lost only one game. And 1939 had been even better. Cornell finished the season undefeated with a perfect 8-0 record and ranked fourth in the country by the Associated Press. Two rating systems, Sagarin and Litkenhous, had declared Cornell the national champion, and it counted among its victories an impressive win over the Big Ten champion Ohio State in Columbus. The team had received an informal bid to the Rose Bowl, which it declined. Its bowl policy, shared by a number of schools, including most of the schools of the Ivy League and the Big Ten, was that eight games per year was an appropriate limit. And Cornell had not lost since the 1938 Syracuse contest, an undefeated

1

stretch of twelve games punctuated only by a Thanksgiving Day scoreless tie with Penn.

As Snavely sketched out in his mind the starting lineup for the Big Red, he had every one of the eleven spots tentatively taken by a senior, and every one of those seniors had started at least one game the year before. In 1939, the team captain, fullback Vince Eichler, had been hurt and lost for the season before the first game, and now, with him healed and ready to return, Snavely saw no opening for him among the starting eleven. Indeed, of the regular starters from the previous year, only halfback Whit Baker was missing due to graduation. The second team, tentatively, was nearly as experienced, with two juniors in an otherwise all-senior lineup. Of the projected traveling squad of 33 players, 24 were seniors. Several prognosticators were indicating that Cornell's team might be even better than the 1939 version.

But Snavely was not an optimistic man by nature, and his biggest obstacle in 1940 could have been the high expectations set by others. The success of the 1939 team, the return of veterans nearly three-deep at every position, and the nearly unanimous opinion of the experts that Cornell would be an eastern powerhouse left Snavely little room for failure. The toughest team on the schedule appeared again to be Ohio State, and the only question from detached observers seemed to be whether the Big Red could repeat its 1939 victory over the Buckeyes. Snavely would not be able to feign weakness. Too many people knew how good his team would be. Stanley Woodward of the *New York Herald Tribune* wrote, "Theoretically this Cornell team is one of the greatest that ever has stepped out ready made on a football field," and added, "Snavely maintains the same mournful mien that he has been so successful in projecting in the past...."[1] *Look*, in its annual preseason football forecast, warned, "Carl Snavely is always moaning. Don't listen to him."[2] Snavely was not beyond trying, however. "We ought to win at least two games this year," was his droll prediction for the season.[3]

Snavely was unusual among major college football coaches of the day in that he was not himself a product of a major college program. Born the son of a minister in Omaha, Nebraska, and raised in Danville, Pennsylvania, he played his college football at Lebanon Valley College in Annville, Pennsylvania, where he was team captain his senior year. California's Stub Allison and Colgate's Andy Kerr were, along with Snavely, among only a handful of major college coaches with small-college backgrounds. Snavely had coached at Bucknell and North Carolina before coming to Cornell in 1936. He shared with his Cornell predecessor Gil Dobie, nicknamed "Gloomy Gil", a dour outlook on life, though not Dobie's abrasive edge. His humor, only seldom coming forth, was of the driest variety. He was often tight-lipped with the press, and served as a brick wall of protection around his players. Though he often gave one-word answers to reporters hungry for a scoop, the press loved to tease him about his peculiar ways, and he seemed to take the ribbing well. He could, from time to time, open up to the point that he was generally well liked, despite his aloofness. John Kieran of the *New York Times* called him "an apple-a-day and early-to-bed fellow of simple rustic background and native habits."[4] Though intense at times, often to the point of being considered unfriendly, he had outside interests, most notably golf. His friends complained of his slow play on the links, since his gridiron perfectionist tendencies carried over to the golf course.

One columnist noted that he had smiled twice during one game, thus using up his allotment for the rest of the year, and had only one chuckle left until November.[5] But they all respected him for his coaching abilities, his fanatic attention to detail, and his demand of perfection. The *New York Times,* in a tribute to Snavely's abilities, called the 1939 Cornell team a "beautifully coordinated unit, thoroughly grounded in the fundamentals of blocking and tackling and almost letter perfect in the mastery of its offensive and defensive assignments."[6] Snavely was a pioneer in the use of movies to analyze his team's performance. His first camera operator had been his wife Bernyce, but he gradually came to trust others. His well-drilled teams exhibited qualities reporters could recognize and respect, and Snavely had a bank of good will built up with them. By the end of the year he would need it.

While many of the coaches, following in the footsteps of Notre Dame great Knute Rockne, built their team around a star player, Snavely rejected the idea. He molded his team based on balance and teamwork, not on the star system, as at Michigan, or on a run-first approach, as at Minnesota, or on startling new ideas, as at Stanford. Snavely differed from Rockne in his approach to the passing game, as well. When it came to passing, Rockne was more guarded as a coach than he had been as a player, and he once said, "The pass is like a lot of dangerous things in life...if it cannot be controlled, it's wisest to stay away from it before it ruins you."[7] Others had equal disdain for passing. "A good running game behind good blocking is the smartest game....Passing is a gambler's game," said Minnesota's Bernie Bierman dismissively.[8] Snavely's approach to football strategy differed as well from that of his predecessor, Dobie. While Dobie's ideas gravitated to simplistic between-the-tackle running, he never acknowledged the need to adjust to new developments, to exploit the passing game, or to develop defenses against it.

Snavely had quality depth at every position, and he loved to pass. Of the two features that would characterize the Cornell team under Snavely, one would be the aerial game. The other was the players' seemingly instinctive brainy grasp of the game. When he praised his team, which was occasionally, Snavely emphasized the players' intellectual qualities. "The boys are far above average intellectually and this gives them additional ability to absorb," he said.[9]

Team captain Walt Matuszczak, called a "flawless blocker and chess-brained field general" by *Illustrated Football Annual,*[10] seemed a perfect man for the job. The youngest of ten children of a dairy farmer from upstate Lowville, New York, on the edge of the Adirondacks, Matuszczak aspired to be a veterinarian upon graduation, and his low-key personality seemed an ideal fit for the situation. Snavely's offense relegated him to the role of signal-caller and blocking back, and he hardly ever carried the ball or even touched it except to hand it to another player. Matuszczak took great pleasure in his work, and he was rivaled in his claim as best at his position in the country only by Michigan's Forest Evashevski. "Matuszczak has few peers as a blocker. He loves to bowl them over," said the Associated Press.[11] As to the obscurity that role brought him, "I have no further ambitions," he said. His idea of fun was to call the signals in the huddle in Polish, a language in which he and teammate Mike Ruddy, but no other player, were fluent.[12]

The football players of the day, due in large part to the limited substitution rule and the single-wing offense, could not claim to be specialists—passers, kickers, defensive backs—but instead of necessity were well rounded football players. Similarly, many of them were not exclusively football players, but versatile athletes, often involved in a number of varsity sports. Cornell provided a good example. The baseball team, for instance, looked much like the football team. Backs Walt Scholl and Lou Bufalino held down the infield corners, third base and first base, respectively; the outfield had end Al Kelley in left field, quarterback Mike Ruddy in center, and Matuszczak in right; center Bud Finneran was behind the plate, and the pitching was handled largely by halfback Walt Sickles and end Ray Jenkins. All these men played prominent roles on the football team. Additionally, Howie Dunbar, starting guard on the football team, was also starting center on the basketball team; and the track team had tackle Fred West, shotputter, and end Jim Schmuck, quarter miler, who were both starters on the football team, as well as Hal McCullough, Kirk Hershey, and Swifty Borhman.

When it came to post-season honors, it was Matuszczak who received attention from the Heisman Trophy balloters, while tackle Nick Drahos, from Cedarhurst, New York, the fifth of 12 children of Czech parents, would be accorded All-America honors for the second year in a row. The mainstay of the team, the man who logged more playing time than any other, was 176-pound center Bud Finneran from Harrison, New Jersey. But when asked which of the Big Red they feared the most, opposing coaches usually identified Mort Landsberg, from Mamaroneck, New York, who played fullback on offense and safety on defense. The speedy Landsberg was given a chance to play when Vince Eichler was injured, and even the former team captain couldn't earn his spot back from him. In the 1940 NFL draft, Mort Landsberg was the last player chosen, but after playing a year of pro football with the Philadelphia Eagles he entered the Navy to become a fighter pilot. In the George Bush Presidential Library there is a photograph, taken in July of 1943, of the ten men of Flight 44, Fort Lauderdale Naval Air Station. In the back row, fourth from the left, stands the future 41st President, George Herbert Walker Bush. Next to him, to his immediate right, stands Mort Landsberg.[13]

Snavely's emphasis on teamwork over individual performance allowed him to play skilled but smaller performers at key positions. While Drahos, West, Dunbar, Hershey, and Matuszczak were well above average in size, Finneran, Landsberg, Lou Conti, Kelley, Scholl, and McCullough were undersized, and their skills might have been lost in the system of another coach.

One reporter, after an interview with Snavely, managed entry into the Cornell locker room and was shocked at what he found. There was a radio playing loud swing music, Bud Finneran was playing a makeshift drum set with a washboard, Al Kelley was tap-dancing on a trainer's table, and the spontaneous joyous party atmosphere was rivaled only by what the reporter said he once saw in the New York Yankee locker room after a World Series victory. Snavely knew all about it, the players claimed, and did not object. The coach might have been dour, but Cornell had a very happy football team.[14]

Football writers, perhaps a bit frustrated by the highly cautious nature of the coaches of the day, especially when discussing their teams' prospects for the season, teased them all mercilessly, and Snavely in particular. His unrelenting pessimism, given all he had to be optimistic about, was more than the writers could abide without resorting to poking fun. They stood by slack-jawed as Snavely pronounced, "Colgate should lick us, believe it or not," and "It's ridiculous for anyone to expect us to beat Ohio State." He said he expected the Buckeyes to "murder us."[15]

"Cornell's football chances for 1940 are doubtful," summed up sportswriter John Lardner. "Texas A&M is doubtful. Georgia Tech is doubtful. Indiana is very, very doubtful. Columbia is extremely doubtful." Lardner teased that those were the only teams whose coaches he had talked to so far. What, in the case of Cornell, whose prospects to any reasonable person seemed so shiningly bright, was doubtful, Lardner wondered.[16] It was the time of year when football coaches donned their sackcloth and ashes and dabbed at their eyes with crying towels, answered the *Reno Evening Gazette*. "There is, of course, the possibility that one or more of the Cornell players will go to a circus and get mauled by a lion," it suggested as the only possible doubt.[17] Snavely took it all pretty well.

Despite outward appearances, Carl Snavely knew he had a team fully capable of winning the national championship by acclaim. But he knew as well that there were many teams that would challenge his for the title. In the next two months some would fall by the wayside, others would unexpectedly join the challenge, and all would be buffeted by the winds of fortune, both good and bad. Talent would be a prerequisite, Snavely knew, but it alone would not be enough. The only thing that could alleviate the preseason anxiety was opening day, when all the loose and airy talk of prospects would be replaced, as it always was, by more solid talk of achievement. Like the autumn leaves on the Ithaca hillsides, the Cornell football team couldn't wait to burst out. But fans, students, alumni, and the players and coaches would all have to wait until October 5, a week later than for most teams.

Some enthusiastic followers expressed impatience that Snavely would not step forward and embrace the great prospects of his team. Others came to his defense. "Nothing quite as promising had been seen since Napoleon started out to Moscow with the Grand Army behind him," wrote athletic manager-turned-columnist Rym Berry of the Cornell team. "But every football coach knows that the road to Moscow leads also to Elba and to St. Helena....The mob wants Napoleon to look at them and say, 'We'll take 'em, boys, we'll take 'em.' But with the inexorable certainty of Elba and St. Helena pressing on his heart, the coach says no such thing. And the mob snarls!"[18]

****

The crowd of 35,401 fans in Memorial Stadium in Berkeley, California, craned their necks to get a better look at Tom Harmon standing on the goal line ready to receive the opening kickoff. It was September 28, 1940, and at last the beginning of one of the most tumultuous college football seasons in history was moments away. The crowd that was gathered to watch the Michigan Wolverines play the California Golden Bears had all heard plenty about Harmon, perhaps the most famous player in America, but few had ever seen him play. By the end of last season his picture had already appeared on the cover of *Time* magazine, which proclaimed him "the No. 1 footballer of the year."[19] Neither had many in the crowd ever seen the powerful Wolverine team play, since its last trip west had been to the inaugural 1902 Rose Bowl. Intersectional games, though not rare, were logistically challenging, often involving three or four days of travel in each direction. The fact that Michigan represented the Western Conference, which played its games 1500 miles to the east, underscored the status of the West Coast as something of an outpost when it came to sports in general and college football in particular. It would be seven years before major league football, and 18 years before major league baseball, ventured west, and visits to the west by distant teams in any sport were significant undertakings.

Great things had been expected of Michigan the year before, until two consecutive losses to Illinois and Minnesota had dashed the Wolverines' lofty hopes. But with the opportunity to start afresh, and with Harmon, runner-up in the 1939 Heisman Trophy race to Iowa's Nile Kinnick, still in the fold, they were again considered strong candidates to compete with Ohio State and Northwestern for the championship of the Western Conference (still nicknamed the Big Ten despite being diluted to nine teams by the departure of Chicago). And they could be expected to contend as well with Texas A&M, the national champion of 1939, at least according to the Associated Press, with powerful southern teams Tulane and Tennessee, and with eastern powers

Boston College and Cornell for what people were calling the "mythical" national championship. The crowd was anxious to see if this man and this team could live up to their advance billing.

In the 1940 Michigan team photo, Tom Harmon, sitting in the front row, is distinctive. His fine though handsomely rugged features are accented by a nose, slightly but pleasantly battered, and by a shock of wavy brown hair. In contrast, to his left, holding the ball that designates him as team captain, sits his backfield mate, Forest Evashevski. Whereas Harmon is all angles, Evashevski, with his lantern jaw and treetrunk legs, is all squareness. At 200 pounds and with a mischievous grin across his face, Evashevski, a converted lineman, looks like he was born to knock an opponent cockeyed, and indeed he once said he didn't want to play football unless he could "crack 'em."[20] If one who knew nothing about Michigan football were asked to pick from that photo the fastest man on the team, his eyes would likely gravitate toward Harmon. His lean 197 pound frame, even from a sitting pose, screamed speed. If one were to pick from the photo the man most likely to lay down the block that would spring him on one of his long runs, the barrel-chested Evashevski would pop from the page. He was black and blue waiting to happen.

On the broad shoulders of these two men rested the hopes that the season would add to the legend created by the one who appears between them. There, dressed in a formal three-piece suit, ankles crossed in a pose practiced for photographers for decades, sits Fielding Yost, the athletic director, a distinctive looking gentleman of advanced age. He could easily be mistaken for a physics professor emeritus.

Fielding "Hurry Up" Yost presided over virtually the entirety of the Michigan football tradition. Forty years before, at the turn of the century, his point-a-minute teams began a streak of five seasons in which they outscored their opponents by a collective margin of 2,821-42. They beat Stanford, the school Yost left to move to Michigan, in the first Rose Bowl, 49-0, in a game terminated midway through the third period by mutual agreement and in which Michigan outgained Stanford 503 yards to 67 (the Rose Bowl was not played again until 1916).[21] Until they were beaten by Chicago in 1905, the Michigan Wolverines dominated the scene of college football. Just as tall tales spread among ancient mariners about giant sea serpents and multi-headed fire-breathing sea dragons who could swallow ships whole, so Wolverine opponents spread stories about eight-ton players with eight pairs of arms who could run 96 miles per hour and toss helpless victims over their shoulder.[22] Yost did little to quell this hyperbole. "Who are they to beat a Michigan team?" he routinely said of his opponents. "They're only human."[23]

Michigan teams continued among the most prominent in the nation for the next three decades, including teams of the mid-'20s that featured Wolverine legends Benny Friedman and Bennie Oosterbaan. But it was not until 1932 and 1933, when it compiled a 15-0-1 record over the two years, that Michigan again claimed the national championship. Yost, who had retired as coach following the 1926 season, stayed on as athletic director, and one of his first acts was to see to completion the construction of Michigan Stadium, a huge 84,000-seat venue, which has been expanded since, a number of times. But those two championships were followed by four years without a winning season, during which time their best player was center and future President Gerald Ford. In 1938 Fritz Crisler took over as coach of the moribund program with change in mind.

Herbert Orin Crisler played his college football at the University of Chicago where his coach was the venerable Amos Alonzo Stagg. One day, after Crisler, who played end, fumbled the ball three times in succession, Stagg bestowed on him the nickname Fritz. Stagg said it was in honor of the German violinist Fritz Kreisler, whose name was pronounced the same but to whose talented artistry the abilities of his charge bore absolutely no resemblance.[24] Crisler bore a lifelong fondness for Stagg, whom he always referred to as "the old man," and kept the nickname he bestowed upon him for the rest of his life. After serving as Stagg's assistant, Crisler moved on to head coaching jobs at Minnesota and Princeton before arriving in Ann Arbor in 1938. In the team photo, Crisler sits off to the side, away from the center, out of the limelight.

One of Crisler's first acts was to restore pride to a fallen program, and he believed no detail too small for his attention. His redesign of the team's helmet, including the winged emblem across the front, has remained the icon of Michigan football. And Crisler's fresh new ideas about employment of the single wing seemed to fit perfectly with his new talented backfield. In addition to Harmon and Evashevski, he also had available to him standout backfield men Norm Call and Bob Westfall. Three years before, Crisler had persuaded Dave Allerdice, whose father had been Wolverine captain in 1909, to attend Princeton instead of Michigan, and after Crisler left, Allerdice remained at Princeton, where he enjoyed a stellar career as a passing halfback. Had Allerdice, too, been in the Michigan backfield, football history might have turned out differently.[25]

Unlike Michigan's first trip to the west coast in 1902, which had taken eight days, this trip was accomplished by a party of 51 members in two days, with a fleet of three United Airlines DC-3 airplanes. It was one of the first times a college football team had ever traveled to a game by air—Pitt had flown to Seattle to play Washington in 1939[26] — and the first time many of the players had ever been in an airplane. Nearly the entire team suffered from airsickness, and the entourage landed for an overnight stay in Denver, both to refuel and to work out a bit, hoping to shake the effects of travel. The team, like a traveling football circus, attracted a throng of curious spectators.[27] The planes were scheduled to make a second stop in Salt Lake City, and by the time they were done, the players had taken a strong liking to the new mode of travel. "Great stuff, this flying," said coach Crisler.[28]

So there at the goal line stood Harmon, on his twenty-first birthday, wearing number 98 on his blue and maize jersey, chinstrap fastened under his leather helmet decorated across the front with the now-familiar Michigan wing. Ankle-high cleats tested the turf, his heavy thigh pads in thick togs stopped just above bare calves, and the cuffs of his long-sleeve jersey were, as always, pushed up above his elbows. It was his personal fashion statement. He looked every bit the football hero he had already been made out to be. If the lofty expectations laid out for him placed any additional weight on his shoulders there was no outward evidence of it. In the stands, the fans waited for their answers. Just how good was Harmon? And how good were the Wolverines?

The referee's whistle sounded, the ball rocketed into the air, and fifteen seconds later, Harmon stood in the far end zone, having taken the ball at the six yard line, picked up a few good blocks and raced untouched 94 yards for a touchdown. Soon afterward, the Wolverines missed a second Harmon touchdown opportunity when one of his passes was dropped on the goal line.[29] Early in the second period Harmon fielded a punt near his own 28-yard line, dropped it, went back ten yards to pick it back up, dodged and darted between the Cal defenders, and then, finally in the clear, dashed for the end zone. He was credited with a 72-yard run, although he may have traveled twice that far. Harmon's third touchdown came later in the second period when he raced 86 yards for a score on a reverse. With six minutes left in the half, Harmon took to the bench, having scored all 21 points in the game, and did not return until the fourth quarter. He then scored a fourth touchdown on an eight yard run, and capped the scoring by throwing a five-yard touchdown pass to Dave Nelson. Michigan won handily by a final score of 41-0. California had a good football team, but the Michigan attack rendered its defense "about as strong as a wet paper bag," said the *New York Times*.[30] On offense, Cal was never able to pass midfield. The fans had their answers.

Harmon's play was magnificent. Not only did he display formidable speed and power, but he combined it with a baffling change of pace and an inner sense of how to follow his blockers in the open field.[31] And though the self-effacing Harmon said of his day, "I played sloppy ball," nobody accepted that assessment. "I've never seen anybody run like Harmon. He was really something special," said Cal end Ray Dunn.[32] If there had been any questions to begin with, neither Harmon nor the Wolverines left any unanswered by the end of the game. They were both for real.

The day had a comical moment to break up the monotony of Michigan dominance. During Harmon's third touchdown run, the 86-yarder, a Cal fan named Bud Brennan broke through lax security and ran onto the field. He was apparently well into his afternoon's libations and was determined to achieve what none of the Golden Bears had been able bring about. He set up his defensive position at the one-yard line and, as Harmon approached

9

with the Bear defenders in fruitless pursuit, the drunken fan took a swipe at Harmon that did little to bolster his later claim that he had once been a football player.

Brennan's version, less truthful but more colorful, appeared with a full photographic spread the following week in *Life* magazine. He seemed genuinely surprised when the men who grabbed him by the neck in the end zone turned out to be two police officers.[33]

Down at the station house, to the delight of reporters, Brennan continued his story. He was determined to celebrate fully his moment of fame, and proved to be a voluble and uninhibited storyteller who delighted reporters with his detailed if fantasized account of his exploit. He was booked for disturbing the peace, and the charges were suspended subject to his good behavior for a year and a day, during which time he was forbidden to leave his seat during a football game. To criticism that his tackle attempt lacked style he admitted to being "a little stiffo." He then contended, "It would have been a different story, though, if I had been cold sober."[34]

Harmon's heroics and Brennan's caper were the highlights of the newsreels that flooded the nation's theaters the next week. The number of people who had not heard of Tom Harmon quickly dwindled. "If I counted the number of people who said they had been in the stands for that game in Berkeley it would have to be three million, easy," Harmon said years later. "If I counted the number of people who said they saw it in their local theater, it would be twenty million."[35]

****

In 1940, a new Studebaker automobile could be purchased for $690, a new Plymouth for $780. Those desiring fancier cars could buy a new Pontiac 6-cylinder Torpedo for $828 or a new Chrysler, complete with cigar lighter, for $895. No man's dress wardrobe was complete without stylish headwear, and a snappy Stetson hat sold for $7.50. A dollar bought four pairs of socks or two ties. A dress shirt cost $2.50, a topcoat $25, and a new men's suit $20. An experienced tool and die maker could earn a dollar an hour, a good secretary got paid $30 per week, an accountant $125 per month. A three-piece maple bedroom set from W&J Sloane on Fifth Avenue sold for $99.50 on sale, and at Gimbel's 98th Anniversary Sale a plush living room chair was available for $44. A seven-room house with a two-car garage in Bergen County, New Jersey, twenty minutes from New York City, sold for $5200, and a nine-room house with detached three-car garage in Hartford, Connecticut, for $7500. Among the hot movies that fall were Bing Crosby and Mary Martin in "Rhythm on the River," Loretta Young and Melvyn Douglas in "He Stayed for Breakfast," and Mickey Rooney and Judy Garland in "Strike Up the Band." Tickets usually cost a quarter, but the matinee at the Aster Theater in Minneapolis, with Cesar Romero starring in "The Gay Caballero," cost only 15 cents. On Broadway,

Alfred Lunt and Lynne Fontanne starred in "There Shall Be No Night." The most popular book of the fall was Walter Van Tilburg Clark's "The Ox-Bow Incident," a western with a message, but most were waiting for the release of the highly touted "For Whom the Bell Tolls," by Ernest Hemingway. Glenn Miller had the two most popular musical hits of the year, "When You Wish Upon a Star" and "In the Mood." Among the most notable innovations of the year were Oldsmobile's clutchless hydra-matic transmission and Borden's new homogenized milk, endorsed by the Dionne quintuplets.

The world has changed dramatically since that fall, and so has the game of football. Its ledger sheet has been completely reconstructed, altering forever its importance to the universities, the fans, the coaches, and the players. College football as played in 1940 was not better or worse than the modern version, just distinctive, with its own unique flavor. Most of the difference centered on the highly restrictive rules of substitution then in effect. Simply put, the rule was this. If a player left the game in any quarter for a substitute, he could not re-enter the game within that quarter. Thus, in one respect, football in 1940 more closely resembled modern baseball than modern football, where substitutions are essentially unlimited.

This factor placed a great burden on the coach to devise an effective substitution strategy within the game. A careless removal of a player could well result in his loss for the remainder of the quarter or the game, and leaving a player in too long in a hard-fought game, like leaving a pitcher in the game too long in baseball, could give a huge advantage to the opponent.

The most obvious impact of the rule was that all players had to be skilled at both offense and defense and play both throughout the game. There was no stream of specialists coming onto the field periodically. When the ball changed hands, the players stayed on the field. Guards became linebackers, fullbacks became defensive backs, and blockers became tacklers. If you couldn't block, you didn't play. If you couldn't tackle, you didn't play. If you didn't have the stamina to last forty or more minutes in the game, you might get some playing time, but you most likely would be relegated to the second or third team, no matter how good you were at any individual skill.

The rule strongly dictated the type of athlete to play the game. The primary attributes of a star player were speed, strength, stamina, durability and, above all, versatility. To meet all these criteria, the players were, as a group, substantially smaller than the players of today. "Football is not and should not be a game for the strong and stupid," explained Knute Rockne. "It should be a game for the smart, the swift, the brave and the clever boy."[36] Nile Kinnick, the 1939 Heisman Trophy winner, was only 5' 8" tall and weighed 170 pounds. The winner of the award the year before, Davey O'Brien, weighed only 150 pounds. The most celebrated linemen of the era, Fordham's Seven Blocks of Granite, which included Alex Wojciechowicz, Vince Lombardi, and Harry Jacunski, among others, were all small, and Al Babartsky was the largest of them at 220 pounds. Wojciechowicz, rated one of the best centers of all time, weighed only about 180 pounds.[37] None of the Four Horsemen of Notre Dame, the most famous backfield from 15 years before, weighed more than 165 pounds. While the size of players, especially linemen, has increased in recent years, such giants had no place in the game of 1940. "You can't carry 300 pounds and play 60 minutes of football," explained Coach T.J. Troup. "You'd drop from exhaustion before halftime."[38] "They'd run out of gas," said Chuck Bednarik of Penn, one of the greatest two-way players of all time. "Before the half, they'd be suckin' and huffin' and puffin'."[39]

There was no room for specialization. Place kickers, holders, punters, nickel backs, third down backs, long snappers, return specialists, drop-back quarterbacks, and behemoth run-stuffing defensive tackles are all integral parts of today's game, and coaches routinely take them out of and put them into the game when specific circumstances dictate. But in 1940, when it was time to kick a field goal, the attempting team had to have somebody among the eleven on the field who could snap, hold, and kick, or risk losing a key player to substitution for a substantial period or the remainder of the game.

And they had to have somebody among the eleven who could punt. The strategy of the day was one of field position, a factor deemed much more important than possession of the ball. Thus punting was more frequent, and often occurred before fourth down, especially when a team had unfavorable field position. The resulting games were low-scoring. When on November 9, 1940, Manhattan beat Marquette by a sore of 45-41, a game that would have been thought of as a high-scoring contest in any era, it was a positively jaw-dropping event.[40] After a coach in a 2009 NFL game made the risky decision not to punt in a critical situation, the *Wall Street Journal* wrote, "Somehow in American football, the punt—a clear and unambiguous symbol of surrender and retreat—has become the hallmark of sensible coaching."[41] In reality it has always been such a hallmark. What has evolved is the punt's status as a symbol of retreat rather than a symbol of attack. In the strategy prevalent in 1940 a punt was often a daring and aggressive move intended to pin an opponent deep in his own territory.

Thus the kicking game played a different role in 1940, less emphasized but more important. In the 1940 season there were more than 40 games decided by a score of 7-6, the winner of each determined by a missed extra point.[42] In the modern game, when every team is well skilled in the extra point, usually with a specialist who has no other responsibilities, it seldom serves as a deciding factor in the game.

Most coaches of the day believed that the ideal offense was the single wing, in which the ball was directly snapped back a few yards to one of the halfbacks, who then ran with it, handed it off, or passed the ball. Like almost everything in football, the single wing was not new in 1940. It had been devised in 1906 by Pop Warner while coaching at Cornell.[43] When Warner moved on to the Carlisle Indian School he used it to take maximum advantage of the skills of one of the finest athletes of all time, the great Jim Thorpe. He called it the Carlisle formation. Three decades later, the single wing had become not just the prevalent offense in college football but also the one almost universally used. But as with all ideas in football, each coach added his own wrinkle or made his own adjustment to suit his preference and the talent at hand. Knute Rockne at Notre Dame, for instance, had his own version, called the Notre Dame Box, which involved a backfield shift just before the snap. His refinement quickly was copied at college after college. The Wildcat Offense, introduced at the University of Arkansas in 2006 by offensive coach Gus Malzahn and now making its way gradually through the college ranks and back into the pro game, is nothing if not a revised form of the old single wing.[44] Predictably, others claim Malzahn knocked off their idea.

The single wing was basically a power running formation that had as its greatest advantage the addition of another blocker in the backfield. Unlike in modern football, where the quarterback's function frequently is simply to hand off the ball, all the backs in the single wing remained involved throughout the play. Some coaches used the formation to inject significant razzle dazzle into the game, using multiple reverses, fakes, and handoffs, while often employing an unbalanced line. Many observers of the 1940 game marveled at the beauty of the ballhandling that some teams could achieve. But the single wing had its disadvantages as well. Most notably, it demanded more skilled play by the linemen. Plays were slow to unfold, and linemen often had to hold their blocks a little longer. Most teams did not pass much, some hardly at all, and what passing there was seldom occurred in the manner familiar to modern fans. Drop back passers with protective pockets were virtually unheard of. Most passing was done by a halfback on the run, rolling out as he looked for a receiver. And forward passing within five yards of the line of scrimmage was prohibited by rule, further limiting the air attack.

The symbol of the era, of course, was the leather helmet. Required by rule only since 1939, it was worn almost always without a faceguard, except by players with facial injuries. Northwestern experimented in 1940 with a resilient plastic helmet,[45] and refinements ever since have been aimed at increasing player safety, with mixed results. An entire uniform in 1940, complete with a full array of safety equipment, cost $56.50.[46]

Immediately noticeable to the modern fan would be the absence of a uniform numbering convention. In modern times, backs wear lower uniform numbers, usually up to 49, and linemen higher numbers above 49. Such a system is seen as an aid to spectators. But in 1940, no such convention existed. In addition to Tom Harmon's famous 98, Cornell backs Walt Matuszczak, Hal McCullough Walt Scholl, Mort Landsberg, and Lou Bufalino wore numbers 88, 63, 56, 53,and 66, respectively, while center Bud Finneran wore 29 and tackle Fred West 23. Ohio State tackle Charlie Maag wore 33, Dartmouth quarterback Don Norton wore 73, and Washington halfback Dean McAdams wore 60. Although the system, or lack of one, placed no apparent burden on the game, 1940 was the last year of its unfettered use. Beginning in 1941, college football began experimenting with uniform numbering keyed to positions, and the result is familiar to every modern football fan.

CHAPTER 2
THE DISCOUNTED

The army that defends on the right is vulnerable on the left;
The army that defends to the front is vulnerable to the rear;
The army that defends everywhere is vulnerable everywhere.

--SUN-TZU, *The Art of War*

That same afternoon, across San Francisco Bay, another key matchup was unfolding. An unusual college football doubleheader had been arranged at San Francisco's Kezar Stadium, with the first game between Santa Clara and Utah and the second between Stanford and San Francisco. The first of the two games was seen as the main event. Santa Clara had won the Sugar Bowl in both 1937 and 1938, each time against Louisiana State, and had played both the San Francisco Dons and the Utah Redskins to ties during the 1939 regular season.

Though it may seem odd, the fortunes of the 1940 Stanford Indians were in large measure forged on the playing fields of the University of Chicago. The Chicago Maroons had a long and rich history in college football dating back to before the turn of the century. They produced the first coaching genius, Amos Alonzo Stagg, one of the first true gridiron greats, Walter Eckersall, the first Heisman Trophy winner, Jay Berwanger, and the first college player ever drafted by the NFL (also Berwanger). After Stagg graduated from Yale, where he was chosen as an end on the first-ever All-America team in 1889, he began his coaching career at the Springfield YMCA, now Springfield College, in Massachusetts.

Stagg was a prolific innovator and inventor. His creations include, among other things, baseball's batting cage, as well as the football huddle, uniform numbers, the tackling dummy, and varsity letters. On the field, his constant tinkering led to the reverse, the end around, the fake handoff, the unbalanced line, the lateral, and countless tactics, formations, and wrinkles that have been passed down through the years. Knute Rockne once said, without fear of error, "All football comes from Stagg."[1] At about the same time Stagg began in Springfield, in 1890, there also arrived on the campus from Canada an enthusiastic young colleague named Dr. James Naismith who, after tinkering with a round ball and a peach basket, promptly set about inventing a game he called basketball. For the two years both men were at Springfield the air in that small YMCA building must have fairly crackled with creative energy.

In 1892, Stagg was handpicked by William Rainey Harper, president of the newly founded University of Chicago, to become its athletic director and tenured football coach. Harper, like many college presidents of the next half-century, saw football as a means to promote his university, with Stagg playing an important role in his strategy. The Maroons became a charter member of the Big Ten, and within two years they were playing football against the team from another newly founded university on the west coast using the same promotional strategy, Stanford. Stagg enjoyed immediate success, and by 1905 his team, led by the 135-pound Eckersall, had brought the national championship to Chicago by winning the final game of the year against mighty Michigan, 2-0. Though the game was played in ten-degree weather in Chicago, it drew an attendance of 27,000, at that time the largest crowd ever for a football game west of Philadelphia. The win snapped Michigan's 56-game winning streak and was such a bitter pill for the Wolverines to swallow that the man tackled for the deciding safety lived a lifetime of despondency. Harper lived long enough to celebrate the victory, but died of cancer two months later.[2]

Stagg's teams won seven Big Ten championships, the last in 1924, but Chicago's enrollment was not large enough nor its recruitment efforts effective enough to allow the football team to compete consistently in the burgeoning Big Ten. In 1929, Robert Maynard Hutchins became president of the university and created a strong emphasis of academics over athletics, seeking to create a top-notch intellectual institution. Hutchins was nothing if not aggressive in pursuing his goals, and Stagg, now an impediment to the president's vision, was soon relieved of his title as athletic director. In 1933 Stagg, still coaching the football team, reached the mandatory retirement age of 70 and, after 41 years with the university, was shown the door.

Clark Shaughnessy, a cerebral student of the game from Loyola University in New Orleans, was hired to replace Stagg. But with little support from the administration the undermanned Chicago team, winner of more Big Ten football championships than any other school, simply was no longer competitive. The team managed to hold its own while Berwanger was in residence, but in the four years since his departure following the 1935 season the team compiled a 6-23-2 record, including a dismal 1-15 record in the Big Ten. The low point of the 1938 season was the added humiliation of a 26-0 home loss to the College of the Pacific, coached by the resilient Stagg. By 1939, the team had reached the depths of despair. The Maroons were beaten by tiny Beloit, managed wins over Wabash and Oberlin, but proceeded to lose games to Illinois, Virginia, Harvard, Ohio State and Michigan by a combined score of 300-0. Perhaps the worst of it was the humiliating 85-0 loss to Michigan, with whom they had vied in their glory years for Midwestern football supremacy, and whom they had beaten 27-0 in Berwanger's day, as recently as 1934. The *New York Times* said of Shaughnessy's teams, "The boys looked so young and scrawny that we couldn't believe they constituted the varsity, but they did."[3] The United Press called Chicago's program "six-man football."[4] Just as bad, the home contest against conference champion Ohio State drew only 1400 fans.[5] The one clear advantage of varsity football, revenue, had ceased to be an advantage at all.

The die was cast. On December 21, 1939, Hutchins, seeing the best opportunity he would ever have and with the support of several key alumni, convinced the Board of Trustees to drop football as an intercollegiate sport. Though Hutchins's plan had been in the works for some time, the hatching of it was a complete surprise to Shaughnessy. The man most personally affected by the move was the most astounded. The *Chicago Tribune* added, "He appeared to be under great strain."[6] To the Associated Press, he said the action was "quite startling."[7] Caught off guard, he was unsure what the move meant for his future with the university.

The move should not have come as a surprise. Rumblings had intensified since the Michigan loss, and football competitiveness appeared to be increasingly at odds with Hutchins's vision. Hutchins had made no secret of his distaste for Chicago's involvement in varsity athletics, especially big-time football. But despite his attitude, Hutchins had done little to interfere with athletics, and Chicago was the only Big Ten school to compete in all thirteen sports sponsored by the conference. He was frequently quoted, paraphrasing an earlier line by economist Thorstein Veblen, as saying that football bore the same relation to education as bullfighting did to agriculture. And he would brag about his coup, "I did not de-emphasize football at the University of Chicago, I abolished it."[8] Chicago's Board of Trustees made its position clear, stating, "The university looks upon all sports as games which are conducted under its auspices for the recreation of the students...the students now derive no special benefit from intercollegiate football."[9] The student body was split if not indifferent to the move, many embracing Hutchins's preference for strict amateurism and recognizing it as incompatible with high-level competition. Others, however, saw football as a necessary diversion from Chicago's rigorous academic grind. "This place will be a seminary in about seven years," complained one.[10] But William McNeill, editor of the student newspaper, the *Daily Maroon*, concluded, "[I]f this school's football has been dead for years, we can only breathe a sigh of relief now that it has its burial."[11] David Martin, also writing in the *Daily Maroon*, likened the action to pulling a tooth. "Now that it's done, it is a good thing," he said.[12] Chicago remained a member of the Big Ten in other varsity sports until after the war, when it withdrew from the Big Ten altogether.

Shaughnessy had been both blindsided and scapegoated. "There is not a football man here but thinks the coaching at Chicago was bad—bad, lousy, rotten—and that Chicago could get enough men and get them on the level to have a good winning team if it had a new coach," wrote one alumnus,[13] who obviously did not know Hutchins well. Stagg, who did, expressed sadness at the turn of events. "It's a great blow to learn that the trustees have been forced to take such action," he said, leaving a hint that he placed some of the blame on the shoulders of his successor. He added, "I never have been happy about leaving Chicago and even have shed tears. I'm foolish enough to believe the action wouldn't have been taken had I been there."[14] But Stagg had already lost one battle of wills with Hutchins, and his comment rang hollow. Shaughnessy had taken a huge salary cut to come to Chicago, and he had every reason to be bitter. When his head cleared it became obvious to him he had no future at Hutchins's university.

Meanwhile, in Palo Alto, the Stanford Indians' football program was also on a losing track. In 1939, the Indians had escaped a winless year by defeating Dartmouth at the Polo Grounds in New York in the last game of the season, and coach Tiny Thornhill's past accomplishments were not enough to save his job. Thornhill, a native of Beaver County, Pennsylvania, had been an All-American tackle at the University of Pittsburgh under legendary coach Pop Warner. He began his coaching career as an assistant at Centre College in Kentucky, and when Warner left Pitt to become head coach at Stanford, Thornhill joined him there as an assistant. When Warner left Stanford, Thornhill became head coach. His first three Stanford teams of 1933, 1934, and 1935 all went to the Rose Bowl, and in the last of those visits Stanford emerged with a 7-0 victory over national co-champion Southern Methodist. The Stanford graduating seniors that year were called the Vow Boys by the press, because as freshmen they took an oath never to lose to Southern California. They kept their vow and won all three of their games against the Trojans. The Stanford football team appeared to be at full throttle, and Thornhill was riding a crest of popularity among alumni and fans. But, after the departure of the Vow Boys, Stanford stumbled through the next four seasons with a 10-21-5 record, and Thornhill became a victim of high expectations. Moreover, Thornhill had lost the team. The players had "absolutely no respect for the authority of their coach for the past three years, either on or off the field," said the student newspaper.[15] The win over Dartmouth was too little too late. Thornhill saw the axe coming. "I am fully aware that I am about to be fired," he said, after a protracted period of silence,[16] but he refused to resign, and on December 15, by a Board of Athletic Control vote of 7-2, his contract, due to expire in April of 1941, was not renewed.

Six days after Thornhill's ouster, the University of Chicago Board of Trustees pulled the rug out from under Shaughnessy, and within twenty four hours Shaughnessy's name was prominent in speculation as a possible replacement for Thornhill. But so were more high-profile names, such as Francis Schmidt of Ohio State, Lou Little of Columbia, Lynn Waldorf of Northwestern, Fritz Crisler of Michigan, Clipper Smith of Villanova and "virtually every coach in the country except Thornhill."[17] Shaughnessy's resume could not compare to the glittery credentials presented by the others. He was not at the top of the list.

Clark Shaughnessy had played his college football at Minnesota, where he had been a Walter Camp All-American in 1912. His university yearbook described him as a "good old war horse...you'll sure make good in that football stuff."[18] He became the head coach at Tulane at age 23, beating out Knute Rockne, who had also applied for the job.[19] For his efforts, he inherited a ragtag program with no field, no equipment, no budget, and no schedule. His annual salary was $1875, in consideration for which he was also athletic director and basketball and track coach. Shaughnessy, out of necessity, discovered first-hand how to build a program from nothing. He learned how to apply grim determination and hard work in the absence of resources, and most important of all, he shed all fear of odds stacked against him. At a young age he learned how to prosper under highly adverse circumstances. By 1925 his Tulane football teams had amassed a winning record, an undefeated season, and an invitation to the Rose Bowl, which was rejected by the university. In 1927 he moved next door to Loyola, receiving a princely contract that would pay him $175,000 for ten years. He accumulated a similarly impressive winning record at Loyola before he left for Chicago and the chance to coach in the Big Ten.[20] Evaluators of his record were left to wonder whether his successful times in New Orleans or his labors in the barren fields of Chicago football were more reliable indicators of his ability. They knew from his New Orleans days that coaches feared him and other employers coveted him, but his record while at Chicago was a huge obstacle for any employer.

The Stanford Board of Athletic Control worked fast and hard over the holidays to decide on a successor to Thornhill, and by the first week of January it had a short list of three highly qualified candidates: Dud DeGroot of San Jose State, Tex Oliver of Oregon, and Buck Shaw of Santa Clara. But when the Board went into executive session on January 7, it could not make a decision. Each candidate was favored by a segment of the nine-member board and was deemed unacceptable by the others. The Board was prepared to offer the successful candidate, if it could settle on one, a salary of $8500 a year for three to five years.[21]

For four days the Board struggled in stalemate, unable to reach an agreement. Finally, on January 11, a fourth candidate, a darkhorse, emerged and was decided upon. Clark Shaughnessy was offered the position at a salary of $7500 per year, a substantial cut from his $9000 salary at Chicago,[22] where he was still employed. He accepted it.[23] In a time when colleges were critically sensitive to accusations of overemphasis of football and professionalization of athletics, his dismal stay at Chicago had been turned into an advantage. No school wanted to be accused of making a coaching change just to win more football games, and with Shaughnessy's record there could be no danger of that.[24] Further, although the three finalists each had great support among factions of the alumni and Shaughnessy had virtually none, those reviewing his resume were impressed by the high regard in which he was held by other coaches. And Stanford was a campus where innovation and fresh thinking were highly-regarded virtues. Shaughnessy's image as football's version of a mad scientist, always one experiment away from the big breakthrough, had a certain appeal in Palo Alto.[25]

But even in Palo Alto not everybody saw it that way, and Shaughnessy's arrival did little to spur enthusiasm among the Stanford fans. The last thing a losing team needed, as they saw it, was a coach from an even worse losing team. With predictable reaction to his slim resume, many expressed outrage. One observer called his hiring "an act of folly comparable to employing an arsonist as fire chief."[26] Prescott Sullivan of the *San Francisco Examiner*, who took note of his weak credentials, claimed that he had made the act of losing "an exact science."[27] A graduating football player, who could have been counted on to be more gracious given the team's record, noted, "I'm rather disappointed in the choice as it seems his record is poor." Another player said, "Who in the world hired him, and why? What were they thinking?"[28] Some alumni looked upon the choice with outright hostility. "Why had the university reached so far beyond the fence for a bad apple when it had two plums (DeGroot and Shaw) in its own backyard?" they questioned.[29] DeGroot, in particular, seemed to have a sterling resume. A Phi Beta Kappa graduate of Stanford, he held a PhD and ran a superb program at San Jose State. In 1939, his team outscored their opponents 324-29, a far cry from Shaughnessy's. In 1924, he had been one of nine Stanford men who had participated on the U.S Olympic rugby team, which won a gold medal in a stunning upset of France. More important, he carried the endorsement of Pop Warner.

Shaughnessy was undaunted. He had been through much worse. If he were the type of man to bend in the face of others' doubts, in the face of extreme adversity, or when the odds were stacked high against him, he would have quit long ago. But there had to be something special in the makeup of a man who could shrug off losses of the type he had endured at Chicago only to come back for more. Far from quitting at Chicago when the going could not have been worse, he would have fought harder and longer if given the chance. "I am not in accord with what happened," he said of Chicago's abandonment of football, "and am one thousand percent for intercollegiate football. I very much regretted seeing that fine university take that step."[30] Though the Stanford football program might have been headed from the frying pan into the fire, he was going to be the coach that led it in 1940.

Then, on March 7, before he had been on campus long enough to find his way around without a map, Shaughnessy dropped a bombshell. He announced that he was doing away with the single wing offense as practiced for years at Stanford by its inventor, Pop Warner, and used by virtually everybody else in college football for years. He would "start from the ground up," as he put it, with his own system.[31] Shaughnessy carried with him to his new job what was to some a troubling belief in an archaic offensive system called the T-formation. Devised before the turn of the century by, of all people, Amos Alonzo Stagg, the T-formation had long ago been put on the football shelf to gather dust in favor of the more versatile and easier-to-teach single wing.

Shaughnessy's time in Chicago had not been for naught. Soon after his arrival he met George Halas, coach of the NFL's Chicago Bears, and the two talked endlessly about how to win football games. Nearly twenty years before, while a player-coach for the Decatur Staleys, forerunner of the Bears, Halas had tinkered with a rudimentary version of the T-formation. Before that he had used a variation of it as player-coach of the Great Lakes Naval Station team that had won the 1919 Rose Bowl. In turn, he had learned it from Bob Zuppke, his coach and mentor at Illinois. Shaughnessy had experimented with a man-in-motion offense with the Maroons, but his talent there was so thin that nothing could be made of his efforts. Halas took on Shaughnessy as a paid consultant for the Bears, at the same time he was coaching the Maroons, and the next year Shaughnessy helped the Bears groom Sid Luckman, a college star at Columbia, as the first modern T-formation quarterback.

The conventional single wing offense of the day began with the ball being snapped by the center to a back five or six yards behind the line of scrimmage, and the original T-formation included a similar concept. It had the quarterback, who received the snap, standing about five yards behind the center with the other three backs lined up behind him parallel to the line of scrimmage. But even in the gifted hands of Stagg the T-formation had been used as a power formation, a method to mass personnel more effectively at the point of a running attack. Shaughnessy had little patience with the single wing or with Stagg's T-formation approach, whose emphasis on power, he thought, was too limited in its focus. What he contemplated was a completely different philosophy of offensive football. Well versed in military history and strategy, Shaughnessy studied the tactics of a variety of military leaders and was convinced of the importance of speed in attacking the enemy. And he saw more possibilities in outwitting the opposition than in overpowering it. Chinese general Sun-Tzu, in his ancient masterpiece *The Art of War*, asserted that the army that defends everywhere is vulnerable everywhere. Shaughnessy's offensive strategy was a simple response: spread the opposition out, make it defend more of the field, launch lightning strikes at the point of attack before the defense could respond, rely on the elements of surprise and deception, and arrive not with more power but with more speed.

In his scheme, the quarterback was not merely another blocking back but a distributor of the ball and launcher of the attack. Unlike with Stagg's approach, the quarterback stood directly under center and had the ball directly snapped to him between the center's legs, enabling him to turn his back to the defense, hiding the ball, as he handed it to a running back. Additionally, by coupling the idea with the man-in-motion concept, he could create several hard-to-defend elements, including quickly developing plays to the outside. It seems fundamental today, but nobody in football had used any part of this system extensively in decades, and nobody had ever put the pieces together as Shaughnessy did.

Shaughnessy proved to be a hungry learner as well as a gifted teacher and observed all he could, each nuance, angle and detail, as Halas installed his system and sprung it on the professional football world. He watched carefully as theory was converted to practice and adjusted as needed. But a year later Halas was still the only coach to use the system which, in the eyes of the traditionalists and the purists, remained unnecessarily complicated and unproven. Blessed with immense self-confidence and outrageous nerve, Shaughnessy left Chicago believing that with the right blend of talent he could make the T-formation, especially with his own personal touches added, work in college football once again.

To some, this was borderline heresy. The grumpy Warner, anything but supportive of the idea of his system being jettisoned, declared that if the system worked, everything he knew about football, which was substantial, could be thrown in the ocean. "Pop was always a stubborn man," wrote sports columnist Red Smith about Warner, "and as he grew old in the game he resisted change, as old men are wont to do."[32] Unwilling to countenance new ideas for his own sake, he was certainly not willing to do so for the sake of a brash upstart like Shaughnessy.

By mid-afternoon on September 28, the 35,000 fans gathered at Kezar Stadium could be forgiven for assuming that, following Santa Clara's defeat of Utah, 35-13, they had seen the best football of the day. San Francisco was favored to beat Stanford in the second game, and many did not expect the game to be close. Local sportswriters thought highly of the Dons, considering them among the best teams in the West, and thought they would make mincemeat of the young and inexperienced line of Stanford.[33] Stanford had only one senior on the line and the Dons were expected to make the Indians pay for that shortcoming. Even the new Stanford uniforms were the subject of scorn by the press. Shaughnessy had dressed them in attractive bright cardinal jerseys and stockings with white helmets and pants, but the press commented that it would be a shame when they were ripped to shreds by the street kids from San Francisco.[34]

As in the Michigan game across the bay, questions abounded. What of this new formation? Was this relic of days gone by just a lot of talk by a coach of a weak team, desperate to try anything in hopes of reversing his and his team's losing trends? Or was it really capable of operating and of catapulting a team to success? Shaughnessy had promised a dubious team in his first meeting with them in March that if they implemented the plan properly it would take them to the Rose Bowl. Was this just boastful talk? And what of the new coach Shaughnessy? Was he for real with these new ideas, the bona fide teacher his new bosses at Stanford claimed him to be? Finally, was Stanford a team of high-potential players held back by an ineffective Thornhill, ready to leap to the top if given a chance under this new magic man Shaughnessy, or were the players really as bad as their record of the last few years would indicate? Nobody knew. Most of all, the Stanford players themselves did not know.

Shaughnessy called the team together before the game and told them that, across the Bay, Tom Harmon had just run back the opening kickoff for a touchdown for Michigan. His message was not subtle. He intended to convey to his men that they were in the same class with Michigan, and that this was pertinent information about a rival on their level. His audacity did not go undetected. "It was something, Shaughnessy putting us in the same class with Harmon," said fullback Milt Vucinich.[35]

When the game started Stanford did nothing with its first two possessions, bumbling along and magnifying the doubts about Shaughnessy and his new system. But at halftime the Indians entered the locker room with a 14-0 lead. The ball movement, the fakes, the men in motion, the razzle dazzle—suddenly it was all working. When Pete Kmetovic scored the first touchdown of the game, he did it untouched on a run up the middle. It is entirely possible he was not even seen. "You could tell by the holes we had that somebody was confused," he said. "We were running right by people who didn't know we had the ball." In the second half Kmetovic returned a punt 60 yards for a touchdown and by the end of the game Stanford had shocked and dismantled San Francisco 27-0, outgaining them 247 yards to eight.[36]

After the game the San Francisco coach, George Malley, looked as if he had seen a ghost.[37] Buck Shaw of Santa Clara hung around to watch the game, with more than a passing interest; Stanford was his Broncos' scheduled opponent two weeks hence, and although Santa Clara was expected to be heavily favored, it was always a good idea to take every opportunity to scout the opposition. He "left as a somewhat subdued individual," said the *Oakland Tribune*.[38] While observers of the game could be certain that they had witnessed a revolutionary new concept—or a revolutionary old concept— it is unlikely that anybody grasped the full significance of what had occurred. What Shaughnessy had pulled from his sleeve had been highly effective, but he was showing no more of his offense and the players that would execute it than necessary. Stanford's offense was so efficient that it had used only eleven plays, but 42 players. To the numerous scouts in the stands, he was "careful to lift only a corner of the curtain."[38] Indeed, he was a fanatic about secrecy. Five decades later, one of his disciples, Richie Petitbon, by then a defensive coach with the Washington Redskins, described Shaughnessy's view: "Don't ever let them play against what they practiced against."[40]

The change was apparent from the very first. "Gone were the recent haphazard willy-nilly performances of recent Stanford teams," noted the press. The clean rhythms of movements and close meshing of parts, not to mention the fresh new ideas on how to win football games, stood in stark contrast to what Tiny Thornhill had dished up, and quarterback Frankie Albert, regarded as a "screwball" the year before, was now seen an effective team leader.[41] Unlike the teams playing across the Bay, Stanford has raised as many questions as it had answered.

****

The Michigan-California game was not the only Big Ten-Pacific Coast Conference matchup of the day. The Washington Huskies traveled to Minneapolis to play the Minnesota Golden Gophers in a game that was equally significant. Thirty three members of the Washington team left Seattle by train at noon on Tuesday September 24 for the long trip eastward, and arrived in Minnesota some forty eight hours later. They stayed in posh surroundings at the Lafayette Country Club and practiced at a local high school as they rested up from their arduous trip.[42]

The game as previewed promised to be an exciting affair. Washington was billed as "...the toughest, trickiest starting eleven in the Pacific Coast Loop."[43] The *Illustrated Football Annual* called them "The King of the Coast" and a team with a good chance to go undefeated.[44] They figured to be in a three-way fight with Southern California and UCLA for a Rose Bowl bid. Though the Huskies had suffered through a losing season in 1939, they had steadily improved throughout the year and, in their last game, had come within a few seconds of beating Rose-Bowl-bound Southern California. Coach Jimmy Phelan had 22 lettermen returning, including eight starters, and two of them were bona fide stars. Halfback Dean McAdams was called by some the finest all-around back in college football. "McAdams is far and away the Coast's premier punter, a brilliant passer, able ball-carrier, and better-than-average defensive cog in the Phelan phalanx," wrote the *Minnesota Daily* .[45] Rudy Mucha was considered by most to be the best center in the country. The *Illustrated Football Annual* called this pair "two of the greatest players in Far Western history" and pointed out that, right behind them, halfback Ernie Steele, "breakaway speedster, is always wrecking games with his jackrabbit speed."[46] *Look* called Steele the second fastest man on the West Coast, behind only Jackie Robinson of UCLA.[47] And Ray Frankowski at guard and Jay MacDowell at end were both All-America candidates.

There was no such optimism in the Minnesota camp. The Gophers had suffered four losses in 1939, an uncharacteristically weak showing for them, and while they expected to be better in 1940, the prognosis for a full recovery was guarded. The 3-4-1 record had been only the second losing record for the Gophers since 1921, and Minnesota fans were simply unfamiliar with losing ways. The Minnesota Gophers had been the most successful team in college football during the decade of the 1930s. Between 1933 and 1938, behind such legendary figures as Biggie Munn, Pug Lund and Bud Wilkinson, the Gophers had gone undefeated three times, won three Big Ten championships outright and had shared a fourth, and had won two national championships outright, sharing a third. At one point in that stretch they had played 28 consecutive games without a loss, and they had a combined record of 39-5-4 over that six-year span. Some have speculated that the 1934 Minnesota team might have been the best college team of all time, and that the second team might have been talented enough to go undefeated as well. Minnesotans had come to view football success almost as a birthright, and set their expectations high, even to the extent of taking for granted undefeated and near-undefeated records.[48] While the slippage of 1939 was certainly not of the magnitude suffered by, say, Clark Shaughnessy, it was enough to set Gopher heads spinning.

Sherm Langley, sports columnist in the *Minnesota Daily*, the student newspaper, reflected the pessimistic mood, citing the long road back for a team so sharply weaker than the Gophers of the glory years recently past. He bemoaned what he perceived as a lack of ends and backs and feared that another four-loss season might be in the Gophers' future.[49] Most other raters of football talent at the beginning of the year concurred with the view that Minnesota, though with some talent, was heading for the middle of the pack in the Big Ten and with, at most, an outside chance for some national recognition. The *Illustrated Football Annual* was dismissive. "Gone are the supersquads of '34-'38," it said. "Bierman now deals with players whose talents, while adequate, are not of a calibre to throw a scare through the circuit. Undoubtedly the wheel will turn back, but not this year."[50] Sportswriter Arch Ward of the *Chicago Tribune* concurred, saying that Minnesota's season would be "much like 1939."[51] All this hand-wringing merely demonstrated that Bernie Bierman had thoroughly succeeded in bamboozling the press, even, and perhaps most especially, his own campus newspaper. "Bierman failed to detect any large amount of improvement on the part of this year's squad over last season's,"[52] reported the *Daily*. In truth, the Gophers were loaded, especially in the backfield. Every coach loves to play the role of underdog, perhaps even catch an opponent by surprise, and now Bierman would have his chance.

True, he had lost to graduation his best player of 1939, left halfback and signal caller Harold Van Every. Winner of the Bronko Nagurski Award given to Minnesota's outstanding player each year, Van Every had made a credible run at the Heisman Trophy won by Nile Kinnick. Through good fortune and a little design Bierman managed to stagger his backfield talent so that each year he had an outstanding senior halfback, a progressing junior, and a promising young sophomore on the rise. This year's senior was George Franck, the fastest football player in the Big Ten, even faster on the straightaway than Harmon. Through a little manipulation Bierman had kept him back a year, essentially red-shirting him, although that phrase and that practice were not in wide use at the time. The spirited Franck rebelled at the practice and contemplated quitting. Early in Franck's sophomore year the junior Van Every was badly hurt—the injury turned out to be a bruised kidney—and Franck became the starting tailback. The next year, with Franck a junior and Van Every a healthy senior, sophomore Bruce Smith entered the scene. Smith spent most of his sophomore year as backup to Franck, and he, Franck and Van Every were a trio seldom in the game all at the same time. In 1940, with Van Every gone, Franck back and Smith a healthy junior, Bierman added sophomore sensation Bill Daley to the backfield. Franck, Smith, and Daley would each earn All-America honors during their collegiate careers, belying the claims of backfield weakness. Bierman also had Bob Paffrath, Bill Sweiger, and Joe Mernik in the backfield, all reliable performers.

The line was almost as talented. Urban Odsen at one tackle was a mainstay. Nicknamed "The Chief" by his teammates, Odsen lived over the top of a fire station near campus and earned his keep by polishing the brass on the fire trucks. Like Franck, he had been kept back a year. Though Bierman hated to start sophomores, he made an exception for Dick Wildung, a strong and talented partner for Odsen at the other tackle. He was labeled "another Ed Widseth,"[53] which was high praise indeed. Widseth had been a stalwart tackle and a two-time All-American performer at Minnesota during the glory years just past, and by 1938, he had been named the Pro Player of the Year while with the New York Giants. And at guard Bierman had Helge Pukema, a 201-pound fireplug who would win All-America honors in 1940. The reality of the team's talent and potential was in sharp contrast to the bunk Bierman had fed the press.

In 1940, Bernie Bierman, who had presided over the entirety of Minnesota's dominant era, was the most successful football coach in the nation. Born in 1894 in Springfield, Minnesota, he played football for the Gophers where he was the teammate and close friend of Clark Shaughnessy, and in 1915, he captained the team. After a brief spell as a high school coach, a stint in the Marines during World War I, and a head coaching job at Montana, he became Shaughnessy's assistant at Tulane. He left to take the head coaching job at Mississippi A&M, then returned to Tulane as head coach when Shaughnessy left in 1927. In his last three years at Tulane he compiled a 28-1 record before losing in the Rose Bowl, and was welcomed home with open arms by his alma mater in 1932, albeit with a pay cut.

Bierman was a hard man to play for. He was cold and intensely introverted, and one of his favorite pastimes was solitaire. He had difficulty communicating with his players, and to get his message across he would often resort to biting, caustic sarcasm. To the press he was no more accommodating. He "consistently refused to extend even average cooperation to a writer or photographer," said one critic. One observer referred to his "arctic exterior." His wife, Clara, it was said, was everything he was not: open, bubbly, emotional, expressive.[54]

He was a perfectionist who drove his team to its physical limits in practice. He was stingy with his praise and lavish with his criticism. He "steadfastly refused to recognize mistakes as part of the human condition," wrote one team historian.[55] "He was a dour person. He was shy and inarticulate; he couldn't speak his mind in front of a crowd," said Bill Daley of him. "But he knew what he was doing, and he was a strong man, and I liked him."[56] As he drove his team to victory after victory, he inspired respect if not affection from his team. "Bierman was not a man to be loved—he was a man you respected," said one player. Team captain Bob Bjorkland summed up the situation perfectly: "We cursed him on the practice field and loved him on Saturday afternoon."[57]

As game day approached and the students filtered back onto campus for the start of classes, the *Minnesota Daily* went back to an age-old tradition, that of the Barber Poll. The barbers at the various shops in town were sought out for their wisdom in predicting the outcome of the upcoming game with Washington. It seemed as good an idea as any. Of the thirty barbers consulted, all of whom were notorious hometowners, 25 picked the Gophers to win, four picked the Huskies, and one predicted a tie.

Bierman wrestled with a harder question until game time, debating what to do two with talented runners, Franck and Smith. He started them both.

Washington, a slight favorite to win by most impartial observers, took the opening kickoff before 46,000 fans, but promptly fumbled the ball on the first play from scrimmage. After Franck quickly scored a touchdown for Minnesota three plays later, both teams settled in to play as the experts expected they would. The two stars, McAdams and Franck, dueled with one another back and forth until, late in the second period, McAdams threw a touchdown pass to put his team in the lead, 14-10. Then, at about the same moment that Tom Harmon was returning his opening kickoff 94 yards in Berkeley, Franck took the following Washington kick at the two-yard line, headed straight up the middle, swerved to his left at about his own 30-yard line, and used all his speed streaking down the sideline for a 98-yard touchdown run that gave the lead back to Minnesota, 17-14.

But the defining play of the game did not occur until the fourth quarter. With Minnesota still hanging on to that slim lead, Washington speedster Ernie Steele, as the Gophers were afraid he might, got loose on a fake punt from his own 21-yard line, crossed midfield, and was looking to go all the way down the sideline for a touchdown and the lead. To add to the moment's intensity, running interference right alongside him was All-America center Rudy Mucha. Further, there was only one Minnesota defender in a position to stop Steele, and he would somehow have to run the Husky pair down, penetrate the interference, and dispatch the ballcarrier. The game, hanging in the balance, depended on his ability to do so. Luckily for Minnesota, that lone defender was Big Ten sprint champion George Franck. That would address the first part of the problem. Steele and Franck were about the same size, but Mucha outweighed them both by about forty pounds. Franck angled across the field at top speed to the same sideline he himself had just streaked along on his own touchdown jaunt, and then, at the critical instant, he hit the two Huskies so hard he knocked them both out of bounds with one shot at the 42-yard line. That took care of the second and third parts. In the process he knocked himself unconscious, and it was five minutes before he could regain his senses and wobble off the field. His game-saving play was later rated one of the four best tackles of the decade.[58]

Adding to Washington's frustration, the Huskies made one last push as the game wound down, and McAdams completed a pass to the Minnesota five-yard line, only to have the ball fumbled away. Minnesota recovered. None of the barbers accurately predicted the final score of 19-14, but Gene at the Union Barber Shop came closest, picking 20-13.

CHAPTER 3
WAR CLOUDS

I have ever deemed it fundamental for the United States never to take an active part in the quarrels of Europe. Their political interests are entirely different from ours.

--THOMAS JEFFERSON

"Hey! Get your football news here!" All across America on September 28, newsboys hawked their morning papers to fans hungry for the latest scoops on the opening day of the college gridiron season. But while readers gobbled up the papers, intent on clawing their way to the sports section, it was the ominous international news on the front page that stopped them cold. The Battle of Britain, raging over London for weeks now, was a familiar story to American readers. But hours before, the German Luftwaffe had changed tactics, launching its daily bombing raid on London in daylight as well as at night, and had subjected the British capital to one of its worse beatings yet. The papers also carried threatening word of Japan entering into a tripartite agreement with Germany and Italy, linking together their political, economic and military futures and delivering a bold and purposeful poke in the eye to the United States. These were the latest in a torrent of menacing events that threatened to draw the nation into the conflict raging among European powers for more than a year, and now engulfing the Pacific as well.

Only months before, while college students were packing their books, clearing their dorm rooms and preparing to leave campus for the summer, the country felt safely isolated from the European conflict. Americans, weary from a decade of economic struggle and still smarting from involvement on European battlefields a generation ago, were content to keep the conflict in a distant corner of their mind, reluctant to contemplate entering the fray, and confident that British and French forces could adequately turn away the Nazi menace. Isolationists such as Senator Gerald P. Nye of North Dakota and aviation hero Charles A. Lindbergh were constantly reminding Americans of the departing advice of George Washington to avoid foreign entanglements, and for the time being, at least, they were winning the battle for American public opinion. But now, with the students returning to campus for the fall, a

29

series of alarming reversals had caused a sharp change in American attitudes. Only a week before, President Franklin Roosevelt had signed into law a bill mandating registration for the first peacetime draft in the country's history. There was hardly a reader of that morning's paper who did not wonder whether the college youth that paraded onto the gridirons later that afternoon would soon be called to a greater and more serious conflict.

Columnist Felix R. McKnight of the Associated Press argued that conscription would ruin football in the Southwest Conference. The "lashings of a wounded world may kick history's most inviting Southwest Conference football race into wreckage," he said. He envisioned nearly a third of the players in the conference being drafted. But Homer Norton, coach of the national champion Texas A&M Aggies, saw it differently. "If the national emergency becomes so grave as to demand conscription, then football would become very unimportant to me," he countered.[1]

In the months leading up to the 1940 football season, the world was hurtling toward its greatest calamity. Following Hitler's rise to power, the Nazi leader made clear his intentions to unite the German people under the banner of the Reich. Through cunning diplomacy, he laid his grip on Austria, a nation populated largely by Germanic people, and then the Czech Sudetenland, most of whose people were also German. But when after military threat he annexed the rest of the Czech territory and then Lithuania, his intentions became suspect.

President Franklin Roosevelt, a consummate master of reading public opinion, was no isolationist. While he may have been constrained in his actions due to an unwilling Congress, he was in no way constrained in his thoughts, opinions, and strategies. Neutrality of thought, unlike with Woodrow Wilson a generation before, was not part of Roosevelt's makeup. The president saw the events in Europe as a real threat to democracy and to American institutions, but he was wise enough to discern that the time was right only for preparation for action, and not for action itself. Events would unfold to change things, he knew, and he would be ready when they did.

On January 4, 1939, Roosevelt addressed Congress on the State of the Union, and directly set himself at odds with the isolationist view. "The world has grown so small and weapons of attack so swift that no nation can be safe in its will to peace so long as any other single powerful nation refuses to settle its grievances at the council table,"[2] he told Congress, while seeking massive new funding to build up an inadequate army and navy. While Roosevelt was careful to couch his comments in terms of national defense—he called the nation's air defenses "utterly inadequate" and hastened to clarify that he had no intention of "taking part in another war on European soil"—it was clear he was talking about arming the nation for possible war, intimating that he would not stand by while dictatorial abuses proliferated.[3]

Polls continued to show that Americans overwhelmingly wanted to stay out of any future conflict in Europe. Despite Roosevelt's determination to stand shoulder to shoulder with Britain and France, a significant barrier kept him from acting further. The Neutrality Law, championed largely by Nye, placed an embargo on arms to all belligerents. The highly popular law had recently been passed in the House of Representatives by a 376-16 vote and in the Senate by a 63-6 margin[4], yet Roosevelt saw it as an impediment to what had to be done.

At dawn on September 1, the German army crashed across the Polish border, and two days later, Britain and France declared war on Germany. Hours after the start of the war, a German U-boat sank the British passenger liner *Athenia* with 1,100 civilians on board. The death toll reached 112, including 30 Americans. But while a similar incident involving the *Lusitania*[5] had helped propel America toward war 24 years before, the *Athenia* incident incited only anger. Nevertheless, Roosevelt proclaimed a state of emergency and laid plans to immediately increase the army, navy, and marines by 100,000 men. By the end of the month, Warsaw had succumbed to assault from combined German and Russian troops, and plans for the partition of Poland between the two conquerors had been laid.

The American public observed the events with "detached distaste."[6] Journalist Vincent Sheean wrote, "the depth of American unconcern in the first winter of the war was immeasurable....The general attitude toward the gathering storm was one of almost inconceivable apathy."[7] A Gallup Poll showed that 84 percent of Americans wanted Britain and France to defeat Germany, 95 percent wanted the United States to stay out of the war, and a solid majority supported repeal of the arms embargo.[8] Americans, it appeared, were willing to help Britain and France win the war, so long as they did not have to fight themselves.

Roosevelt used his fireside chats to assure yet caution the American people. "Let no man or woman thoughtlessly or falsely talk of America sending its armies to European fields," he said. But he also added, "When peace has been broken anywhere, the peace of all countries everywhere is in danger....Passionately though we may desire detachment, we are forced to realize that every word that comes through the air, every battle that is fought, does affect the American future."[9]

On December 1, 1939, the 1940 Olympic Games were officially canceled. Helsinki, the scheduled host city, was indisposed at the time, being accosted by Russian troops intent on invading Finland.

The American public did not take seriously the prospect that Germany could win the European conflict. "It has been a tacit assumption of American thinking that Germany would lose the war," wrote George Soule in the *New Republic* on April 22, while warning his readers that the unthinkable—a Hitler victory—might yet occur.[10] "During the first six months of the war, most Americans took for granted that Hitler would be defeated," said the *New Republic*.[11] In late October 1939, polls showed that 90 percent of Americans had faith in a British-French victory.[12] There was also belief that even if Hitler prevailed on the continent he would not dare attack Britain.[13] Unlike their leader, the American public judged poorly both the likelihood of German victory and its consequences.

Soon this entire house of false assumptions came crashing down. On April 8, the German blitzkrieg began to advance into Denmark and Norway, and a month later moved swiftly through Holland, Belgium, and Luxembourg and into France. An ocean away, Americans huddling before their radios were met with a steady stream of bad news as the situation worsened, seemingly by the hour. By the end of May, the British Expeditionary Force was stranded on the beach at Dunkirk, the last open port in Flanders. Between May 29 and June 5, in one of the most remarkable efforts in the history of warfare, a makeshift fleet of British, French, and Dutch fishing boats, shrimp boats, rowboats, fireboats, whaleboats, pleasure craft, and every other imaginable manner of floating device, aided by rainy weather that kept the Luftwaffe at bay, systematically crossed the English Channel and evacuated 340,000 Allied soldiers from the beach. The vulnerability of the force opposing the Nazis could not have been more evident. By June 14, the Nazis were in Paris, and France, its military shattered, was through as a major resisting force to the Germans. The prospect of Nazi supremacy in Europe was never more real.

What only weeks before had seemed impossible had come to pass: Hitler had Europe in his grip, and there was no telling where it would all stop. The dramatic turn of events had an immediate and profound effect on American public opinion. "Until last week the possibility of allied defeat was a distant threat," wrote Freda Kirchwey in *The Nation*. "Last week it pushed forward and demanded consideration."[14]

Noting the sharp and recent departure in American public opinion from its recent isolationist apathy, *Time* characterized the current stance as this: "Hitler was invincible in Europe, Britain was facing probable defeat, the U.S. had best look to its own security."[15] Polls showed that suddenly only 30 percent of Americans believed in an Allied victory, and 63 percent believed that Hitler would eventually seize territory on the American continent.[16] In short order America came to understand that isolationism in the form it so recently had embraced was an empty policy. Journalist Elmer Davis succinctly explained what had happened: "The unrecognized premise of a good deal of American isolationism was a conviction that the Allies were going to win anyway so we needn't worry about how the war would come out. That conviction, recently, had been shaken; and accordingly a lot of people are worried for the first time."[17]

By mid-June, polls showed that Americans, stunned by the inadequacy of their nation's military to meet the challenge of war, were strongly in favor of rearming. A *Fortune* survey claimed that more than 93 percent of Americans were supportive of spending whatever was necessary to build up the military as quickly as possible.[18] The nation was nearly in a state of shock, its complacency roughly torn away and replaced by a sense of unity and desperate urgency. The *New Republic* warned, "Today we are awaking into the world of military powers, where victory goes, not to the side with the highest moral qualities, but to the one that gets there first with the biggest guns and the fastest planes."[19] *Time* continued to pound away at the same message: "As in few times of peace the Nation spoke as a whole and the voice came clear to Congress: Arm. Arm the U.S. for what may come."[20]

On May 10, Winston Churchill became Prime Minister of Great Britain. The blunt choice set before him and the British people was whether to fight on or to seek peace terms from Hitler. Both Neville Chamberlain and Lord Halifax favored seeking terms.[21] On June 4, after the evacuation of Dunkirk, Churchill gave his answer: "We shall go on to the end. We shall fight in France; we shall fight on the seas and oceans; we shall fight with growing confidence and growing strength in the air; we shall defend our island, whatever the cost may be. We shall fight on the beaches; we shall fight on the landing grounds; we shall fight in the fields and in the streets; we shall fight in the hills; we shall never surrender."

For the United States, the choice was whether to arm and support Britain, in hopes Churchill could succeed, or to prepare to face the Nazi menace themselves. Churchill continued to warn Roosevelt that, without American aid, all of Europe could fall in rapid order. The clear implication was that the Nazi wolf would then be at America's door. "If this country was left by the United States to its fate, no one would have the right to blame those then responsible if they made the best terms they could for the surviving inhabitants," said Churchill, hinting that his greatest bargaining chip was the British fleet.[22] Thus America's stake in Britain's struggle was redefined.

Roosevelt's choice was equally clear. He knew that there was a well-founded fear in the United States that providing arms, ships, and planes to a weak and failing Britain might be tantamount to handing them over to the Nazis. But Roosevelt had to find a way to protect Britain. It was from there, his military strategists held, that a future attack upon the European continent would have to be launched. If only for geographic reasons, Britain was essential. On June 10, Italy joined the war on the Axis side. That same day, Roosevelt, in a commencement address at the University of Virginia, gave his answer. In his speech, he announced that he would "extend to the opponents of force the material resources of this nation."[23] Roosevelt knew he was speaking and acting in accord with the changed views of his constituency. *The Nation* said the speech marked "a new phase of relationship of this country to the struggle in Europe."[24] The *New Republic* claimed it marked the formal change of American foreign policy from one of neutrality to one of partisan non-belligerency.[25] *Time* again led the cheer. "Last week," it reported, "more and more U.S. citizens were determined that the U.S. should aid the allies."[26]

Complicating the picture was that Roosevelt was in the last months of his second term. Churchill regarded Roosevelt as Britain's best friend, and he fervently hoped he would seek reelection to an unprecedented third term. But Churchill knew that Roosevelt's chances for reelection hinged on Roosevelt's compliance with the fleeting demands of American public opinion, at least in action. Churchill said of Roosevelt, "I expect he wants to get reelected, and I fear that isolationism is the winning ticket."[27] Churchill knew that without American help he could not hold on. His nation's fate was in the hands of the American people.

Churchill had help over the spring and summer. Journalists such as Quentin Reynolds, writing in *Collier's* magazine, and broadcasters Edward R. Murrow and Eric Sevareid, both working for CBS, pushed hard to bring the war home to Americans and to garner support for aid to Britain. Dorothy Thompson, writing in the *Saturday Evening Post*, energetically portrayed Hitler as a ruthless and treacherous brute. Freda Kirchwey wrote an article in *The Nation* titled "Supposing Hitler Wins," in which she painted a horrific view of the potential future, including the execution of Churchill.[28] George Soule's article, "If Germany Wins" was published in the *New Republic,*[29] which also ran an article titled "If Hitler Writes the Peace."[30] On July 16 an article in *Look,* by Drew Pearson and Robert S. Allen, "Can We Keep Hitler Out of the Americas?", addressed the issue of what would happen should Britain's defenses fail. Their answer to their question: No.[31] A week later, on July 22, *Life* ran an article by Walter Lippmann titled, "The Economic Consequences of a German Victory," which detailed the destruction of U.S. capitalist institutions under a totalitarian regime.[32] The August 13 issue of *Look* included an article by Vincent Sheean, "What a Hitler Victory Means to the United States," and predicted worldwide transfers of territories, hunger in Europe, and constant and growing threats to America.[33] These articles had the effect of driving home to a complacent public that although the struggle was in Europe, the future of American democratic principles and security was hanging in the balance.

By the first week in June, even before Paris fell, the first Nazi planes were sighted over northern counties in Britain, probing defenses but as yet doing little damage. Two weeks later they were over the Thames, dropping a scattering of incendiary bombs. On June 18, Churchill warned, "The Battle of France is over. I expect the Battle of Britain is about to begin."[34] By late June, Liverpool, Newcastle, and Southampton each had experienced bombing attacks.[35] On June 23, the *New York Times* ran an article detailing how the Battle of Britain would be fought. "[B]ritain, facing a continent dominated by her enemies, prepared for a fight to the death," the article began ominously. It was no secret that the air assaults were but a prelude to a land invasion designed to take possession of the British Isles and put an end to Britain's empire.[36] By early July, the action had progressed to all-day air raids over the British coast. "For the first time in a hundred and twenty five years a powerful enemy was now established across the narrow waters of the English Channel," wrote Churchill.[37]

By July 11, action over the English Channel between the Luftwaffe and the Royal Air Force had intensified to the point that observers said that the sky was "black with planes."[38] Then, on July 16, Hitler declared what everybody suspected: "As England, in spite of her hopeless military situation, still shows no signs of willingness to come to terms, I have decided to prepare, and if necessary to carry out, a landing operation against her."[39] His plan, dubbed Operation Sea Lion, was predicated on the ability of the Luftwaffe to defeat the RAF. If Hitler's plan was to frighten the British people into backing down as they had done before, he miscalculated their tenacity and the grit of their new leader.

The next day, the news from Europe was temporarily pushed off the front page as Roosevelt accepted the Democratic Party nomination to run for an unprecedented third term in office. The Democrats adopted a strong anti-interventionist plank in their platform, vigorously opposing sending American troops to fight in Europe, but pledging to send aid to those nations attacked by aggressors.

The intensity of the air war immediately picked up. On July 29, Berlin announced to the world that its invasion of Britain was "days, if not hours, away."[40] But it never came. Instead, the attacks by air continued with increasing ferocity.

In Washington, another battle raged. On June 20, a compulsory service bill had been introduced by Sen. Edward Burke of Nebraska, and on July 31 it came to the floor of the Senate for discussion. Secretary of War Henry Stimson urged rapid adoption of the bill, warning of the potential fall of Britain within thirty days and the loss of her fleet to Germany.

The presidential election was only ninety days away, and as the debate on the draft bill raged in the Senate, the air battle raged in the skies over Britain. Where previously the Germans had sent a hundred planes a day across the Channel, mostly to disrupt British convoys, the RAF was now facing 800 planes a day, and holding its own. On August 15, the Luftwaffe sent the biggest attack yet, in which a thousand German planes swarmed over the London docks, and more than a hundred of them were shot down. The next day the Luftwaffe sent a thousand more planes to the same target, losing 71 more, as it gradually shifted its emphasis of attack toward London. For the next few weeks, with little letup, the London suburbs were pounded, attack after attack, day after day. But the Luftwaffe continued to suffer painful losses at the hands of the British defenders, as the Messerschmitts and Stukas were met in the air by defiant Spitfires and Hurricanes. Addressing the House of

Commons, Churchill praised the RAF by saying, "never in the field of human conflict has so much been owed by so many to so few."[41]

Nearly as hotly contested was the battle in the U.S. Senate over the draft bill. Protests in the streets mounted, one of the most notable on Fifth Avenue in New York, where a banner proclaimed, "The Yanks Are Not Coming—Our Fight Is on the Sidewalks of New York."[42] Finally, on August 28, by a vote of 58-31, the Senate approved the bill. It was expected to be taken up within the week by the House.

On Saturday afternoon, September 7, Londoners looked into the sky at 4:30 and saw a sight that they would remember for the rest of their lives. Nearly a thousand German planes, covering 800 square miles of sky, were streaking for the center of the city.[43] Later tallies showed that 348 bombers and 617 fighters were involved in the attack. After darkness fell the raids continued, and by morning London had absorbed its worst beating of the war. That first night, 430 Londoners were killed and 1600 wounded. The next night, and the night after, and the night after, London felt more of the same.[44]

Hitler had decided to abandon the strategically sound effort of destroying the RAF air bases in order to take the war directly to the people. His plan was to terrorize London into submission. The assault on London would go on for 57 nights in near-perfect weather, setting the city on fire in a thousand different places, burning up the Thames, burning up the docks, Westminster, the churches, the apartments, the homes, the theaters and libraries and museums.[45] Buckingham Palace and the House of Lords were hit, as was 10 Downing Street, the Prime Minister's home. By the end of the Blitz, as the Londoners came to call it, 16,000 houses in London had been destroyed, another 60,000 damaged, and 300,000 Londoners were in need of shelter.[46] But the city held on.

On September 14, the U.S. Congress passed the Burke-Wadsworth Bill, establishing the first mandatory military draft in the history of the United States, intending to induct 800,000 men between ages 21 and 35 into the military beginning about November 15. Roosevelt signed the bill on Monday, September 16, and suddenly college students returning to classes for the fall faced a new challenge. On October 16, each male over the age of 21, which included most college seniors, would be required to register for the draft. The world had changed dramatically since the students left campus in the spring. The evolution of American attitude toward involvement in the war, though not yet complete, had cast their future, and the world's future, into grave doubt.

As thousands of college football players on campuses all over the country suited up and headed onto the playing fields on September 28, it was not only thoughts of the gridiron but also thoughts of what lay ahead that swirled through their minds. Their lives and the lives of their classmates had suddenly been tossed upside down. All the debates in Congress, the newspaper columns, the speeches and political pronouncements that filled each day's news were no longer just about the nation's future, but about them and their future. If the nation were attacked, if the American people were dragged into the war, if the conflict spread, the brunt of the responsibility to fight would fall upon their shoulders and those of their classmates and others of their generation. What only months ago appeared as the beginning of a carefree college year, the joyous culmination of their youth, dimmed only slightly by the clouds of a distant war, now appeared ominously like the prelude to a future they could not foresee, control, or understand.

Some of them accepted their fate and willingly prepared to defend their country, perhaps even anxious to do so, as idealistic youth often are. Some worried about their families and the horrors suffered by the people of Europe, fearing the same fate might befall them and their loved ones. Some hoped, maybe even believed, that the crisis would all blow over and life would go on as they had always known it. Some must have been grateful they had football to take their mind off the unsettling subject. Some relied on their faith or on other stoic resources to settle themselves. There must have been anger, even fear, of how they would react if called upon to face death. Could they kill another man, or would they have to? Some counted on being lucky. Others looked for a way out. Almost every one kept his true feelings deep within himself, hidden perhaps behind a façade of false bravado, or of manufactured indifference. But most must have felt, as they gathered on the playing fields of America that fall, that they was preparing to enjoy the fruits of youth one last time.

CHAPTER 4
THE MONEY

Just follow the money.

--WILLIAM GOLDMAN, *All the President's Men* (screenplay)

When thieves broke into the office of the University of Kansas athletic director after halftime of the 1928 homecoming game against Nebraska and made off with the cash box holding the game's receipts, they got away with $4000-$5000, a substantial percentage of the school's athletic revenue for the year.[1] Today, more than anything else, the magnitude has changed. In 2012, the two football teams in the BCS Championship game, LSU and Alabama, collected annual revenue of $69.4 million and $72.8 million, respectively.[2] Decades ago, the debate on the proper role of football on college campuses raged, as it does today. And rules regarding recruiting, scholarships and the support of athletes are still criticized from every quarter, as they have always been. But the greatly increased streams of revenue have substantially raised the stakes and have led to a heightened importance of winning.

In 1927, the Yale football team shared the national championship and generated $1,033,212 in revenue, a record at the time. All other sports at Yale generated combined revenue of $86,068. After expenses were subtracted, football still showed a profit for the year of $549,000. Each of the other sports, once their expenses were subtracted, operated at a deficit. They were supported and made possible by a profitable football program.[3]

Between 1933 and 1936, Cornell athletics, with a less successful football team, lost $125,000.[4] This loss stressed the university budget for non-paying sports. Similarly, Colgate, unsuccessful in football since being undefeated in 1932, and thus with less attendance at football games, was forced to run its entire athletic program with a net operating loss.[5] By 1938, Cornell athletics, enjoying the benefits of a resurgent football team, generated $269,100, and the resulting surplus allowed for the start of construction on a new university golf course.[6] In 1939, Cornell was again successful, and it received revenue of $203,291 from football and $80,573 from all other sports. As at Yale, Cornell football made a substantial profit and all other sports lost money, and as at

Yale, the sports that lost the most were track and rowing.[7] By 1940, a winning football team was already a critical part of the university budgetary process.

One tried-and-true method of promoting winning football was to aggressively recruit and subsidize the most talented football players. Benefits not generally shared by the student body at large, such as generous athletic scholarships, lucrative jobs, and in some cases outright salaries for playing sports, helped attract talented football players to schools interested in such image enhancement. But not all schools shared the same attitude toward athletics. Some, like Chicago, rejected the economic appeal of winning football in favor of a continued emphasis on the academic goals of the institution, and their philosophy of strict amateurism was often seen as praiseworthy adherence to a higher ideal. Writing of Chicago's dismal team, columnist Henry McLemore wrote what everybody knew but few wanted to admit: "None of its players was fought over because students do not make the best players."[8] But the opinion battle raged hotter in academia than among the fans. Most supporters had no concern for such matters and saw no harm in the recruiting practices of aggressive schools, especially if the result was entertaining football. "If colleges give scholarships for debating, why not football?" questioned journalist Francis Wallace.[9]

There was no shared view of the proper relationship between athlete and university. The National Collegiate Athletic Association passed a resolution condemning recruiting and subsidizing,[10] but as for enforcement or investigation, it had absolutely no capabilities. Only by joining a conference of like-minded participants could schools have any assurance that they would be playing against competitors on relatively equal footing. Schools of the Big Ten, the Pacific Coast Conference, and the loosely organized Ivy League generally agreed among themselves to policies of amateurism, although there was some disagreement as to exactly what that meant. Strict amateurism and its opposite, subsidization, were separated by a line of uncertain location. What was called a scholarship by some was termed a salary by others. Andy Kerr, respected coach at Colgate, continued to favor athletic scholarships up to a certain point, because they provided means to an education for many youths that would not otherwise be available.[11] Many shared Kerr's view.

The differences in attitude showed up in other ways. At the end of each year the college presidents of the ten Pacific Coast Conference schools chose a representative to play in the Rose Bowl, and the chosen representative then invited its opponent. But the choices were slim. Desiring to play against schools on equal competitive footing, they found that both the Big Ten and the Ivy League schools had policies prohibiting bowl competition, and they were almost forced to play against opponents who did not share their competitive philosophy. One proposed strategy, with a two-pronged outcome, was to coax the Big Ten into a long-term Rose Bowl relationship. First, it would provide a highly popular, even-handed competition and, second, it would provide an incentive for the "bad boys," as some saw them, to clean house and thus become eligible for the $100,000 bonanza provided by the Rose Bowl.[12] Though it would take some time, such an arrangement did indeed come about by 1947. Meanwhile, the issue of subsidization remained a source of great anguish to most college administrators.

The University of Pittsburgh was a school deeply invested in the strategy of subsidization and found that these practices came at a steep price. Between 1931 and 1938, under its coach Jock Sutherland, Pitt amassed a record of 63-7-6, including two undefeated seasons, a national championship, and two Rose Bowl appearances. "Sutherland fielded great teams because he knew what it took to keep his cattle in clover," wrote football historian John Sayle Watterson.[13] But the football program was being cast in an increasingly poor light, despite its on-field success, by continued allegations, largely true, of generous subsidization to the players.[14] Much of this criticism was the work of Francis Wallace, who wrote in the *Saturday Evening Post* singling out Pitt for particular attention.[15]

There was some feeling that those who criticized the most loudly were equally at fault. In 1935, rumors spread that the entire Ohio State football team was on the state payroll as legislative pages.[16] The rumors were never substantiated. Further, many felt that what went on under the table, out of sight and in the absence of any regulation or control, more accurately defined the situation than did official policy. There was no telling, in the minds of these doubters, how many young quarterbacks had their tuitions paid, in whole or in part, by wealthy alumni benefactors. And there were just as many who saw no evil in such practice. To these people the entire question of reform was an exercise in shortsightedness and hypocrisy.

Pitt not only wanted to compete with the schools in the Big Ten, but also very much wanted to become a member of the conference. But in 1936, the Big Ten, whose schools gravitated strongly toward a policy of highly restrictive amateurism in athletics, now headed in exactly the opposite direction. It severed athletic relations with Pitt, citing a sharp difference in athletic philosophy. To add to this embarrassment, after Pitt won the national championship in 1937, it was invited for the second consecutive year to play in the Rose Bowl. The players publicly declined to play, holding out for increased financial rewards. Sutherland strongly supported his players in their request, but their demands were refused.[17] The players' rejection of the invitation cost the school about $100,000 and some very red faces.

Chancellor John Gabbert Bowman immediately instituted a series of changes to the school's athletic policies. Sutherland, now sharply at odds with him and the athletic department, was stoically tolerant at first while remaining a staunch supporter of subsidization. The new regulations restricted spring practice, put college athletics under faculty control, and required that athletes make normal progress toward their degrees. They included a ban on married players (of which there were many at Pitt, a sure sign, some thought, of undue luxury) and a requirement that players hold down jobs in exchange for their tuition and board.[18] And they eliminated 35 annual football scholarships for freshmen and restricted football coaches from newspaper writing, radio appearances, and endorsement of athletic goods.[19]

"We're convinced that Pittsburgh has turned over a new leaf and is doing a good job," said Ohio State Athletic Director L.W. St. John.[20]

Sutherland had had enough. In March of 1939, though enjoying strong popularity with the student body and the alumni, he resigned, citing "athletic evangelism gone wild,"[21] and moved on to a career in the National Football League, where such problems were not an issue. He served as head coach for eight years with the Brooklyn Dodgers and the Pittsburgh Steelers.

Pitt, now back in the good graces of its critics, was eager to schedule Big Ten teams again, so anxious to do so that it dumped West Virginia, its second longest rival, from its schedule. Rumors began to spread that Pitt would be admitted to the Big Ten beginning in 1941 to replace Chicago,[22] and others hinted that they were "fairly itching" to do so.[23] But it was only a tease.

****

The popularity of sports in America hardly needed help from broadcasting to take root. Shortly after the turn of the century, nurtured mainly by reporting after the fact, through newspaper and other similar publications, sports such as baseball, boxing, and football had developed robust followings. But soon after the end of the Great War, sports popularity spread simultaneously with quantum improvements in radio technology. In September of 1920, experimental radio station WWJ in Detroit was the first to report results of a sporting event over the air, a Jack Dempsey-Billy Miske heavyweight fight. By September of 1927, first-hand accounts of the second Jack Dempsey-Gene Tunney championship fight were heard by over 50 million sports fans around the world. In 1922, the United States had 60,000 households with radio sets; by 1930, it had 12 million.[24] The Golden Age of Sports flourished.

But an even bigger advance was about to take place. In 1927, a 21-year-old inventor named Philo T. Farnsworth, working in his laboratory in San Francisco, developed a crude version of what he called an image dissector. David Sarnoff, president of RCA, acquired the right to use Farnsworth's technology, and on April 30, 1939, at the World's Fair in Queens, New York, television was unveiled to the world. President Franklin Roosevelt took the podium to inaugurate the event, and his image was broadcast by Sarnoff's television system throughout the New York metropolitan area. It was estimated that as many as 200 television sets were tuned to the event, and as many as 1000 people may have witnessed the broadcast. That year, Sarnoff sold 3,000 sets.[25]

41

Problems with the new technology abounded, and *The Nation* referred to the "half-ready art of visual broadcasting."[26] The new sets stood about 4 ½ feet tall and, depending on whether one purchased the five-inch screen or the nine-inch screen, cost between $250 and $675, nearly matching the cost of a new car, at a time when the nation was not yet fully recovered from the Depression. The picture quality was poor. It flickered, it was dull, it had a greenish tint, the horizontal lines that made up the picture were quite visible, and the viewable image was tiny. The innovation was labeled "an expensive and impractical toy."[27]

"The economic base for television has yet to be found," remarked Edgar M. Jones in *The Nation*. "Diehard radio men refuse to believe that the American people will sit in darkened living rooms to accommodate sponsors of television programs."[28] Six years later Darryl F. Zanuck of 20th Century Fox, still holding to that view, said, "Television won't be able to hold on to any market it captures after the first six months. People will soon get tired of staring at a plywood box every night."[29] In 1940, when there were about 29 million radios in a nation with about 35 million households,[30] it was clear that radio was still king.

It is difficult to peg when the first college football game was telecast, but it probably happened on September 30, 1939, when Waynesburg College played Fordham at Randalls Island Stadium in the Bronx. The only outwardly noticeable evidence of what was going on was a structure that looked like a railroad boxcar near the 40-yard line and a camera on a tripod. The participants and fans were oblivious. Referee Jack McPhee had this to say: "When I returned home I told my wife about it. She was all excited, asking me what television was and how did it work. Of course, I did not know." The game was viewed by about 9000 fans in person and an estimated 200 viewers on television.[31]

In December 1941, when production due to the war was halted, about 10,000 families in the United States owned television sets.[32] By 1948, there were 170,000 new televisions in the country.[33] Sets by then were still immensely expensive, costing $299.95 and up, and a homeowner could purchase a new refrigerator and a new electric range for the cost of a new 21-inch television.[34] But the screens were getting bigger and better, and television stood on the brink of an explosion of popularity.

College football officials continued to view the prime relationship between the game and the fans to be one of attendance in the stadium, and they feared that television, instead of enabling and promoting the relationship, would undermine it. Not until 1951 did the NCAA allow football games to be televised on Saturdays, and it only allowed one game in each area per Saturday.[35] As time wore on and understandings of the new world evolved, that restriction would significantly loosen.

By the end of the 1950s, 90 percent of all American households owned at least one television set, a clear sign that the innovation had taken a firm hold.[36] This swift spread of popularity changed the nature of communication forever. A seemingly ever-expanding stream of revenue would reshape the world of sport, of communication, and of fandom, promising more to come.

A half-century later, the implications of this relationship have become enormous. College football's modern balance sheets stand in sharp contrast to their counterparts in 1940. By 2004-05, the University of Texas football program, the country's most profitable, took in $53.2 million in revenue and made a profit of $38.7 million.[37] By 2010, Texas had increased its coach's salary from $3 million to $5.1 million. "He's in the entertainment business," said one prominent booster.[38] At the start of the 2009 season there were three football coaches in the country who earned more than $4 million, and 56 who earned more than $1 million. By 2009, salaries for head football coaches in the Southeastern Conference averaged more than $2.6 million each in total compensation.[39] In some cases these salaries are augmented by huge bonuses tied directly to winning. In December of 2010, the Oregon football coach received $4.3 million in bonuses and contract extension tied to the outcome of one game, a victory over archrival Oregon State.[40] At some colleges the salaries of assistant coaches exceed the presidents' salaries,[41] and by 2010 six assistant coaches were earning at least $700,000.[42]

All this was made possible by immense television contracts that in turn greatly expanded the number of viewers. The Big Ten Conference signed a ten-year, $1 billion deal with ABC/ESPN, and every school in the conference in 2008 received at least $15 million.[43] The Southeastern Conference, too, has a new 15-year deal with ESPN and CBS.

In 2009, ABC averaged more than 6 million viewers per game for the 31 college football games it televised, and CBS approached 7 million viewers for its 16 games. The SEC championship game attracted nearly 18 million viewers to CBS. In 1941, Bruce Smith was awarded the Heisman Trophy in a ceremony attended by 900 people. In 2009, the Heisman Trophy award telecast was viewed by nearly 6 million on ESPN.[44] Meanwhile, bowl games proliferated from five in 1940 to 34 plus a BCS Championship game in 2012, and a total of nearly 225 million viewers tuned in.[45]

Tickets to a top game in 1940 cost about three dollars. By 2010, they were unavailable at the most competitive schools except through a seat-licensing program whereby the right to buy tickets was sold in multi-year bundles that literally involved taking out a mortgage.[46] Television helped transform college football from a popular campus diversion with major financial implications for the universities into a huge industry, its product viewed by tens of millions of people each week, with outsize salaries for its key non-student performers.

In 1940, the NCAA charged each of its member institutions $25 per year in dues; its largest source of revenue was the new NCAA basketball tournament, from which it made about $10,000, its clerical charges for the year came to $325, and its cash on hand was $10,346.61. It had no executive director or permanent staff, and thus no real role except to publish books of rules it could not enforce.[47] By 2006, the NCAA was spending nearly $1 million per year chartering private jets.[48] In 2008-09, the NCAA budget shows $590 million in television and marketing rights fees, not including championships, 95 percent of which is returned to the member institutions. The modern financial world of college sports, awash in revenues and with a new emphasis on winning to capture them, bears little resemblance to the version of 1940, in large part due to the plywood box of Philo T. Farnsworth.

CHAPTER 5
CONTROVERSY

*You can tell the character of every man when
you see how he receives praise.*

--SENECA, *Epistles*

Unlike Minnesota, Ohio State had every reason for optimism. It was coming off a successful 6-2 season in which the Buckeyes were Big Ten champions, and in 1940 they were favorites to repeat. Their final game of the year against Michigan was expected to decide the Big Ten title. They were led by their All-American quarterback Don Scott on both offense and defense. An excellent passer and punter on offense and a tackler tough enough to play linebacker on defense, Scott, a graduate of McKinley High School in Canton, Ohio, was *Look* 1940 preseason Player of the Year. Likewise, Francis Wallace of *The Saturday Evening Post*, in an article previewing the season, named him the back of the year. When Scott made the All-Big Ten first team in 1939, he finished second in the balloting, behind Nile Kinnick but ahead of Tom Harmon. On his shoulders as the season began was the burden of proving to the football world that he was worthy of such lofty praise. Scott, a likeable team leader who purposely did not read the newspapers hyping him, welcomed the challenge as an opportunity to free up his teammates to excel. "If they keep watching me," he reasoned, "Strasbaugh and Langhurst will run their ears off."[1] As expected in the opener against Pitt, Scott, playing only sparingly, threw two touchdown passes in the third quarter, one for 45 yards and one for 18 yards, to seal the victory before the second and third string came on.

On Wednesday, October 2, the World Series began in Cincinnati, pitting the Reds against the Detroit Tigers. The Series, a tight and well-played affair, was won by the Reds in seven games played over seven consecutive days. Between 1935 and 1944 it was the only World Series not involving at least one New York team—three Series during that stretch involved two—and the New York press seemed a bit bored by it. On Sunday, October 6, following the Reds' 5-2 victory in the fourth game, the bulk of the Series coverage appeared on page 8 of the *New York Times'* sports section. College football, far more compelling, received top billing.

45

On October 5, Ohio State opened the defense of its Big Ten crown with a game in Columbus against the Purdue Boilermakers. The Buckeyes were a big physical team, and they were heavily favored over an outweighed and outmanned Purdue eleven. Purdue was not without its resources, however. Halfback Mike Byelene and end Dave Rankin were both All-American performers, and any team hoping to beat Purdue would have to deal with these two standouts.

Using long sustained drives, Ohio State scored in the first quarter on a 65-yard drive, and again in the second quarter, moving 73 yards. The second touchdown was scored by Jim Langhurst on a three-yard run right after Ohio State sent a group of new substitutes into the game. There were 41 seconds left in the half.

The second half was completely different. The Boilermakers came roaring back. Borrowing a page from Ohio State's book, they took the opening kickoff of the second half and marched down the field 72 yards for a touchdown, then tacked on another touchdown in the fourth quarter to tie the game. But Ohio State, with 28 seconds left in the game, had the ball on the Purdue 12-yard line. Coach Francis Schmidt sent into the game Charlie Maag, his starting right tackle, a second-team All-Big Ten performer the previous year, and an excellent field goal kicker. Maag proceeded to kick the winning field goal. The Buckeyes had sweated more than they thought they would, but although outgained in total yardage for the day by Purdue, they came away with their second victory of the year.

A few days later, Gordon Graham, sports editor of the *Lafayette (Ind.) Journal and Courier*, wrote in his column that something about the game was sour. He contended that just prior to Ohio State's second touchdown at the end of the second period, when the Buckeyes made a group of substitutions, one of the players brought into the game was Charlie Maag. Maag, he contended, had already played in the second period and had been taken out of the game, and was thus ineligible to re-enter the game until after halftime. The rule of the day, dramatically different from today's free substitution rule, was clear: "A player may be substituted for another player at any time, but a player may not return in the same period or intermission in which he was withdrawn." This was not an obscure rule. It was at the heart of how the college game was played in 1940, and had been in the rule book in some form since 1922. It was akin to the baseball rule that prohibits a player from re-entering the game after being lifted for a pinch-hitter. The only problem was that nobody had taken particular notice of the substitution at the time.

A subsequent review of the game films showed that Graham was correct in his contentions, and thus the rest of the rule, which spells out the penalty for violation, becomes relevant: "The penalty for this illegal entry is that the player shall be suspended from the game and his team penalized fifteen yards." So Ohio State had enjoyed two illegal advantages in scoring its second touchdown. First, they had Maag, the first stringer, and not Jack Stephenson, his backup, in the game. Second, they had the ball at the three-yard line and not the 18-yard line. One could argue that the first advantage was minor. After all, the Buckeyes had moved the ball down the field 70 yards just fine with Stephenson in the game and Stephenson, it turned out, would be a starter for much of the remainder of the season and team captain the next season. There is no reason to believe that Ohio State could not have moved the ball an additional three yards. But the second advantage—operating from the 18-yard line instead of the three—is substantial. There can be no conceding a touchdown from the 18-yard line, especially when there are only 41 seconds to play.

The Buckeyes enjoyed a third, even greater, illegal advantage. Maag, who came into the game to kick the game-winning field goal (although he should have been disqualified), had experience with game-winning situations like this—he had beaten Minnesota the previous year on such a play. Who can say whether a different player would have kicked the field goal?

With the error exposed, people wondered what Ohio State would do about it. When confronted with the facts, Schmidt readily admitted the error. He agreed that Maag was illegally in the game. "However," he added, "the illegal substitution was an oversight and purely unintentional. It's unfortunate, but nothing can be done about it now. I'm really sorry that it happened."[2]

Under the rules of the Big Ten, the coaches, not the referees on the field, were responsible for monitoring the substitutions on an honor system basis. Referees hated the substitution rule, claiming that, with all they had to do on the field, it reduced them to bookkeepers; they were happy with the Big Ten rule that reassigned the responsibility. L.W. St. John, Ohio State athletic director, blamed both Maag, who should have been aware of the situation, he contended, as well as the student manager in charge of monitoring substitutions on the bench.

Schmidt's sentiment, that it was a serious error but nothing should be done about it, was widely shared. The Purdue coach, Mal Elward, was at least outwardly in agreement. "That game is over at least as far as we are concerned," he said valiantly.[3] He was, he said, willing to "forgive and forget."[4] Major John L. Griffith, the Western Conference commissioner of athletics, was just as definite. "If Maag was illegally substituted it was a mistake about which nothing can be done....[I]t's too bad. The incident is closed," he said.[5] The Cornell student newspaper, which would soon have more dealings with disputes and with the principals in this one, agreed. "[T]hat game is over and nothing can be done about it now. But the memory lingers on," it said.[6] But others were not so quick to dismiss the concern. "It's as illegal as a 12-man team," pronounced the United Press.[7] "Honor is on trial in the Big Ten," proclaimed the *Capital Times* of Madison, Wisconsin, which concluded that the game should have ended in a 14-14 tie.[8] Ohio State might have come away

47

with a win, which could not be appealed, but the victory had come at a cost of loss of face for the Buckeyes.

Columnists had great fun with the incident. Declaring the occurrence to be fantastic, John Kieran of the *New York Times* wrote, "No movie script writer could have thought up any such complicated comedy." First, he exonerated Maag and the student manager, judging the substitution practices too complicated to track. Then he expressed regret that fate had given Ohio State such a decided edge, especially on the final field goal. Finally, he concluded, as others had, that the final result had to stand. "That water is under the bridge. Let it go," he concluded.[9]

By the end of the season, Kieran would learn much more about fantastic occurrences. The entire incident was a grim foreboding of things to come.

****

Cornell's first game of the season was on October 5 against the Red Raiders of Colgate, a team that had come closer than any other to defeating the Big Red the year before, falling only 14-12. The closeness of that 1939 game, in which the margin of victory was Colgate's two missed extra points, was all the clearer when one noted that Cornell, too, had both its extra point kicks blocked. The true margin of victory was that, after the first blocked kick, Cornell's Whit Baker, who had just scored the touchdown, was able to pick up the loose ball and run it into the end zone, thus preserving the point. On the second blocked kick Colgate was ruled offside and Cornell, given a second chance, opted to run for the extra point rather than risk a third block, and Baker again took it in for the point. Cornell then had to hang on for its life as Colgate missed a 33-yard field goal on the last play of the game.

So as Carl Snavely's charges took the field they were well on guard against overconfidence. By the end of the afternoon, however, the scoreboard read 34-0 in favor of the Big Red. Cornell outgained the Red Raiders in total passing and rushing yardage by 406 yards to 103, scored four of their five touchdowns on passes, completed 11 passes for 248 yards, intercepted five Colgate passes, limited Colgate to four pass completions in 18 attempts, and was simply superior in every facet of the game. But the most important point was how many players were involved in the victory. Five different players (Landsberg, Bufalino, Schmuck, Kelley, and Scholl) scored touchdowns, and in addition to these players, Hal McCullough, Kirk Hershey, and Walt Matuszczak seemed to be in the middle of everything. Cornell's line was superb on offense and defense. Snavely's team had served notice that it had depth at every position and knew how to use it.

Cornell suffered a number of nagging injuries against Colgate, but was nevertheless heavy favorites to beat Army on October 12. The Big Red boarded a train in Ithaca on Thursday night and headed to Cornwall, New York, where they stayed and worked out at the Storm King School, then headed for West Point for their game at 2 pm. Meanwhile, Army officials were hard at work adding additional temporary seating capacity to Michie Stadium in expectations of the largest crowd ever to view a game at West Point. An overflow crowd of more than 27,000 was expected. The two teams had played only once before, in 1907, and Cornell had won that contest, 14-10.

The Cornell coaching staff continued to be on guard against overconfidence. Assistant coach Ray Van Orman cautioned the Big Red players that, despite Army's record, the Cadets could be counted on to be tough, well-conditioned, and full of fight. Van Orman, who played in the 1907 game, related his experience to the team. "I remember when I played against them myself," he recounted, "and woke up in Jersey City."[10]

What the record crowd witnessed was the worst defeat in the proud 51-year history of Army football as Cornell won easily, 45-0. After establishing a decisive edge, the Big Red spent much of the afternoon punting on second and third down. The recipe Snavely's team used was identical to that of the week before. Seven different players scored seven touchdowns; six different passers completed thirteen passes; and the aerial attack scored touchdowns on passes of 45, 65, and 35 yards. Walt Scholl threw two of those passes and caught the third. In attendance at the game was former president Herbert Hoover, who in his time had seen notable collapses. Hoover stayed for three quarters of the game before leaving.

Cornell had displayed a powerful and diversified offensive to the football world, one capable of striking from anywhere, and when the first Associated Press rankings of the year came out on the following Tuesday, the Big Red were ranked first in the nation. Texas A&M, Michigan, and Northwestern followed in the next three spots.

CHAPTER 6
HARMONIZED

Good speed to your youthful valor, boy!
So shall you scale the stars!

--VIRGIL, *The Aeneid*

There are those that feel that Tom Harmon was a victim of jealousy and resentment throughout his college career, both from those outside the Michigan team and from his own teammates. When he arrived on the Michigan campus at Ann Arbor in the fall of 1937, he was the most famous and sought-after high school athlete in the country. Born in Rensselaer, Indiana, and raised in Gary, Indiana, some 40 miles to the north, Tom Harmon was one of seven children. His father was a steel mill security guard.[1] He earned 14 varsity letters at Horace Mann High School in Gary; he was all-state quarterback for two years, captain of the basketball team, and state champion in the 100-yard dash and 200-yard low hurdles; he pitched three no-hitters for the baseball team his senior year. In an era when recruiting was strongly frowned on in many circles, Harmon received offers from 54 colleges.[2] Turned off by the size of the Notre Dame program, he narrowed his choice to Purdue, where two of his older brothers had gone to college, and Michigan, at his high school coach's urging. He finally settled on Michigan where his celebrity, though hard earned, was resented by many.

Harmon received no easy ride. He worked hard for his money. He labored in the steel mills in the summer, worked in the bookstore on campus during the school year, and got up at 5 am every morning to work for three hours in the Michigan Union washing dishes before class. It was the same for all the other football players. Harmon's teammate and best friend, quarterback Forest Evashevski, recalled that football practice had to stop each day at 5:30 so that the players could get to their jobs on campus.[3]

As soon as he arrived in Ann Arbor, the rumors began to spread that Harmon was being recruited to leave Michigan to attend Tulane, where another brother had gone to school. These rumors did nothing to calm the uneasy relationship the arriving celebrity had with the rest of the student body. Harmon started out as a blocking wingback in Fritz Crisler's offensive scheme, partly, it has been suggested, to deal with the intense jealousy among at least some of his teammates.[4] He made the All-Big Ten team as a sophomore in that role in 1938, and midway through his junior year, Crisler moved him to tailback, the featured position in the single wing. His already illustrious career began to shine even brighter. By mid-season, *Time* had labeled him "the number one footballer of the year."[5] He finished the 1939 season with a prodigious 13 rushing touchdowns and one by interception return, and he passed for six more.

Harmon had an athlete's cockiness, but he went to great pains to assure it was never mistaken for arrogance or conceit. "So afraid is he of being considered high-hat that he waves to everyone he meets on campus," declared *Time*.[6] Apparently he didn't always succeed. His football talent seemed to work against his popularity as much as for it. He did not have the personality to embrace celebrity and showed no great comfort with it. He went out of his way to praise his teammates, especially Evashevski, for his accomplishments. After one particularly sterling performance in 1939, in which he scored 27 points, he told the press, "Anybody could have done it with that Evashevski and those others in there blocking like that."[7] Still, the acerbic John Lardner, in a profile written for *Newsweek*, expressed the thought that Harmon's celebrity rubbed his teammates the wrong way. He observed, "In pregame practice at Harvard, one of the boys looked over his shoulder and said, 'Here comes Harmon. Now the practice can begin.' " Lardner added, in a kinder note, that Harmon had a "pleasant, self-effacing way about him which preserves him a mild popularity."[8]

Later in the year, Harmon and All-Star teammate Frank Reagan of Penn caused a stir at the East-West Shrine Game, held in San Francisco, by missing a few practices to go to Los Angeles. Their supposed purpose was to drum up support for another all-star game to support British War Relief.[9] The game never came off. His all-star teammates suspected that Harmon was negotiating a movie contract, a purpose for which he had also dropped out of school temporarily,[10] but the complaints were dismissed by many as mere jealousy. East coach Andy Kerr scoffed at the allegations.[11]

In 1940, it was Evashevski, not Harmon, who was chosen as team captain. And later that year Evashevski, running against Harmon, was elected senior class president by a landslide.[12] Harmon was "no mental meteor," the sniping Lardner said,[13] but he got decent grades. He was an honor student who earned a B average while taking 18 credit hours his junior year.[14] Evashevski, on the other hand, had graduated from high school in Detroit at age 16 and won the Big Ten Medal for excellence in academics and athletics. He graduated from Michigan with a major in sociology and a minor in psychology. Despite this apparent rivalry, the two remained close friends for life.

Harmon was as gracious when he lost as when he won. He seemed to have the knack for saying the right thing, even if his answers to questions sometimes strained credulity. When asked at the end of his senior year, he stated that his greatest thrills in football came from a tackle he made in 1939 against Ohio State and from a block he made for teammate Paul Kromer, also against Ohio State (this in a game Harmon left to a standing ovation from the Buckeye crowd). When asked who the best back was he'd played against all year, he named Frank Reagan, a man he dominated in a head-to-head matchup. Only when that answer was poorly accepted by his audience did he change his answer to Bruce Smith. A reporter at the event commented that he seemed "as modest and retiring as the fifty-ninth sub on a squad of sixty."[15]

But not everybody saw that quality in Harmon. Professor James B. Lane, in writing a history of Gary, Indiana, Harmon's home town, attributed to Harmon "vanity and aloofness" and criticized his "self-congratulatory fanfare."[16] Lane rated Harmon as the second most famous war hero from Gary, behind well-known combat photographer Johnny Bushemi, who was killed in 1944, in a mortar attack on Eniwetok in the Pacific. Bushemi gave his life for his country, and there can be no minimizing his standing. But there was a certain meanness expressed toward Harmon. Apparently his charm, though embraced by some, was less than universal in its appeal.

In the middle of the 1939 season, after Harmon had outshone Iowa's Nile Kinnick in another head-to-head matchup of great stars by scoring four touchdowns and all his team's points in a 27-7 victory, *Time* ran an article that acknowledged Harmon's performance as the best of the day, then called it "as magnificent a display of fancy field running, passing, blocking and place-kicking as has been seen on a college football field since the days of Red Grange."[17] While not quite amounting to a comparison between Harmon and Grange, the remark paved the way for the debate to begin, one that would keep football fans fully occupied for the next season and a half. The remark sparked immediate interest, amounting to heresy in the minds of some, and introducing a worthy subject for debate in the minds of others. Whether Harold "Red" Grange of Illinois was the greatest college football player of all time was, in 1939, an open question, but he, along with George Gipp, Willie Heston, Jim Thorpe, and a small handful of others, was prominently considered for the mantle. Grange's career record of 31 touchdowns stood along with Babe Ruth's 60 home runs as a symbolic record of the sporting era. To be considered comparable to Grange, or even mentioned in the same breath, was perhaps the greatest praise a college football player could receive.

Grange weighed 165 pounds when he began his college career and about 180 pounds at its end. He worked each summer as an iceman, sinking tongs into huge blocks of ice and hauling them up flights of stairs to his customers. But Harmon was at least twenty pounds heavier and every bit as fast. Once in the open field, both seemed to have a sixth sense that calculated the positioning and movement of each opponent and blocker and charted a course through them down the field. While Harmon seemed more analytical and conscious of what he was doing, Grange seemed all instinct. "I don't remember one thing I ever did on any run I made," he later explained.[18]

In an era when even play-by-play radio broadcasts strained technological capabilities to the limits, Grange nevertheless managed to capture the adoration and imagination of the burgeoning crop of college football fans of the day. Along with Ruth and Jack Dempsey, Red Grange formed the triumvirate of sports heroes that ruled the decade of the 1920s, the Golden Age of Sports. After he made Walter Camp's All-America team as a sophomore, Grange's defining performance came on October 18, 1924, in the third game of his junior year. It happened on the same day that Grantland Rice anointed the Four Horsemen of Notre Dame at the Polo Grounds. Playing for Illinois against Michigan at the newly dedicated Memorial Stadium in Champaign, Grange turned in perhaps the greatest single performance in the history of college football. It was elegant in its simplicity. He returned the opening kickoff 95 yards for a touchdown. Then, in rapid order, he ran for touchdown runs from scrimmage of 67 yards, 56 yards, and 44 yards. Before the game was 12 minutes old, he had accounted for 282 yards in total offense, including the two runs on which Michigan somehow managed to tackle him. He did not return to the game until the third quarter when he ran 13 yards for his fifth touchdown, and then in the fourth quarter passed for his sixth touchdown of the day. In 42 minutes of playing time he accounted for 402 yards in rushing and kick returning and passed for another 64 yards.

"It is doubtful if anything near its equal has been seen in the West since the days of Walter Eckersall," said the *Chicago Tribune*. "It made old time football people think of Heston of Michigan," the *Tribune* added.[19] The Associated Press report called Grange's performance "the most remarkable exhibition of running, dodging and passing seen on any gridiron in years."[20] The praise poured in from every quarter. "The greatness of the Illinois star, the thing that causes him to stand among the elect of all time, lies in his ability to encompass the layout of the field ahead of him and to adapt his movements accordingly," said sportswriter Lawrence Perry.[21] "It is impossible to find words to describe the brilliance of Harold 'Red' Grange of Wheaton, Ill.," wrote Henry Farrell.[22] In another column Farrell added, "Beyond all doubt, Grange is the greatest football player that has come up in the last ten years at least....Gipp could kick better than Grange but he could do nothing else better."[23] Amos Alonzo Stagg said, "That was the most spectacular single-handed performance ever made in a major game."[24] He later added, "Grange, beyond all doubt, is one of the greatest players ever developed," and Knute Rockne chimed in, "I never heard of any player scoring four touchdowns in the first period of such an important game."[25]

There is no telling how sports history would read had Grantland Rice been in Champaign that afternoon instead of at the Polo Grounds. As it was,

Rice bestowed on Grange, before he ever saw him play, the resonant label "The Galloping Ghost."

But Grange was not a one-game wonder. Two weeks later he rushed for 300 yards and passed for 150 more as Illinois tied the Chicago Maroons. Many thought his greatest game was the next year against Penn when he ran for 363 yards and introduced himself to the eastern football establishment, many members of whom had belittled his previous accomplishments as mere "western football." That Grange turned in his performance against a team that some had favored by as much as four touchdowns—Illinois won, 24-2— was all the more significant. "This was delivering the goods," wrote an impressed Paul Gallico.[26]

"Red Grange was the most sensational, the most publicized, and, possibly, the most gifted football player and greatest broken field runner of all time," wrote W.C. Heinz.[27] Damon Runyan wrote, "Twenty years from now when we all have long gray whiskers, we will be harking back to Mr. Red Harold Grange as one of the greatest that ever lived."[28]

In the week following the Michigan game an article appeared in the *Chicago Tribune* titled, "Does Red Grange Outrank Grid Heroes of Other Years?" The article is significant for two reasons. First, its author was Walter Eckersall, a *Tribune* sports columnist who, while a player at Chicago, clearly was among the premier grid stars of his day. Second, Eckersall made no attempt to answer his posed question, leaving the reader to gather that it could not be answered and, more important, that there seemed to be no point in answering it. The joy of the matter to Eckersall, and apparently to his readers, was in raising the question, for it led to reminiscing among the great names of the past (he diplomatically left out his own name), and not in the answering of it.[29] The debate would be great fun.

Fifteen autumns later, the issue was reopened. Harmon's coach, Fritz Crisler, had coached against Grange as an assistant at Chicago under Amos Alonzo Stagg and so was in a position to have an informed opinion. "I saw Red Grange, and (Tom) Harmon is better. He's not only a runner, but he can also pass, block, and tackle. Grange was chiefly a ball-carrier, and even in that department, Grange had no edge over Harmon," he said.[30] Later, he stuck to his message. "He was better than Red Grange, the 'Galloping Ghost'. Tom could do more things. He ran, passed, punted, blocked, kicked off, and kicked extra points and field goals. He was a superb defensive player."[31]

Grange's coach, the venerable Bob Zuppke, was not eager to enter the debate. "It's difficult to compare them," he said. "Harmon runs in angles and Grange was the snaky type."[32] Zuppke and Grange, it should be noted, did not part company on good terms. After Grange quit school at Illinois to play pro football for George Halas and the Chicago Bears, the two men shared a strained relationship for many years, not speaking for most of the time. Zuppke was profoundly opposed to professional football, and especially to his star leaving school before graduation to enter that shady world, but Halas, Zuppke's protégé, was more persuasive. When Zuppke gave a talk at a Rotary Club dinner in Champaign expounding on his views, Grange, deeply wounded by his comments, abruptly walked out, leaving behind the letter sweater he had been awarded earlier that evening. Later in his life, after the two had reconciled, Zuppke acknowledged Grange as the greatest football player who ever lived,[33] and Grange expressed as one of his few regrets not ever having a letter sweater.[34]

John Lardner, for one, was not buying the Harmon line. "I cling steadfastly to my belief that no man, including Harmon, ever could carry a football with the smooth speed and elusiveness and sure, blazing instinct of Harold the Iceman," he concluded.[35]

Others, such as William D. Richardson of the *New York Times*, declined an opinion, admitting that Harmon was sensational, but claiming that as of midseason 1939 he had not been tested. Michigan's line was so superior to its opponents, he reasoned, that "a one-legged man might have gone hopping to town."[36] This argument was later buttressed by the fact that Michigan's two losses in 1939 came with an injured Evashevski out of the lineup.

There is no question that Harmon enjoyed great blocking. E.W. Midgett, coach at Tennessee State College, was in attendance at the 1940 Michigan-Ohio State contest, Harmon's last college game, and what he observed made a lasting impression on him. When Harmon instinctively reversed his fields and dashed into the open on one of his long runs, he then cut behind a wall of blockers and, said Midgett, "you could hear those blocks in the second tier of seats."[37]

But Richardson's view was exactly the view that set others off. While many observers heaped credit on Harmon's blockers, most notably Evashevski, there was plenty of evidence that Harmon ran as well, whether Evashevski was in the lineup or not. "I don't want to belittle Evashevski's value," wrote Henry McLemore of the United Press, "but Harmon can go with or without him."[38] Whitney Martin of the Associated Press agreed. "Other backs have had fine blocking, yet have been no Granges or Harmons," he pointed out. "No matter how good the blocking, a star ball carrier must have something," he added.[39] There was a difference, they reasoned, between having great blocking and knowing how to use it.

Some looked for other excuses. After Harmon had decimated California in the 1940 opener, Cal coach Stub Allison was asked whether the Bears' poor tackling might have contributed to Harmon's looking like a second Red Grange. "No sir!" answered Allison. "That Harmon is a great halfback—one of the fastest and best I've ever seen. When he's having a great day like he did against us he will make any team look bad....He was just plain dynamite."[40]

Grange had faced exactly the same doubts and misgivings in his time. His key blocker, fullback Earl Britton, had been much bigger and more versatile than Evashevski, and equally deserving of praise. "While admitting that he is one of the greatest players in the country, many western critics claim that he has his great interference to thank," wrote Henry Farrell of Grange, then added, "but it will have to be admitted that every runner has to have interference."[41] Lawrence Perry admitted he was at first tempted to regard Grange as "the greatest running back who ever wore cleats," but then decided to defer judgment, reasoning that Grange had yet to play against stiff competition. "To poor end play thus may not a few of Grange's long runs be ascribed," he said.[42] But Michigan had entered the game against Grange with a 20-game unbeaten streak, and together with Illinois and the Chicago Maroons were the cream of the Big Ten. The more than 400 yards Grange gained against the Wolverines was more than all Michigan's opponents combined had gained the previous season. Grange had accomplished his feat against competition as stiff as there was.

Harmon was acutely aware of the problem presented by such talk, since it only heightened the resentment against him, and avoided the issue at every opportunity. He could challenge on the football field the other luminaries of his time—Reagan, Kinnick, Franck, Smith— but he could not beat a legend of another era when his only weapon was print. He wrote this note on an autographed photo he gave to Evashevski: "I know I'm no Red Grange, but the sporting world has never seen a greater blocker than you. You deserve the world on a string. From Ol' 98—and the man you made."[43]

In 1962, Alfred Wright, writing in *Sports Illustrated*, took on the Herculean task of identifying the best college player of all time. In the process, he said, "Harmon is the only other broken-field runner who can be spoken of in the same breath with Grange."[44] But though attempts have been made,[45] there is no clinical way to compare players of different eras, such as Grange and Harmon, even when they were separated by less than two decades. The differences in rules, strategies, strength of schedules, and customs of the day make such attempts suspect. During the 1940 season, George Pfann, star of Cornell's national championship teams of 1921 and 1922, only a year before Grange's ascendency, was interviewed for the Cornell student newspaper. The changes in the game over the eighteen years since his departure had been remarkable, he thought. The game had become faster and more technical, in his opinion, but the players were softer. "We had more stamina, I believe. We used to get in there and play all sixty minutes straight....the boys don't seem to be as hard today as they used to be, automobiles and all that," he remarked.[46] And comparisons of modern players to those of either past era would be even more difficult. With the demise of one-platoon football, modern players are all specialists. "[W]e haven't the faintest notion whether [Jim] Brown knows how to pass or punt or tackle," wrote Wright in 1962. Nevertheless, Wright chose Ernie Nevers of Stanford as the greatest, surely a minority opinion.[47]

On November 27, 1939, the All-Big Ten team was announced. Harmon was selected by the Big Ten coaches to the first team for the second consecutive year, finishing third in the balloting behind the senior Nile Kinnick of Iowa, the only unanimous choice, and junior Don Scott of Ohio State. The next day, with virtually no fanfare ahead of time or comment or analysis afterward, the Heisman Trophy for 1939 was awarded. It went to Nile Kinnick. Kinnick was a brilliant player, and as well-rounded in his football skills as any player of any era. And he was something that Harmon had never been—warmly popular with the fans and sportswriters. Further, it was Kinnick, grandson of a governor, who wore the mantle of underdog to Harmon, son of a security guard. In 1939, the Heisman Trophy was only five years old, and its traditions and significance had yet to be established. Only in later years would choices be scrutinized and debated and some of the choices considered dubious. The senior Kinnick's popularity had managed to overcome the junior Harmon's clear statistical edge and his superiority in their head-to-head matchup. As the years went by, it became increasingly difficult to deny Kinnick the legitimacy of his award, but at least one observer, football historian Mark Purcell, has offered his view. "Harmon, not Archie Griffin, should have been the first two-Heisman winner and in a breeze," he wrote.[48]

Harmon approached the 1940 season like a man possessed. After his performance in demolishing California in the opening game, he continued his assault on the rest of the football world. The next week he scored all his team's points in a 21-14 victory over Michigan State in a performance the *New York Times* called "virtually a one-man show."[49] The following week, at Harvard, it was "strictly a personal matter," the *Times* again reported, as Harmon once again ran, passed, and kicked for all the team's points in a 26-0 victory. The Michigan team as a whole was unimpressive in the game, fumbling repeatedly and missing blocks with regularity. But Harmon was sterling. "Harvard now joins California and Michigan State as a doormat for the upbuilding of the Harmon tradition," said the *Times*.[50] "Harmon Still Untamed," said a heading the next day.[51]

Against Illinois on October 19 he slowed a bit, as if to catch his breath, scoring only ten points in a wind-driven rainstorm as the Wolverines won easily, 28-0. That night a huge party was held in Ann Arbor for Michigan's retiring athletic director, Fielding Yost. Attending were the great Willie Heston, one of Yost's first stars from the turn of the century, and Harmon, his latest luminary, forty years younger. In their remarks during the affair, both stars emphasized the important contributions their teammates made in making their accomplishments possible.

On October 26, Michigan faced its toughest test yet. The stage for the Michigan-Penn game had been set the year before. The 1939 game between the two teams had ended in an unsatisfactory manner as a melee of players and angry fans pouring onto the field had threatened to turn a good game into a slugfest. Penn had scored a touchdown with less than a minute to play and trailed only 19-17. The Quakers had recovered a short kickoff and had at least a chance to score again. But a dispute about the play came up, one the officials could likely have easily dealt with, and although the head linesman had signaled for the clock to stop while the dispute was settled, it kept running and time expired without another play being run. Some pushing and shoving ensued, fans got into it, and while order was quickly restored, Penn left the game feeling it had been short-changed.

The linesman for the game had been Joe McKenney, a former head coach and star player at Boston College. McKenney said he had signaled for the clock operator to stop the clock at thirteen seconds, but the clock operator said he had seen no signal and had kept it running until time expired. Rules official Wilmer G. Crowell later stated, when asked why the clock simply could not be reset to the correct time, "The referee does not have the right under the rules to turn back the hands of the official clock."[52] Thus rigid adherence to the rules, no matter how injurious to fairness, even if an official's error was thus validated, and even if the error could materially change the outcome of a game, appeared more important than establishing a fair outcome.

The enthusiasm leading to the 1940 game was not misplaced. Penn had a strong team and was a worthy challenger to mighty Michigan. The rivalry between the two teams had been evenly played over the years. Moreover, the game was seen as an appealing showdown of sorts between two great halfbacks, Tom Harmon and Penn's Frank Reagan, fresh off a six-touchdown performance against Princeton, and a chance to measure their greatness against one another. Their 1939 matchup had been scintillating, and football fans were hungry for more. Reagan had rushed for 85 yards and had passed for 188 more, while Harmon had run for 202 yards. "Harmon didn't have a thing on Reagan," said the Associated Press.[53] In 1940, they showed similar statistics: ten touchdowns for the year so far for Reagan, eleven for Harmon, and 156 yards per game rushing for Reagan, 158 for Harmon. Indeed, *Time* billed it as the "Duel of the Century."[54] Allison Danzig called the matchup between the two players "irresistible."[55] The United Press pronounced the game a "double-barrelled bell-ringer" matching the reputations of the teams' respective "miracle men."[56]

Francis Xavier Reagan, it had been rumored, had already signed a contract to play baseball for the New York Yankees. The Yanks, it was said, were willing to pay him $7500 to catch in their organization.[57] The son of a factory foreman, one of eight children, Reagan grew up in Philadelphia. He was described as restrained and bashful, and was highly religious, playing an active role in Catholic students' organizations. He lived in the priests' house of St. Bede's chapel on campus. "He looks like his name and lives like it," a writer said.[58]

But Penn played a miserable game, Reagan was not a factor, and Michigan overwhelmed the Quakers 14-0. Harmon once again accounted for all of Michigan's points, played all sixty minutes on offense and defense, rushed for 142 yards, and was clearly the dominant factor in the game. He "played football of a type that few individuals have played on any gridiron," according to the day's press coverage,[59] and left little doubt as to his greatness as a football player. He passed for one touchdown to Ed Frutig, and his touchdown run, in which he ran 20 yards across the field, 20 yards back, and then 80 yards down the field, was later called by Fritz Crisler the greatest play he had ever seen.[60] Reagan, on the other hand, gained only ten yards in the game on twelve carries. Some observers saw extenuating circumstances. "Penn's Francis Reagan couldn't equal Harmon's pace because of the fundamental difference between most rival backs—a superior line," said Wilfrid Smith, sounding again that old tune.[61] Grantland Rice had a different theory. "[O]ne sight of Tom Harmon apparently threw the Penn squad into a panic, including Frank Reagan," he observed.[62] Henry McLemore agreed. Reagan was a superb punter, but as a result of his attempts to keep Harmon from returning his punts, his whole kicking game "went blooey," he thought.[63]

Both Reagan and Penn came under heavy criticism for their subpar performances. Apologists offered the view that had Penn played the game at home it could have done better.[64] But the Michigan game was Penn's only game away from home all year, and no team hoping to be considered of championship caliber can expect such an advantage. Good teams win on the road as well as at home. While Penn and Reagan had been forcefully expelled from the top rung of the season's performers, future opponents would underestimate them at their peril.

Meanwhile, the praise for Harmon came rolling in. One writer advised readers, if they could not think of three backs to accompany Harmon on the All-America team, "Don't worry. He doesn't need 'em." Even the referees had things to say. Mike Layden, an official in the Penn game, said that he had lost 12 pounds trying to keep up with Harmon on the field.[65]

Harmon's dominance of the scene had become so complete that the press came up with a new description of Michigan's defeated opponents. They had been Harmonized.[66]

CHAPTER 7
DISCOUNTED NO MORE

Before honor is humility.

--PROVERBS, 15:33.

In the fall of 1940, if there was anybody in America thought capable of challenging Tom Harmon for the Heisman Trophy it was George Franck of Minnesota. "Franck has everything Harmon has except the publicity," wrote one observer.[1] One of the few people ever to upstage Harmon on the football field, Franck was the star of the 1939 head-to-head matchup at Ann Arbor, as Minnesota upset Michigan and ended any hopes the Wolverines might have had for the Big Ten championship. While Harold Van Every and Bruce Smith both scored touchdowns for Minnesota as well, it was Franck's 59-yard touchdown run that took the heart out of the Wolverines, and when Harmon and the rest of the Michigan offense was held in check, the Gophers went on to a 20-7 upset victory. Franck had also run right past Harmon on another 30-yard gain, faking Harmon to the inside while he ran outside, only to be tackled two yards short of the goal line by Paul Kromer.[2]

Born and raised in Davenport, Iowa, George Henning Franck, nicknamed "Sonny" by his mother, had been an all-state football player in high school. When the University of Iowa, his first choice, showed interest in him only as a track star, Franck went instead to Minnesota, where he played football and ran track. He could run the 100-yard dash in 9.6 seconds and was a Big Ten track standout for his three varsity years. In the spring of his junior year he ran the anchor leg on Minnesota's Big Ten champion mile relay team and finished third in the Big Ten championships in both the 100-yard dash and 220-yard dash. In the winter of 1941 he won the Big Ten indoor 60-yard dash championship. More than 25 pounds lighter than Harmon, Franck nonetheless had an array of skills and a hardnosed style of play that made it difficult for opponents to contain him. Bernie Bierman, attracted by his speed, converted him from end to halfback, although he puzzled over how his power offense could best use the swiftest runner he had ever coached. "We were all fast in that backfield," said teammate Bill Daley, "but Sonny was really fast."[3]

By his own admission Franck was somewhat abrasive and hard to get along with at times. "My teammates always thought I was a self-centered S.O.B. and cocky. I probably was," he later admitted.[4] Though he shared a German ancestry with Bierman, he was often Bierman's favorite target for abuse. Franck, however, just laughed it off. He showed himself to be not only a prolific rusher and talented punter but also a vicious tackler on defense, launching his thin frame at opponents with abandon. With stars aplenty, there was room for a variety of opinions about them, and Daley had his: "George was the best football player Minnesota ever had."[5]

The team showed an interesting array, as well, of attitudes toward athletic honors. When Tom Harmon won the Heisman Trophy, he was deeply impressed by its significance. "It has always rested in the center of my desk since the day I won it, and I saw what it means in the eyes of youngsters who came to my home....They would walk to the trophy and feel its outline, like it had a power they could touch," he said.[6] Clearly Harmon had a point. But some others didn't see athletic honors that way. Dick Wildung, Minnesota's great two-time All-America tackle, served two years in the Navy, played for seven years with the Green Bay Packers, then operated a hardware store in his wife's home town. Only upon his death did his son, going through his grandmother's scrapbooks, discern the magnitude of his father's athletic achievements. "If you didn't ask, he would never volunteer anything about himself," said Dave Wildung, whose nephew added, "He was such a humble man."[7]

The most remarkable man on the team, the one who prompted the greatest accolades and garnered the most honors, was Bruce Smith. His array of athletic skills provided a potent complement to Franck's. While Franck's forte was blazing speed, Smith had an unusual running style that confounded every defense he faced. To Franck, Smith always seemed to be off balance. "His feet seem to swing at right angles to his body," Franck explained. While his upper body seemed to be going in one direction, his lower body was headed in another.[8] His swivel-hipped, stop-and-start style, coupled with plenty of speed—he could run the 100-yard dash in ten seconds flat—made him an elusive target for tacklers. Smith was a better passer than Franck, a skill that had limited value in Bierman's offense, but he could also drop-kick extra points, a skill he learned from his father as a child.

Smith's personality provided an interesting counterpoint to Franck's as well. He was a humble man to whom athletic achievement was much less important than the lessons he was taught as a youth. His father, Lucius Smith, had also played football for Minnesota in 1910 and 1911, where his teammate and backup had been Clark Shaughnessy. Growing up in Faribault, about 35 miles south of Minneapolis, Smith was an excellent high school athlete, lettering in baseball, basketball, golf, and football. His high school football coach called him "head and shoulders above anyone else in the state of Minnesota."[9] As his football career blossomed, he was dubbed by the admiring press the Faribault Flyer, but his teammates could discern no distinction in his demeanor. Smith could have been the king of Fraternity Row, the toast of every campus party. Instead, he chose to live in Pioneer Hall, a dormitory on campus, and spent most weekends at home in Faribault with his family. He was the most well-liked member of the team, and his quiet leadership style proved to be an inspiration to them. He told his father that every man ought to spend at least an hour a day with God, and he regularly stopped in to pray at church before and after games.

The praise from those who knew him came equally for his football ability and his sterling character. Said teammate Dick Wildung of Smith, "He was an All-American boy—everyone liked him and had a lot of respect for him. He was as good a running back as I've ever seen, including the pros." Judd Ringer added, "Bruce was a kind of plain clothes guy, who by nature was above glory chasing and pettiness....He led quite simply by showing us how to win when the going was the roughest."[10] Pug Lund, a star in his own right, said, "Bruce Smith is the one I'd like to be in terms of football ability."[11] Tom Harmon added, "Not only was he a great talent as a football player, but he was a clean living, religious, fine guy off the field as well. He was a champion in the true sense of the word."[12]

****

After their upset win over Washington, the Gophers had no chance to relax. Their next opponents were the Nebraska Cornhuskers, thought by many to be one of the premier teams of the Midlands, as football fans then called that portion of the country. Nebraska was deep and experienced, with a line anchored by All-American tackle Forrest Behm, but was notably lacking in talent at end. Some experts nevertheless tagged the 1940 Cornhuskers as the best ever assembled at Lincoln. Others expected them to improve as the year went on, but found it difficult to peg just how good they were in the early going. As for Minnesota, Bernie Bierman constantly tinkered with how to get the most out of his deep and talented backfield. He decided to start the reliable Bob Paffrath at fullback, but planned to give the young but promising Bill Daley plenty of playing time. Bierman had warmed to the idea of playing halfbacks George Franck and Bruce Smith at the same time, especially since Smith appeared finally to be coming around, albeit slowly, from the effects of a bothersome chest injury, and both would start against Nebraska.

After a scoreless first period, Bill Daley entered the game in the second quarter and ripped through the Nebraska line for a 48-yard run to the Cornhusker five-yard line, carrying a Nebraska defender on his back for the last 15 yards. He then scored the touchdown two plays later. After Nebraska tied the score, it was not until the fourth period that Minnesota took control of the game, as Bruce Smith threw a 42-yard touchdown pass to Bill Johnson for the winning score. The Gophers had one bit of luck in the game. A 66-

yard touchdown run by Nebraska's Butch Luther was called back when both teams were offside on the play.[13] Minnesota's line play was superb in the game, both offensively and defensively. Behind the blocking of Dick Wildung, Urban Odsen and their mates, the Gopher backfield was able to use its speed, and on defense the line shut down Nebraska's late-game threat by throwing the Cornhusker ballcarriers for two big consecutive losses to seal the victory. Odsen, one of the few Gophers from outside Minnesota—he was from Clark, S.D.—later said that he thought the Nebraska game was the best game he had played so far.[14]

Minnesota's first two games, impressive wins over tough teams, signaled to many observers that the Gophers were back. "Put Minnesota down, tentatively, as the No. 1 team," wrote Allison Danzig in the *New York Times*,[15] perhaps out of habit. But to others such talk was premature, and more evidence would be needed. The distance from where the Gophers began the season to the top was too great to be made up in only two games. Many football fans were thrilled that so many big games were being played early in the year. Such contests as Minnesota-Washington, Michigan-Cal, Pitt-Ohio State and Minnesota-Nebraska were huge showdowns. But some traditionalists preferred the season to work to a crescendo and for such games to be played later. "That's what's happening in football these days," bemoaned William D. Richardson.[16] But in a year with so many great teams it was hardly possible to avoid big games early in the schedule.

After a week off the Gophers headed to Columbus and to just such a game with Ohio State, the defending Big Ten champions, who had lost a tough one to an excellent Northwestern team the week before. The game was seen as a head-to-head contest between Don Scott of Ohio State and Franck, both vying for All-America honors. With two weeks to tune up for the game, Bierman's practice sessions frequently featured a backfield of Paffrath, Sweiger, Franck, and Daley. Having Franck and Smith in the same backfield had produced an impressive offensive attack, but having Daley and Paffrath in the same defensive lineup gave the Gophers two vicious tacklers to go along with Franck. Bierman may have decided how he would start the game, but no clues could be discerned from how he ran the practices. Clearly he enjoyed the versatility that so much talent provided him, and he saw the advantage of being ready to adjust should injuries strike. Both lines were impressively big, averaging over 210 pounds per man. Oddsmakers rated the game a tossup, and warning was given to Minnesota. "There's an old football saying that goes, 'Beware of a beaten team,'" counseled the *New York Times*.[17]

In a cold driving rainstorm, the same storm that plagued the Illinois-Michigan game, the Buckeyes, behind the sterling play of Don Scott, outplayed Minnesota but came out on the short end of a 13-7 score. Ohio State outgained the Gophers, 346 yards to Minnesota's 246, and made 16 first downs to Minnesota's ten. Still, while Ohio State drove the ball inside Minnesota's 11-

yard line five times in the game, they were able to score only one touchdown. Minnesota, on the other hand, had only two scoring opportunities and made good on both.

Bierman elected to start with both George Franck and Bruce Smith in the backfield again, sitting Daley initially; Franck, calling signals in the game, gave most of the action to Smith. The strategy paid off immediately. The Gophers scored on their first possession when Smith faked a pass from his ten-yard line and ran off right tackle for a touchdown, but his drop-kicked attempt for the extra point failed. Ohio State nearly came back to score immediately. With the help of a devastating block from Don Scott, who took out two defenders, Dick Fisher of Ohio State ran 55 yards deep into Minnesota territory. But when Scott, on fourth down from the one-yard line, failed to make it into the end zone, Ohio State had nothing but its first of four wasted scoring opportunities. Later in the first period, on fourth down from the Minnesota 19-yard line, Scott threw a touchdown pass to Charley Anderson, kicked the extra point, and Ohio State led in the game, 7-6. Minnesota took the following kickoff and marched the length of the field to score its second touchdown, again scored by Bruce Smith. Except for a 30-yard kick return and a nine-yard run by Franck, all the rest of the yardage was gained by Smith, including a pair of 23-yard runs, on which he was tackled from behind by Scott each time. When the extra point was kicked, Minnesota had the lead back, 13-7.

But it would not be that easy. Minnesota would never again get the ball past the Ohio State 25-yard line, while in the third period Ohio State moved the ball to Minnesota's 11-yard line and again to the four-yard line, both times without scoring. But the real thrill for the crowd came in the last minute of the game. Once again Ohio State drove the ball deep into Minnesota territory, threatening to score and at least tie the game. On second down Don Scott took the ball around left end, heading for the goal line, when George Franck, coming at top speed from the middle of the field, and Bob Paffrath knocked him out of bounds with a game-saving tackle at the one-yard line. The Buckeyes botched the next play, losing 12 yards, and then their last attempt, a pass into the end zone, was knocked away by Paffrath. The Gophers had their hard-earned victory.

Franck would later call his tackle of Scott one of the most memorable plays of his career.[18] With the win, Arch Ward of the *Chicago Tribune* became a believer in the Gophers. "Out of the rain, the chill, and the damp that pervaded Ohio State stadium today, came a great Minnesota football team," he wrote.[19] As for the frustrated Buckeyes, they were out of the Big Ten race, and there was no letup in sight. Their next date was in Ithaca, New York, against the number one team in the country.

Of 35 barbers polled in Minneapolis before the game, 25 picked the Gophers, eight picked the Buckeyes, and two predicted a tie game. Vic at Oscar's Barber Shop hit the winning score on the nose, 13-7 Minnesota.

The year before, in that difficult season of 1939 for the Minnesota Gophers, the most painful defeat of all had been at the hands of the Iowa Hawkeyes at Iowa's homecoming game. Not only did the loss to Iowa guarantee a losing record for the year, but the Gopher fans had considered the game won when, entering the fourth quarter, their team held the lead 9-0 and had denied Iowa any offensive success. But what followed was one of Nile Kinnick's most memorable quarters in his march to the Heisman Trophy. He threw a 45-yard touchdown pass to cap a four-play, 80-yard drive, drop-kicked the extra point, and then moments later threw a 28-yard touchdown pass to cap an 88-yard drive. In the two drives Kinnick was involved by passing, running, and kick return, in all plays but one. Then, to finish off the day, with time running out, he intercepted Harold Van Every's pass, as Minnesota desperately tried to come back. As the Gophers saw it, they had lost to an inferior team with one superior player.[20] Bernie Bierman was beside himself in frustration, and although George Franck had scored the only Gopher touchdown of the day and had intercepted a Kinnick pass on his ten-yard line, Bierman singled out Franck for special blame and berated him in front of the entire team.[21] Franck later said that as part of his tirade Bierman accused him of throwing the game to Iowa.[22]

Now, on October 26, 1940, it was Minnesota's homecoming as Iowa came to town. The Gophers, and George Franck in particular, were bent on revenge. It was his chance to strike back at the team that had humiliated him a year ago and the school that had rejected his football talent when he was in high school. The team spent the night off campus to avoid the homecoming parties, then returned just before the start of the game. Bruce Smith had carried a heavy load in the game against Ohio State, aggravating earlier injuries, and it was feared he would be unavailable for the Iowa game.[23] But Smith, although he did not start, threw two long touchdown passes to Franck, and Franck scored two other touchdowns as Minnesota won easily, 34-6 before an overflow crowd of nearly 63,000 fans. Franck's revenge, in perhaps his greatest game as a collegian, was won. When the Associated Press rankings came out on the following Tuesday, Minnesota, about whom so much doubt had been expressed earlier, had risen to fourth in the nation.

****

Clark Shaughnessy could finally rest a bit easier. After Stanford's big upset win over San Francisco, feelings toward him of curiosity, mild doubt, roaring apprehension, and downright hostility could be tempered with at least a bit of validation. True, he had won only one game with his new system, but he had won it in overwhelming style. San Francisco, as it would turn out, was overrated—they would win only one game in 1940—but his system had worked to perfection and his players had taken to the system and performed beyond any reasonable expectations. He felt confident enough to jettison his emergency backup plan, a conventional single-wing offense to be employed if his T-formation fell flat. Stanford would be a T-formation team for 1940, and greater challenges lay ahead.

He could not have fully appreciated it in March, when he committed to the T-formation, but he had inherited a group of players that were not just compatible with the new idea, but perfectly suited to it. Perhaps Shaughnessy was due a bit of luck after his travails in Chicago. He knew he had to find the right quarterback and teach him the right skills to make the system work. In Frankie Albert, who had been a mediocre single-wing halfback in 1939, Shaughnessy had the ideal man for the job. Diminutive even by the standards of the day, the brassy left-handed Albert turned out to be a slick ball handler, a hard worker, and a quick learner. He slept at Shaughnessy's house in the offseason and often stayed up until 6 am studying with his coach.

The T-formation had certain personnel advantages as well. Whereas the single wing demanded well-rounded football skills of all its backfield personnel, the T-formation was more specialized, demanding less of some skills and more of others. In Norm Standlee, Shaughnessy found a strong straight-ahead runner who flourished in the T-formation, where he could take an extra step to accelerate before being handed the ball. Jim Blewett, UCLA backfield coach, said at the start of the season that he expected the toughest back he would face all year, tougher than Dean McAdams of Washington or John Kimbrough of Texas A&M, would be Norm Standlee.[24] Pete Kmetovic was a smaller back who had great outside speed and pass-catching ability, but who could not block so well as the others. He would thus be a liability in the single wing, but the T-formation brought alive his specialized skills. By year's end Kmetovic had amassed a body of accomplishments that, although they did not win him All-America honors, possibly placed him among the most underrated backfield performers of all time.[25] Henry McLemore of the United Press called for every All-America team without Kmetovic, the best back he saw all year, to be dropped in a river. "Make sure it's a deep river," he emphasized.[26] Lastly, Hugh Gallarneau was a well-rounded back who could have excelled under any system. During the Depression, Gallarneau was forced to drop out of high school for two years to labor in the Chicago stock yards, and he played football for the first time when he finally reached Stanford. He made the team as a walk-on by demonstrating to Tiny Thornhill and his coaches that he could beat every other back on the field by four yards in the 100-yard dash.[27] With the four of them in place, Shaughnessy believed he had the perfect group of backfield operatives to make the T-formation work.

Later in the season, Washington coach Jimmy Phelan expressed doubts that any other system but the T-formation could have worked for Stanford and its mix of personnel. And Frankie Albert, he said, who did not run or block well but was a master of everything else, might not have been able to start in his Husky backfield, where the single wing demanded well-rounded skills of all players.[28]

As with installing any new system, Shaughnessy had huge obstacles to overcome, most notably the absence of any model to copy. No other college team was using the system. But opposing teams were at an equal or greater disadvantage. They had to figure out how to stop the T-formation, and they had no model either.

The rules of the day, set up to govern the predominant single wing, did not favor him. It was not legal in 1940 for a back within five yards of the line of scrimmage to throw a forward pass or to hand the ball to another player except in a backward direction. For a single wing back who received a direct snap from center and who was usually already five yards behind the line of scrimmage, that rule presented little problem. But for a T-formation quarterback who took the snap directly under center, the rule was daunting. The ballhandling skills demanded of a T-formation quarterback were substantial, yet they happened to be exactly the skills Albert possessed in plentiful supply. Not only were his physical skills superb, but he was a tough little man with a chip on his shoulder and ice water in his veins. It was, in short, a fortuitous marriage of man and opportunity.

Shaughnessy had more than a group of talented players. He also assembled an excellent coaching staff, the two key figures of which were Phil Bengtson and Marchy Schwartz. Like Shaughnessy, Bengtson had started his college football career as an All-American at Minnesota, where he played tackle alongside Bud Wilkinson on the great Gopher teams of 1933 and 1934. While Wilkinson went on to be one of the greatest college coaches of all time at Oklahoma, his linemate Bengtson developed into a defensive genius who later plied his trade in the NFL, spending nine years as defensive assistant to Vince Lombardi during the glory years of the Green Bay Packers. He became the Packers' head coach after Lombardi left. Marchmont Schwartz had been one of the greatest players in Notre Dame history, playing halfback on Rockne's superb undefeated teams of 1929 and 1930, and earning a spot on many all-time Notre Dame teams. Schwartz had been the head coach at Creighton before coming to Stanford and added needed expertise in the complicated workings of Shaughnessy's backfield.

On October 5, Stanford, underdogs again, hosted Tex Oliver's team, Oregon. Shaughnessy would have a chance to go head-to-head against one of his chief rivals for the Stanford coaching job. Stanford dished up more of the same, beating the visitors 13-0 as the T-formation hocus pocus was too much for the Oregon players to deal with. At times they were chasing two or three Indian players at once.[29] It was one razzle dazzle play after another, said the Associated Press.[30] The key plays in the game were Standlee's long pass to Albert, which set up the first touchdown, and Gallarneau's long run, which set up the second. After the game, Oliver pronounced, "Until I see a better one, Stanford is the best team on the Coast."[31]

It was almost too much to believe that, in only two games, Shaughnessy had made such a turnaround from the depths, both his and Stanford's, of 1939. Only two weeks before, the team had been "provoker of polite snickers," wrote Russell Newland of the *Los Angeles Times*.[32] The T-formation razzle dazzle system had been universally dismissed as too complicated for a college team to learn, and now it had sent two seemingly solid teams to defeat.

To make sure such talk was not taken too seriously, Santa Clara was scheduled to come to Palo Alto the following week. Most observers felt that Santa Clara, who had not lost to a Pacific Coast Conference rival in three years or to Stanford in five years, and whose combined record since the beginning of the 1936 season was 29-5-3, including two Sugar Bowl victories, was still a stronger team than Stanford and would put an end to such loose talk. Certainly the oddsmakers thought so. They installed the Broncos as solid favorites. To add flavor to an already zesty matchup, Shaughnessy would have the chance to coach against Buck Shaw, yet another one of his rivals for the Stanford job.

The Broncos fared no better. On a hot, sunny, day they too went down to defeat 7-6 before the wide-open style of the Indians. Though the margin of victory was but a missed extra point, Stanford won in their now-typical fashion. In the second period, with the ball on the Santa Clara 12-yard line, Stanford set up with one end spread wide, and then spread two flankers out to opposite sides. Spreading out to defend against what it felt sure was a sweep, Santa Clara could only watch helplessly as the powerful Standlee rushed the ball straight up the middle for the winning touchdown. Art Cohn, sports editor of the *Oakland Tribune*, pointed out that the score was misleading, that Stanford should have scored two additional touchdowns. As the game ended, they had the ball on the Broncos' nine-yard line.[33] The win left Stanford as the only undefeated and untied team on the West Coast and what Russell Newland termed "the hottest team in football pants."[34]

It was Shaughnessy's nature to heap praise upon his team, and he took this opportunity to say to the press, "These kids astound me. I've never seen such spirit, such scrappiness, such charge." Asked to identify stars of the game, he replied. "Stars? Every last one of 'em."[35]

Stanford had the need to travel out of northern California to play their schedule only twice during the year, and on October 19 they made the trip to Pullman, Washington, to play in Washington State's homecoming game at Rogers Field Stadium. But Stanford spoiled the Cougars' day with a 26-14 come-from-behind victory. It came as no surprise that the Indians won by trickery and slick maneuvering. Near the end of the first period, they pulled off a particularly deceptive play that seemed to fool the entire Cougar team, and the resulting 28-yard run by Pete Kmetovic set up the first Stanford touchdown.[36] Kmetovic also had another 52-yard run in the game, but Bill Sewell of Washington State, a fine passer and punter, kept the Cougars in the game for most of the afternoon. The only needling about Stanford that day came in the form of guffawing from the news media over their football pants. Stanford's fashionable all-white uniforms with red stripes, attractive but perhaps a bit ahead of their day, made them look, said the press, like gas station cadets.[37]

After the game, the praise began pouring in. "It looks as if Clark Shaughnessy has a team of destiny in his first year at Palo Alto," wrote Allison Danzig.[38] He had apparently overcome odds that, a month ago, gave him as much chance as "those of a mouse dumped down in the center of a convention of cats," added Russell Newland.[39] Others suggested the magicians' union require Shaughnessy to take out a card and pay dues.[40] Four weeks into the schedule the United Press reported that Shaughnessy had put Stanford "right aboard the Rose Bowl Special."[41] Even Pop Warner began coming around. "Shaughnessy is entitled to the fullest credit for the phenomenal way he is making use of the T-formation," he said. His memory spurred by Shaughnessy's success, he suddenly played a very different tune. "The formation is almost as old as football itself. We used it when I played at Cornell from 1892 to 1894 and when I started coaching the next year at Iowa State and Georgia."[42] Failure is an orphan, Shaughnessy learned long ago, and now he saw that success has a thousand fathers.

The Wow Boys, as the press now called them, had football fans on the west coast fully in their thrall. The story of these down-and-out players, coupled with an even more down-and-out coach, rising up to smack down the football bullies of the West Coast, captured the imagination of even the coldest of fans. They were now even bets, along with the Washington Huskies, to go to the Rose Bowl, a prospect no fan had dared contemplate only weeks before, lest his sanity be questioned. On Tuesday, October 21, the Associated Press Poll had the Stanford Indians ranked ninth in the country, just behind the Penn Quakers and just ahead of Boston College.

But the mountain kept getting steeper. The Indians' next game was against the mighty Southern California Trojans. The defending Pacific Coast Conference champion, winners of the Rose Bowl the last two years and undefeated in their last 17 games, figured to be Stanford's toughest challenge yet. The same team had beaten Stanford 33-0 the year before, and the matchup in Palo Alto would provide an accurate reading of how profound a change had been made to the Stanford team. The Trojans were depleted by graduation, but the backfield, headed by Bob Robertson and Jack Banta, was still powerful. And they, too, were still undefeated.

Stanford won the game with defense. Frankie Albert opened the scoring by connecting with Pete Kmetovic for a 60-yard touchdown pass in the first quarter, but only a few moments later the Trojans pushed the ball to the

Stanford 29-yard line. On the next play, Hugh Gallarneau was called for pass interference on the goal line, a call that was highly questionable. The newspapers' still photographs the next day revealed that Gallarneau was nowhere near Trojan receiver Joe Davis when the ball sailed over his head. The Trojans were awarded the ball on the one-yard line, and when they scored a touchdown the game was tied. From there Stanford's defense clamped down on the Trojans for the rest of the game. Stanford's constantly changing defensive scheme was as befuddling as its offense, and the Trojans gained only 30 yards on the ground in the second half. Their stifling defense made the Trojan backfield "look like handcuffed high school runners," said the *Los Angeles Times*, and Southern California did not complete a pass during the game.[43]

Though Stanford dominated play, the score remained deadlocked until the final four minutes of the game. A tie would have been dearly welcomed by the Indians the year before, but Shaughnessy disdained any such thought. "We're not playing for a tie. We're going to win this ball game," he said to his team. Setting aside any conservative playcalling, with the ball on their own 20-yard line and after Albert had been thrown for a nine-yard loss trying to pass, the Indians elected to keep passing the ball. Their risk paid off, as Albert led them 80 yards in six plays, and they scored the winning touchdown with 90 seconds left to play. Then, twenty five seconds later, as the Trojans mounted a desperation comeback attempt, Albert intercepted a pass and ran it back for the Indians' third touchdown of the game and a 21-7 win. As he came off the field, Albert was hoisted off the ground by a jubilant Shaughnessy, who planted a big wet kiss on him.[44] The Palo Alto fans who had been so slow to embrace Shaughnessy now had taken him to their hearts.[45]

On Tuesday, Stanford leaped to sixth in the Associated Press ranking, just behind Texas A&M and ahead of Tennessee. Stanford now found itself in rarified air. Each member of the poll's top ten was undefeated. If the Indians could beat the two-time Rose Bowl champions, the reasoning went, they could go to the Rose Bowl themselves. Of their chances, the Trojans' vanquished coach Howard Jones said, "I'll string along with Stanford until a better team comes along. It is the most improved team in one year I have seen in years." And of Shaughnessy's suddenly evident coaching genius, all the West Coast press could say was, "Thanks, Chicago."[46]

CHAPTER 8
THE GENTLEMEN'S AGREEMENT

*The inequities in human relationships are many, but the lot
of the Negro is one of the worst....May wisdom, justice,
brotherly love guide our steps to the right solution..[1]*

--NILE KINNICK, 1939 HEISMAN TROPHY WINNER

The growing popularity of college football caused many schools to gradually include intersectional games on their schedules as a surefire method to increase revenue, fan support, and team prestige. But when it came to playing teams from southern schools, it was necessary to overcome the great barrier of sharply divergent societal views of the regions. Black athletes were a rarity on college teams of the time anywhere; in the South they were nonexistent. Further, teams from the South firmly and universally refused to compete against black athletes. The only tool to bridge the regional divide with southern schools was an odious arrangement coyly called, of all things, a gentlemen's agreement. Southern schools were willing to compete with their northern counterparts, if the northerners agreed to keep their black players out of the competition. While socially conscious people of the time found the southern stance to be repugnant, equally as troublesome was the ready willingness of northern universities to comply with the demands of their southern counterparts.

For decades the gentlemen's agreement ruled and made possible the realm of intersectional football, but it frequently created great difficulty and controversy. A school at the heart of this controversy was New York University. NYU prided itself on being a progressive institution of liberal ideals with an active student body inclined to become involved in their promotion. It also had a competitive football team that was a leader in intersectional play, and NYU frequently had black athletes on its teams in all sports. The formula was just right for conflict.

On November 9, 1929, the NYU Violets were scheduled to play an important intersectional football game against Georgia at Yankee Stadium. But, about three weeks before the game, rumors began to circulate that Georgia had objected to NYU's including its black backfield star Dave Myers in the game lineup, and that NYU had responded by agreeing not to play Myers.

71

What followed was a farcical charade and the first serious objection to the use of the gentlemen's agreement.

When presented with the rumors, Prof. Giles C. Courtney, chairman of the board of athletic control at NYU, boldly stated, "New York University will tolerate no discrimination against Myers....NYU has no agreement with Georgia, either written, verbal, or implied, in regard to Myers' non-participation in the game here November 9." He further stated that if Georgia were to show such poor sportsmanship as to demand that Myers be removed from the lineup, the game would be canceled. Courtney's statement was a perfect expression of the longstanding philosophy of his university. The NAACP sent a letter to NYU, in which it labeled any such agreement, should it exist, "official sanction of race prejudice in its crudest and ugliest form."[2] Its position was solidly in line with NYU's philosophy. Courtney's stance was clear. NYU had high standards on such matters and intended to adhere to them. It was a matter of honor for the university.

But that same day, Dr. S.V. Sanford, dean of the University of Georgia, spoke to the press and insisted that Georgia did indeed have a gentlemen's agreement with NYU precluding Myers' participation, and that it had been reached with the NYU football coach, Chick Meehan. "The matter has been amicably adjusted," he said, "and we anticipate no unpleasantness whatsoever."[3] Courtney and Meehan, it was clear, were not in alignment on how matters were to be run at NYU. Meehan refused to answer questions directly about the matter but did indicate he was concerned for the safety of Myers should he take the field against the southerners. His fear was that the Georgia players would try to purposely injure Myers and put him out of the game.

Exactly what occurred in the discussions that followed between Courtney and Meehan is not known, but the outcome is clear. The clash of ideas was aired out, and the next day Courtney clarified his previous statement. "The head football coach has full jurisdiction over the selection of his players for each game scheduled," he said, in full retreat.[4] Meehan, now on center stage, flatly declared that Myers would not play. "There will be no unpleasantness in the Georgia game," he said, using the Georgia dean's language, "as we did not intend to play Myers when the game was scheduled and he is not going to play in the Georgia game."[5] He added, "We understand the feeling of southern colleges in regard to playing against negroes, and I made up my mind then that Myers would remain out of that game. The name of Myers did not enter into negotiations with Georgia."[6] Meehan's statement was carefully crafted so as not to technically contradict Courtney's, yet also to align with Sanford's. He seemed to draw a distinction between an arrangement where a concession is demanded and given and one where it is not demanded but is given anyway. Certainly there was no distinction of effect, and no correlation to NYU's philosophy. The honor of the university appeared to have been compromised by the football coach.

Earlier in the season, after a loss to Fordham, Meehan had shifted Myers from the line to the backfield, and the results were immediate and sensational. The press had instantly warmed to him, affectionately but condescendingly dubbing him "the ebony-hued cyclone," and had given him credit for nearly single-handedly defeating Penn State the next week. When he was being harmed, the press came to his defense. One writer called the matter "a strange commentary on our 1929 civilization and 'commercialized' athletics."[7]

That commentary was written on October 28. On October 29, the stock market collapsed. Teetering for days, stocks shed billions of dollars of value in a matter of hours, in a day to be forever known as Black Tuesday. The world was thrown into economic turmoil from which it would require more than a decade and a world war to recover. But a few blocks to the north of Wall Street, the Dave Myers controversy continued at full throttle.

Members of the NYU student body were outraged and ready to act, and they rapidly joined the growing chorus of opposition to the University stance. "To the minds of all who believe in good sportsmanship and fair play, this 'agreement' puts the stamp of unmistakable intolerance on the University of Georgia. What is more serious, however, is the fact that it jeopardizes New York University's reputation for upholding, at all times, the doctrine of racial equality," wrote the Cosmopolitan Club of NYU. The students circulated a petition asking that no more games be scheduled against schools objecting to the participation of any player, regardless of race.[8] Meehan's logic, and thus the university's position, seemed to rest on the distinction that it was he, and not Georgia officials, that initiated Myers' benching, separate and apart from any agreement. It rested on the hopes that nobody would think that the benching was a prerequisite to Georgia's agreeing to play.

Congressman Emanuel Celler of New York entered the fray and wrote a letter to NYU officials, in which he termed their position "disgusting." Others agreed. "Because this United States is and has been a free country, race or pigment of the skin should have no direct conflicts on the gridiron,"[9] wrote one newspaper. Another editorial began, "Who is the boss of the modern American university—the president or the football coach?" The editorial laid out the outstanding liberal traditions of New York University, and how this last incident was starkly at odds with them, then concluded, "New York University may have its traditions but none more compelling than this one: 'We must have a winning football team and big gate receipts.' "[10]

Early in the week leading up to the game, NYU ran its practices without Myers present. The team began preparation for the Georgia game expecting that neither he nor end Charlie Marshall, out with a broken leg, would be available for the game.[11]

Matters were even worse than they appeared. Only half of the problem had been exposed. NYU's next opponent after Georgia was Missouri, a school no more likely than Georgia to accede to Myers' participation. Incredibly,

73

nobody outside the university had yet thought to ask Meehan what agreements he had made with Missouri, and nobody inside the university had thought about how to deal with the hail of protest sure to be unleashed once that question was answered.

The entire matter had reached a critical peak, and William H. Nichols, acting chancellor of NYU, heretofore silent, decided to become involved. He replied to Congressman Celler's letter, saying, in part, "It is the purpose of our athletic authorities to place the best available eleven on the field next Saturday. We hope and expect that the colored lad, Myers, will be of that number." His statement, directly contradicting Meehan's, wrested control of university policy from the football coach and appeared on the surface to safeguard university honor. Then Courtney followed with a memorandum of his own, reasserting his role as well. He denied that a gentlemen's agreement with Georgia ever existed. Suddenly it appeared that Myers would play and that NYU's status as a liberal institution dedicated to racial equality was intact.[12] The next day, Meehan dutifully put Myers out on the practice field running through plays.[13] But there was face-saving to be done. The university chancellor had made statements categorically opposed to those of his football coach and to those of the dean of another university. Somehow these matters had to be rectified.

Then, either an incredible stroke of luck occurred or a devious plot was hatched, depending on what one wished to believe. On Thursday, after three days of practice, Dave Myers developed a sore shoulder. An Associated Press report termed his participation in the game "unlikely" due to the injury, and Myers himself said he thought he would not be able to play. NYU officials, hoping to guard against accusations of fabricating an injury, took an unusual measure. They said that two outside physicians with no connection to the university would be brought in to examine Myers' shoulder, and that their decision on his condition would be final.[14] Courtney made clear that Myers would play "if his condition permits." The injury, said Courtney, was suffered against Penn State and aggravated against Georgetown.[15]

On Friday, not two but three surgeons entered the picture, one from the American College of Surgeons, one from St. Vincent's Hospital, and one from the French Hospital. NYU could not be too careful. The surgeons' conclusion was that Myers had suffered a serious shoulder injury, was unfit for duty, and could possibly miss the remainder of the season, which of course included the Missouri game. They also indicated a danger of permanent injury should he play.[16] Myers was out, and the issue of a gentlemen's agreement was moot.

Playing without Myers, NYU defeated both Georgia and Missouri, and in the week of Thanksgiving, was readying for its game against Rutgers. Myers's career-threatening injury, thanks to the miracles of medicine, had completely healed right after the Missouri game, and he resumed his starting position in the backfield. NYU again won, and before the game was over, Myers had made a brilliant 35-yard run and two 50-yard runs, one of which was for a touchdown.

On October 17, 1936, in another game played at Yankee Stadium, the University of North Carolina football team competed, for the first time, against a black athlete, fullback Ed Williams of NYU. North Carolina teams had faced black opponents in track and boxing, but never on the gridiron. That nothing had been done to protest Williams's presence in the game caused a degree of stir back home. The willingness on the part of university officials to have North Carolina athletes play on the same field as blacks, if only on the road, represented a softening of southern policy attributed, said the *Gastonia (NC) Daily Gazette*, to the fact that recently there were more northern players on southern college football teams, and they "feel no qualms about playing against negroes, or going to school with them, etc., etc." But the policy change "might cause some of the old rip-roaring, rabid, fire-eating Southerners of a generation ago to rise up out of their graves," it clarified.[17] While there might have been a grudging willingness to allow such competition to take place on northern fields, there was none whatsoever for it to occur in the South.

Some observers claimed that in the game, won 14-13 by North Carolina, Williams was severely roughed up, as Meehan had feared would happen to Myers, and had to be taken unconscious from the field.[18] But the record shows that Williams, though he did not start in the game, played well, and by midweek appeared to have earned a starting assignment against Georgetown the following Saturday. "It appears almost certain that Williams, on his showing against North Carolina and his continued improvement all season, will be at the fullback post when the game begins," predicted the *New York Times*.[19] On Saturday, he started against Georgetown and again played well. The severity of Williams's injuries, and whether they were inflicted by racially motivated opponents, remains a subject of speculation.

On October 4, 1940, two notable events took place in New York City that, taken together, help describe the world of athletic competition for the black athlete in America at that time. At Madison Square Garden, Fritzie Zivic, a hard-punching boxer from Pittsburgh and a 3-1 underdog, won a unanimous 15-round decision over Henry Armstrong, a black man, and took Armstrong's world welterweight title belt. The bout marked the end of an era.

On October 29, 1937, Armstrong knocked out Petey Sarron in the sixth round to win the world featherweight championship at 126 pounds. On May 31, 1938, he moved up two weight classes and decisioned Barney Ross, himself a great champion, in a 15-round bout in Long Island City to win the world welterweight title at 147 pounds. On August 17, 1938, in Los Angeles, he won a 15-round split decision over Lou Ambers and the world lightweight belt at 135 pounds. At that moment Henry Armstrong had achieved what no other boxer in the history of the sport, before or since, regardless of race, had ever achieved. He was the simultaneous world champion of three weight categories at a time when there were only eight.

Three months later Armstrong, now committed to the heavier weight classes, relinquished his featherweight title. And on August 22, 1939, Ambers won a clear 15-round decision against him to take back the lightweight belt. On March 1, 1940, Armstrong fought world middleweight champion Ceferino Garcia to a disputed draw in Los Angeles, nearly winning a world title in his fourth weight class.

Since capturing the welterweight title from Barney Ross, Armstrong had successfully defended the belt, his last one, 19 times. So on October 4, he climbed into the ring for one more defense, a 15-round bout, this time against Zivic. Armstrong's most recent bout had been less than two weeks before, when he had knocked out Phil Furr in Washington. Furr had damaged Armstrong's eye during the bout, and two weeks later it still had not healed. But Armstrong wanted to fight, and his manager Eddie Mead put him back in the ring. Zivic knew where Armstrong's weak spots were and concentrated his attack on the scar tissue around his eyes and mouth. Armstrong bled heavily throughout the bout and by the tenth round his eyes, battered by Zivic's blows and hampered by the injury he had suffered against Furr, were so swollen it was doubtful he could see.

But Armstrong fought on for five more rounds, largely on a sheer will to win. "Through five of the most brutal rounds ever seen in the Garden, Armstrong took his bloody punishment," wrote *Time*. After 14 rounds, Referee Arthur Donovan and Judge Marty Monroe had the bout even, seven rounds for each boxer. But in the fifteenth, Armstrong, nearly out on his feet and unable to see, went to the canvas just as the fight came to an end. The unanimous decision was not in dispute. Henry Armstrong had lost his last belt and would never again hold a world title. Sportswriters suggested a fitting epitaph: "He went down fighting."[20]

Armstrong's accomplishments are among the greatest in the history of the sport. He is often named as, pound for pound, the greatest boxer of all time, an elusive title that requires comparisons over decades as well as weight classes, and his fans would be challenged in that regard by the supporters of such greats as Sugar Ray Robinson and Willie Pep. Robinson, ironically, made his professional debut on the undercard of the Armstrong-Zivic fight. One thing is certain. Between 1938 and 1940, Henry Armstrong was among the greatest boxers on the planet.

The very same day that Armstrong lost his last title, the *New York Times* ran an article describing a second notable event. A few blocks down Broadway, on the campus of New York University, Dr. Marvin A. Stevens, coach of the Violet football team, was discussing the prospects for the upcoming season before the media. Stevens was a prominent bone surgeon and former head coach at Yale, and still held a post as part-time professor in the Yale Medical

School. He had been a leader in the early fight against polio[21] and enjoyed high standing and strong connections in the New Haven community. The NYU Violets had planned an aggressive schedule for 1940, and the squad was thin and inexperienced. As he went through his list of concerns, largely centering on NYU's offensive inefficiencies, Stevens eventually came to the issue of one of his best players, sophomore halfback Leonard Bates, and discussed a particular dilemma in an almost offhand way. Bates would not be playing in the game against Missouri scheduled for November 2 in Columbia.

Stevens indicated that Missouri had not given permission for Bates, a black man, to play. Missouri had not yet requested that Bates stay home, but all indications were that the game would be played without him.[22] This time there was no place for NYU to hide. The university had, by its own admission, entered into a gentlemen's agreement with the University of Missouri and had bartered away the right of one of its students to participate in the game. While southern schools were begrudgingly willing to tolerate playing against blacks in northern venues, they would not tolerate blacks on southern playing fields.

The NYU-Missouri game had been booked before Bates arrived on campus, and the two schools had agreed to play twice, both games to be in Columbia. Upon adding Bates to the team, NYU officials tried to get both games changed to New York so that Bates could play. NYU Graduate Manager Al Nixon succeeded in switching the 1941 game to New York, but the 1940 game would be held in Columbia, as scheduled, with Bates's involvement subject to Missouri's approval, which was not expected. Alluding to the Dave Myers incident of 11 years before, the *New York Times* said, "The NYU authorities...refuse to fake a Bates 'injury' and feel that it is up to the host team to decide who plays and who doesn't."[23]

The indication was clear. Leonard Bates, because he was a Negro, was not going to be permitted to play against Missouri. Further, his school, even though committed to principles of racial equality, was not about to stick up for him. When Henry Armstrong was given a chance to compete, he reached a level of performance unattained before or since by any other man. When he lost, he lost on merit. But Leonard Bates was being denied the opportunity to compete, when he was in fact a mainstay of the team. Bates had become a starter before the Holy Cross game, and of his abilities the *Illustrated Football Annual* stated, "His crushing, 203-pound body-blocks are sheer devastation."[24] He was one of three players brought with some degree of fanfare to NYU by Stevens from high school careers in New Haven.

It wasn't as if NYU had talent to spare. The roster was so thin, and the team so banged up, that it was questionable at times whether there would be eleven healthy men available to suit up. In agreeing not to play Bates, a multi-talented backfield man, the Violets were not only caving in to the base demands of another university, ceding to another school the right to determine its roster, they were also practically assuring they had no chance to win the game. The *St. Louis Post-Dispatch* said, "The New Yorkers are nothing to cheer a coach's heart this season and without Len Bates in their backfield they're strictly 'suckers' for a passing team. And since the contract with Missouri stipulated that the Negro ballcarrier would not play, Bates is not being taken on the trip."[25] And Missouri, with its All-American star Paul Christman in the lineup, was an accomplished passing team. Indeed, after Missouri had defeated NYU the year before, the New York press ranked Christman as a passer on the same level with Sid Luckman, Benny Friedman, and Sammy Baugh.[26]

The entire idea did not go down well with the NYU student body. Protests on the campus multiplied, as twenty undergraduate organizations circulated petitions demanding that the school cancel the Missouri game. With passion outpacing the letter-writing and the flood of anger of 11 years before, during the Dave Myers incident, it was the first time that such a substantial organized opposition to the gentlemen's agreement had been voiced. Some 2000 students, many carrying protest signs with such messages as "Bates Must Play" and "No Missouri Compromise," picketed the NYU administration building. Bates found himself in the middle of this unrest, and after a two-hour meeting on October 18 with Professor E. George Payne, dean of the School of Education, where Bates was enrolled, he wrote a letter to the student groups declaring that he had previously stated his wish not to participate in the contest. The NYU administration was quick to make the letter public, hoping to defuse the incident. Officials at northern schools had become used to complacent reaction, or no reaction, to their treatment of black athletes and had never before been faced with such strenuous opposition to their policies. The reaction on the NYU campus to the exclusion of Dave Myers had been mild compared to what they were now facing. Payne told the Negro Culture Group on campus that Bates, when he enrolled, had been told in a perfectly friendly manner that he would not be allowed to play against Missouri, and that he had agreed.[27] Stevens emphatically told the assembled students that Bates would not be in the lineup against Missouri. "Bates knew of the situation when he came out for football," Stevens explained.[28]

This explanation did nothing but inflame the protestors. They were being asked to accept the logic that discrimination, so long as the victim had been sufficiently browbeaten to accede to it, was acceptable. This was coupled with the ostensible logic behind the exclusion, that black athletes placed in a racially charged hostile environment were more prone to injury by assault, and thus the victims of such assault, and not the perpetrators, should be punished.

The protestors would have none of it. On October 21, a mass meeting was held on campus where undergraduate leaders vowed to continue their efforts.[29] The All-University Committee on Bates Must Play, as it called itself, passed four resolutions: that Bates be allowed to decide himself whether to play; that

NYU never again contract with Jim Crow schools; that the University clarify its views on this issue; and that, failing any of these things, there be a boycott of all home games for the remainder of the season.[30] The circulated petitions ultimately had 4000 signatures.[31]

Not everybody agreed with the position of the protesting students. Jim Herbert, a black man and a recent world class track star at NYU, was a member of some considerable standing in the NYU athletic community. He was world record holder in the quarter mile and 400-meter indoor events and a member of the NYU relay team that, in the spring of 1940, set world records in the mile relay and 1600 meter indoor relay. He refused to sign the Committee's petition, believing that the chance of injury against Bates or other athletes placed in his position was a real concern.

Others thought the point of the protest's arrow was aimed at the wrong target. The issue was not whether Bates should play, in their minds, but whether liberal institutions like NYU should schedule athletic contests against schools inclined as Missouri was. It was the very same point NYU protestors had made 11 years before, this time with more force.

Meanwhile, the students' protests garnered attention and support off campus. Letters to the editor began raining in. A European refugee, disgusted by the idea that a man could be excluded from participation in a football game because of the color of his skin, wrote a scathing commentary on the matter and said that any school endorsing such practice "should not only be ignored in the future by the contestants immediately concerned, but should also be boycotted by every college and university whose ideas and ideals range beyond narrow-mindedness."[32]

The student newspaper of the University of Minnesota, a school whose black athletes had been forced to sit out in the past, sounded off against the practice, perhaps encouraged by a concert appearance on campus on the day of the editorial by actor and baritone Paul Robeson. Robeson had been a great football star at Rutgers, and as a black man had been similarly held out due to the gentlemen's agreement. But a reader responding to the editorial piece made an even more important observation, attacking the northern universities that were cowed into accepting the southern policies: "[Concentration on southern school policy] serves the evil purpose of diverting attention from the lackadaisical attitudes toward racial questions which have long prevailed in the North—attitudes which actually foster racial intolerance by allowing southern schools to dictate to northern schools conditions under which intersectional games are to be played. Had our own athletic department taken a more uncompromising position in previous games with Tulane and Texas, Reed and Bell, our own colored athletes, would not have suffered the humiliation of having to sit on the bench, and this great democratic university would not have had to humble itself before the mighty southern god of White Supremacy."[33]

Often, critics attempted to separate the students from the college administration. A letter to the *New York Times*, calling the matter "an outrage of the rankest order," and "a walk along the road of vicious racial inequality" suggested that the exclusionary attitude toward black players existed among controlling university officials but not among the university students or sports fans.[34] This dubious position does not square with the catcalls aimed at black athletes during competition or with the abuse Jackie Robinson experienced on the baseball diamond later in the decade. Unmistakably, racial attitudes were deep-seated and widespread.

Some members of the University of Missouri student body seemed to sympathize with the plight of Bates and the NYU students and agreed that Bates should be allowed to play. Perhaps their sentiment was genuine, but clearly the students could rest with the sure knowledge that the University was not about to change its course.

The Varsity Club at the City College of New York spoke out in support of the NYU student protestors: "One would think that the field of sports, above all other endeavors, would hold no brief for racial prejudice within its ranks. At a time when democracy is at stake throughout the world we discover right here in our own back yard, supposedly a stronghold of democracy, the most vicious type of bigotry and intolerance." It then passed the following resolution: "The City College Varsity Club condemns all form of racial discrimination and therefore looks with disfavor upon schools that practice Jim Crowism in the conduct of their athletic programs."[35]

The mainstream newspapers, aside from printing letters sent in by their readers, showed no interest in the social issues presented by this dilemma. The job of the press, as they saw it, was to give their readers what they wanted, which was the scores and accounts of the athletic contests. Some need was felt to account for Bates's absence, much as an injury would be reported that might keep a player out of a game. It seemed that while other athletes were expected to miss some contests with sprained ankles or bruised shoulders, Leonard Bates was expected to miss the Missouri game with Negro blood. But the black press, including such papers as the *Baltimore Afro-American* and the *Chicago Defender,* were much more thorough in their coverage, and they did not go lightly on either Stevens, the white coach, or Bates, the black player. They attacked both Stevens's character and Bates's manhood.

On October 29, as the last comment in a walkup article to the game, the *New York Times* noted tamely that the demonstrations seemed to have abated.[36] But the reduction in student protests may have been mostly due to a persistent rain. The student leader of the movement, Guy A. Stoute, together with an English professor, addressed a small group of drenched protestors in Washington Square the next day. That night, the NYU Student Council passed a resolution by a 6-1 vote urging that Bates be allowed to play on Saturday. Dr.

Julius Yourman, faculty representative, cast the lone dissenting vote, offering the astonishing reason that "it would only make for ill feeling."[37]

On October 31, thirty one NYU football players made their way to the University Heights station of the New York Central Railroad to set out on their trip to Missouri. Leonard Bates was not among them. They were met by a small band of protesting students carrying "Bates Must Play" signs. The *New York Times*, in one last attempt to defuse the situation, pointed out that his absence was in accordance with agreements between NYU and the University of Missouri and between NYU and Bates.[38]

Missouri handily defeated the depleted Violet team, 33-0. More painful to the students than the on-field loss was the stubborn refusal of the university administration to budge an inch on the issues presented. Further, by this time Bates had recanted on a portion of the contents of his letter the administration had so enthusiastically made available. His position, he said, was that he was amenable to the gentlemen's agreement as explained to him, but that he would prefer to play. The decision not to play, he said, was not his. Further, he made a prepared statement in which he asserted his "unquestionable right" to play.[39]

Even though the football game was now in the past, the unrest continued, fueled by the determination of the university to ignore the protesters. Their ire was directed at the university chancellor, Harry Woodburn Chase, and at Professor Philip O. Badger, head of the athletic department. Not only did the students find themselves ignored, they soon discovered that the NYU administration had every intention of applying the gentlemen's agreement to the basketball team as well. Jim Coward, a black star of the basketball team, was declared ineligible for upcoming games against Georgetown and North Carolina. More massive demonstrations with several thousand demonstrators followed. But the protests were doing little to diminish the standing of Badger among college leaders nationwide. Though he was seen by the NYU students as the face of rigid adherence to Jim Crowism, at the end of December he was elected by his peers across the nation as president of the NCAA, where he served from 1941 to 1944.

The problem came to a head when students discovered that the track team was also to be subject to this treatment. George Hagans, co-captain of the team and a black man, would not be allowed to participate in a track meet at Catholic University in Washington, D.C. scheduled for March, 1941. Other black athletes, including David Lawyer and Fabian Francis, would also be ineligible. Each of these three was a standout in his event: Hagans in the 440-yard run, Lawyer in the 100-yard dash, and Francis in the 120-yard high hurdles. Hagans was one of four NYU track men who, in the spring of 1940, set the world record in the half-mile relay.[40] While the football team aspired to greatness, the track team was one of the best in the country. The Violets, with all members of the team performing, had won the 1940 IC4A Championship.

Leonard Bates, too, was on the track team, specializing in the field events, where he consistently placed in the hammer throw, the shot put, and the discus. Bates finished third in the discus at the 1941 IC4A Championships. In 1943, his senior year, Bates finished sixth in the nation in the discus at the NCAA championships, and NYU as a team finished fourth. In the spring of 1941, Bates would not compete against Catholic University.

In one sense, track was a different story. There were a handful of black athletes playing football in the country in 1940, but while it could not be said that blacks dominated the sport of track, they were much more prominent. In 1936, eight African-American track and field stars took the Berlin Olympics by storm, winning ten individual medals—six gold, two silver, and two bronze—with Jesse Owens winning three of the individual gold medals. Barney Ewell of Penn State, NCAA champion in the 100-yard and 220-yard dashes and an outstanding broad jumper as well, was arguably the greatest collegiate track star of 1940. That same year, the NCAA title in the 120-yard high hurdles was won by Ed Dugger of Tufts. Mozel Ellerbee of Tuskegee was one of the best 60-yard dash performers, Archie Harris of Indiana University won the NCAA discus championship, and Jackie Robinson of UCLA was the NCAA broad jump champion. All these men were black. So a school's track team refusing to play against another school's black athletes was likely to be refusing to play against their best athletes. The concept of competition was severely compromised.

The protest machine was again in full throat, and it was not just students doing the screaming. On March 3 the Council for Student Equality circulated a petition calling for a halt to discrimination against Negro students by the administration. When warned to stop, they persisted. On March 6, seven students—Argyle Stoute, a black man and the leader of the Bates Must Play Committee, and six white students— Naomi Bloom, Jean Bornstein, Mervyn Jones, Robert Schoenfeld, Anita Krieger, and Evelyn Maisel—were suspended by the University for three months, in part for spreading perceived untruths about the track program. In years to come, this group would become known as the Bates Seven.

On April 3, 1941, some 900 NYU students met in the Judson Church auditorium in Washington Square to discuss the suspension of the seven students. Guest speaker at the event was the First Lady, Mrs. Franklin D. Roosevelt. At the time of the protests she kept an apartment on Washington Square, close by where the demonstrations had taken place. She rebuked the students for their protest. "Mrs. Roosevelt told the students that had they taken less spectacular means of registering their protest 'perhaps it would have turned out better and there would have been no martyrs.' She added, however: 'I think it's unfortunate to suspend students for doing foolish things; I hope they get taken back.' " Thus the First Lady focused her attention on the protest and not on the cause for which the protest had been launched. The lack of communication with the students was brought further to light by her following prepared comments, which urged them, "Never be afraid to change."[41]

Eleanor Roosevelt was no stranger to protests on behalf of the causes of black people. Unlike her husband, who was constrained by the need to hold together a political coalition, she had an independent mind and championed the cause of equality for minorities. "[S]he dared the awful scorn reserved for those who associated politically with southern blacks," wrote John Kenneth Galbraith.[42] She had resigned her membership in the Daughters of the American Revolution when the DAR refused to allow black contralto Marian Anderson to perform at Constitution Hall, a venue the DAR controlled. Eleanor Roosevelt had the clarity of vision to recognize the prejudice and to act accordingly. And as First Lady she had access to alternatives. She had the power to see to it that Anderson, in compensation, was given the special opportunity to perform at the Lincoln Memorial on Easter Sunday 1939, where her talent dazzled a crowd of 75,000 people, both black and white, in a powerful symbolic statement. At times Anderson, too, had access to alternatives. Though denied the opportunity to enroll in schools of her choosing, stay at hotels of her choosing, or eat in restaurants of her choosing for most of her life, when she was turned away from a room at the Nassau Inn in Princeton, New Jersey, she stayed at the home of Albert Einstein.[43] The students at NYU had no such alternatives available to them. Their only course of action was to take advantage of the limited tools at their disposal. Eleanor Roosevelt may have found their actions foolish, but in a cause on par with hers, those actions were all they had.

On March 30, 1941, the National Council for Democracy in Education, meeting in Cambridge, Massachusetts, passed a resolution calling for the immediate and unconditional reinstatement of the seven suspended NYU students.[44] The resolution was to no avail.

The week after the Missouri game, Bates was back in the starting lineup for NYU against Franklin and Marshall as if nothing had happened. He distinguished himself with a number of fine runs on offense and an intercepted pass on defense, and the Violets won for only the second time. The newspaper coverage gave no clue that anything out of the ordinary had occurred. NYU would finish the year with a mediocre 2-7 record. Early the next year Bates would suffer a season-ending injury, but not before making a long kick return against Texas A&M, in a game NYU lost. In 1942, Bates's senior season, NYU suspended its football program because of the war. While Leonard Bates's football career was at an end, he and his supporters had made a mark in the early struggles for civil rights.

The exchange between the students and the First Lady, the opposing attitudes among the various student groups and the administration, the recurring conflict between principle and expediency, the distinct vantage points of the powerful and the powerless, and the profound differences of values among the participants in the debates all foreshadowed the long and arduous road ahead. By the time the civil rights movement reached its hottest moments, a generation in the future, these issues had been replayed thousands of times over. The students and protesters at New York University served an important role in beginning the painful process of righting the societal wrongs that, while highly visible in the world of sport, were pervasive in the society of the time.

****

As Cornell approached its game with Syracuse on October 19, its undefeated streak was at 13 games, and it was well aware that its last loss had been to the Orangemen in 1938. That year, Cornell was undefeated and was comfortably ahead of Syracuse 10-0 midway through the fourth quarter when a talented Syracuse halfback named Wilmeth Sidat-Singh enjoyed perhaps his greatest moments as a collegian. Passing for three touchdowns in the fourth quarter, Sidat-Singh led Syracuse to a startling come-from-behind upset of Cornell, 19-17, his team's second consecutive upset of the Big Red.

"Woe, woe, unutterable woe!" lamented one columnist.[45] "Those who witnessed this exciting struggle...will long sing the praises of Sidat-Singh,"[46] said another report. "It Don't Mean A Thing If It Ain't Got That Singh," sang a third.[47] Grantland Rice, the great sports chronicler, was gushing in his praise. "A new forward-pass hero slipped in front of the great white spotlight of fame at Syracuse today. The phenomenon of the rifle shot event went on beyond Sid Luckman and Sammy Baugh. His name is Wilmeth Sidat-Singh," extolled Rice.[48] Cornell would not lose again for more than two years.

The year before, Wilmeth Sidat-Singh had had a secret divulged that materially changed his career and his life. In 1937, it was Sidat-Singh's pass to Marty Glickman, the star of the Orange team, that had set up Glickman's second touchdown, as Syracuse scored a huge upset over Cornell, 14-6, one that had the press saying, "If the wind had blown the roof off Willard Straight Hall into Lake Cayuga...it wouldn't have caused as much surprise...."[49] That game would be the last before the secret came out. Sidat-Singh was a dark-skinned man who many assumed, given his name, was a Hindu. But on the day before the Syracuse-Maryland game of 1937, a writer named Sam Lacy divulged his secret in the *Washington Tribune*, a weekly black newspaper. An hour before game time, already dressed in his uniform and with his family in the stands, Sidat-Singh was informed that he would not be allowed to play against Maryland.

Years later, Glickman described the scene in the locker room. "Wil is sitting alongside me; we're starting halfbacks in the single wing. Ossie Solem and Lew Andreas (coach and AD, respectively) come in and tell us Maryland knows Wil's not a Hindu; they know he's a black man."[50]

Wilmeth Webb was born in Washington, D.C. to black parents, Pauline and Elias Webb, in 1918. His father, a pharmacist, died of a stroke in 1925, and after a time his mother married an Indian doctor from New York City named Samuel Sidat-Singh. Wilmeth took the name of his new father, and the family moved to Harlem.

He went to Syracuse on a basketball scholarship, and when his skills in throwing a football became apparent to an assistant coach on the football team—he was seen throwing the ball 60 yards flatfooted in an intramural game—he began competing on the gridiron as well. His Hindu-sounding surname was seen as an advantage to Syracuse, since he could be passed off as what he was not.

But all that came crashing down when Lacy's headline hit the street. "Negro To Play U. of Maryland," it screamed. "They Call Him A Hindu" was the sub-heading. Sidat-Singh had never made a secret of his heritage, and all his friends from Harlem were well aware of his family history. "He never told anybody he wasn't black. Syracuse came up with that on their own, they put that word out," said sports historian James Coates.[51]

Sidat-Singh was often referred to as the "Brooklyn Hindu,"[52] although he was neither from Brooklyn nor a Hindu. On the basketball court earlier in the year he had been hailed as the "Hindu Hoopster" and he was said to be "probably the only Hindu playing intercollegiate basketball."[53] In the fall, one newspaper said he was "probably the only Hindu player in football today."[54] In another, he was called, "the only Hindu footballer in captivity."[55] He was a great curiosity, and his photo often appeared in the paper under such headings as "Hindoo Magic"[56] and "Hindu Half."[57]

But all that came to an end on October 23, 1937. "The schools had an agreement," explained Coates. "It wasn't a color line that they had drawn into the contracts; it was an anti-American Negro line. If you were black and from the Dominican Republic, or black and from Cuba, or a native American, or Hindu, you were allowed to play against Maryland. If you were an American Negro, you couldn't play."[58] Syracuse acceded to the pressure, and Sidat-Singh did not play. And it wasn't just football. When the basketball team played Navy the next year in Annapolis, he was also not allowed to play, despite being the team's leading scorer.

There was another convention at play, a code of silence among mainstream northern newspapers. The gentlemen's agreement was not discussed in the press. Similarly, the athletes' absence, if possible, was simply ignored. The Maryland-Syracuse game had been highly anticipated, and there had been a number of articles in the paper leading up to the game. "Jack Hinkle will be ready for the southern trip and is expected to see some action, although Wilmeth Sidat-Singh will probably get a major share of the work," said one a few days before the contest, while the secret was still intact.[59] But when he sat on the bench for the entirety of the game with a wet towel over his head, no explanation was offered in the press as to why the hero of the week before had made no appearance. Through a series of half-statements over the next week, readers were left to surmise that Sidat-Singh had somehow lost his starting job to Hinkle but that, with Hinkle "ailing," he would be back in the lineup the next week against Penn State.[60]

Maryland won the game, 13-0, but the next year, with the game played at Syracuse, the Orangemen avenged the loss, 53-0.

That was the week before Sidat-Singh's three fourth-quarter touchdown passes did in Cornell. In that game he was not the only high-achieving black player on the field. Cornell's two-time All-American end, Brud Holland, would go on to compile an illustrious career after football. Dr. Jerome Holland served as president of Delaware State University and Hampton Institute, later Hampton University; he was national chairman of the American Red Cross until his death; he served as United States Ambassador to Sweden; he was the first black member of the board of the New York Stock Exchange; he was a member of the Cornell University Board of Trustees; he was vice-chairman of the National Conference of Christians and Jews; he was recipient of the National Football Foundation's Distinguished American Award. But when stories about the 1938 All-America team ran in southern newspapers, they were often accompanied by only ten photos of the eleven-man team.

The black community expressed outrage at Lacy's actions in revealing Sidat-Singh's situation, feeling that he had deprived them of the chance for one of their own to excel. But Lacy stood firmly on principle, insisting that he had done the right thing.

When he graduated from Syracuse, there was no job for Sidat-Singh in the National Football League, which had a strict ban against black players. He played for whatever professional or semiprofessional team was available. He played basketball for the New York Renaissance, an elite barnstorming team of all-black stars that routinely held its own against the best teams in the world, and for the Lichtman Bears, another elite all-black barnstorming team based in Washington. While in Washington, he also played football for the semi-professional U Street Lions. After the war started, he joined the D.C. police force.

His experience with discrimination was not unique among the Orangemen; teammate Marty Glickman had already suffered a similar sting of discrimination. Years later, Marty Glickman would become well known to America through his long and distinguished career in sports broadcasting. A fixture in New York City and nationwide, he served as the voice of a range of professional New York sports teams, and for HBO. But few knew that in 1936 Marty Glickman had been a world-class sprinter who was kept from competing with the rest of the United States representatives at the Berlin Olympics, because he was Jewish.

It all began during the Olympic trials when Glickman, according to the films of the race, finished third in the 100-yard dash, thus qualifying for that event in the Olympics. But the official ruling was that he had finished fifth and would go to Berlin with the Olympic squad only as a member of the 4x100 yard relay team. Then, in Berlin on the day before that event, he was told that he and Sam Stoller, another Jew from the University of Michigan, were being replaced in the event by Jesse Owens and Ralph Metcalfe, respectively. Owens was a faster runner than Glickman, but for two weeks Glickman and his teammates had practiced the handling and passing of the baton, a critical skill in a relay, and Owens had not. Owens protested, but to no avail. The U.S. team won the gold medal by a wide margin. It did not need the extra speed Owens provided, but needlessly risked everything to faulty baton handling. Glickman, deeply bitter, could only sit on the sidelines and watch.[61]

So a Jew like Glickman could not compete for his country in the Olympics but a black man like Jesse Owens could, while a Jew like Glickman could play football against the University of Maryland but a black man like Wilmeth Sidat-Singh could not.

As Glickman sat on the bench next to Sidat-Singh in the locker room that day in October 1937, he knew, more than anybody, the anguish and humiliation. Glickman finishes the story: "I say to myself, 'Marty, get up and say if Wil doesn't play, I don't play.'...I didn't say anything. I'm ashamed of it. That stays with me still, the one thing I'll always regret."[62]

****

The 1940 Syracuse team was in no position to duplicate the momentous upsets of 1937 and 1938, and on October 19, fresh from a 40-0 pasting by Northwestern, it was the Big Red's next foe. Again Cornell scored four touchdowns by passes of 57 yards, 37 yards, three yards, and 30 yards. And their other touchdown was scored by Bill Murphy on a beautiful end reverse run of 44 yards, as the Cornell blockers mowed down the defenders with precision. The long pass play was becoming the Cornell trademark, and there was no telling how or where it would strike. Scholl to Landsberg, McCullough to Schmuck, Murphy to McCullough, McCullough to Jenkins, McCullough to Bufalino, and Stofer to Ruddy—each combination netted long gains. And as in their previous games, Cornell's five touchdowns were scored by five different players. By the fourth quarter, Carl Snavely put all of his substitutes in the game, but Cornell still amassed 542 total yards in the game, 311 of them on 15 completed passes. By the time it was over, the Big Red had prevailed, 33-6.

After the game, Syracuse coach Ossie Solem was effusive in his praise. "It's the greatest passing attack I've ever seen," he said. "There are so many players on that team that can pull down anything they can get their hands on. You have to take into consideration the number of guys who can chuck that ball too. My gosh but they're wonderful." Another observer added, "They are probably the greatest passing team of all time," rating Cornell with Rockne's Notre Dame teams of a decade before and with Michigan's teams of the same era with Benny Friedman.[63] A continent away, Clark Shaughnessy seemed to have the perfect team for the T-formation, and in Ithaca Carl Snavely seemed to have the perfect array for the single wing—a bevy of well-rounded athletes skilled in each aspect of the game who could do almost anything asked of them.

On Tuesday, the Associated Press poll again showed Cornell as the leading team in the nation with 80 first place votes to 30 for Notre Dame and 18 for Michigan.

****

On September 29, Charles Seymour, President of Yale University, wrote an article, "War's Impact on the Campus," that appeared in the *New York Times Magazine*. Seymour expressed his view that the college students of the day were willing to fight to defend their country but unwilling to contemplate fighting in Europe. He further felt that they had an insufficient appreciation of the strong relationship between the well-being of Britain and that of their own country, but could be brought to understand it better in time. He advocated stronger emphasis on the moral lessons of history, and felt certain that when such took place the advantages of compulsive military service would become evident. Seymour wrote, "Clarify the issues, explain the dangers our American ideals face, emphasize the obligation to leadership which rests upon him and the undergraduate will respond to the call."[64] Seymour would soon have the chance to test his ideas.

October 16, 1940, was a momentous day in the history of the United States. Three weeks before a presidential election, all over the country, in fire stations, hotel lobbies, county buildings, public schools, and on college campuses, men between the ages of 21 and 36 lined up to register for the nation's first peacetime draft. Some huddled in the early morning chill, eager for warmth, or ducked into doorways to keep dry from a passing shower. Taxi drivers in from their red-eye runs, factory workers home from the midnight shift, farmers eager to get to their fields, office workers anxious to complete the job and get back to their desks, even duck hunters in a hurry not to miss opening day of the season, all stood in lines snaking down hallways and out onto sidewalks to fulfill their responsibility. The nation had never seen anything like it. Celebrities, hospital patients, even a man in an iron lung[65] signed up. Unlike the draft during World War I, when force had to be used to restrain protestors, the process went smoothly virtually everywhere in the country. A handful of draft resistors were detained by authorities, but in the main the day was notable for its well-organized efficiency. And unlike the draft of a generation later, it was broad in nature. "Wealthy leaders and ragged men from the Bowery...men from the gutters and men from great mansions"[66] were all registered, said the *New York Times*. Following the same theme, the *Chicago Tribune* noted, "Millionaires' sons and ditch diggers' sons stood in line...."[67] Indeed, the key theme of the press coverage of the day was the breadth of the impact on the American people.

The world of sports was fully involved. New York Giants center Mel Hein took his entire football team to the registration center. Bob Feller, Joe Cronin, Whizzer White, Byron Nelson, Joe Louis, Max Baer, Billy Conn, Ben Hogan, and Hank Greenberg were among the famous athletes who came forward and put their name on the line with everyone else. In the world of entertainment, Tyrone Power, Orson Welles, Henry Fonda, Artie Shaw, Benny Goodman, and Woody Herman all signed up. Laurence Rockefeller and John D. Rockefeller III both signed up in New York, at a local fire station, while their brother David Rockefeller registered at P.S. 79. The sons of the ambassador to Britain signed up as well: Joseph Kennedy, Jr., signed up on the campus at Harvard, and his brother John F. Kennedy registered at Stanford.[68]

Students were guaranteed exemption from service until July 1, 1941, but no later. It was made clear that married registrants would not be among the first chosen. On October 29, Secretary of War Henry L. Stimson was to draw the first number to establish the order in which 16 million men would be considered for conscription into the armed services.

The nation had changed in its attitude toward mandatory registration, prodded in no small measure by the relentless bombardment under which London and other British cities found themselves. Both major presidential candidates, Roosevelt and Willkie, were supportive of the draft. Carr's, a Minneapolis men's clothing store, offered a Defense Cooperation Money Back Certificate, a guarantee of credit or full refund on merchandise purchased between September 16 and November 1, if the purchaser were drafted and entered the service before January 1, 1941.

On campuses the atmosphere was quiet, as those willing to comply with the law outnumbered those eager to object to it. Cornell students placed a coffin on campus, intending to send it to President Roosevelt in protest against America's trend towards entering the European conflict. The coffin attracted moderate interest from passers-by. Meanwhile, about 1,500 students registered at six registration booths on the campus. The process appeared orderly, and no disturbances or protests were in evidence. At the University of Minnesota, the process went equally smoothly as over 2,000 people registered, and officials were delighted that nobody had to wait more than ten minutes. Registrants there were told their chances of being inducted into the service were about one in 20. At Harvard, too, the process went off without a hitch, despite the presence of a handful of conscientious objectors, as 4,700 students and faculty members registered.

One incident at Cornell, notable for its mildness, helps define, at least in part, the mood of the day. One of the important traditions at Cornell is the daily chime concerts from atop the McGraw Bell Tower, whose pealing bells could be heard all over campus. The classical or popular pieces to be played by the chimemaster are usually publicized in advance and culminate with the playing of the alma mater. On October 16, the concert from 12:50 to 1:00 pm was to include excerpts from *Le Secret* by Gautier, *Tambourin* by Rameau, and *Le Cinquintaine* by Gabriel-Marie. As the male students over 21 lined up to register, the chimemaster, who was a junior and too young to be subject to the draft, climbed the stairs to the bell tower and played instead *"We're in the Army Now," "Show Me the Way to Go Home,"* and *"I Didn't Raise My Boy to Be a Soldier."* The incident, more in the nature of a prank than a protest, was nevertheless roundly criticized by the student newspaper. The protests of another war a generation later, at Cornell and on campuses all over the country, involving sit-ins, takeovers, bonfires, destruction of presidents' offices, hangings in effigy, and much worse, make the mild expressions of 1940 pale in comparison.

Women's colleges were active as well. At Barnard in New York City the day was set aside to organize practical service. Students engaged in such activities as knitting socks and sewing children's garments, and the proceeds were sent to British War Relief.

Meanwhile, voluntary recruitment was at an all-time high. Between September 1 and September 24, more than 3,100 men volunteered for military service in New York, New Jersey, and Delaware, including 700 in one day, sending recruiting officers to seek more resources. That figure was surpassed in the first three weeks of October, when nearly 4,300 men signed up. Similar figures were reached in recruiting offices throughout the country, with the San Antonio, Atlanta, and Chicago headquarters being most active.

But amid all this sudden patriotic fervor a different and perhaps more realistic facet of the times peeked through. On October 23, in New York City, three trainloads of soldiers from the Army's 27th Division were scheduled to depart from Grand Central Station en route to Camp McClellan, Alabama, for one year of training. As they entered the rotunda of the station, present to greet them were about 4,000 of their friends and relatives, separated from the troops by a police line. The troops were given 25 minutes to say their goodbyes, but when it was time for them to fall in, many of the women broke through the police lines, reached their men, and refused to let go. Some became hysterical and could be separated only by having the men form up and double-time out of the rotunda. "It was apparent that those who had come to say goodbye to them feared that something more serious than training was ahead of them," explained the newspaper.[69] The reality would gradually become clear to more Americans as the days wore on.

CHAPTER 9
THE LEGEND

Oft expectation fails, and most oft there
Where most it promises.

--SHAKESPEARE, *All's Well That Ends Well*

The exact moment that the football fortunes began to skyrocket for a small little-known Catholic college from the midwest, and indeed for the entire game of college football, can be identified with precision. On October 30, 1913, a party of eighteen men—fourteen football players and a handful of coaches and trainers—boarded a train in South Bend, Indiana, bound for West Point to play the mighty Army football team, the very embodiment of the eastern football establishment.

Notre Dame had enjoyed consistent success in football over the years on a regional level, but never before had the team ventured so far from South Bend and never before had it played an opponent of such national standing. Army had agreed to pay Notre Dame $1000 to cover travel expenses and had invited the Catholics, as they were then called, to fill a vacancy on its schedule. When the weary contingent from South Bend got off the train in West Point at 8 am on game day, it was judged by their hosts to be acceptable warm-up material.[1]

According to legend, two roommates at Notre Dame had been tossing a football around, while on their summer job as lifeguards at the Cedar Point resort on Lake Erie in the summer of 1913, when they happened upon a critical discovery. They found a technique by which the ball, rounder and more cumbersome than today's modern version, could be gripped and accurately thrown from one to the other over great distances. When one would run a predetermined route and the other would time his throw just right, the ball could be caught on the run. They theorized, according to this legend, that this technique could be used to greatly expand the effectiveness of the forward pass as an offensive football tool.

The forward pass had been effectively used in college football for some time prior to the teammates' discovery, but in modified form. But most coaches hated the idea of passing the ball, resorting to it only when all else failed. The accepted method of play, especially in the East, involved what was called at the time "straight football," that is, power blocking and running mostly between the tackles, with an underhanded shovel or short overhand toss to a stationary receiver used perhaps once or twice a game. But unlike the previous Notre Dame coach, John Marks, who was only mildly tolerant of the concept, the new coach, Jess Harper, not only tolerated such revolutionary schemes as his two players had devised, he embraced them.

To be sure, it was not Notre Dame who introduced the pass to Army. Indeed, the first touchdown of the game, scored by Army, was set up by a completed pass.[2] But Notre Dame had different ideas as to its use. The magic moment occurred midway through the first period of the game. Notre Dame quarterback Gus Dorais, a frail 145-pounder, whose first two passing attempts had gone awry, faded back from the Army 25-yard line and hit his roommate, captain Knute Rockne, with a perfect pass at the goal line, just as they had practiced at Cedar Point, and Notre Dame had its first touchdown against an astounded Army team. This was not a short toss to a stationary target but something revolutionary, seldom seen before and never before practiced with such precision—a well-timed long throw to a distant receiver on the move. Notre Dame was not done. For the entire afternoon, it seemed, Dorais launched long passes to either Rockne or Joe Pliska, who were regularly catching them on the dead run. Notre Dame was moving the ball 30 yards or more at a time, and Army seemed quite unsure how to defend against this new technique. The revolutionary new offense, said the *Chicago Tribune*, "was a source of much discomfort to the cadets."[3] The *New York Times* agreed, calling Notre Dame's play "the most sensational football that has been seen in the east this year."[4]

The outcome was not long in doubt. By the end of the game, Notre Dame, using only twelve players, had buried Army 35-13, and all five Notre Dame touchdowns had been scored by forward pass. The visitors also found that by using the pass they made their "straight football" skills more effective. "When the whistle ended the game they were smashing the Army line to pieces," reported the *Chicago Tribune*, adding that Notre Dame had attempted the unheard of number of fourteen passes, completing twelve.[5] Other sources indicate that Notre Dame had completed fourteen of seventeen passes for 245 yards.[6]

After the game, football men could not stop talking about what they had seen. Among them was Bill Roper, former head coach at Princeton, who had been an official in the game. Such a performance under the new passing rules had often been considered theoretically possible, Roper thought, but the execution of the concept by Notre Dame had approached perfection.[7] The game, said John Kieran of the *New York Times* years later, as he contemplated its importance in football history, "wakened the conservative east to the worth of the forward pass in football."[8]

The game of football had been changed forever, and a radical new offensive strategy had been introduced. Notre Dame, which completed an undefeated season in 1913 (Army would lose only to them and would go undefeated the following season) had burst on the scene as a powerful football force, never again to be relegated to secondary status. With its $1000 advance in the bank, Notre Dame had netted $85 on the trip,[9] but the benefit to its football program and to college football in general was incalculable. And a compelling new rivalry had been given life. Over the next four decades, some of the most important and notable games in college football history would be played between Army and Notre Dame. The fans in attendance that day had seen merely the first.

Born in Voss, Norway, in 1888, Knute Rockne had been a few years older than most of his teammates. After graduating magna cum laude from Notre Dame with a degree in chemistry, Rockne stayed on as graduate assistant in chemistry and assistant football coach, and helped Jess Harper continue the process of innovation, most notably with a series of formations and shifts known as the Notre Dame Box. In 1918, Harper unexpectedly resigned as Notre Dame head coach, and the job was given to Rockne.

Arriving on campus that year was a group of seriously talented players including end Eddie Anderson and guard Heartley "Hunk" Anderson, who would both start as freshmen under the relaxed eligibility rules brought about by the Great War. Both, like Rockne, were sons of Norwegian immigrants and were best friends. Also on the team that fall, having arrived on campus in 1916 as a 21-year old freshman on a baseball scholarship, was a larger-than-life, boozing, gambling, carousing, practice-skipping, pool-hustling, poker-playing academic no-show prima donna of immense football talent named George Gipp. Never has an individual contributed more to the Notre Dame legend over the years than Gipp, but if a little bad-boy image is a good thing for a legend, Gipp went far beyond that. Seldom attending classes, Gipp preferred the action at Hullie and Mike's, a local pool hall. He bet on the games, smoked cigarettes on the end of the bench, and unlike the other players who supported themselves with jobs in the dining hall or bookstore, Gipp subsisted comfortably on his winnings from poker and three-cushion billiards, at which he was also immensely talented. Some versions of the legend have him sharing his winnings with needy or less fortunate classmates, thus lending a Robin Hood air to the story. But when he drop-kicked a 62-yard game-winning field goal his freshman year, his football talents commanded top attention, and to Rockne nothing else mattered. Rockne loved him and treated him with kid gloves.[10]

The 1918 season was truncated due to a national flu epidemic, and participation that year did not count against players' eligibility. The Notre Dame team went undefeated in 1919, won a share of the national championship, and was set for a glorious year in 1920 against stiffer competition when a complication arose. On March 8, Gipp, newly chosen as team captain for the upcoming year, was expelled from school for failure to attend classes. Rockne had to intervene and argue strenuously for his reinstatement, which he finally gained, but Gipp, it was made clear, would not be captain of the football team.

Notre Dame was undefeated as well in 1920 when it came up against its now-familiar rival, Army. In what was probably his finest game, Gipp matched football talent with the great star of the Army team, Walter French. Gipp scored the first two Notre Dame touchdowns, French the first two Army touchdowns, and when French kicked a field goal Army led at the half. Gipp's passing and running in the second half set up the last two Notre Dame touchdowns and the final score was 27-17 in Notre Dame's favor. Gipp accounted for 332 yards in rushing, passing, and kick returning.

The game was significant for one more detail. According to one version of the legend the fans, excited by a Notre Dame lineup which included names like Coughlin, Kiley, Garvey, Barry, and Shaw, repeatedly chanted "Let's Go Irish!" The chant caught the ear of influential sportswriter Arch Ward of the *Chicago Tribune,* and he decided to hang on the team from South Bend a new nickname. It stuck.[11]

Notre Dame played Purdue the following week, and Gipp, playing less than a half, gained 171 yards passing and 250 by running, including touchdown runs of 80 and 92 yards.

Then things turned both better and worse at the same time. At Indiana, the Irish came from behind to beat the home team 13-10, and the *Chicago Tribune* offered this succinct version of the win: "George Gipp, who had left the fray in the third quarter with an injured shoulder, came back and carried the oval across for a touchdown. He then kicked goal."[12] The legend is a bit different. With Notre Dame trailing 10-0 and the ball on the two-yard line, says the legend, Rockne sent Gipp, who had either broken or separated his shoulder earlier in the game, back in with explicit instructions to act as a decoy and not to touch the ball. Gipp promptly took the ball and plowed over for the winning touchdown, injured shoulder and all. It was later determined that the shoulder was broken and doctors said Gipp would miss the rest of the season.[13] Gipp continued in the game and later passed to Eddie Anderson at the one-yard line to set up the winning touchdown.

Gipp did not return home with the team, and instead took a side trip to Chicago. When he finally arrived in South Bend, having been on a three-day bender, he had an increasingly bad cough and a high fever.[14] The legend incorrectly attributes his condition to injuries from the Indiana game.

Rockne decided not to play him in the upcoming game against Northwestern. According to the legend, however, Gipp drop-kicked ten successive field goals from the fifty-yard line in pregame warm-ups before retreating to the bench.[15]

Notre Dame had the game in hand in the fourth quarter when fans cheering for Gipp got the better of Rockne. In accord with their loudly expressed wishes, he inserted Gipp into the game in the fourth quarter. The legend says Rockne again instructed him to take it easy and again Gipp disobeyed orders. He promptly threw a 35-yard touchdown pass to Eddie Anderson, the end's third score of the game, and then a 54-yard touchdown pass to Norm Barry. Notre Dame won 33-7. It would be Gipp's last game.

By the next week Gipp was too sick to play against Michigan State on Thanksgiving Day or to pose for the team picture commemorating the second consecutive undefeated season and second consecutive shared national championship. His tonsillitis and strep throat turned into pneumonia, and when his condition steadily worsened he was hospitalized. By the end of the month he was fighting for his life. "Physicians See Slim Hope For Gipp's Recovery," the *Chicago Tribune* headlines read on December 2. If he could make it through the night he had a chance, but a slim one, doctors reported.[16] He hung on for two more weeks. Meanwhile, on December 11, he was named to Walter Eckersall's All-America team and was told, before it was published, that he had been named as well to Walter Camp's All-America team. He was the first Notre Dame player so honored. The student body held vigils outside St. Joseph's Hospital. Hunk Anderson, who also went to high school with Gipp, donated blood. For the last twenty-four hours his mother, his sister and brother, and Rockne were constantly at his side. The end came on December 14 at 3:30 am. He was 25 years old.

Classes at Notre Dame were suspended. His funeral was attended by 1500 people before a train took his casket home to Laurium, Michigan. Burial took place in Lakeview Cemetery, a bleak hillside overlooking Lake Superior, in snow driven by gale force winds. The casket was carried nearly five miles to the cemetery on a horse-drawn sled through snow that was eight feet deep.[17]

Notre Dame had won its first two games of the 1924 season when the Irish again faced Army. What had begun eleven years before as a chance encounter had bloomed into a fierce and immensely popular rivalry, one that had outgrown the small confines of the facilities at West Point, even as Army's brand new and much larger Michie Stadium was under construction. As the popularity of the rivalry continued to grow, school officials sought progressively larger venues. In 1923 the game was moved to Ebbets Field in Brooklyn where it was attended by 35,000 fans; to the Polo Grounds in Manhattan the following year, where 55,000 spectators were present; and finally in 1925 to Yankee Stadium in the Bronx, where it found its traditional venue and was viewed annually by more than 75,000.

The Polo Grounds game, played on October 18, 1924, added a critical chapter to the Notre Dame legend. The Irish had a powerful team that year led by a talented and well-balanced backfield of Jim Crowley, Jim Miller, Elmer Layden, and Harry Stuhldreher, and they beat Army 13-7 behind their strong running. Walter Eckersall of the *Chicago Tribune* called it "one of the most powerful running attacks seen in recent years."[18] Eckersall had a good view of the game. He not only reported for the newspaper, but also served as the linesman on the officiating crew. Another account of the game, more subdued, merely pointed out Notre Dame's superior team speed and commented, "Stuhldreher at quarter starred for Notre Dame."[19] Walter Camp wrote an account of the game that likewise mentioned Notre Dame's team speed and a great team effort, but singled out no player or players for particular mention.[20] Modern football commentator Beano Cook later characterized it as an "unremarkable game."[21] Nevertheless, the contest was immortalized, not by the players on the field, but by sportswriter Grantland Rice of the *New York Herald Tribune*, who had a decidedly different and memorable description of the day's events.

In language that would be considered mawkish today but nevertheless stands as perhaps the most famous paragraph in the history of sports journalism, Rice wrote: "Outlined against a blue-gray October sky the Four Horsemen rode again. In dramatic lore they are known as famine, pestilence, destruction, and death. These are only aliases. Their real names are: Stuhldreher, Miller, Crowley, and Layden. They formed the crest of the South Bend cyclone before which another fighting Army football team was swept over the precipice at the Polo Grounds yesterday afternoon as 55,000 spectators peered down on the bewildering panorama spread on the green plain below." When a few days later Notre Dame press agent George Strickler had the four players pose atop a quartet of borrowed workhorses and snapped what would become an iconic photograph, the Four Horsemen became permanently enshrined in Notre Dame legend. Cook called them the most famous quartet of the twentieth century until the Beatles. The photo was so popular that in 1998 the United States Postal Service chose it to appear on a postage stamp, one of a set of fifteen printed to be representative of the national culture of the 1920s. In 1924 Notre Dame would remain undefeated, win a share of the national championship again, and beat Stanford and the great Ernie Nevers in the Rose Bowl on New Year's Day, as Elmer Layden scored three touchdowns, including two on interception returns of 70 and 35 yards.

Notre Dame finished out the decade with undefeated seasons in both 1929 and 1930, behind such players as Frank Carideo and Marchy Schwartz, winning the national championship each year. But then, on March 31, 1931, the Notre Dame legend took a tragic turn when Knute Rockne boarded a plane in Kansas City bound for Los Angeles. The plane crashed in a wheatfield near Bazaar, Kansas, killing everybody on board. Rockne was 43.

Rockne's legacy as a coach was stellar. Between 1918 and 1930 he compiled a record of 105-12-5, including five undefeated seasons, six national championships, and a Rose Bowl victory. Just as significantly, during his tenure, Notre Dame was a veritable launching pad for coaching talent. His old roommate Gus Dorais, who served as an assistant under Rockne, coached for many years at the University of Detroit. During Rockne's first year as head coach his freshman fullback was Curly Lambeau, who went on to coach the Green Bay Packers and was a founding figure in the National Football League. Norm Barry similarly coached the Chicago Cardinals of the NFL, and Adam Walsh coached the Cleveland and Los Angeles Rams, as well as Santa Clara and Bowdoin in the college ranks. Hunk Anderson succeeded Rockne as coach at Notre Dame. Three of the Four Horsemen—Harry Stuhldreher at Villanova and Wisconsin, Jim Crowley at Fordham, and Elmer Layden, who would succeed Hunk Anderson at their alma mater—followed in their coach's profession. Eddie Anderson at Holy Cross and Iowa, Jack Chevigny at Texas and the Chicago Cardinals of the NFL, Joe Bach at St. Bonaventure and the Pittsburgh Steelers of the NFL, Buck Shaw at Santa Clara, Harry Mehre at Georgia and Mississippi, Rip Miller at Navy, Chet Wynne at Creighton, Auburn and Kentucky, Tom Lieb at Florida, Moon Mullins at Loyola of New Orleans and St. Ambrose, Rex Enright at South Carolina, Marty Brill at LaSalle and Loyola, Slip Madigan at St. Mary's, Jim Phelan at Purdue and Washington, Frank Thomas at Alabama, Frank Leahy at Boston College and Notre Dame, Marchy Schwartz at Creighton and Stanford, and Clipper Smith at Santa Clara and Villanova were among those head coaches who learned their football at Rockne's knee. During the 1940 season, no fewer than 28 men who had played with or under Rockne served as head coaches in college football. Not only had Rockne taken his alma mater from obscurity to the zenith of the college football ranks, his coaching talent was broadcast like seeds in the wind, spreading the mystique of Notre Dame football throughout the country.

Perhaps the single greatest contribution to the Notre Dame legend came not from the playing field, or the press booth, but from the movie studio. On October 5, 1940, timed to coincide with the start of the football season, Warner Brothers released a movie titled *Knute Rockne, All-American*. A young actor named Ronald Reagan, whose thin resume included such recent films as *Brother Rat* and *Boy Meets Girl*, won out at the last minute over Henry Morgan for the role of George Gipp. The film, a paean to Rockne and Notre Dame, is a mixture of exaggeration and fabrication held together by a thin glue of fact, and was warmly received by the hero-hungry public. Most notably, the film asserts that Gipp whispered to Rockne on his death bed his wish that Notre Dame would some day, when the going was tough, win a game for him. Further, it claims that at halftime of the 1928 Army-Notre Dame game, yet another classic between the two teams, with Army leading 6-0, Rockne made a speech to the team highlighted by the line, "[S]ometime, when the team is up against it, and the breaks are beating the boys, tell 'em to go out there with all they got and win just one for the Gipper."[22] The movie then has an aroused

Notre Dame team rallying to defeat Army 7-6. It brought tears to the eye of the most hardened football fan.

Like many good legends, the win-one-for-the-Gipper story enjoys a long and spirited history of debate about whether it ever actually happened. Each side has its proponents, its theories and its arguments, and the more the debate goes on the greater the legend becomes. The game was played in the heart of the sport-crazy and hero-crazy 1920s, and both Rockne and the press of the day were highly prone to exaggeration and outright fibs to create a good story. Certainly Grantland Rice and Paul Gallico played important roles as sportswriters in creating the legend, and both routinely produced flowery descriptions of the heroes of the day. Rockne was certainly present at Gipp's deathbed, but it is not known what words, if any, were exchanged between the two, and Rockne never made any previous mention of it if there were. And Rockne certainly gave a spirited talk at halftime, as he often did. If it did happen, it was certainly not as the movie portrayed. Notre Dame was not losing at halftime—the score was 0-0—so Rockne certainly did not urge a come-from-behind effort. The final score actually was 12-6.

But if it didn't happen, the screenwriters certainly did not invent it. Almost immediately after the game the buzz began about a great halftime speech, and there is no question that Gipp had a hold on the emotions of the day that can hardly be imagined in today's world. A teary poem about him, for instance, appeared in the *Chicago Tribune* soon after his death, and reruns of it had appeared on demand periodically thereafter, including on the day after the 1928 Notre Dame-Army game.[23] The screen writers had only to take the loose threads of the story and weave them into what would become a well-established fable. At least according to Gallico's version, Gipp hated Rockne's halftime speeches, much preferring a quick cigarette in the hallway to the type of melodrama he supposedly urged on his deathbed.[24]

In the game as it was really played, one of the heroes for the Irish was Jack Chevigny, who scored the tying touchdown. It could not be known to the mythmakers in 1928, or to the moviemakers in 1940, but Jack Chevigny was later to die as a Marine lieutenant on Iwo Jima in 1945, a hero's death, quite frankly, far nobler than Gipp's.

In one last ironic note on the game, the referee for the contest was Walter Eckersall, the former Chicago Maroon great and *Chicago Tribune* journalist who had named George Gipp to the 1920 All-American team. It was possibly Gipp's strongest connection to that game. But maybe not.

****

Notre Dame struggled through the decade of the 1930s, successful, but certainly not Rockne-like, until fortunes again began to pick up late in the decade under coach Elmer Layden, the former Four Horsemen star. The 1938 Notre Dame team finished with an 8-1 record, losing only to Southern

California in the last game of the year. Though ranked fifth in the nation by the Associated Press, the Irish were rated by the Dickinson System as the top team in the nation.

Four weeks into the 1940 season, after the games of October 26, it appeared that Notre Dame would once again be a team in contention for the national championship. For the prior two weeks, the Irish had held on to the number two ranking by the Associated Press, just behind Cornell, on the strength of impressive wins over Pacific, Georgia Tech, Carnegie Tech, and Illinois. Preseason prospects for a much-improved season were coming to fruition. Senior captain Milt Piepul from Thompsonville, Connecticut, "a speed-and–power marvel of ribbed-steel construction," said one publication, was the fullback and team star, and he broke with a Notre Dame tradition that a lineman be team captain.[25]

There was hardly room on the Notre Dame bandwagon for more supporters. "[T]his team may be ranked up with the Four Horsemen outfit or the later group that Frank Carideo drove to glory," wrote John Kieran in the *New York Times*.[26] Robert F. Kelley, also in the *Times*, wrote, "[T]his is the greatest of modern Notre Dame teams, and ... Milt Piepul is the greatest fullback of the college's history."[27] That assessment included Piepul's coach, Layden, who was the fullback among the Four Horsemen. A third *Times* columnist, Allison Danzig, added his piece: "Notre Dame may have its finest eleven since Rockne's blocking masterpiece of 1930," he pronounced.[28] "It's true what they say about Notre Dame—great down to the second team," said Steve Snider of the United Press.[29] "Irish Appear Headed For Unbeaten Year," screamed the headlines over an article written by Earl Hilligan of the Associated Press, with five weeks still left in the season.[30]

The praise appeared to be constructed on solid ground. On October 5, the Irish had taken apart the Stagg-coached College of the Pacific team 25-7 with a second-half onslaught of three touchdowns. Piepul had scored twice, but had received plenty of help from Steve Juzwik and Bob Saggau. A good Georgia Tech team was no match for the Irish. Notre Dame was "looking more like potential national champions than in any recent campaign," said the *New York Times* after that one.[31] Their potent running game and long passes downed the Yellowjackets, 26-20, as the Irish scored three touchdowns in the second period, then the next week overwhelmed an outmanned Carnegie Tech team 61-0. Against Illinois the Irish again won easily, 26-0, as Juzwik set the pace with two touchdowns. The second and third teams were getting as much playing time as the first stringers.

Preseason forecasts also pointed out a key factor for the Irish. "[T]his may be a Notre Dame team in which sophomores eventually may play an important role," said one.[32] One of the most promising was end George Murphy. By 1942, in his senior year, George Murphy would become Notre Dame team captain, and that year he teamed with future Heisman Trophy winner Angelo

Bertelli to form a potent passing combination. With Bertelli passing and Murphy catching, it was "like Rockne and Dorais of yesteryear,"[33] said one historian.

****

On November 2, the Notre Dame Fighting Irish took their swagger, their legend, and their undefeated record to Yankee Stadium to face Army for another chapter in their great long rivalry. The Cadets could not be blamed for harboring ill feelings toward the schedule maker. Two weeks previously they had faced the top ranked team in the country, Cornell, and had absorbed the worst defeat in their history, 45-0. Now they had to face Notre Dame, the second-ranked team, and although their rivalry with the Irish through the years included hard fought games, Army looked particularly incapable of withstanding the attack of the highly praised Irish. Army had managed to win only an opening game squeaker against Williams and had tied a weak Harvard team, while losing the rest of its games; at no time did it exhibit the strength necessary to combat a team as strong as Notre Dame appeared to be. The pregame talk centered not on who would win the game, but by how much the Irish would prevail. Oddsmakers accordingly established Notre Dame as 6-1 favorites.

So it was with no small amount of surprise that the 78,000 fans watched the Cadets proceed to push the bigger, stronger, and faster Irish all over the field for four quarters, only to lose 7-0. A driving rain had stopped just before the game began, making the field too muddy for the Cadet marching band to perform, but the condition of the field did not appear to affect play. Making the best of their superior blocking and tackling, Army limited the Irish offense to 62 total yards, including only three yards in the first half, while gaining 237 yards of their own, and they outpaced the Irish, 15 first downs to four. But what cost Army the game was a series of tactical blunders that all but delivered the contest into the hands of the outplayed Irish. After recovering Notre Dame's fumble on the opening kickoff, Army pushed the ball to the four-yard line, and on fourth down decided to try for a field goal instead of a first down, only inches away. The attempt was missed. Then, after getting the ball back and pushing to the Notre Dame 20-yard line, Army tried a dangerous pass into the left flat, and Army halfback Henry Mazur carelessly threw it right into the hands of Irish defender Steve Juzwik, who ran it back 80 yards for a touchdown. Army failed to stop the clock at the end of the first half, when more judicious time management could have given them another chance to score, and then, late in the game, when it again had the ball on the Irish four-yard line, it ran four plays without seriously threatening to score, playing right into the hands of the Notre Dame defense each time. In all, Army took the ball to the Notre Dame four-yard line twice and inside the Notre Dame 21-yard line three other times, but never scored.

The game put to rest what Allison Danzig called "the myth of Notre Dame's super-greatness,"[34] a myth his earlier highly charged articles had helped to create. The Irish performance, he felt, had been "a distinct disappointment."[35] Suddenly, Notre Dame's standing, deemed so lofty by so many prior to this letdown, was in full retreat. As for the Army quarterback's questionable play-calling that ultimately cost the Cadets the game, Minnesota coach Bernie Bierman quipped, "It's a good thing that boy isn't a general yet."[36]

For the Irish, lucky to escape, it was on to Baltimore the next week for a chance to redeem itself against another service academy, Navy. Undeterred by the sobering events at Yankee Stadium, the oddsmakers installed the Irish as favorites once again. It was difficult to figure against an undefeated Irish team, even though Navy was much stronger than their brethren from West Point and was coming to the game with its best team in over a decade and a strong 5-1 record. Even in its lone defeat the week before, against a talented Penn team, Navy had thoroughly outplayed the Quakers. Despite advancing past the Penn 30-yard line seven times, they could not score and somehow managed to lose 20-0. Navy figured to present a formidable challenge to the suddenly wobbly Irish.

Notre Dame played a game eerily similar to their contest against Army the week before. Navy dominated play for more than three quarters, surrendering only a first-quarter touchdown, but although it drove inside the Notre Dame fifteen-yard line twice in the second period they, like Army the week before, could not score. It was not until the early moments of the fourth quarter that the Middies took a 7-6 lead and appeared headed for victory, since the Irish had shown no spark whatsoever in the game.

Then, as if somebody tinkering under the hood of the Irish football engine finally found and reconnected the loose wire that had robbed them of their power, Notre Dame sprung to life with half a quarter to play. In perhaps their most impressive offensive showing of the year the Irish marched the ball 79 yards down the field, and when Bob Saggau scored on a seven yard touchdown run the Irish escaped with a 13-7 victory. Notre Dame won the game, but the glory belonged to Navy. It had topped Notre Dame in yards gained, 223-175, and in first downs, 13 to 6. That most of what the Irish achieved came in the last drive emphasizes the degree of dominance Navy exercised for more than three quarters.

The Irish limped home to South Bend with their prestige deeply bruised. Significantly outplayed two weeks in a row by lesser teams, they could claim that they were still among the dwindling ranks of unbeatens, but the exuberance and unbounded optimism of the first half of the season had melted away in the heat of competition. They had dropped to seventh in the Associated Press rankings.

CHAPTER 10
IT GETS PERSONAL

Veracity is the height of morality.

--THOMAS HENRY HUXLEY, *Universities, Actual and Ideal*

The Georgia-Columbia game of October 19 was a beauty. In the second period, Hayward Allen of Georgia connected with Lamar Davis on a 65-yard pass play that had Davis shaking loose from and threading his way through a number of Lion defenders to run the last 42 yards. Then came a goal line stand by Columbia, when the Bulldogs had the ball first and goal at the one yard line but could not score. "There is something brave and tingling about a goal line stand such as that," wrote Arthur J. Daley in the *New York Times*.[1] Before the game was done there were four lead changes. But the best play of the game, and the play that ultimately would be the most controversial, was the play that sent the Baker Field crowd home happy and satisfied.

Early in the fourth quarter, with the score 13-12 in favor of Georgia, Columbia had the ball on the Bulldog 40-yard line. Columbia fullback Len Will took the ball and crashed forward into the Georgia line, only to be stopped after a five-yard gain. Before he went down he lateraled the ball to his teammate, Phil Bayer, who ran the rest of the way for the game-winning touchdown without being touched by a defender. When the game ended with the final score 19-13, the hometown Columbia fans went home confident they had watched one of the great games of the year.

The game featured perhaps the two best sophomores in the country, Frank Sinkwich of Georgia, who in two years would win the Heisman Trophy, and Paul Governali of Columbia, who would finish right behind Sinkwich in the Heisman balloting and would win the Maxwell Award. Neither disappointed. Sinkwich passed for a touchdown and recovered a fumble on defense, while Governali likewise threw a touchdown pass and intercepted a pass in the end zone on defense. Governali, it was agreed, was the star of the game.[2]

But controversy immediately erupted. On the following Tuesday, Georgia cameraman Buster Birdsong sat down to review his game films. When he was done, he announced his finding that the lateral on the game-winning play actually traveled several yards forward. That would have constituted a pass that, if Birdsong were correct, should have been ruled illegal by the game officials on the spot, thus nullifying the touchdown. But the officials had either not seen the play or had deemed the lateral not to be forward, and had done nothing about it. Georgia coach Wallace Butts considered the matter closed. Likewise, Columbia officials had no comment on the matter. The operative view at the time was that the game was in the hands of the officials, who were in the best position to make judgments. Even if an error had been made, there was nothing to be done about it after the game was over, and nobody was about to take action.[3]

****

All season long Cornell had been embroiled in a series of complaints, charges, gripes, and accusations, large and small. To some, this problem was simply a necessary outgrowth of the team's success, to be brushed off as the cost of winning. To others, this turmoil was beginning to take its toll. It began simply enough with a charge by an Associated Press writer that the numerals on the front of the Cornell uniform jerseys were not large enough. The charge was met with the assurance that the numerals were the requisite height.

Then, during the Syracuse game, on a run around right end by Cornell, one of the Syracuse defenders suffered a broken leg when blocked to the ground by the Big Red's Mike Ruddy. Several of the Orange players were adamant that Ruddy had used an illegal block from behind to injure their teammate and accused him of dirty tactics. The matter was taken seriously by Cornell, but review of the film after the game exonerated Ruddy, showing that his block was not from behind as had been alleged. Although Ruddy was called for a penalty on the play, the penalty was for holding and not for an illegal block.[4]

But Cornell's end-around play itself, which was one of the Big Red's favorite and most effective plays, was a subject of further controversy. Perfected by Brud Holland, Cornell's All-American end of 1938, it involved a snap to the fullback, who rushed forward to the line and handed the ball to one of the tackles pulling backward into the backfield. The tackle then lateraled the ball to one of the ends coming around the play, and the blockers had a great opportunity to provide him a lane for a big gain. Under the rules of the day, which prohibited a forward pass or handoff within five yards of the line of scrimmage, the exchange between the fullback and the tackle had to be a backwards handoff; that is, the tackle, moving backward, had to be past the fullback, moving forward, before he received the ball. Any other type of exchange was deemed an illegal forward pass. Michigan had a similar play in its arsenal involving Westfall, Evashevski, and Harmon, and had used it to score a touchdown against Penn. Some officials claimed that Michigan's play, too, was illegal.[5] Perhaps its most vocal critic over the years had been Pitt's Jock Sutherland. The play required precise timing, sure ballhandling, effective blocking, and plenty of practice, but it was devastating when used correctly. Some said it also required a blind eye from the referee. The more successful the play was, the more bickering it engendered, but an infraction was seldom called against Cornell. In contrast, when the Cornell freshman team ran the play in its games, it was almost always called for an infraction.

By no means were Cornell and Michigan alone in being criticized in this way. California used a technique called the "rocker shift," in which its linemen, after coming set at the line of scrimmage, rose up from a low crouch to a high crouch and in the process frequently pulled the other team offside. The technique was widely criticized but no action was taken during the season. After the season the rules committee declared it illegal. And as the season wore on, Stanford's Frankie Albert became the subject of increased scrutiny for his handoffs, many of which, his detractors insisted, were forward handoffs and thus in violation of the rules of the day. The next year the rule prohibiting a forward handoff in the backfield would be stricken from the rulebook.

On October 14, Ogden Miller, chairman of Yale's board of athletic control, gave a talk to the Football Writers Association at Toots Shor's restaurant in New York City, in which he reiterated Yale's stance against overemphasis of football. "In carrying any sport, and in particular football, to extremes we can be certain that we must compromise the principles on which most colleges were founded and for which they are believed to exist....We believe that athletes who need help should be treated neither better nor worse than nonathletes."[6] This talk followed by two days the crushing defeat of the Yale team by Penn, 50-7. It was one of the worst defeats in Yale's football history, and the timing of his comments was at first suspect. But Miller's remarks were greeted by columnist John Kieran in the *New York Times* as "much ado about nothing."[7] They were taken as a well-intended statement of longstanding Yale policy, and there was no hint of a disparaging tone toward any other institution, although it was well noted that there were many schools in the country that did not agree with Yale's philosophy.

Nevertheless, on October 15, the Harvard student newspaper, the *Crimson*, saw this as an excuse to unleash an attack against Cornell and Penn, Harvard's Ivy League brethren, alleging illegal recruitment of football players and the awarding of scholarships to athletes. The *Crimson* labeled both schools "outlaws" and stated, "It was an unequivocal declaration that the University of Pennsylvania is sponsoring professional football, and that the Elis want no further grid relations with their Quaker neighbors."[8] This sentiment was in fact far removed from anything expressed in Miller's comments.

The next day, the same day that the first Associated Press football ranking poll of the year was released showing Cornell as the number one team in the country, the attack continued. In an unsigned article the *Crimson* claimed that Penn and Cornell used "Yawkey style" methods to pursue wins,[9] referring to Tom Yawkey, owner of the Boston Red Sox and his high-spending ways.

These successful teams were buying their football players, the newspaper charged. Some observers at Cornell took the matter lightly at first, countering with the accusation that Harvard's polo team was buying its horses.[10] But instead of accepting the assault for what it was, a series of factless barbs, the *Crimson's* counterpart, the *Cornell Daily Sun,* took the bait. Greatly agitated, its writers fired back a telegram that, though perhaps unnecessary, was instructive. It contended that the allegations against Cornell were baseless and that only three men on the first team were receiving scholarship aid, in the form of regional scholarships of $100, $250, and $500. "No other man on the first team receives any financial help, and each has signed an affidavit so stating; as is the policy of all Ivy League teams," it concluded.[11] The winds of fortune blow hot and cold, the rebuttal reasoned, and at the present they favored Cornell and Penn, whereas in the past weekend Yale and Harvard lost by a combined score of 76-7. It characterized the entire matter as, among other things, sour grapes.

In 1940, the Ivy League was bound by nothing more than a loose understanding among representatives of eight particular universities in the east. Neither the grouping nor the name was the work of the schools themselves. The term was applied to the eight schools by sportswriter Caswell Adams of the *New York Herald-Tribune* in 1937.[12] That the eight universities seemed to share common understandings and values was not so much an operational template in 1940 as it was a foreshadowing of things to come. The public, however, and the schools themselves, identified strongly with the informal designation.

Perhaps frustrated by a lack of official attention or response to its charges, the *Crimson* changed tactics and began a personal attack on Coach Carl Snavely. On October 24, two days before his—and Cornell's—biggest challenge, when the Big Red was scheduled to meet Ohio State, the *Crimson* accused Snavely of being directly responsible for subsidizing Cornell's football program. It charged that while he was head coach at North Carolina one of the coaches handed out alumni money to the players. The practice continued when he moved to Cornell, it alleged, and "Snavely and subsidization traveled hand in hand." It cited a President's Agreement banning travel by coaches to recruit players, then stated, "Carl Snavely is the biggest traveling salesman that ever wore the rubber off the tires of an automobile....He hit all the football high spots, and the little spots, and the little football heathens from the hinterlands who had never heard of Cornell, gathered 'round to hear the Ithacan apostle spread the golden word. And, like Caesar, Carl came, saw, and conquered [sic]."[13] Snavely did not respond.

The ethics of the day were tortured. There were no agreed-upon rules as to how athletics should be funded or athletes supported. If, as Yale's Ogden Miller suggested, athletes should be treated no better or worse than non-athletes, and if the student body as a whole were awarded a certain number of scholarships based on need or academic performance, then it would seem that athletes should be eligible for a certain share of them, as would any group on campus. But there was no agreed-upon rule that separated the reasonable awarding of scholarships from the dreaded offense of subsidization. Further, there was no agreement from the general public that Yale's stance was the right answer, although Cornell had largely agreed to abide by it. "The process of recruiting is not looked upon with horror in all gridiron circles," wrote one columnist.[14] If a talented cellist or budding chemist could be encouraged to attend a given school, then so should a gifted athlete, some reasoned. "Why should the process of getting [players] be regarded as shady?" asked another, who also suggested Harvard should join Chicago on the sidelines.[15] The lack of common rules exposed schools with successful teams to the type of sniping leveled by the *Harvard Crimson*. As Pitt discovered, the most effective force was peer pressure.

The charges against Cornell and Snavely presupposed that the Big Red's superb team was built by luring recognized football stars to Ithaca with offers of rich scholarships and other bounties. But what Cornell had were good athletes melded into a superb team by Carl Snavely's keen football insight, gems in the rough polished to a luster by his coaching skills. As for stars, there were none. Snavely's unit succeeded because he had formed it into a well-coordinated team.

Years later, reflecting on the team's success, end Jim Schmuck wrote, "I've always wondered how a group of mostly average players turned into such a great team. I have just two answers. First, they were smart. Smart players coupled with a smart coach in Carl Snavely created a synergistic effect. Second, everyone was a 100-percent team player."[16]

Snavely did establish a system of regional scholarships when he arrived at Cornell, but as the *Cornell Daily Sun* pointed out, only three men on the first team—Walt Matuszczak, Hal McCullough, and Bill Murphy— and only six men on the entire squad received assistance from them. After his freshman year Alva Kelley, an honor student in the engineering school, was awarded a scholarship due in large measure to his academic achievement. As for football talent, it was Snavely's keen eye that allowed the right people to be put in the right places which made the difference. On other teams, "some of the leading Big Red players would be tossed into the bone pile," said one observer.[17] Bud Finneran came to Snavely as a halfback, too slow to contribute, and Snavely turned him into one of the best centers in the country. Lou Conti, who had never played football in high school, wanted to play halfback as well, but Snavely, after diligent film study, noted his blocking talent and made him into a standout guard. He switched Howie Dunbar from end to guard, and Kirk Hershey from guard to end. When the team captain went down with an injury the year before, Snavely reached all the way down to the jayvees to pluck Mort Landsberg to replace him. His films showed the 175-pounder, 30 pounds lighter than the man he replaced, had the drive he was looking for. That is how Snavely built Cornell's superb team, and the football experts saw it clearly. As for the charge by the Harvard newspaper, Jack Miley of the *New York Post* called it "the laugh of the week."[18] Eddie Breitz of the Associated Press labeled it "preposterous."[19] "Cornell is to be congratulated on its frank stand," wrote Harry Grayson, NEA Service Sports Editor.[20] The accusation, wrote Robert McShane of the Western Newspaper Union, "is one that any winning coach may expect."[21]

But members of the Cornell football team were furious. Bud Finneran and a number of the other players went to the office of Athletic Director James Lynah to discuss the issue, and to ask what Cornell was going to do about the attack. Lynah was out of town serving on the National Defense Board in Washington, and Assistant Athletic Director Robert Kane, in his stead, heard the players out. According to *New York Times* columnist Allison Danzig, Finneran's complaint was as follows: "We came to Cornell because we wanted to come here. We are paying every nickel of our expenses. We've worked hard to make Cornell a good team, and because we win they are calling us a bunch of pros. Our friends are reading that all over the country. How do you think we feel, seeing that rot in the papers? And how do you think our families feel?"[22]

The 27-year-old Kane was a graduate of Ithaca High School and a former track star at Cornell. That he had been trusted to act in Lynah's absence was testimony to the faith others had placed in his judgment. His answer to the players was that the charges were not to be afforded the dignity of a response, and that Cornell's books were open for anybody to review. They would show, he said, that Cornell was giving as little aid to football players as any college in its group. Danzig also noted that "Cornell had received a letter from the athletic director of a sister institution expressing his regret over the recklessness of its student editors."[23] This was a matter that went beyond winning and losing football games; it was a matter of personal and institutional honor and Danzig, it should be noted, was a Cornell graduate, Class of '21.

The consternation this incident caused among Cornell officials can most clearly be viewed against a background of the history of the Cornell football program over the previous two decades.

In July of 1919, Romeyn Berry, who had graduated from Cornell in 1904 and who was fresh from a successful law career on Wall Street, was hired as Graduate Manager of Athletics. Berry found himself almost immediately steeped in controversy. One of his first moves was to hire a new football coach, and when Cornell turned to Gilmour Dobie as its choice, both Berry and the entire Cornell community were immediately introduced to the sweet and sour of their new relationship.

Gil Dobie's record over the years had been, to say the least, unusual. He had accumulated one of the longest winning streaks of all time at the

University of Washington and had built a record nearly as good in his three-year stay at Navy, but due to his dour and abrasive personality he also left behind a trail of grudges and hard feelings. His spats with the mayor of Seattle during his long stay at Washington and with imperious admirals during his short stay at Navy are legendary. His stay at Detroit lasted three days.[24]

One incident during his time at Navy stands out. In 1918, during a game against the Great Lakes Naval Station, whose player-coach was the soon-to-be-renowned George Halas, a Great Lakes player was streaking down the sideline for a touchdown with no chance of being stopped. As he passed the Navy bench, a Navy substitute jumped onto the field and tackled him. The referee, at a loss as to how to handle the infraction, allowed himself to become entangled in an argument between Dobie, who asserted that a simple penalty should be assessed, and Halas and his teammates, who argued a touchdown should be awarded. Dobie won the argument, and the referee stepped off a penalty. But the Naval Academy superintendent, Captain Edward Walter Eberle, stormed onto the field and overruled both his coach and the game official. It was a touchdown, he declared, as a matter of honor, and he forced the referee to change his ruling. The resulting touchdown cost Navy the game against the Rose Bowl-bound Great Lakes team.[25] Dobie was not used to such interference, and he spent an unhappy three years at Navy. It would not be the last time in his career that Dobie's voracious hunger for victory would be tempered by administration officials when that hunger conflicted with institutional values.

Dobie's arrival at Cornell came with a significant catch—he was still under contract to Navy. Dobie had represented to Berry that he had a side understanding with the secretary of the Navy Athletic Association, Commander Bull Halsey, that allowed him to get out of the contract any time he wanted. Halsey denied that any such arrangement existed, but Navy, in a quandary, reluctantly released Dobie from his contract. The doubts, the accusations, and the allegations were unpleasant, and it was left to Rym Berry to smooth things over.[26]

Dobie came to Cornell as advertized. His winning ways, as well as his caustic and cantankerous demeanor, so evident during his Navy and Washington years, were on full display in Ithaca as well. Off to a rocky start, Dobie soon delivered three successive undefeated seasons and two national championships. But problems remained. Future Athletic Director Bob Kane wrote of him, "Those who liked him and admired him were staunch; those who didn't were staunch....No one was indifferent to Gilmour H. Dobie."[27]

The relationship endured on a certain course so long as Dobie was winning football games, but by 1933, in the throes of the Depression, Cornell's athletic fortunes had sunk to unprecedented depths and its athletic program was deep in debt. Suddenly Dobie's verbal harassment of his players, his abrupt dismissal of alumni concerns, and his stubborn refusal to cooperate with faculty and administrators were seen in a different light. By 1934, when football receipts fell to less than $100,000, change was inevitable.

In September, 1935, following a reorganization of the university's athletics, James Lynah was hired as the school's first Athletic Director. Lynah had been captain of the Cornell football team in 1904 under Coach Pop Warner and had retired from private industry at the age of 48, having enjoyed successful careers at DuPont and General Motors. His business acumen was sorely needed. Rym Berry was an eccentric and much-beloved figure on campus, and responsible for, among other things, the team nickname, "The Big Red." He was retained in a different capacity until he retired a year later. He continued to write popular columns for alumni publications for several years.

Dobie's 1935 football team went winless, and his comment on the team's poor prospects in the *Cornell Alumni News* surely raised eyebrows: "Dobie reiterate[d] that under present conditions it is difficult to build a winning football team primarily of students."[28] That philosophy was starkly at odds with Cornell's approach, and at season's end it was decided that, despite his long-term contract, Dobie had to go. George Pfann, star of Dobie's last national championship team, was dispatched to Dobie's house to break the news that he had been fired, but when he arrived, Dobie gleefully produced a copy of a brand new contract he had just signed to coach Boston College.[29] Thus Dobie left the same way he arrived.

In March of 1936, Cornell hired Carl Snavely from North Carolina to replace Dobie, and Lynah was quick to praise his new hire. He cited Snavely's ability to work with and gain the respect of the students, alumni, and faculty, as well as his pleasing personality, a not-so-subtle contrast to Dobie's. Snavely would prove to be no less taciturn and morose than Dobie, but he did prove to be genuinely well-liked. Lynah also made clear the future course of the school's athletic program with this remark about the selection process: "It is highly significant that, without exception, all those with whom we had personal interviews expressed themselves as strongly in favor of pure amateurism in college athletics and opposed to proselytizing in any form."[30] Additionally, Lynah's policy was strongly against recruitment. He forbade coaches and players to visit high schools, except their own, to avoid the "evils of gossip, recruiting, and subsidization." His policy was further spelled out in this public comment: "It is not the function of a coach to recruit matriculants....I want the coaches to be men of such character, personality and capability as teachers that through their work with students, as evidenced by the manner in which the members of our teams conduct themselves in contests and elsewhere, boys of the desired types will be encouraged to come to Cornell and participate in our sports."[31] Lynah's statements, when coupled with Dobie's alleged parting comment, that coaches couldn't win football games with Phi Beta Kappas, made clear the nature and extent of the chasm.

By June of 1937, Lynah had also replaced the basketball, tennis and boxing coaches, and in July, Edmund Ezra Day succeeded the retiring Livingston Farrand as president of the university. Thus, in a few short months, Cornell had completely broken its ties with both its championship days and the downtrodden days of the past, and at the same time had established with clarity its course for the future of athletics. The choices were difficult and painful. Had Cornell chosen to seek victories over other considerations, it had only to retain and empower Dobie.

While some may have viewed Lynah's corporate background and Snavely's history at North Carolina with suspicion, questioning whether Cornell's program was perfectly pure, that view sharply differed with the declared direction Lynah had set for Cornell's athletic program. Accusatory student commentary thus carried additional sting. Lynah spent a great deal of time in the fall of 1940 in Washington dealing with war preparation efforts, and in his absence Kane continued to bear the brunt of the attacks.

****

Ithaca readied itself for perhaps the biggest day in its history. The Ohio State Buckeyes were coming, and the sleepy city of 30,000 at the southern tip of Lake Cayuga would be called upon to host an influx of an additional 30,000 people. There were 95 special railroad cars dispatched to bring the visitors to town. Three major newsreel companies, nine radio stations, and a host of prominent news reporters would all be in attendance. There were 38 direct telegraph wires set up for the game.[32] The roads, the restaurants, the accommodations, and every other element of supporting infrastructure and service, despite the best efforts of the university and the community, were overwhelmed. There was not a room reservation to be had anywhere in the area. Not all went smoothly, and complaints were rampant.

But there was more. The two teams had agreed in advance, according to custom, that Ohio State would wear red jerseys in the game and Cornell their traditional white home jerseys. But when the Buckeyes arrived at their hotel in Watkins Glen they had with them only their white jerseys. Cornell would have to wear red. This was a minor bit of gamesmanship, it appeared, but the irritations were beginning to mount. Ohio State complained that it had not been provided adequate seating for its band, which had accompanied the team from Columbus. Cornell responded that sufficient tickets had been sent to Columbus to seat the band in the stands, but Ohio State had apparently sold them. Makeshift seating for the band had to be arranged at the far end of the field, much to the expressed dissatisfaction of the visitors. Then the Buckeyes complained about the team benches. The Cornell team traditionally sat along the western side of the field facing the large Schoellkopf Crescent, and the visiting team along the east side with the Crescent to its back. This caused the afternoon sun to shine in the eyes of the visitors, and since the temperature for the day was in the 50s, the sunshine was not seen as the godsend it sometimes was on a crisp October Ithaca afternoon. It was suggested that Cornell had switched sides on Ohio State, and dissatisfaction was expressed accordingly.

Not all was negative, however. On the Friday before the game, in keeping with its tradition of planting a tree on the campus of each school it plays, Ohio State planted a buckeye tree near the entrance to Schoellkopf Field. Groundbreaking was performed by Cornell Professor Emeritus Paul M. Lincoln of the School of Electrical Engineering and the captain of the first Ohio State football team in 1894.[33]

When Lynah first agreed in January of 1936 to enter into a home-and-home football series with Ohio State, his idea was met with wholesale criticism from those who lacked a taste for getting clobbered. Even incoming Cornell President Day later urged him to cancel the contract, a point on which the two clashed so sharply that Lynah threatened to resign over the matter.[34] Lynah saw the move as an important element in his plan to place the Cornell athletic program on firmer footing, largely by greatly increasing the stream of revenue entering its coffers and by scheduling a different and more attractive set of opponents, and Day reluctantly agreed with him. There was even talk of scheduling the second game in Cleveland instead of Ithaca, a move that would reportedly have guaranteed an attendance of 70,000. In 1939, Notre Dame played Navy before 80,000 fans at Cleveland's Municipal Stadium, netting each institution more than $76,000.[35] A contest between the top-ranked team in the country and the reigning Big Ten champion could be expected to produce similar results.

During Cornell football's nascent years, Cornell's first president and co-founder Andrew Dickson White, who intensely disliked football, famously said of a proposed trip to Cleveland, "I refuse to let forty of our boys travel 400 miles merely to agitate a bag of wind."[36] Lynah's reasons for avoiding Cleveland were different. He saw that the wiser course of action was to play the game in Ithaca, albeit with less attendance and revenue, and strengthen football's bond with the student body and the Ithaca business community.[37]

When the throng finally began to file into Schoellkopf Crescent and the specially constructed stands around the field on Saturday for the 2 pm kickoff, it was indeed the largest in the stadium's history, estimated to be about 33,500 strong, some three thousand more people than saw Cornell play Dartmouth in 1938. Among the fans were about 15,000 Cornell alumni. Tickets for the game had gone on sale on October 21, but the crowds had begun to gather outside the ticket office as early as October 9, when they became rowdy and were chased away by university officials. Officials told 32 fraternity representatives to disperse and return on the 13th, when a lottery would be held for the tickets. A good ticket for the game cost $3.30.

Ohio State was hoping to avenge its loss to Cornell in Columbus the previous year when Buckeye coach Francis Schmidt had been so confident of victory that he excused himself from the last day of practice on Friday and went duck hunting.[38] In 1939, Ohio State had been installed as a 2 to 1 favorite, and Schmidt evidently was even more confident than that. But, the *New York Times* had noted, "it would be an awful shock here if Ohio State should lose after taking Minnesota, Northwestern, and Missouri over the jumps." Columbus, like Ithaca the following year, had been in a state of high excitement over the game and had been flooded with broadcasting and press representatives. The city had "taken on aspects of the national football capital" for the game, said the *New York Times*, and developments in the European war were displaced from the headlines in favor of the latest gridiron updates.[39]

The 1939 game had had a definite David and Goliath flavor to it, and when Ohio State took a 14-0 lead early in the game, largely on the passing and running of Don Scott, the Buckeyes' All-American quarterback, Cornell appeared doomed. But suddenly 159-pound Cornell backup halfback Walt Scholl, spurring a comeback, broke loose for a 79-yard touchdown run down the right sideline, aided by picture-perfect downfield blocking by his teammates. Only three minutes later Scholl shrugged off a Buckeye pass rusher, spotted his fellow backup Swifty Borhman, who had gotten behind two Buckeye defenders, and lofted a long pass that hit Borhman on the dead run, completing a 63-yard touchdown play. Borhman, true to his nickname, outraced the Buckeye defenders for the last 40 yards. The comeback resulting in a 23-14 win was the greatest in Cornell's undefeated season and one of the most memorable in its football history. "This was one of those games that go down in red letters to become legendary in the book of football," wrote Allison Danzig.[40] The victory caused the Big Red's football prestige to skyrocket, and Lynah to beam. The game also drew national attention to the outstanding play of tackle Nick Drahos, who outwrestled the larger Buckeye line all afternoon, taking a huge step toward becoming a two-time All-American tackle, and to the amazing depth of the Cornell team. It became a measure of Cornell's status that Scholl and Borhman, as talented as they were, could never crack the starting lineup.

One of the highlights of the 1939 trip to Columbus had been the exploits of the Cornell team mascot, a female bear cub named Touchdown IV. Her three predecessors had reigned supreme at Schoellkopf Field between 1915 and 1920, but despite student protests, Lynah, ever cautious, had refused to allow a live bear in Schoellkopf, no matter how tame she appeared. Officials at Ohio State had no such reservations, however, and had allowed the bear to accompany the team to Columbus and to frolic inside the stadium during the game, which she did without incident.[41] But during the postgame celebration in Cleveland she escaped from, or more likely was enticed from, her cage and entered a nightclub in the Hotel Cleveland. There, to the astonishment of the clientele, she entertained herself by eating popcorn and climbing a potted palm until she was apprehended after a brief chase. A few days later the bear, which had been purchased by two Cornell students from a New Hampshire animal farm for $50, was taken to the Pennsylvania mountains and released into the wild.[42] The Cornell team, without its bear, was greeted upon its return at the Ithaca train station by an ecstatic mob who accompanied the team, with bands blaring, up the big Ithaca hills to the campus, arriving just as the bell tower on campus sounded the midnight hour.

The 1940 game promised to be a matchup just as exciting until Ohio State lost the previous two weeks, to Northwestern and Minnesota. Some, but not all, of the glamour was gone. The Buckeyes were still the defending Big Ten champions, and it was the opinion of many that Ohio State had outplayed Minnesota, to whom they lost by six points while squandering four scoring opportunities. Cornell was well aware that Ohio State had been looking forward to this chance for revenge for a year, and reacted with justified caution. The *New York Times* pointed out the danger, mostly in the form of the Buckeyes' multiple formations and other types of razzle-dazzle, as well as in the form of their fine quarterback, Don Scott.[43] The Big Red posted a picture of Scott on their locker room wall with the caption "205-pound substitute for Superman."[44]

All week Ohio State concentrated its practice on defense. The Buckeyes feared they could not win a high scoring game against the Big Red and were particularly concerned about Cornell's passing attack. In the past two weeks, the Buckeyes had lost to Northwestern, which threw only two passes all game, completing neither, and to Minnesota, which used no passes in the game at all. Now they were up against the most formidable passing attack in the country, one which had completed an astounding 40 of 60 passes in its three games. Schmidt was dissatisfied with the defensive aggressiveness of Jim Langhurst and Tom Kinkade, and installed Don Scott as linebacker in a revised scheme. Thus Scott was counted on to bear a heavy burden on both offense and defense.

But of Ohio State's chances in the game, Syracuse coach Ossie Solem, a college teammate at Minnesota of both Bernie Bierman and Clark Shaughnessy, said, "I don't see how the Buckeyes can stop them. I don't see how anyone can." Carl Snavely, in his usual restrained and pessimistic mood, said, "You can quote me as saying we have a chance."[45]

Ohio State-Cornell was the second of two big Ivy League-Big Ten matchups of the day, the other being Penn-Michigan, and the football world was in a state of high excitement. The two games taken together were seen as the best pair of matchups not only of the 1940 season but for the past several seasons.[46] The press called it a football drama in two acts, "The Collisions of the Titans," and reckoned Cornell and Michigan as the favorites in two close contests.[47]

Not everybody saw the Cornell-Ohio State game as a decided question. It was at least possible that Ohio State could exploit an undiscovered flaw in Cornell's armor, thought Allison Danzig. The Buckeyes, with two close losses to Minnesota and Northwestern, and still stinging from their upset by the Big Red the previous year, certainly had the motivation. But Cornell, in Danzig's opinion, was even stronger than people suspected. They were "a team that may take its place high up on the roll-call of the gridiron great," he reasoned.[48]

The discord continued all the way through the pregame events. John Lardner, picking up on the tension between the two schools, wrote a tongue-in-cheek piece in the *New Yorker* about the game. "Before the game, the bands of the two universities massed on the field and played the national anthem. The Cornell musicians were off like a flash, and were leading by perhaps half a note right up to 'the rockets' red glare'; then Ohio State, coming up fast on the outside, caught Cornell and finished the stronger of the two."[49]

The bands relinquished the field, and then the game began with a weird twist. Ohio State, preparing for the opening kickoff, lined up with 22 men on the field. Then, just before the referee blew the opening whistle, 11 of them peeled off and went to the sideline.[50] It was one last bit of gamesmanship. Once the blocking and tackling began, the game displayed eerie similarities to the game of the year before. After Cornell punted, Ohio State started by driving down the field for a touchdown, moving 89 yards on 19 running plays, most of them by Captain Jim Langhurst. It was clear the Buckeyes intended to abandon their passing and razzle dazzle and use their superior size to simply muscle the Big Red out of the way. At first, their strategy worked. Cornell fumbled the following kickoff, and Hal McCullough was unable to evade the Buckeye passrushers for most of the first half. When McCullough was able to get his passes away, Don Scott was effective in defending them, and things, as they had in Columbus, looked bleak for Cornell. But then, near the end of the first half, Mort Landsberg returned a Don Scott punt into Ohio State territory. McCullough was able to complete a pass to his end Jim Schmuck who, with the help of a jarring block from Walt Matuszczak and a great fake on Scott, scored the tying touchdown, completing a three-play drive of 47 yards.

Near the end of the third period, Bud Finneran, who played all sixty minutes for Cornell, as he did in Columbus, made one of his three interceptions of the day. Walt Scholl, the hero of Columbus, played sparingly, since his smaller size was a particular disadvantage against the husky Buckeyes, but when he did he again provided the spark that carried Cornell to victory. Scholl, a senior from Staten Island, was a critical cog in the Cornell machine. "Pop was a kind of a flamboyant guy," said guard Lou Conti of Scholl. "He was a little guy. I think all little guys are aggressive in the sense that he had a lot of talent, but he was not above advertizing himself. Most of the other guys on the team were not that way."[51] Inserted into the game when Snavely sensed the Buckeye defense was tiring, Scholl completed a pass to Ray Jenkins, then made the best run of the day. Helped by Matuszczak's second great block of the game, he took the ball 33 yards off tackle to the Ohio State six-yard line to end the third period. "Scholl clearly wanted to try to make the touchdown, but he is a broken field runner, not a plunger, and Big Ten football seems to call for realism, not sentiment. Out of the game he went, angrily protesting...."[52] reported John Lardner. Lou Bufalino, his substitute, scored a touchdown standing up on the next play and shortly thereafter, when Hal McCullough made one of his two pass interceptions of the day, Bufalino ran the last fifteen yards for the game's final touchdown, securing Cornell's 21-7 victory.

Ohio State, whose rushing game was so superior on the opening drive, did not make a rushing first down in the second half, had only two in the second half by passes, and never crossed the Cornell 30-yard line after the opening drive. It was the biggest defeat suffered by the Buckeyes in seven seasons under Francis Schmidt. "It was their reserve strength that licked us," said Schmidt. "Their second string line was just as good as the first and I believe the second backfield, especially that Bufalino, was better than the starters.... Landsberg must be the fastest fullback in the country, and is probably the most valuable man on the squad." As for Snavely, he thought the difference in the game, as it had been in Columbus, was Walt Scholl, who only played for a few minutes but put new life into the team when he did.[53] The *Cornell Alumni News* agreed. Scholl had been in the game, it said, "long enough to set off the fuse of victory."[54]

After the game, Allison Danzig felt vindicated in his aggressive stand on Cornell's superiority. Ohio State had shown itself to be the physically stronger of the two, but the Big Red had demonstrated it could absorb the Buckeyes' best blows. Cornell's poise and superior execution made the difference, he said, and further observed, "Ohio State scored one touchdown on nineteen successive running plays. Cornell scored three touchdowns on nine plays."[55]

Wilfrid Smith of the *Chicago Tribune* added his praise. He was particularly impressed by Cornell's ability to bottle up Don Scott's passing and singled out Bud Finneran for his fine defensive play. And, like Danzig, he took note of Cornell's explosive power. "The speed with which Cornell struck was astonishing," he wrote.[56]

The venerable Grantland Rice joined the chorus. "Cornell belongs as one of the best teams of many years," he wrote. "It has the four main ingredients—speed, smartness, spirit, and excellent coaching. It is a team that has resilience and versatility above any team I've seen, including Michigan and Ohio State."[57]

But then, immediately after the game, minor problems that had plagued Cornell leading up to the big showdown turned major. Ohio State Athletic Director L.W. St. John and Coach Francis Schmidt leveled a blistering charge against Carl Snavely. They reported to the *Columbus Post-Dispatch* that throughout the game the Cornell coach had sent in plays from the bench to his players in violation of the rules. Such action on Snavely's part, they contended, showed poor sportsmanship and bad ethics.

St. John alleged that Snavely had used a light-colored cylinder he held in his hands, and that each position of the cylinder indicated a different play. By displaying the cylinder held a certain way in his hands, St. John contended, Snavely was communicating a corresponding play to his team on the field. St. John's contention was buttressed by Dr. E.P. Maxwell, an Ohio State alumnus and former game official with 24 years' experience. Maxwell was also on the sidelines with St. John and contended that "we were able to call every play they ran toward the end of the game." The two did not contend, however, that Snavely's actions had any effect on the outcome of the game.[58]

This time Snavely responded immediately. "Mr. St. John's charges are unwarranted and contrary to fact," he answered. "The officials of this game were perfectly competent and were empowered by the rules to take action in the case of illegal activity on the bench or sidelines. If Mr. St. John had any complaints, they should have been made to the officials during the course of the game."[59]

St. John detailed his charges further. He said that Snavely used the cylinder by "grasping it by the end for a pass play, in the center for a sweep, in both hands for a line smash, and then crossing his legs and swinging one foot when he wanted a kick." Schmidt went even further. "It was a…crime. But it was so obvious and so amateurish that we had to laugh. We finally got to the place where we could call practically every play, Snavely's actions were so bald-faced. Some guys are foxy about pulling stuff like that, but everyone in the stadium could see this."[60]

It was suggested by Cornell officials that the cylinder in question was an elaborate substitution chart, a not-so-veiled dig at Schmidt for his substitution error in the Purdue game. It must have been particularly galling to Snavely and Lynah to have these charges brought by Schmidt and St. John, who had so cavalierly dismissed Ohio State's own earlier game-altering rules transgression in its contest against Purdue.

Rule 11, Article 1 of the rules of the game in 1940, considerably more limiting than today's rule, states succinctly, "There shall be no coaching, either by substitutes or by any other person not participating in the game." The rule had been in effect since 1917. The referee in this case, W.H. "Red" Friesell, Jr., was empowered by the rule, if he found Snavely to be in violation, to assess a fifteen-yard penalty against Cornell or, in the case of a flagrant act, to eject Snavely from the field of play. Finding no evidence, he did neither, which is what Snavely argued. After the game Friesell was clear that he had seen no signaling from the bench and had received no protest concerning signaling during the game.[61]

St. John immediately filed an official protest with Asa S. Bushnell, executive director of the Eastern Intercollegiate Association, citing a gross violation of the official football rules and a breach of sportsmanship. St. John noted to reporters that officials had been asked to watch for signaling, but that they were too busy with business on the field to take notice. He expressed the belief that no other Cornell officials were involved. St. John sent a copy of his official protest to his counterpart at Cornell, James Lynah.

Bushnell had recently been involved in a roller skating accident in Trenton, New Jersey, and was in a Princeton hospital having his broken arm set. Lynah did not immediately receive a copy of the protest, as he was still in Washington serving with the National Defense Council. Thus the matter stewed for a few days.

For St. John and Schmidt, both their timing and their tactics were suspect. Schmidt was involved in an ongoing heated and bitter dispute with the local Columbus press concerning the quality of play of the Buckeyes in what so far had been a disappointing season. And the pair added fuel to the fire by discussing the issue exclusively with one newspaper while leaving other local writers out in the cold. For this, the press was "looking daggers" at St. John.[62] If he and Schmidt were seeking support from an increasingly adversarial press, they would soon be disappointed.

As for the appeal to Bushnell, St. John placed himself in a position where he could not win. Bushnell had no recourse but to base his position on the statements of the game officials, whom he had queried, and the officials had already spoken. There was no other evidence. Bushnell was being asked to undercut his own officials without anything on which to base his action. The outcome could not be reasonably in doubt.

But Dick Dashiell, sports columnist of the *Asheville (N.C.) Times*, recalled that, when he was a player for Snavely at North Carolina, Snavely was caught red-handed by Wallace Wade, the Duke coach, at such tactics in 1935. Snavely was observed sending plays into the game with the trainer and waterboy, and Wade went on to the field to protest it. But Dashiell expressed his belief that Snavely would never make the same mistake twice, especially with a team as talented as Cornell, and doubted that the current charges were valid.[63]

The matter was made worse on Tuesday when, speaking to a group of alumni, James L. Renick, Ohio State publicity director, said that Ohio State had been tipped off before the game that signaling by Snavely might occur, and that the game officials had been notified.[64] But Red Friesell, speaking that same day, refused to corroborate that claim, reiterating that no protest had been lodged with the officials.[65] "Had the Ohio State coach made a complaint, we would have looked into the matter," he said.[66]

The *Harvard Crimson*, with its bloodthirsty predilection toward Snavely, found the entire matter to be fresh meat. First it advocated the formation of a new Ivy League excluding Cornell and Penn and including Army and Navy in their place.[67] Then it renewed its personal attack on Snavely, saying that his denial of the charges were "to be taken with several grains of saline....The

117

world loves a winner, but not one who violates not only the football rules but the gridiron's code of fair play as well."[68]

But the student newspaper was virtually alone in its position. Sportswriters from all over the country found the Ohio State position to be full of holes. The practicality of sending in plays in the manner suggested seemed dubious and more likely to create confusion than anything else. The need was also questioned. Walt Matuszczak was seen as perhaps the best playcaller in the country, and it did not seem likely that his judgment could be improved upon from the bench. Moreover, Matuszczak, when questioned, steadfastly maintained that he was never, in the course of the game, influenced by any action on the bench, and football people were inclined to believe him.[69] Why, people wondered, did Schmidt not say something to the officials during the game, when something could have actually been done about the matter? And why were the Ohio State players not alerted, as they obviously were not? Finally, that Ohio State, which had achieved victory in the Purdue game under questionable circumstances, would lecture another team on sportsmanship provoked reaction ranging from amusement to outrage.

One by one the sportswriters of the country were heard from. "We're inclined to sympathize with the unhappy Mr. Snavely," wrote Robert McShane of the Western Newspaper Union.[70] "Slightly out of line," the *New Castle (Pa.) News*[71] said of the charges. "Bunk, nothing but bunk," pronounced the *Syracuse Herald-Journal*.[72] "Ridiculous," claimed the *Alton (Ill.) Evening Telegraph*.[73] "Ridiculous," echoed Grantland Rice in his syndicated column.[74] "Extremely silly," opined the *Syracuse Herald-Journal* a second time.[75] "Absurd," chimed in Harry Grayson, NEA Service Sports Editor.[76] William D. Richardson, in his *New York Times* column, commented, "The intelligence quotient of the Big Red must be 150 (par for a genius) if they can remember his [Snavely's] signals as well as their own."[77] A *New York Times* reader said St. John "convicts himself...of stupidity" and is "seeing banshees."[78] Wilfrid Smith of the *Chicago Tribune* deemed the entire matter "bitterly humiliating" for Ohio State and the likelihood that Snavely was guilty of the charges "incredible."[79] In his *New York Times* column, John Kieran poked fun at St. John and the rule, calling it, with some validity, unenforceable and the entire affair "mildly amusing."[80] Dillon Graham of the Associated Press claimed that Cornell's greatness was due to its superior football instincts and reasoned, "Snavely can't signal his boys to reverse their field while they're on the dead run."[81] John Lardner in *Newsweek* wrote a column titled "Study in Semaphore," in which he lampooned the entire affair. His concluding remark on Snavely was, "If he does signal, it's like what Lincoln said of Grant— 'I wish all my generals drank the same signals.' "[82] Nor would *Time* rise to the bait: "Few winning coaches have escaped such a charge.... [W]igwag or no wigwag, Cornell is the No. 1 team of the year."[83]

On November 1, Bushnell completed his review of the complaint and found in favor of Snavely. "The reports of the official, now at hand, include no evidence of coaching from the sidelines and some definite indication of opinion that it was nonexistent," he wrote.[84]

But the matter was not done. On Saturday, November 2, Lynah returned to Ithaca for Cornell's homecoming game against Columbia, and he was livid. On November 5, he fired off two letters. The first, to Bushnell, was a defiant defense of Snavely. The second, to St. John, was a scathing accusation of ungentlemanly behavior in the way he brought the charges. The letters were quoted in their entirety in several newspapers across the country.

Whether Snavely signaled from the sidelines or not, it is clear that Cornell and its officials were weary of all the friction. To be attacked by a band of Harvard undergraduates is one thing, to be involved in a clash over jersey colors is one thing, but to be attacked by the athletic director at another university is quite another. The *Syracuse Herald-Journal* observed, "[M]ost Cornell football fans are wandering about in a daze speculating if they wouldn't be better off with a loser like Syracuse and Colgate have been."[85] This sentiment carried over to some degree to the student body. One unsigned column in the *Daily Sun* read in part as follows: "...[W]e feel that a large proportion of this university's undergraduates will breathe a deep sigh of relief a week from today [after the last home game], and settle into a more staid routine. Our comments here are not meant to detract from the wonderful showings of the Big Red team. We merely are looking at the football situation on the campus from a slightly different angle momentarily. It behooves us to take note and comment on the wearying effect a winning eleven has had on the campus, to the undergraduates and the tired, but happy alumni too."[86]

When the flap had finally been replaced in the press by other events, it was clear that St. John and Schmidt had embarrassed themselves by trying to make a football felony out of an incident of jaywalking, and an unsubstantiated incident at that. Years before, Knute Rockne had termed the practice of signaling from the bench "...abominable. It cheats the boys and ruins confidence in their self-reliance."[87] But the prohibition was strictly drawn and loosely enforced. Indeed, Clark Shaughnessy was said not only to have signaled from the Stanford sideline but also to have occasionally sent in plays on index cards. One additional wrinkle to the substitution rule of the day prohibited new substitutes from speaking in the huddle until one play had been run, surely an unenforceable provision. When pressed about the matter, Shaughnessy owned up to it, admitting that he had sent substitute guard Ken Robesky into the game against Southern California with a written message to Frankie Albert on a card stuffed in his helmet. But Shaughnessy maintained that the message, complete with diagram, was not given to Albert until one play had been run, thus, at least in Shaughnessy's opinion, making the act legal.[88] Nothing was ever said or done about it. Whitney Martin of the

Associated Press wrote in his column, "We saw Elmer Layden call the signals on a half-dozen consecutive plays in the Notre Dame-USC game last year, using players as carrier pigeons."[89] The *Burlington (N.C.) Daily Times-News* reasoned that signaling from the bench was a common occurrence and that "to make a case against one engaged in it would be difficult."[90] True, Snavely's detractors had his incident at North Carolina to point to, the implication from which was clear: cheaters don't change. But the response from St. John's detractors was that he had leveled similar charges in the past against tiny Wooster when that school had had the effrontery to tie the mighty Buckeyes 7-7 in 1928, and the implication there, fair or not, was equally clear: St. John was a sore loser. As the days wore on, the issue became stale, and a month later Whitney Martin wrote this in his syndicated column: "Mr. Carl Snavely is whitewashed of the charge that he calls signals from the Cornell bench."[91] Finally, this ditty, which appeared in many newspapers nationwide, brought an appropriate end to the controversy:

> Carl Snavely sat upon the bench,
> And clutched his trusty papers;
> But that is all, for it's a cinch,
> He tried no funny capers.[92]

****

Francis Schmidt had problems of his own. At a time of the season when speculation normally arises about coaches whose jobs might be in jeopardy, Schmidt's name was at or near the top of many lists. Not only were the losses mounting for the highly rated Buckeyes, and not only had his accusations backfired against him and tarnished his image, but dissention in the Buckeye locker room had been boiling for some time as well. Schmidt was a screamer whose style did not sit well with all of his players. The charge that filtered out from the players to the public was that Schmidt ran lax practices where plenty of loafing took place, but the suspicion was that there was more to it than that. Throughout Schmidt's tenure, the Buckeyes had suffered from a trend of being upset by at least one underdog, almost annually. After the Buckeyes' loss to Northwestern, but before additional losses to Minnesota and Cornell made the situation worse, Sherm Langley of the *Minnesota Daily* pointed out, "[T]he football fanatics of Ohio haven't liked that state of affairs one bit."[93]

In the loss to Minnesota, the Buckeyes failed repeatedly to score from close range, and Schmidt was taken to task by the press for too much trickery and not enough basics. After fancy plays inside the five-yard line fizzled, the press wondered why more straightforward power football wasn't used. Upon his arrival at Ohio State, he was dubbed by the press, "the zaniest, maddest, most imaginative coach ever to hit the Big Ten."[94] The same practices that had drawn admiration now sparked criticism. That the Buckeyes outplayed

Minnesota was of little consequence. Moral victories were insufficient to satisfy the demands of the critics.

Then, amidst the playcalling flap in the loss to Cornell, a new wave of criticism hit Schmidt. The Buckeyes were out of shape, said the critics, a direct slap at his coaching techniques, which did not include toughening scrimmages during the week. Moreover, the criticism was supported by his own people. After the Northwestern game, 55 Buckeyes held a players-only meeting, and when they emerged, Captain Jim Langhurst had this to say: "We just don't have enough hard work and bodily contact during the weekly practices. The result is that we aren't ready for tough games on Saturday."[95] James Renick, Schmidt's own publicity chief, stated, "Our team is poorly conditioned...our boys seem to lack the pep to play more than half the game at full speed," this, in the same talk to alumni in which he claimed an advance notice to officials of Cornell's signaling transgressions. Schmidt was duly peeved, but the facts bore Renick out. In the last four games the Buckeyes had been outscored in the second half by a margin of 34-6, and half their points had come on the questionable field goal against Purdue. Though Renick lay some of the blame for the team's failure at the feet of Don Scott, calling him "sensitive and modest"[96] and unwilling to involve himself as signal-caller in key plays, others saw Scott's performance as one of the few saving graces of the season. His play, particularly on defense, had been superb, especially against Minnesota, where he had made seven out of ten tackles in the secondary, saved two touchdowns by running down Gopher backs from behind (it was Bruce Smith both times), and whose passing and running spurred the offense all day.[97] One wonders where the Buckeyes would have been without Don Scott. Then Dillon Graham of the Associated Press said of Ohio State after the Cornell loss, "It just didn't have the same football instinct or will-to-win."[98] Ohio State was being called the football enigma of the year. With as much talent as anybody and a top star of the first magnitude, it was puzzling to observers how the team could fail to win any of the big games. Such comments can never be construed as favorable to the coach.

Some alumni came to Schmidt's support, alleging that the press had overrated the Buckeyes from the beginning and had unfairly held Schmidt responsible for the team's failure to live up to inflated expectations. The press, they contended, had fired Schmidt without consulting the Ohio State officials. But members of the press responded by pointing out that high preseason assessments of the team did not originate with them, but had been expressed by other Big Ten teams, coaches, and alumni and, further, were valid and accurate. "The press never satisfies the also-ran," wrote Hank Casserly of the *Capital Times*, but noted no squawk from Minnesota, Stanford or Tennessee all year long.[99]

The conclusion was inevitable that Schmidt had a poor relationship with the press. Additionally, the relationship between St. John and Schmidt had never been a warm one, and the stress of recent controversies only made the chasm wider. Schmidt was on thin ice.

CHAPTER 11
THE EAGLES SOAR

All for one, one for all, that is our motto.

--ALEXANDRE DUMAS, *The Three Musketeers*

For Boston College, 1940 was a year of opportunity. Ever since the death of Knute Rockne in 1931, Notre Dame had been unable to cling to national supremacy or to go unchallenged as football leader of the nation's Catholic schools. While Minnesota dominated the national picture through the decade of the 1930s, the quest for supremacy among the Jesuit schools was not so clearcut. Boston College made a credible run, compiling a 44-18-3 record in the seven years of Joe McKenney's stay as head coach, including an undefeated season in 1928, but the competition was not seen as top-notch. His victories over the likes of Boston University, Manhattan, Canisius, and the Connecticut Aggies were not so convincing as those of his competitors. Others making bids to supplant Notre Dame at the top were western power Santa Clara, and more convincingly, Fordham. The Rams, coached by Jim Crowley, a member of Notre Dame's famous Four Horsemen backfield, played three memorable games against Pitt in 1935, 1936, and 1937, each at the Polo Grounds, each ending in a 0-0 tie. Jock Sutherland's 1936 Panther team had won the Rose Bowl, and the 1937 team had captured the national championship, when the tie was the only blemish on its record. Fordham was able to compete because it had the Seven Blocks of Granite, a line as tough as any in the nation. Anchored by Alex Wojciechowicz at center, it also featured future coaching legend Vince Lombardi at guard. The line was in large measure the creation of Fordham's assistant coach, Frank Leahy. Like Crowley, Leahy had been a Rockne disciple, but his playing days at Notre Dame had been cut short by injury.

During Joe McKenney's stay through 1934, the Eagles also had a strong propensity to play their games at home, a trend that did not diminish after McKenney's departure. Starting in 1935, resolving to break out of their regional confines, they became a leader in intersectional play, scheduling Michigan State, North Carolina State, Kansas State, Kentucky, Indiana, Florida, and Auburn. Though representing an upgrade in schedule toughness, none of these opponents had yet achieved the competitive status they would enjoy in later decades, and each of these games was played in Boston. From 1934 to 1939, Boston College played a total of six regular season games on the road.

McKenney, though successful, was not paid well, earning only $2500 his final year, and after the 1934 season he left to take a position with the Boston Public Schools, a better paying job, and to become a game official. In 1936, following a year with two short-term coaches, Boston College hired Gil Dobie from Cornell, paying him quadruple the salary earned by the likeable McKenney.

Independently wealthy, Dobie had apparently lost his edge by the end of his stay in Ithaca. His last team at Cornell had been winless, and while his three teams at Boston College compiled a respectable 16-6-5 record, his contrary ways wore heavily on those around him. "A leopard can't change his spots," warned Allison Danzig of Dobie.[1]

At the end of Dobie's first year at Boston College, an event occurred that shook him to his core. On December 1, 1936, after a long night of partying, he crashed his car into a bridge abutment in Boston's Kenmore Square. Both he and his passenger, an assistant coach, were propelled through the windshield, each suffering a broken jaw and facial lacerations. Dobie spent three weeks in the hospital and underwent extensive plastic surgery. His assistant coach, who was at first not expected to survive, stayed longer. By 1939, Dobie was gone, and in his place Boston College hired the young and promising Leahy from Fordham.

Frank Leahy had this in common with Carl Snavely at Cornell. Each had inherited a lackluster program from Gil Dobie and each had returned it to national prominence almost immediately. Leahy's first team compiled a 9-1 record against a tougher but still light schedule, losing only to Florida, and earned a trip to the Cotton Bowl, its first bowl appearance, where it lost to Clemson. But below the surface there was much more to it than that.

One of the key players on Leahy's 1939 team was a lightning-fast 160-pound halfback from Brockton, Massachusetts, named Lou Montgomery, the first black athlete to play any varsity sport for the Eagles. Montgomery, a highly touted high school star, never got much attention from Dobie, who preferred larger backs, and in his sophomore year under Dobie he logged only six minutes of playing time, getting into only one game. But when Leahy arrived on campus in February of 1939, one of his first public statements was, "I intend to teach much that I have been taught," and observers took that to mean a more open Notre Dame-type offense for the Eagles, one into which Montgomery's skills would fit perfectly.[2] Indeed, Montgomery excelled in early season workouts, and Leahy warmed to him immediately.

But the third game of the 1939 season was against Florida, a mediocre team the Eagles had beaten the year before, 33-0. Lou Montgomery, it was announced, would not play in the game. The gentlemen's agreement had raised its ugly head once again. More than seven decades later, it seems impossible to countenance the language used to describe the dilemma, or to appreciate the emotion or lack of it that drove the actions of the day. Ordinarily, even in 1939, the agreement precluded the participation of black players in southern venues, but this game was to be played in Boston. Perhaps with its unusual home-weighted schedule the Eagles had to make unusual concessions. "The B.C. team plays Florida and in deference to their feelings the Brockton flash will be kept on the sidelines," a local newspaper blithely announced.[3] The notice was buried deep in the sports incidentals, along with mention of the Arlington High cheerleaders and the bowling scores at the Putnam Street alleys. With hardly a ripple of attention or a breath of protest Lou Montgomery was benched, for no other reason than his skin color. The Eagles, weakened by his absence, were shut out by Florida, 7-0, suffering their only regular season loss of the year.

Montgomery returned to the team and excelled in practice, and Leahy decided to start him against Temple. He played well for two more weeks until Auburn came to town, and again he was held out of the game against the southern team, this time with even less discussion. The next week he returned to the lineup, and Leahy again decided to start him against Detroit. When Boston College completed the regular season with a 9-1 record, the Eagles won a bid to the Cotton Bowl in Dallas to play Clemson. But on December 16, Curtis Sanford, president of the Cotton Bowl A.A., said, "In view of the general attitude towards Negroes in Texas, it was deemed advisable that Montgomery refrain from playing. We conferred with Boston College officials and Montgomery will come to Texas with the team but will not play."[4] His own school had bartered away his right to participate, not for the first time but for the third time that year. Montgomery decided not to honor the arrangement and, not surprisingly, opted to stay home instead and get a job for the holiday season. It was pointed out in the *Brownsville (TX) Herald* and other newspapers that the move was a "courtesy gesture" to the southerners.[5] To make up for the slight, or perhaps to calm consciences, Montgomery was scheduled to receive a sportsmanship, citizenship, and athletic ability medal from the Veterans of Foreign Wars in January in light of his "self-effacement" in withdrawing from the Cotton Bowl trip.[6]

Even more startling than what was said and done was what remained unsaid and undone. There was virtually no comment, no protest, and no reaction of any type from the northern press, who, like their southern brethren, simply accepted Montgomery's exclusion as a routine item in the course of business. When Jack Miley of the *New York Daily News,* one of the few writers to even mention the incident, termed the action "spineless, mealy-mouthed, craven, weak-kneed," Albert Reese of the *Galveston Daily News* fired back that it was none of the northerner's business. "Odd how easy it is to write a lot on a subject you know absolutely nothing about," Reese wrote.[7] Five decades later, Bob Lobel, the host of a popular radio call-in show, "Calling All Sports," on WBZ in Boston, confessed he had never heard of the incident and quizzically wondered, "Boy, times have changed. Didn't anyone protest?"[8]

It was left to the *Paris (TX) News* to lay the matter out. "It is our opinion Boston's Negro halfback should be allowed to play. The way we see it the Cotton Bowl booked Clemson and Boston College to clash in the 1940 classic and not the white men on Boston's squad to play Clemson. Montgomery is part of the Eagle team....This corner always thought the fundamental principle of sport is: 'May the best man win.' Or is it: 'May the best WHITE man win?'.... We believe any sportsman will agree that Montgomery should play against Clemson."[9]

On December 26 the team left for Dallas amid much celebration by alumni and speechmaking by the Boston mayor. Montgomery was there to see the team off. Six days later, missing one of their key offensive weapons, the Eagles lost to Clemson, 6-3. Nevertheless, despite this defeat, from a standpoint of wins and losses, it had been one of the most successful seasons in the history of Boston College football.

By 1940, Leahy had an even better team. The Eagles made some late adjustments to their schedule, pushing up the opening game against Centre until September 21, a week earlier than most teams started, and fitting in a trip to New Orleans to play Tulane. After easily dispatching Centre, 40-0, the Eagles got down to the business of dealing with the Green Wave. In one scheduling move, Frank Leahy had given his team exposure to football in the south, which he learned was valuable at bowl time, provided his team's only road game of the year, and hoped to put to rest the talk about a weak schedule. The press would later refer to him as Frank "I Fear St. Anselm's" Leahy.[10]

Of course, the Eagles would have to face Tulane without Lou Montgomery, who again would be excluded from the trip south. The *New York Times's* comprehensive preview of the game and of Boston College's chances for the season named every prospective participant nearly down to the second string ball boy, but omitted Montgomery, a sometime starter in 1939 who had scored a touchdown the week before. Perhaps the omission was easier than explaining his absence. Boston College could hardly afford the luxury of benching him. Leahy, it was said, was "going through the mental torture of the football coach who knows he is expected to turn out a world-beater and honestly distrusts that he has the wherewithal to do it."[11]

The experts had Tulane pegged as the best team in the South, but Boston College made quick work of the Green Wave as well, 27-7. "The mighty Wave of last year was but a ripple," said the Associated Press.[12] The Green Wave had seemed to have nearly as optimistic a future as Cornell. The team that had finished 1939 ranked fifth in the nation, undefeated but with one tie against North Carolina, and a 14-13 loss to national champion Texas A&M in the Sugar Bowl, had most of its strength back for 1940. The game between two bowl teams of the year before had been seen by football fans as a splendid way to begin the 1940 season, and the win as a glorious victory for the Eagles. But, hampered by injury, Tulane lost the next week as well to Auburn, 20-14. Then, on October 10, tragedy struck. Tulane was scheduled to play Fordham in New York City that weekend, and the parents of co-captain Tommy O'Boyle were driving from their home in Gary, Indiana, to see their son play. In Coudersport, Pennsylvania, they were involved in an auto accident that killed O'Boyle's father and aunt and seriously injured his mother, who died within a few hours.[13] Later, the star-crossed O'Boyle ended his college career when he broke his leg in the East-West Shrine Game. The Green Wave never recovered from its wobbly start and was never a factor in the 1940 season. By the time Tulane's record reached 0-3, they were being dismissed as just another mediocre team, and Boston College's attempt to bolster its strength of schedule was frustrated.

After a week off, the Eagles smothered Temple, 33-20 in a game not as close as the score indicated, and Montgomery was back on the field. Then followed four consecutive shutouts against familiar weak competition: 60-0 against Idaho, 55-0 against St. Anselm's, 25-0 against Manhattan, and 21-0 against Boston University. On a roll, the Eagles had now won seven straight and were set for a November 16 showdown with a team undefeated since 1937: Georgetown. The football world eagerly awaited.

CHAPTER 12
RANKINGS

Those who'll play with cats must expect to be scratched.

--CERVANTES, Don Quixote

College football was born and reared in the shadows of the ivy-covered walls of the elite institutions of the East. But with time the popularity of the game, and soon the balance of power, spread westward. Stanford, California, and Washington on the West Coast and Michigan, Chicago, and soon Notre Dame in the Midwest challenged the established eastern powers of Yale, Harvard, Princeton, and Army for football supremacy. But, as if the game were evolving on remote islands, there was little interaction between teams of different regions. The limited transportation capabilities of the age saw to that. Only gradually, through the 1920's, would intersectional competition increase and became a popular and lucrative enterprise.

Texas and football, it has been said, were made for one another, and as the game grew in popularity elsewhere, it sprouted in the Southwest as well. But the expansive geography of the region made football in Texas even more insular than elsewhere, and intersectional matches were few. Moreover, they did not go well for the Texans. The University of Texas travelled to Chicago to play the Maroons in 1904 and lost, 68-0; Notre Dame traveled to Austin twice, in 1913 and 1915, and beat the Longhorns handily both times; and a trip by Texas to Harvard in 1931 resulted in a 35-7 loss at the hands of the Crimson. Baylor lost to Boston College in Dallas in 1921 and in Boston the next year, both by lopsided scores; to Notre Dame in South Bend, 41-0 in 1922; and to Purdue, 20-7, in Lafayette in 1930. Southern Methodist traveled to West Point in 1928 and to South Bend in 1930, and came home with two losses. The unmistakable conclusion by the football establishment was that football in the Southwest was a lesser product, not up to the standards observed elsewhere.

All that changed in the first half of the 1930s. Texas traveled to Notre Dame in 1934 and surprised the Irish, 7-6. It was the second game for the Longhorns' new coach, former Notre Dame star Jack Chevigny. Texas Christian made a trip to California and beat a well-regarded Santa Clara team, and Southern Methodist ran off an impressive string of intersectional wins against Indiana, Navy (twice), Syracuse, and Fordham.

By 1935, two teams—Southern Methodist and Texas Christian—had emerged not only as regional leaders but as national powers as well. Playing a twelve-game schedule in 1935, Texas Christian finished 11-1, then beat Louisiana State in the Sugar Bowl. The Horned Frogs' high-powered offense, led by passing sensation Sammy Baugh, captured the attention of fans all over the nation, and their only loss was in a head-to-head matchup with Southern Methodist. The Mustangs finished with a perfect 12-0 record and shared the national championship with Minnesota. They became the first team from the Southwest invited to the Rose Bowl, where they lost to Stanford's Vow Boys.

In 1938, Texas Christian again led the nation with a perfect 10-0 record, this time behind the passing of the diminutive Davey O'Brien. When the team won a piece of the national title, shared with Notre Dame and Tennessee, and O'Brien was selected for the Heisman Trophy, football in the Southwest had won full acceptance.

In 1939, Texas A&M took the baton, and the Aggies compiled a 10-0 record and a national championship shared with Cornell and Southern California before defeating Tulane in the Sugar Bowl. It was the third national championship for Southwest Conference teams in five years. Unlike the aerial teams of Texas Christian, Homer Norton's Aggies won with a solid running game, featuring guard Marshall Foch Robnett blocking for one of the toughest runners ever to take the field, halfback John Kimbrough, and a rock-solid defense. In the regular season, only Villanova had managed to score as many as seven points against them.

But in 1940, the Aggies, who had nine of 11 starters returning from an undefeated national championship team, did not get the respect, even within their own region, they would seem to deserve. Experts considered the Southwest Conference race to be wide open.[1] Many thought the Aggies were lucky to have defeated Southern Methodist in 1939—a blocked punt rolling along the goal line was recovered for a safety instead of a touchdown in a 6-2 win—but all good teams enjoy a degree of luck. By the end of October, the undefeated Aggies were lurking behind Cornell, Notre Dame, Michigan, and Minnesota in the Associated Press poll, and they had expectations of going undefeated once again, earning a Rose Bowl bid, and winning a second consecutive national championship. Unless somebody figured out how to stop the powerful Kimbrough, or how to score more than a touchdown against them, those expectations seemed likely to be realized.

****

The title hopes of the Ohio State Buckeyes had been dealt a fatal blow. Losers of three games in a row, Francis Schmidt's team was in a tailspin, and its standing was not helped by the controversy from its tainted win over Purdue or from the lack of support for its protests against Cornell. The defending Big Ten champions could only watch as the 1940 league title was decided by three better teams. Michigan and Northwestern, who had expected to be there, and Minnesota, who had not, would play three games among themselves over a period of three weeks. The three games, a round robin[2] among the undefeated teams, would determine the Big Ten championship and possibly the national championship as well. One thing was for sure. They would be three very tough games.

Sports editor Walter L. Johns of the Central Press devised his own ranking system, which he applied to the college teams across the country. Involving point spreads and other factors he deemed important, it was an objective rather than subjective system. On October 30, his rankings were released. Based on his formulas, he determined Michigan to be the best team in the country, to which he awarded 992 points. Tied for second were two teams, Northwestern and Cornell, with 990 points each, and in fourth place was Minnesota with 972 points.[3] If Johns's system was accurate—and who could say it wasn't—three of the four best teams in the country would be involved in this round robin. Football fans salivated.

The first game was played on November 2 in Evanston, and as anticipated, it was an evenly played contest. The Gophers entered the game a slight favorite over Northwestern, despite not having won in Dyche Stadium since 1929, and it was partly their size that convinced the oddsmakers. Wildcat coach Lynn "Pappy" Waldorf had a scrappy bunch of players that were 25 pounds per man lighter than their Gopher counterparts, but as their nickname implied, were full of fight. Ohio State's Francis Schmidt, who by this time had played and lost to both teams, thought Minnesota the better team. "That Bruce Smith is as neat a ball carrier as I've seen in a long time," he added.[4]

In addition, the Wildcats were expected to get only limited service from one of their key players, junior halfback Bill DeCorrevont, hobbled by an injured ankle. Recruited from Austin High School in Chicago, the national high school champion, DeCorrevont was the most celebrated high school player of his time, even more than Tom Harmon. He had been "given more newspaper space in his high school days than Hedy Lamarr," claimed the Associated Press.[5] He had scored 34 touchdowns his senior year in high school (the state record at the time was 36, held by Red Grange) and once scored 57 points in a single game (Grange had scored 59). In college, DeCorrevont started slowly, was hampered by injuries, and only occasionally showed the brilliance of which he was capable. But that brilliance, when on display, was considerable. It was his long run the year before that had helped Northwestern beat Minnesota, 14-7. And earlier in 1940, when the Wildcats had beaten Waldorf's alma mater, Syracuse, 40-0, DeCorrevont had run wild. "This DeCorrevont is all they say he is," said Syracuse coach Ossie Solem. "He's a great back. The one weakness he had last year was starting slow, that is, he waited for the holes to open up before he started to really move, as only he can, but this year there was none of this hesitation, he just grabbed the ball and zing—with no time wasted."[6] Other observers noted that DeCorrevont had changed his running style, running less between the sidelines and more up and down the field, making him an effective slasher on off-tackle runs.

But DeCorrevont might not have been the best back on his own team. That distinction probably belonged to Oliver "Red" Hahnenstein, a more versatile and durable performer. Certainly Minnesota thought so. "This Red Hahnenstein is much more dangerous than DeCorrevont," said Minnesota backfield coach Sheldon Beise.[7] In addition, the Wildcats had, on their bench, an injured sophomore halfback of exceptional passing ability named Otto Graham. Beginning the next year, 1941, a healthy Graham would tear up the Northwestern record books.

The first half of the game could be described as a tale of two missed tackles. Northwestern struck first when, from the Minnesota 43-yard line, Hahnenstein hit DeCorrevont's substitute, Tuffy Chambers, with a pass at the 25-yard line. Chambers put a move on safety George Franck, who had already saved two games for the Gophers with his sure tackles, and slipped away from his grasp for the first touchdown of the game. Fullback Don Clawson missed the extra point by inches, and the score stood at 6-0. The missed extra point did not appear to be consequential, until Minnesota advanced in the second period to the Northwestern 20-yard line, moving the ball slowly but surely down the field. George Franck was tackled there, short of the first down, but on fourth down the Gophers decided to go for it. Bruce Smith broke the tackle of Wildcat end Al Butherus and got to the 12-yard line for a first down, from where the Gophers scored their first touchdown on the first play of the second period. Reliable Joe Mernik kicked the extra point, and Minnesota had a 7-6 lead.

The Gophers threatened again in the second period, when Bruce Smith lofted a long pass into the end zone to Warren Plunkett. Whether the pass hit Plunkett in the chest and he dropped it[8] or whether defender Paul Heimenz batted it away[9] depends on the newspaper coverage.

Minnesota scored its second touchdown in the third period when the Gophers' Bob Paffrath intercepted a Hahnenstein pass near midfield and took ten plays to score. The key play was Franck's pass to end Bill Johnson at the two-yard line. When Gordon Paschka missed the extra point kick, Minnesota had a 13-6 lead.

The most impressive football of the game took place in the second half as Northwestern took the ball 80 yards in 15 plays to score their second touchdown, the smaller but quicker Wildcat linemen having their way with the weightier Gophers. Most of the yardage was gained on runs by Hahnenstein and fullback Don Clawson, but the biggest gain of the drive was on Clawson's pass to Hahnenstein, Clawson's first pass as a collegian. Then, on the last play of the third quarter, with the ball on the Gopher one-yard line on third down and the game in the balance, the Gopher defenders smothered the fullback Clawson before he could get into the end zone. Gopher fans could exhale, Wildcat fans could nervously twist their game programs, but both would have to wait for the teams to move to the other end of the field for the fourth-down play. There Hahnenstein, not to be denied, plowed over his right tackle, relying on second and third efforts, for the touchdown that brought the Wildcats within one point.

A nervous George Benson prepared for the extra point that, if made, would tie the game. He could feel the eyes of 48,000 fans on him. All activity on each sideline came to a halt as the teams lined up. Fans could hear a pin drop. The ball was snapped, he got the kick away and...he missed! The *Chicago Tribune* said the ball sailed just outside the left upright.[10] The United Press report said he sliced it just outside the right upright. But both agreed he just barely missed. It was "by little more than the width of a man's hand," said the UP.[11]

And that was the margin of Minnesota's victory. The 13-12 win left the Gophers undefeated and Northwestern wondering what might have been.

****

Late in the afternoon of November 2, word came from the West Coast that Stanford had defeated UCLA 20-14. The news was a surprise to nobody. With the day's work complete, Stanford's record stood at 6-0 and UCLA's at 0-6. Stanford had taken UCLA's anticipated spot at the top of the Pacific Coast Conference standings, and UCLA had taken Stanford's at the bottom.

Frankie Albert played a different sort of game, using as much deception as ever but sticking largely to the ground, and most of Stanford's success was based on straightforward running by Hugh Gallarneau, who scored two touchdowns, each time using the same play, and by Pete Kmetovic and Norm Standlee. Standlee's 44-yard run, in which he leaped over UCLA's Jackie Robinson, was his longest of the season. Robinson, ironically, was the reigning NCAA broad jump champion and arguably the finest all-around athlete ever to play college football, starring also in baseball and basketball. Albert completed only two passes in the game, but one went for a touchdown after a more typical Albert maneuver on a fake reverse. Both of UCLA's touchdowns were scored against Stanford's second and third teams. Robinson had two fine punt returns in the game, one for 32 and one for 42 yards, and passed for one of the Bruin touchdowns.

The win set up, for November 9, the second major showdown of the day, both unanticipated at the beginning of the season. At the same time that Minnesota would face off with Michigan for supremacy of the Big Ten, Stanford would go head-to-head with once-beaten Washington for the top position on the West Coast and a clear path to the Rose Bowl. Although Washington had been idle the week before and thus well rested, Stanford, the preseason pick to finish last in the Pacific Coast Conference, was expected to beat the preseason favorite Huskies. Washington had rebounded nicely from its opening day loss to Minnesota, shutting out its next three opponents and downing California 7-6. But the oddsmakers' choice sat well with Husky coach Jim Phelan, who preferred the underdog role. Instead of trying to stop the Stanford offense, he planned to wear down the tired Indians by running constantly at their middle and eventually outscore them.[12]

While the weather in Minneapolis was abysmal, the day on the west coast dawned sunny and cool, full of uplifted spirits. It was not until the beginning of the second period that either team was able to assert itself. The Huskies were pinned back to their own nine-yard line by Albert's fine punt, and were without their starting fullback, Walter Harrison, injured earlier in the game. Still, they began a 91-yard drive highlighted by a 56-yard run by Harrison's substitute, Jack Stackpool. Stackpool broke free from the defenders, and would have scored had he not violated Satchel Paige's old rule. He looked back to see if anyone was gaining on him and allowed the speedier Kmetovic to catch him from behind. Norm Standlee was also out of the game for Stanford, and Dean McAdams, exploiting Standlee's absence backing up the line, followed with a 36-yard pass to substitute end Earl Younglove. Younglove broke loose from Albert and ran the final 15 yards for the only touchdown of the first half.

Standlee, like Harrison, had been lost to injury in the first period, and prospects for Stanford, already dim, turned darker. Although nothing official had been announced, Standlee had already been photographed for his spot on Grantland Rice's All-America team, and his loss was a bitter one for the Indians.[13] In the third period, bogged down in its own territory, Stanford lined up to punt on fourth down. Center Vince Lindskog was injured with a badly cut hand, and he had already made one shaky snap on a punt; this time he snapped the ball over the head of Frankie Albert. The Huskies took over on downs on the Stanford 19-yard line. After the ball was advanced to the 8-yard line, John Mizen kicked a field goal, and Washington led, 10-0.

Deep in the third period, the Indians appeared doomed. Perhaps the goal of reaching the Rose Bowl had been too brazen. The six wins they had tallied so far might have to be balm enough for the stinging defeats of years past. They had been lucky all along, as Clark Shaughnessy had often reminded them, and perhaps their luck had finally run out. Time and again they had threatened to score, only to be turned away. Albert had missed a short field goal, a fourth-down pass had been dropped, another pass had been intercepted by Dean McAdams near the goal line, and yet another drive stalled deep in Washington territory. Now, Washington had the ball and was driving again, having reached the Stanford 30-yard line. Every sign pointed to the impending end of their amazing streak.

With three minutes left in the third quarter, the Huskies held on to their ten-point lead, and many a reporter in the press box, trying to get a jump on his deadline, clacked away feverishly at his typewriter, framing a story of upset, dashed hopes, and the Huskies in the Rose Bowl.

But Stanford was not finished. All they needed was a turning point, something to reverse the tide of fortune and start the momentum heading in their direction. It was Chuck Taylor who provided it. With only a yard needed for another first down, Washington was stopped three plays in a row, each time on a jarring tackle by Taylor. On fourth down, Taylor stopped Stackpool inches short of a first down.[14]

Stanford had yet to score. It appeared that the mystery of the T-formation had finally been solved, that Jimmy Phelan, the old Notre Dame mastermind, had finally found a way to shut it down, and many a typewriter hammered out that message in the press box. But this was Frankie Albert's time. After calling two running plays, Albert tossed a short pass to Pete Kmetovic, who caught it just past midfield, evaded a lunging Dean McAdams, and ran untouched the rest of the way for a touchdown. When Albert kicked the extra point, Stanford was trailing by only three points, 10-7. The tide had turned. As soon as Washington got the ball back, Albert intercepted a pass, and Stanford had the ball again at the Washington 41-yard line as the third quarter came to an end. This time Albert kept the ball on the ground, calling consecutive running plays that took the ball to the Washington nine-yard line, where Stanford had a fourth down and three yards to go for a first down. Albert's sure bet, with momentum on his side, would be to kick a field goal and tie the game.

But the short odds did not appeal to Albert's personality. He was a gambler to the depths of his soul, and while his exploits occasionally left his team in a hole, they more often netted big rewards. Shaughnessy, fully understanding Albert's love of the big risk and his knack for making it pay off, did little to curtail this tendency. He was no stranger to the emotion himself. Nervous Indian fans, always on the edge of their seats, would alternately cringe and exalt as Albert tempted fate time and again. Sam Jackson of the Associated Press suggested that the most heard comment regarding Albert was, "You never know what that guy will do," the tone of voice varying with the outcome of his last roll of the dice.[15] Art Cohn of the *Oakland Tribune* called him "a gambling fool...a gimlet-eyed sharpshooter, as cold-blooded a gambler as ever spun a wheel at Monte Carlo."[16]

On fourth down, Stanford broke the huddle and Albert settled in under center; it was clear to everybody in the stands that he was going to take one more risk, with the game and a probable trip to the Rose Bowl on the line. Needing three yards, and with the injured Standlee on the sidelines, he handed the ball to Gallarneau, who made four over right tackle. But when the Huskies' defense again stiffened, Albert found himself once more with a fourth down, this time from the one-yard line. In for a dime, in for a dollar, he figured, and he called on Gallarneau again. The two lines collided, the players piled up on the goal line, and when the bodies were cleared away, Gallarneau lay in the end zone, the ball having cleared the line by inches. Albert calmly kicked the extra point, and with a little over four minutes to play in the game, Stanford suddenly had a 14-10 lead. From one end of the press box to the other the sound could be heard of copy paper being ripped from typewriters, balled up and tossed in a corner. Frankie Albert had rewritten the story. Repeating what it did against Southern California, Stanford applied the coup de grace by running back a pass interception for another touchdown late in the fourth quarter. This time, it was Pete Kmetovic who took it 40 yards, and Stanford had a 20-10 win. After the game, the ever-confident, ever-cocky Albert, who seemed never to have doubted the outcome, or to let on if he did, said to a reporter that Shaughnessy's chin had been trembling "like a kite in a hurricane."[17]

The victory shook Shaughnessy from his usually undemonstrative shell. "That Albert's a hell of a great ball player," he gushed. "Did you ever in your life see a kid like that?" Former Stanford great Ernie Nevers was in the locker room after the game to offer his congratulations on one of the biggest Stanford wins he had seen, and added, "Please, Clark, don't do it this way again. Go out there and get the lead early. It's too tough on the heart." But when reporters tried to get Shaughnessy to comment on his suddenly increased prospects for a Rose Bowl trip and to have his picture taken with a bouquet, he immediately reverted to his former conservative self, figuring he had tempted fate enough for one day. "Nothing doing," he retorted hastily.[18]

****

Cornell was able to take out some of its frustrations in the middle of the St. John controversy in the homecoming game against Columbia on November 2. The Big Red had practiced particularly hard and late all week, mindful of an upset threat from the Lions. In last year's game only a blocked punt by Mike Ruddy, after which Ruddy outraced the Columbia players to the ball and covered it in the end zone, allowed Cornell to sneak by, 13-7. It had rained hard all Friday afternoon, and more rain was expected for the homecoming festivities. Cornell decided to wear red jerseys again, making a celebration out of the previous week's irritation. The game was not close. The rain held off until a deluge in the fourth quarter, and by then the Big Red had scored four touchdowns, all on passes. By game's end they had outgained the Lions 441 yards to 108, much of their yardage coming in 20-and 30-yard chunks, and had outscored them 27-0. The defense had intercepted four passes in the game.

The entire team continued to receive rave reviews. Sports commentators marveled at its near-perfect coordination and teamwork, as well as its formidable depth.[19] The team was called, "one of the great elevens developed in the East" and "pass masters of the country."[20] It was the last home game for eighteen seniors on the first and second team, and they left without ever having lost a game at Schoellkopf Field.

Cornell was now being called in some circles, "the best all-around football team in the last ten years."[21] Some called Cornell the greatest team in eastern football history.[22] "Cornell Appears Cinch to Have Unbeaten Season," announced one headline.[23] When some hinted that Cornell had been lucky, others answered that Cornell was "lucky the same way a steamroller is lucky when it meets a peanut. It seems to have the authority."[24] On Tuesday, the Associated Press ranked the Big Red number one in the country for the fourth week in a row.

After the game, Coach Snavely made one change in his starting lineup in preparation for the upcoming Yale game. At the beginning of the year, junior tackle Ed Van Order had hardly been mentioned for playing time. Well down the depth chart, mired on the third team, he gradually worked his way up to share some time on the second team. But his continued hard work in practice and steady performance when he was inserted in the games convinced Snavely to place him in the starting lineup. He was the only junior to start a game for Cornell all year. Snavely had not had to wear any rubber off the tires of his automobile to recruit him, either. He was a graduate of Ithaca High School, about a mile from the Cornell campus.

The history of Yale football extends back to the very roots of the college game. Dating back to 1891, when Walter Camp was the coach and Pudge Heffelfinger the star, Yale had won or shared the national championship 13 times, most recently in 1927. Cornell had never beaten Yale in football. The two teams first played in 1889, when a polished Yale team that included Amos Alonzo Stagg beat ragtag Cornell 56-6 and then in a rematch 72-0. More modern matchups went only marginally better for Cornell, resulting in a 23-0 shutout in 1936 and a 9-0 shutout in 1937, when Larry Kelley and Clint Frank won two consecutive Heisman Trophies at Yale. But 1940 was a decidedly down year for Yale. Polite people said that Yale was "rebuilding her grid fortunes" under coach Ducky Pond.[25] The Elis had won only one game, against Dartmouth, while losing four.

Yale at its best was no match for Cornell, but to make matters worse the Elis were hobbled by injuries that caused the betting line to go to 10-1 against them. As for the prospects of a competitive game, the *New York Times* noted, "This is a good time to go back to a good book."[26] Herb Barker of the Associated Press called the game "batting practice" for Cornell.[27] Rather than the outcome of the game, the speculation was whether Cornell would exceed the 50-7 beating that Penn inflicted on Yale. "If any team is going to beat Cornell it will have to be Penn," said one expert. "It looks to be a bigger job than Yale or Dartmouth can handle."[28]

Ithaca was socked in with deep snow, a continuation of horrid November weather on the east coast, and travel plans were endangered. The Big Red left Ithaca with 34 players and took a bus to Sayre, Pennsylvania, to work out. From there they took a train to New York City where they stayed at the Governor Clinton Hotel for two nights, planning on taking the train into New Haven on Saturday morning for the game. Friday night they took in a show, *"Hellzapoppin'*," which was enjoying a successful run at the Winter Garden Theater on Broadway (the Wisconsin team, in town to play Columbia, saw the same show that weekend), and on Sunday afternoon they saw an NFL game at Ebbets Field between the Brooklyn Dodgers and the Washington Redskins before returning home to Ithaca. In between the festivities they played their worst game of the season. They fumbled and stumbled their way through an uninspired 21-0 win over a surprisingly competitive but thoroughly outmanned Yale team. "Cornell took the football game and Yale took the glory"[29] was the way the papers read the next day. "For the first time this season, Cornell lacked the poise and precision that marked its earlier conquests," admitted the *Cornell Alumni News*.[30] All Cornell had to offer was that it could play poorly and still win. Still, Ducky Pond said of the Big Red, "Cornell has probably the best balanced team I think I've ever seen"[31]

****

Back in the Midwest, in the rain and the cold, the Michigan Wolverines left their hotel rooms in Minneapolis and readied themselves for the second act of the Big Ten's three-act play. At stake, among other things, was the Little Brown Jug. Left behind in the dressing room by Michigan, after playing Minnesota to a 6-6 tie in 1903, the water jug, according to legend, was found by equipment manager Oscar Munson and has served as a trophy awarded to the winner of each year's game between the two teams ever since. It is believed to be the oldest trophy in football. In November 1940, Minnesota had held the trophy for six years in a row, and Oscar Munson was still on the sidelines, serving as team equipment manager.

But there was much more at stake than the Little Brown Jug. With only two games remaining, the winner would have a strong advantage in pursuit of the Big Ten title. Wolverine seniors could not forget that, in each of the past two years, Gophers victories had knocked them out of the Big Ten race. And a national title was not out of the question for either team. Although the chase had been winnowed down to perhaps half a dozen teams, the slightest stumble by any of them could catapult one of the others into the top position. Minnesota, with 18 first-place votes, was ranked second in the nation by the Associated Press poll, while Michigan, with 11, was ranked third. The only team ahead of them was Cornell, which had lengthened its lead in the voting the week before, and had 119 first place votes.

Additionally, the relationship between the two coaches was civil but frosty, stemming from events during the 1931 season. In 1929, Fritz Crisler had been an assistant to Stagg at Chicago when Robert M. Hutchins became

Robert J. Scott and Myles A. Pocta

university president. Stagg, seeing the handwriting on the wall, urged Crisler to move on. Crisler pursued the vacant head coaching job at Minnesota and got it. But Crisler did not fit in with the Minnesota culture, and after a losing record in his first season the Gophers decided to replace him. In September of 1931, Bernie Bierman, still coaching Tulane, agreed to become Minnesota head coach beginning in 1932. But nobody told Crisler or Tulane officials about this arrangement, and when the story leaked midway through the season, hard feelings erupted all around. Crisler, offered the athletic director position, instead moved on to Princeton.[32]

Although the game was rated even, Crisler downplayed his team's chances. "It will be a dogfight all the way," he said, "and I'm afraid they have too many reserves for us."[33] The absence of injured Wolverine guard Milo Sukup was enough to worry Crisler and tip the scale for many observers. It appeared that the contest, like the Michigan-Penn game, would be a personal duel between two great stars, George Franck of Minnesota and the Wolverines' Tom Harmon. Bernie Bierman saw the weather as a critical factor. Rain in the days before the game had soaked the playing field. Michigan, with its complex blocking schemes and Harmon's cutback running style, needed a dry field more than Minnesota did.

The rain started up again early Friday afternoon as the leading edge of an ominous weather system moved in, and by game time on Saturday, with the temperature in the low 40s, it was still coming down and getting steadily worse. Minnesota opted to go on offense first, hoping to take advantage of the field before it turned into a quagmire, but to no avail. For the first quarter Michigan dominated the back-and-forth action but could not score.

All the significant events of the game took place in the second period. In the soaking downpour, Michigan still managed to drive from its own 15-yard line to the Minnesota five-yard line where it had first down and goal to go. Michigan decided to rely on its greatest strength and for three tries Harmon pounded into the Minnesota line, only to be thrown back, first by Bill Daley alone and then by gangs of Gopher tacklers. Then, on fourth down from the one-yard line, with a huge hole opened for him, Harmon slipped in his own backfield and was downed short of the end zone. It was a dilemma that would plague the Wolverines all day long.

Forest Evashevski lamented later that he had repeatedly opened holes for Harmon, holes of the type he had run through easily all year, but Harmon kept slipping trying to get to them. Later, when interviewed about the game, Harmon said of the field, "Your cleats would be full of mud after two steps."[34]

Minnesota, now with possession of the ball at its own goal line, immediately punted and Harmon, this time keeping his footing, returned the kick to the six-yard line. Three plays later he fired a perfect touchdown pass to Evashevski in the corner of the end zone, and Michigan had the lead. Harmon lined up for the extra point, slipped again in the mud, and missed the kick just to the

138

left of the upright. He missed "by inches," said the Associated Press report.[35] Michigan's lead as the deluge continued was 6-0.

A minute later, Ed Frutig of Michigan blocked George Franck's punt, and Michigan recovered on the Minnesota three-yard line. The tide of battle had turned Michigan's way, and a touchdown here could seal the game. The field was getting more slippery by the minute.

But then, in the span of three plays, the entire game, the entire season for both teams, and the national championship chase experienced a complete reversal of fortune. Seeking what could have been a clinching touchdown, Harmon launched a pass into the end zone and Bob Paffrath of Minnesota, as he had done the previous week against Northwestern, came up with an interception. The ball came out to the twenty-yard line, and from there came the play that, at least for the two teams involved, was the single most important play of the year and for Bruce Smith perhaps the single most important football moment of his life.

Franck called a reverse play, but as the team broke the huddle and headed for the line of scrimmage, he called to Smith, "Boo, switch halfbacks with me." Suddenly it was Franck and not Smith in the tailback position, and the Michigan defense immediately picked up what had happened. The year before, pulling a similar switch with Harold Van Every, Franck had taken the ball 65 yards for a touchdown, but this time the Wolverine defense, on full alert, would be ready for it. Smith moved to the wingback position to Franck's right, but Michigan stacked up the defense to guard against what it was sure would be a Franck run. Franck took the snap and headed right, pursued by the Michigan defense. But Smith cut behind him and took Franck's handoff on a reverse. Smith cut over the left side of the Minnesota line, broke Evashevski's tackle, then cut toward the left sidelines, right through where Harmon, playing right defensive back, should have been. But Harmon had committed to stopping Franck, and Smith blew past him on his way to the open field. Smith navigated through the mud and rain all the way to the Michigan 40-yard line where he slipped through the grasp of Bob Westfall, and then continued the rest of the way untouched, completing an electrifying 80-yard touchdown run on which seven Wolverines had a shot at tackling him. Summing up the play years later, Franck said, "[T]he greatest mistake Michigan could have made they made."[36]

As he did against Northwestern, Joe Mernik, substituted for Smith, kicked the extra point, and Minnesota led at halftime, 7-6.

During the halftime intermission the rain, already coming down in sheets, intensified. Nearly 64,000 fans braved the game-long downpour, huddled under newspapers, umbrellas, and makeshift coverings of every sort. One fan had fashioned a makeshift poncho from an oilskin tablecloth. Others simply surrendered themselves to the elements; few were inclined to miss any part of the classic struggle simply to stay dry. One observer likened it to "climbing into the Saturday tub en masse."[37] On the field, the Minnesota marching band trampled the field's last vestige of integrity. If the first half had been played in a driving rainstorm, the second half was played in what one observer called "a Rangoon monsoon."[38] The *Chicago Tribune* said it "was coming down in torrents in the fourth quarter."[39] For thirty more minutes the two teams just got wetter and muddier, but neither could score again, and the Gophers emerged with yet another critical one-point victory, secured once again by a margin of a few inches.

Lost in all the celebration was Bob Paffrath's interception and George Franck's spontaneous improvisation, but Bruce Smith was showered with adulation and, said one observer, could have been elected governor.[40] Yet, it was not in his nature to allow praise to affect him. Indeed, he was embarrassed by it. "His predilection for humility produced an innate aversion for ostentation," wrote one observer. "His was a serene and uncomplicated nature. He eschewed the campus social life in which he undoubtedly would have been lionized."[41] Instead of basking in the glow of the most important touchdown run in Gopher football history,[42] he returned to Faribault to spend the weekend with his family and savor his mother's home cooking. Later, his only comment on the game was to express sympathy for Tom Harmon, since he thought the loss must have been a bitter disappointment for him.[43] He was right. Harmon later said of the play, "It was the greatest run I ever saw and the greatest disappointment I ever suffered."[44] The game hinged on one play involving three men who were not just great football players. In later life, one would win nine battle stars in combat in the Pacific; one would win the Silver Star in aerial combat over China; and one would be nominated for sainthood in the Catholic Church. An indication of the respect between the three men is that, years later, the license plate on Franck's wife's car read, "54-98," the uniform numbers of the two greatest figures he ever played with.[45]

****

In early November, a strange series of events occurred. It was as if Mother Nature, looking down on the global carnage caused by men at war, decided to remind the human race that the earth still belonged to her. Beginning on Sunday, November 3, for a period of eight days, she unleashed a series of four devastating incidents across the globe. The first incident was just a warm-up. Beginning at 4 o'clock on Sunday morning, a giant typhoon, the worst in 40 years, struck the Pacific island of Guam, a prosperous U.S. possession and home to 23,000 natives and about 1000 Americans. For twenty hours, it raked the remote but strategic outpost 1500 miles east of Manila with torrential rains and winds of between 110 and 150 miles per hour. More than 15,000 Chamorro natives were made homeless. The banana crop, 90 percent of the coconut crop, and all garden crops were wiped out.[46] Miraculously, there were no deaths attributed to the storm. As to damage to Japanese forces and facilities on surrounding islands, the Japanese chose not to divulge them.[47]

On Thursday, November 7, the second chapter unfolded. The Tacoma Narrows Bridge, the world's third longest suspension bridge opened only four months before, connecting the Washington mainland to the Olympic Peninsula, collapsed in heavy winds. The structure began oscillating even while being built. Curiously, the action was more pronounced in gentle breezes of 4 miles per hour than in heavier winds.[48] The engineers expressed no worry, and the bridge, which immediately acquired the nickname "Galloping Gertie," became a tourist attraction.[49] Then, on the morning of November 7, winds on the Puget Sound howled at over 45 miles per hour, and undulations reached three to five feet in magnitude. At 10 am officials closed the bridge. Almost immediately a second oscillation was introduced, which increased the magnitude of the undulations to 28 feet and began to twist the span 45 degrees back and forth from horizontal. At 10:30 the center span dropped 195 feet into Puget Sound, and by about 11:10 all that remained were two towers. Remarkably, there were no human casualties.

Early on the morning of November 10, residents of Bucharest, Rumania, saw a blinding flash of blue light, which was followed by three to five minutes of violent shaking. The most destructive earthquake in Rumanian history destroyed most buildings in a 5,000-square-mile area, set oil fields in the Ploesti region ablaze, and killed an estimated 2,000 people. Virtually every structure in Bucharest was damaged or destroyed,[50] and countless people were made homeless by the quake, its aftershocks, and raging fires.

Within hours of the end of the Minnesota-Michigan game on November 9, the temperatures in the Midwest began to climb into the 60s and the torrential rains tapered off. The unexpected warmth was enough to coax duck hunters on and along the Minnesota lakes to shed their outer clothing and settle in for what they hoped would be a long pleasurable Armistice Day holiday weekend. On Monday, November 11, the weather forecast for the day called for flurries across most of Minnesota, but the day began with a slow warm drizzle, perfect for duck hunting. Then about midday, the mercury began to drop. The drizzle turned to sleet and the sleet to snow. Instantly the wind picked up and almost immediately reached tornado strength. People all across the central states from the Great Lakes to the Gulf Coast suddenly had a raging wind-driven blizzard on their hands. In Chicago, the temperature dropped from 63 degrees to 32 in four hours, and a few hours later would fall to 15. Temperatures dipped below zero in Nebraska and the Dakotas, Wyoming, Colorado, and Montana, and reached twenty degrees below zero along the western Canadian border. Highways in Minnesota, Iowa, and Nebraska became impassable. The Cimarron Valley in Colorado received three feet of snow. Waves reached six feet in height on the Mississippi River. Before the storm was done, Minneapolis received 16.7 inches of snow, with drifts in the outlying areas of twenty feet and more. Buildings collapsed, airplanes and trains crashed, power lines were downed on top of cars. Whipped by the ferocious winds, fires raged uncontrollably. The wall of wind hit Chicago precisely at 11:01 am, and within two hours there were 600 emergency calls to the fire department. Over a million Thanksgiving turkeys perished. Three freighters sank on Lake Michigan, drowning 66 sailors. Duck hunters, wet, stranded, and underclothed, froze to death by the score. The broadcast tower of WJR Radio in Detroit, at 733 feet the tallest structure in Michigan, succumbed to 53-mile per hour blasts. In Chicago, a ten-story tall Hiram Walker Whiskey sign, one of the largest electric signs in the world, crashed to the ground. El Paso experienced a sandstorm with 70 mile per hour winds, and in Buffalo the winds were clocked at 55 miles per hour. In total, along its thousand mile wide swath, the Armistice Day Blizzard left more than 150 people dead.[51]

On the campus of the University of Minnesota, classes were still officially scheduled, despite rumors and radio broadcasts to the contrary, but numerous buildings were closed, and few professors showed up. Only three or four students, many of whom skied to class, made it to most classes before they were cancelled; food services were greatly limited, and the road system was largely inoperable. Many students had left campus for a three-day weekend, and most were unable to get back. Bruce Smith, stranded at home in Faribault, was among them. The campus was, in a word, desolate. Dean Malcolm Willey hitchhiked a ride to campus and arrived by 8:15, but he was in the distinct minority. The weather forecast called for continued cold weather throughout the week without any chance of thaw.[52]

As Minnesota dug out and tallied its losses, there was at least some good news. The latest Associated Press polls were released, and they showed that the Gophers had supplanted Cornell as the top-ranked football team in the country. Their win over Michigan had been so impressive that Cornell, though it was still undefeated and had outscored its opponents to date by a margin of 181-13, garnered only 45 1/3 first place votes to Minnesota's 55 1/3. Michigan dropped from third to sixth.

****

The ranking of football teams was a practice started by Walter Camp near the turn of the century. Camp often included his personal opinion of team rankings at the same time he offered his personal opinion of All-America player selection. His work carried with it no greater pretense than that. It was just one man's opinion, plainly labeled as such. Many other sports figures of the day offered their individual views as well. The practice was common, and often rendered highly diverse outcomes.

In 1936, Alan Gould, the sports editor of the Associated Press, introduced the Associated Press weekly poll of football teams, based on voting by various sports editors from around the country. Gould's purpose was to entertain the public and to generate debate among the fans, at which his poll was highly successful. It roughly paralleled the advent of the Heisman Trophy in 1935, also awarded based on the voting of sports editors.

Although it carried with it the aura of scientific basis, since points and votes were tabulated, the poll was nothing more than a compilation of individual personal opinions. The public clearly understood that most of the people voting, even though they were sports editors, had no opportunity to view most of the teams or players they were voting on, and thus the basis for their votes was understood to be limited. Both the voters and the sports public were subject to the same technological limitations of the time and understood them well. There was not, and indeed could not be, any pretense of finality or official coloring to their acts. A team that emerged on top of a recognized poll or rating at season's end was said to have won the "mythical" national championship.

Gould explained his purpose: "It was a case of thinking up ideas to develop interest and controversy between football Saturdays....That's all I had in mind, something to keep the pot boiling."[53] In the world of modern football, the polls are thought of as a means to resolve controversy, not develop it, and as a means to hype interest in the televised coverage of games, something not on the minds of the sports public in 1940. Instead, newspapers of the time were filled with debates among columnists and readers, fictitious discussions and opinions, and a healthy delight in the give and take. The post-season bowls, instead of being part of the crowning of a champion, as in the modern setting, were distinctly separate from it. The mythical national champion was chosen before the bowl games were played. The debate was much more important than the answer. It was, in short, exactly what Gould had in mind, and it was great fun.

On November 15, an article written by Henry McLemore, staff correspondent of the United Press and as knowledgeable a football man as any, appeared in many papers. It seemed at first glance to be a whimsical look at team ratings, their proliferation, and their weaknesses. But behind the whimsy was an important message. Rankers didn't know very much about many of the teams. McLemore was tempted to list his top five teams as many others had: Texas A&M, Notre Dame, Cornell, Minnesota, and Tennessee, but then confessed he really had nothing on which to base his work. "To hell with it," he concluded. "Let's forget it. Nobody knows who is best."[54] The year before, Allison Danzig had written a similar piece in the *New York Times* in which he identified Tennessee, Texas A&M, Southern California, Cornell, and Tulane as the five best teams in the country for 1939, but he could not find any factor to separate any one of them from the others. To anybody who would attempt to do so, "heaven help him," he warned.[55]

With their losses to Minnesota, Michigan had slipped to sixth in the Associated Press poll, and Northwestern to tenth, but it was unclear what that meant. The Minnesota student newspaper, delighted by its team's top ranking, still was able to wonder how a missed extra point could cause Michigan to plummet so far. "If Minnesota is the number one team in the country after last Saturday, then Michigan should certainly be no worse than number two,"[56] it empathized. But Northwestern, after its two missed extra points against Minnesota, had a similar argument. After the undefeated Big Red dropped out of first place, the Cornell student newspaper lamented that the only basis of comparison between the Big Red and the Gophers was their common opponent, Ohio State, whom Cornell had beaten more convincingly.[57] Columnists, editors, and fans from each corner of the country joined in the debate. What about the other highly regarded undefeated teams, Boston College and Georgetown? Stanford, on the West Coast, was also still undefeated. Who could say they didn't deserve top ranking? And if any team in the country had a gripe, it would appear to be Texas A&M, the undefeated defending national champions, at least in the eyes of the Associated Press. They rated no better than third. But some said Tennessee had an even bigger gripe. By mid-November, Tennessee had won 29 consecutive regular season games and had been unscored upon in 1939. Yet they finished second in the voting in 1938 to TCU and second again in 1939 to Texas A&M. In 1940, again undefeated, the Volunteers were in fifth place, the victim of a weak schedule.

CHAPTER 13
SETTLED ON THE FIELD

We are not interested in the possibilities of defeat.

--QUEEN VICTORIA

On November 9, Harvard and Penn faced off at Franklin Field, in a match that joined the increasingly long litany of games with controversial outcomes, officiating lapses, and lack of communication. Once again the referee was the estimable Red Friesell, the same official who had handled the Cornell-Ohio State game two weeks before.

The game was expected to be a one-sided thrashing. But what remained unsettled was whether Penn would play as it had in its splendid wins over Yale, Princeton, and Navy, or whether it would play another flat game as it did in its only loss of the season to Michigan. Harvard had beaten only Amherst and had played ties against both Army and Princeton. Penn was as much as a three-touchdown favorite. But in this game Harvard clearly held its own. Nine of the starting eleven men played all sixty minutes for the Crimson, and they used a six-man line to slow down the Penn running attack. Frank Reagan and the rest of the Quakers had a rough time all afternoon against the resourceful Crimson. The game ended in a 10-10 tie, Harvard's third of the year, but the real story of the day was how it got to be that way.

Late in the third period, trailing in the game 10-7, Harvard intercepted a Penn pass on the Penn 29-yard line and advanced the ball in a few plays to the seven-yard line, where it faced fourth down. Harvard opted to attempt a field goal to tie the game, and sent in Henry Vandereb, its best kicker, for that purpose. His try was successful, but Penn was declared offside on the play. The head linesman, G.R. MacDonald, reportedly asked an unspecified member of the Harvard team whether he would take the penalty, and he declined it. Thus the score stood, 10-10, and that ended up being the final score of the game. But the Harvard acting captain, Bill Brown, who should have been the player consulted by McDonald, stated after the game that he never knew about the penalty until ten minutes later and would have accepted it if he had been given the choice. An accepted penalty would have resulted in the three points being taken off the board and a Harvard first down at the two-yard line, which could well have led to a winning touchdown. Friesell was unsure which of the Harvard players had made the decision to decline the penalty.[1] Clearly a member of Friesell's crew had been careless in handling the issue.

A modern fan might well be puzzled by such a problem, wondering how a player on the field could not know that a penalty had been assessed. The answer is shocking in its simplicity—the penalty flag had not yet been invented. In the modern game there is perhaps no phrase more familiar than "Flag on the play!" It is an instant and unmistakable signal to every player, to the benches, and to the fans, that a penalty is about to be enforced by a game official. It gives the referees clear control over the moment. But the first penalty marker was not used in a game until the next year, 1941, when officials in the Youngstown-Oklahoma City game used one fashioned out of red and white cloth from an old Halloween costume.[2] There is some indication that variations had been used sporadically before that, but when Irma Beede, wife of Youngstown coach Dwight Beede, sewed the first penalty flag and weighted down one corner with weights taken from a set of drapes, she in effect became the Betsy Ross of football.[3] So in the meantime Friesell, MacDonald, and all their refereeing brethren were at a distinct disadvantage when it came to matters of signaling to the players that a penalty was being enforced. They were relegated to using a whistle, exactly the same signal they used to mark the end of a play, or some other vocal signal easily lost in the noise generated by an excited crowd.

Although this confusion was unfortunate and probably affected the outcome of the game, it cannot be said for certain how. By giving up three points and taking the ball on the two-yard line, Harvard could just as well have lost the game as won it. Or perhaps, given a moment to reflect, Harvard would have declined the penalty anyway and settled for a well-earned tie. Nobody will ever know. The Harvard-Penn game would not be the last that year in which uncertainty about a penalty call would play a factor in the outcome.

****

In Britain, it had been a hellish autumn as Londoners defiantly took the daily lashings from the Luftwaffe. Bombs raining on them tore up their homes, their churches, their factories, and with no rest even for the dead, their cemeteries. Even worse than the physical devastation, in the opinion of some, was the thorough disruption of the daily patterns of life. Sleepless nights were commonplace; meals were routinely eaten cold; the residents' daily flight to shelter, wrapped in blankets and with suitcases and children in tow, often began before the sirens sounded, and for the lucky led to a night spent on a folding cot or in a sleeping bag. After the all-clear siren came the heartbreaking process of damage assessment, fire fighting, rubble clearing, the rescue of the injured and the recovery of the dead. And each day Londoners tried as best they could to keep some semblance of normality until evening when the sirens sounded again.[4]

The façade of normal life was critically important, and the British did not lose their sense of humor. Amenities such as golf courses continued to operate, if anybody had the capability or inclination to partake of them. One such golf course on the outskirts of London modified the ground rules for the times. "Players may pick out of any bomb crater, dropping the ball no nearer the hole, without penalty. Ground littered with debris may be treated as ground under repair," the new regulations read.[5]

The travails of the British were thoroughly chronicled in the American press, and the attitude of the American public slowly shifted toward a more supportive stance. Its views of the issues would be seen through the prism of their presidential election scheduled for November 5.

The campaign of 1940 unfolded in the context of this rapidly deteriorating international scene. In the Far East, the United States embargoed wheat shipments, the British threatened to send aid to the Chinese in defiance of Japanese warnings, and American citizens abroad were advised by the State Department to leave the Orient. Japan, under her new prime minister, the passionately anti-American Hideki Tojo, was now clearly aligned with Germany and Italy. On October 9, a statement appeared in the newspaper, attributed to, but denied by, the Roosevelt administration, that war with Japan was perhaps fifteen days away.[6] On October 25, labor leader John L. Lewis, whose unions had regularly regarded the New Deal favorably, threw his support to Willkie, stating his belief that Roosevelt's intentions were to lead the nation to war. On October 28, Italy invaded Greece, bringing further escalation in global tension, and the fear of war at home. From late September to mid-October, Roosevelt's support had slipped, from a double-digit lead to a six-point lead in the polls.[7] Now, although he had remained mostly aloof from the campaign, he set out to make a number of speeches in the closing days to bolster his position. On October 30, he told a crowd assembled in Boston, "Your boys are not going to be sent into any foreign war."[8] Willkie responded: "If his promise to keep our boys out of foreign wars is no better than his promise to balance the budget they're already almost on the transports."[9]

On Tuesday, November 5, more than 50 million Americans streamed to the polls, the fate of the world in their hands. By nightfall, Roosevelt had won a sweeping victory with 449 electoral votes and nearly 55 percent of the popular vote, the first time in history that an American president had been elected to a third term. His stage from which to direct national policy, unencumbered by electoral pressure, was secure.

Less than two weeks later, John Edward Lawton of Boston, an unemployed plumber's helper, was the first of 800,000 men sworn in to the service as part of the Peacetime Conscription Program, planned to continue until June 30, 1941.

On November 16, Americans awoke hoping to enjoy a rousing football Saturday, a needed respite from the pressures of the worsening world condition. The day dawned cold and wet over most of the country. Fans in State College, Pennsylvania, were told to expect snow for the Penn State-NYU game, and they got it. In New England, it had rained and snowed all week, and more was expected. The Midwest, still reeling from the Armistice Day Blizzard, was getting another blast of winter.

The football season had unfolded in an unanticipated manner. At this late date there were still 11 major undefeated teams, and two of them, Boston College and Georgetown, were scheduled to face one another at Fenway Park in Boston. Notre Dame, still undefeated, aimed to right itself after two wobbly performances. In the west, Stanford was hoping to solidify its startling claim to a Rose Bowl berth. But the week's horrible weather all over the country had left gridirons everywhere a series of soggy swamps. Arthur J. Daley, in the *New York Times*, gave ample warning. "In football mud is the great equalizer," he said. "Hence upsets are probable."[10] November 16 would turn out to be a day of reckoning in college football, one to be remembered for decades.

Americans may have been looking forward to a big football celebration when they awoke that Saturday morning, but the news that greeted them was far from festive. Overnight, the Luftwaffe had reduced the British city of Coventry to ashes and rubble. Feinting toward London and then veering inland to the city of a quarter million people, 500 German bombers had dropped 600 tons of explosives and thousands of incendiaries on the city. Homes, businesses, and much of the city's remarkable medieval architecture were obliterated. The city said to be the site of Lady Godiva's famous ride was devastated, and one of its most noted buildings, St. Michael's Cathedral, which dated to the fourteenth century, was destroyed. Taking advantage of the full moon, the Luftwaffe also sent 200 planes to pound London, subjecting the capital to what the United Press called "its heaviest and most protracted bombing in a month." Scores of fires were set and hospitals damaged before the "all clear" signal sounded at 7 am.[11] Hitler threatened to similarly "Coventrate" other British cities, and immediately turned his attention to Birmingham.[12] The news from Europe was gloomier by the day, the war closer.

****

When 36 Northwestern football players arrived in Ann Arbor for the third game of the round robin among the three best teams in the Big Ten, there was a temptation to view the November 16th game against Michigan as a consolation. Each had lost to Minnesota, each by a missed extra point, each by a matter of inches. Yet both teams knew that, should Minnesota falter in either of its last two games, the winner of this contest would be in a position to capture a share of the Big Ten championship. Most observers figured the game would be closely contested, with a slight edge to Michigan, based on

Tom Harmon's presence and Michigan's nine-pounds-per-man edge in size on the line. Harmon had been limping all week, the result of an ankle injury suffered against Minnesota, but vowed to play. After spending a night in the hospital, he showed up for practice on Monday, long enough to proclaim to the press, "I'm going to play against Northwestern Saturday, and you can print that in capital letters." But Fritz Crisler would not allow him on the practice field, and sent him back to the hospital.[13] By Saturday he was ready. On the Northwestern side, Bill DeCorrevont planned on more playing time, since his injuries were healing, but was not expected to start. Both teams were ground-oriented in their offense, but Michigan had allowed only one touchdown by rushing all year.

Although the blizzard early in the week had finally abated, it was snowing again all across the Midwest, and a strong northerly wind added to the day's distinctly wintry feel. Even so, 77,000 fans showed up, including Red Grange, present for the first time to see Harmon play. Harmon entered the game with 29 career touchdowns, two fewer than Grange's career record, and the Galloping Ghost had a keen interest in the events of the day.

The Michigan-Northwestern game epitomized the day's prevalent field-position football. Michigan won, 20-13, because it kept the Wildcats bottled up in their own end of the field for most of the game and because it displayed a superior kicking game. All three Michigan touchdowns resulted directly from Wildcat punts from their own end zone into a swirling wind, and the longest of their three touchdown drives was 26 yards. Both Wildcat scores came from long range.

The scoring began midway through the first period when Ollie Hahnenstein, punting already for the second time from his own end zone, had his punt blocked by Ed Frutig, and the ball rolled out of bounds on the one-foot line. Tom Harmon ran it into the end zone from there, his thirtieth career touchdown, then kicked the extra point, and Michigan led 7-0. Minutes later, Hahnenstein, again punting from his own end zone, managed a punt of only thirty yards into the wind, and it was returned to the Wildcat 5-yard line. Bob Westfall of the Wolverines made easy work of it from there, and the first period ended with the Wolverines leading 14-0.

On the first play of the second period, Northwestern's Bill DeCorrevont, newly substituted into the game, threw a 48-yard touchdown pass, with the wind at his back, to Bob Motl, and when the extra point was missed Northwestern had climbed to within 14-6. Later in the second period DeCorrevont, again with the wind at his back, got off a poor punt from his own end zone. The ball carried out only to the 26-yard line. Six plays later Bob Westfall scored his second touchdown of the day for the Wolverines, and when Harmon missed the extra point, they led 20-6.

Michigan had lost to Minnesota the week before because it had given up an 80-yard touchdown run by Bruce Smith, and this week they gave up another. This time it was Ollie Hahnenstein who, in the final period, took a handoff from Don Clawson at his own 20-yard line and sped around right end on a reverse that left every Wolverine behind but Harmon. Hahnenstein raced all the way to the 35-yard line before Harmon got close to him, but a trio of Wildcat blockers knocked Harmon out of the play. Down now only 20-13, the Wildcats got the ball back and began driving again. From their own 21-yard line they carried the ball, on their only sustained drive of the day, to the Michigan 15-yard line, where they had a first down with three minutes left in the game. In three plays Hahnenstein moved the ball nearly ten yards, and the Wildcats had a fourth down and inches to go for a first down. The game appeared to hang in the balance as Hahnenstein threw himself at the Wolverine line for the fourth time. But Bob Westfall, Michigan's offensive hero of the game, showed his mettle on defense as well, and threw him for a two-yard loss, effectively ending the game.

As expected, the game was settled on the ground, with DeCorrevont's touchdown pass being the only significant aerial effort of the day. Although Northwestern outgained Michigan in rushing and passing by over 70 yards, the Wolverines' punts were far more effective, and Northwestern was able to return only one of ten. Red Grange went home still the holder of the all-time career touchdown record.

****

Undefeated Notre Dame was ripe for an upset. After being showered with praise by nearly every sportswriter in the country for four weeks, then eking out wins against Army and Navy, the Irish were suddenly finding it difficult to justify their standing among the nation's elite, their undefeated record notwithstanding. But even the most negative of analysts found it hard to foresee that any comeuppance would be administered by the lowly Iowa Hawkeyes.

Over most of the past two decades Iowa had found its customary home deep in the second tier of Midwestern teams, venturing forth from that humble station only occasionally. The Iowa team had savored a brief taste of football superiority in the early years of the 1920s when it amassed a 20-game winning streak, a Big Ten championship and a share of a second, as well as a share of the national championship in 1921. But in 1930 the team began a decade of crushing adversity marked by a suspension from the Big Ten for a year due to league rule violations, only two winning seasons, and a woeful 6-28-6 record against Big Ten opponents. Even the lowly Chicago Maroons did better, winning seven times. During the two-year coaching tenure of Irl Tubbs in 1937 and 1938, after Ossie Solem left for Syracuse, the Hawkeyes' record nosedived to 2-13-1, and Iowa did not score a touchdown in the last five games of 1938. And as the 1939 season approached, the beleaguered fans saw only a more difficult schedule ahead of them, one that included powerhouse Notre

Dame for the first time since 1921. They were left to recollect wistfully their last glorious era, when among their most cherished victories was their 10-7 win that year against the undefeated defending national champions from South Bend, a game that snapped the Irish 20-game winning streak. Iowa's new and unheralded coach for 1939 remembered that game well. He was Dr. Eddie Anderson, and he had been the Notre Dame captain that day. It was the only losing game that Eddie Anderson experienced in four years as a college player.

Eddie Anderson, it can safely be said, was a man apart. The son of Norwegian immigrants, he was born in Oskaloosa, Iowa, and moved to Mason City as a young teen. When he arrived on the campus at Notre Dame he became part of Knute Rockne's first team, and when he left, he was team captain and All-American, firmly indoctrinated in the Rockne way of football.

He was unsatisfied in excelling at only one thing. By 1939, he had been head football, basketball and track coach at Columbia College in Dubuque, Iowa; captain of the NFL champion Chicago Cardinals; football, baseball and track coach at DePaul University; a medical student at Loyola University; head football coach at Holy Cross in Worcester, Massachusetts; a staff member as an ear, nose, and throat specialist at Massachusetts General Hospital; and head of the ear, nose and throat clinic at Boston's Veterans' Hospital. Along the way he compiled a sparkling 47-7-4 record in his six years coaching Holy Cross. In 1939, Eddie Anderson became head football coach at the University of Iowa and a staff member at the University of Iowa ear, nose, and throat clinic.[14]

The first sight of Anderson showing up for afternoon football practice in his hospital scrubs no doubt convinced the Iowa players that they had entered a new era. Anderson could be emphatic, sarcastic, gruff, and warm all at the same time. Applying both his medical and his football background, Anderson was known to adjust broken noses and pop dislocated joints into place on the sidelines and send the repaired player back into the game.

One of the defining characteristics of Anderson's coaching style was his disdain for substitution. With his early teams at Columbia College, he often played only 11 men. When he moved on to Holy Cross, he continued the practice, but was often criticized for it. His entire Iowa roster at the start of the 1939 season numbered only 20 players, and he had no plans to use all of them.[15] "There is no reason, barring accidents, why any boy who is a football player shouldn't be able to play a full game," he said. "It requires excellent conditioning, but represents no particular strain on them physically."[16]

Then, in 1939, to the delight of underdog lovers everywhere, the Hawkeyes built a 6-1-1 record and threatened, until the last day of the season, to win their first Big Ten title in nearly two decades. For one brilliant explosive season, the Hawkeye fans were lifted from despondency, transported by one heart-stopping win after another. Sports fans have always had a special fondness for teams resurgent from ineptitude and for the stars that lead them.

The most creative casting director in Hollywood could not have conjured up a more glorious leader, a more charismatic champion, a more heroic figure than the player who led the 1939 Iowa Hawkeyes, Nile Clarke Kinnick, Jr., of Adel, Iowa. If the 1939 Hawkeyes were college football's version of the Impossible Dream Boston Red Sox or the Miracle Mets, then Kinnick was their Yastrzemski, their Seaver. He found ways, sometimes seemingly impossible ways, to hoist his team to victory after improbable victory. Off the field he was a deep intellectual, a brilliant student, senior class president, and devout practitioner of his faith.

Kinnick was the oldest of Nile and Frances Clarke Kinnick's three sons. Frances's father, George W. Clarke, had been governor of Iowa until just before Nile was born. Kinnick excelled as a youth in athletics in Adel, a small farming community just west of Des Moines. He played catcher on the local American Legion baseball team when the pitcher was the precocious Bob Feller, from nearby Van Meter.[17] The duo enjoyed a magical year in 1939, and while Kinnick's exploits lit up the gridiron, Feller was winning 24 games for the Cleveland Indians. When the Depression swallowed the Kinnicks' farming operation the family moved to Omaha.

When it was time to think about college, Kinnick found that his size, at 5' 8" and 170 pounds, and relative lack of speed were insufficient to impress college coaches. After Bernie Bierman rejected him, Kinnick found himself at Iowa, a setting he warmed to strongly and immediately. Though he quickly became a mainstay of the football team, he was not yet the star performer. That distinction belonged to end Erwin Prasse, from Chicago.

In the first game of the 1939 season, although against lesser competition, Kinnick ran for three touchdowns (one on a 65-yard run), passed for two more, and drop-kicked five extra points against South Dakota in a one-sided 41-0 victory. The next week, the Hawkeyes faced a tougher Indiana, led by the best passer in the Big Ten, halfback Hal Hursh. Kinnick got off a 73-yard quick kick, passed for two touchdowns (one of 30 yards and one of 50), and ran three yards for another after setting it up with a 55-yard run. Trailing 29-20 beginning the fourth quarter, Kinnick marched Iowa 73 yards for a touchdown. Then, late in the fourth quarter, facing a fourth down and 15 from the Hoosier 18-yard line, Kinnick faced the key play of the game. Opting against a tying field goal, he instead passed for the winning touchdown. The Hawkeyes won a thriller, 32-29, beating the Hoosiers for the first time since 1921. It was the first Big Ten win at home for Iowa in six years.

Kinnick could not match Tom Harmon, however. The next week, against Michigan, in their head-to-head match, the powerful Wolverines prevailed 27-7. The two stars accounted for all the points in the game. One of Harmon's touchdowns was scored on a 90-yard return of an intercepted Kinnick pass. But Kinnick's effort was second to none. For the second week in a row he played all 60 minutes.

The next week, the Cornbelt Comet, as the press labeled him, put the Hawkeyes back on track. Again playing all sixty minutes, he threw for three touchdown passes of 19, 39, and 24 yards, and Iowa beat Wisconsin, 19-13. After the press noted that he had used only 18 players in the game and that six had played every minute of Iowa's four games to date, Anderson said he was coaching a team of "ironmen,"[18] a term that would serve as the defining label for this great team over the decades to follow. Junior tackle Mike Enich, perhaps the toughest of the ironmen, had collapsed on the field in the Indiana game, but ended up playing every minute of the last six games of 1939, and the entirety of ten games in his last two years.[19]

In the next game, after a week off, Iowa's 14 men beat Purdue with the help of a pair of blocked punts by the improbable score of 4-0 on two safeties in the fourth quarter. "Shucks. We didn't even need that second safety. We just wanted to make it decisive," deadpanned Iowa line coaches Jim Harris.[20] One-liners like this are plentiful when things are going well.

The next week, Notre Dame, ranked second in the country but no longer feared by the suddenly confident Hawkeyes, came to town for a game the Irish once envisioned as a soft spot on an otherwise difficult schedule. The game offered several interesting sidelights. Elmer Layden, before returning to his alma mater, had succeeded Eddie Anderson as coach at Columbia College, and now the two former Notre Dame greats were to square off. The two teams would meet for the first time since Iowa's great 1921 victory over Anderson's Notre Dame team. For Layden, it was a homecoming of sorts, and the Irish team stayed in nearby Davenport, Layden's home town, until hours before game time.

The game turned on one play, a matter of split-second judgment. Late in the second period, Irish defender Steve Sitko intercepted a Kinnick pass in the end zone. But instead of downing it for a touchback he tried to return it and fumbled it away on the four-yard line. Moments later, Kinnick ran for the only Hawkeye touchdown with 40 seconds left in the half, lowering his shoulder into an Irish defender on the goal line just as a photographer tripped his camera's shutter. Copies of the resulting picture, which perfectly captured the Hawkeyes' defiant resurgence, hung in Iowa homes for years to come.[21] Kinnick then drop-kicked the extra point. Notre Dame switched to green jerseys for the second half, but it did no good. In the fourth quarter, from his own 30-yard line, Kinnick sealed the victory as time in the game ran out with his 16th punt of the day, a 63-yard kick that soared over safetyman Sitko's head and rolled out of bounds on Notre Dame's six-yard line. It was probably the greatest punt of Kinnick's career, in the greatest game of his career. The Hawkeyes had knocked the Irish from the undefeated ranks, 7-6, and hung on them their only loss of the year. Of the 11 Iowa starters, eight played the entire 60 minutes. For Kinnick, it was his fifth consecutive 60-minute performance.

The excitement on campus was so intense, the joy so unbounded, that the Iowa Board of Deans cancelled Monday classes.

Fans and teammates loved him. Said Hawkeye quarterback Al Couppee of Kinnick's clinching punt, "I have played in 147 football games, college, service, and pro, but that was the single most exhilarating moment I've experienced in sports."[22] Dr. Jerry Anderson, son of the Iowa coach, said years later, "I know every kid in Iowa went to his mother the next week and asked her to sew a number 24 on his shirt so he could pretend to be Nile Kinnick."[23] Iowa's defeat of Notre Dame was the greatest upset of the 1939 college football season and elevated Kinnick above a host of contenders to the top candidate for the Heisman Trophy.

The next week, at Iowa's homecoming, Kinnick's fourth quarter performance against Minnesota in his last home game turned the crowd of 50,000 wild with joy. With the Hawkeyes trailing 9-0 beginning the fourth quarter, he began by moving his team 80 yards on three passing plays, finishing with a 45-yard touchdown pass to Erwin Prasse. The pass, thrown on the run from the far right hand side of the field to the far left, was caught by Prasse on the 8-yard line before he ran untouched for the score. Then, with four minutes remaining, Kinnick set the Hawkeyes off on another drive, this one resulting in a 28-yard touchdown pass, also thrown on the run, to sophomore Bill Green. "I was two steps from running out of the end zone," Green later said, "and the throw was right on the money."[24] Kinnick then stifled Minnesota's comeback attempt by intercepting Harold Van Every's pass with less than 30 seconds left in the game. The Associated Press called it an "almost unbelievable finish."[25] Another story reported the score, "Nile Kinnick 13, Minnesota 9" and called the contest "the most spectacular football game in modern Big Ten history."[26]

The exultant homecoming fans streamed onto the field and carried the Hawkeye team to the locker room. It was Iowa's first win over Minnesota since 1929. For the sixth consecutive week Kinnick played all 60 minutes, and six other starters also played the entire game. Eddie Anderson used only 17 players. By the end of the season, 13 different players had played all sixty minutes of at least one game.[27]

On the final weekend of the season, with the Big Ten championship still within reach, Kinnick separated his shoulder in the third quarter against Northwestern, bringing to an end a string of 402 consecutive minutes played. Iowa and Northwestern tied, 7-7, and the Ohio State Buckeyes were Big Ten champions. But the setback took little luster off the season. Kinnick was acclaimed as the back of the year, Anderson the coach of the year, and the Iowa team as the "fightin'est group of sixty-minute men of the campaign."[28] The *New York Times* summed up their performance by saying, "For a team that was the whipping boy of the conference, its rocket-like ascent stands as one of the biggest success stories in recent football history."[29]

When Gil Dobie, the frustrated football coach at Cornell, left at the end of the 1935 season to take the job at Boston College, one of his parting remarks was, "You can't win games with Phi Beta Kappas."[30] So on December 6, 1939, when Nile Kinnick, soon to be elected to Phi Beta Kappa, ascended to the podium at the Downtown Athletic Club in New York to accept the Heisman Trophy, the moment was one of some irony. Though fans in future years would cast doubt on whether Tom Harmon, and not Kinnick, should have won the award, such discussions are common any time awards are bestowed. The entire matter surrounding the six-year-old award was met with little fanfare, but it should be noted that Kinnick was the only unanimous choice by Big Ten coaches for the All-Big Ten team and, in addition, the Associated Press selected him as 1939 male athlete of the year over such stars as Joe DiMaggio, Joe Louis, and Byron Nelson. He also won the Walter Camp and Maxwell Awards. If any mistake was made in judging the quality of Kinnick's achievements, there were plenty of people making it.

Kinnick was drawn to the law and, like his grandfather, to politics. He was an immensely thoughtful and perceptive person who was deeply interested in the war in Europe, certain that America would soon be involved, and eager to do his part. "Nile said it was going to be our duty," team captain Prasse later recalled.[31] "He was Jack Armstrong and Frank Merriwell rolled into one," quarterback Al Couppee said of him. "There was just an aura about him. He didn't try to create it, it was just there. You really had the feeling you were in the presence of someone very special."[32] Remembrances of him range from the special care he took as a camp counselor for the most poorly coordinated kids in camp[33] to his gift of his All-America sweater to an 18-year old football player who had just had his leg amputated.[34] Kinnick's charisma was seemingly boundless.

Kinnick's Heisman acceptance speech was greeted with awe by those in attendance. How a young man could be so selfless, so thoughtful, so mature, was a mystery. The clinching line of his speech revealed an ability to appreciate the world situation and his place in it with a degree of wisdom uncommon in people of any age: "I'd like to make a comment which, in my mind, is indicative perhaps of the greater significance of football and sports emphasis in general in this country. And that is I thank God I was warring on the gridirons of the Midwest and not on the battlefields of Europe. I can speak confidently and positively that the players of this country would much more, much rather struggle and fight to win the Heisman award than the Croix de Guerre."[35]

His later writings would indicate even stronger feelings about his responsibility as an American and as a citizen of the world. Preparing for military service, he wrote, "It is not only a duty but an honor....May God give me the courage and ability to so conduct myself in every situation that my country, my family and my friends will be proud of me."[36] Of the responsibility to fight he wrote, "Lincoln was a moral and upright man. He was a pacifist at heart. But when there was no other alternative he did not equivocate nor talk of peace when there was no peace." Of the popular leaning toward isolationism he wrote, "We are not people apart."[37] After the Heisman ceremony, Bill Cunningham of the *Boston Globe* wrote of him, "This country is OK as long as it produces Nile Kinnicks. The football part is incidental."[38]

By the fall of 1940, Kinnick had graduated, had turned down a $10,000 offer from the NFL's Brooklyn Dodgers to play pro football, and had entered law school at the University of Iowa. In his absence the 1940 version of the Iowa football team had regressed to its old losing ways, and by the time the Hawkeyes traveled to Notre Dame, they had lost four games in a row. But Anderson's tendency to play his ironmen had not lessened. By the Notre Dame contest, nine Hawkeyes had played every minute of two or more games.[39]

Still undefeated and clinging to the seventh spot in the Associated Press poll, it was the Irish who were suddenly difficult to figure. They were surely not so good as they looked winning their first four games, nor so bad as they looked winning their last two. Against Army and Navy, Notre Dame had learned a valuable lesson. A team may dominate play, gain more yardage, and impose its will on its opponent for most of the game, but it does not win if it cannot find a way to score. That was the principle upon which Notre Dame, dominated by each of them, had forged its two wins against the service academies. On November 16, it saw that lesson at play once again. The Irish, wrote Associated Press reporter Steve Snider, "battered the underdog Hawks from one goal post to the shadows of the other."[40] Five times the Irish launched threatening drives, and each time they were thrown back. In the first period they reached the Iowa 15-yard line, only to lose the ball on downs, and then fumbled the ball away near midfield. After playing almost the entire third period in Iowa territory, Notre Dame sealed its own defeat by turning the ball over five times in the fourth quarter. First it drove to the Iowa 1-yard line and, for the second time in the game, lost the ball on downs when Jim Walker and Mike Enich tackled Milt Piepul there on fourth down. Walker, a black man playing in his home town of South Bend, had been denied admission to Notre Dame,[41] and he was, no doubt, playing with extra incentive. When the Irish got the ball back, they advanced to the Iowa 10-yard line before they again fumbled the ball away. Iowa captain Mike Enich picked Milt Piepul's fumble out of the air and returned it nearly to midfield. Once Iowa was forced to punt, Bob Saggau of the Irish promptly threw an interception, picked off by Al Couppee. Iowa could not advance and missed a field goal attempt, but Notre Dame, on the first play after it got the ball back, fumbled it away 24 yards from its own goal line. It was recovered by the Hawkeyes' Ken Pettit. This time Iowa did not squander the opportunity and took the ball into the end zone in four plays. The touchdown was scored by Bill Green, who accounted for nearly all the Iowa offense for the day. Then, to cap off the day, leading 7-0, the Hawkeyes' George "Red" Frye intercepted another Bob Saggau pass, and Iowa was able to run out the clock. Notre Dame, too inconsistent to mount an effective scoring drive, lost to a team it outgained by more than a 2-to-1 margin but who was able to capitalize on errors. The Irish, for the third successive time, lost their undefeated season to the Iowa Hawkeyes.

****

Stanford's victory over Oregon State on November 16, its eighth of the year, was significant for a number of reasons. First, it demonstrated clearly the strength of the system Clark Shaughnessy had built. Injured players were replaced by substitutes without missing a beat. The slightest letdown in tackling efficiency was met by immediate attention from the coaches. The players readily absorbed plays inserted by the coaching staff just before the game. It stood in stark contrast to the Stanford-Oregon State game of the previous year, which had given the press ample opportunity to criticize the sloppiness of the 1939 Indians. "Stanford turned in a loosely played game," the Associated Press had criticized. "Its aerial sorties generally failed to function, and ground plays often found the linemen tangled with the backs."[42] By contrast, the well-oiled machine of 1940 emerged from the locker room at halftime tied 7-7 and scored three touchdowns in the next nine minutes, putting the game out of reach. The Beavers, under coach A.L. Stiner, had entered the game with a 5-1-1 record, losing only to Washington and tying Southern California, and were correctly thought by the Stanford coaching staff to be a formidable opponent. But while everybody assumed Stanford would go to a passing attack with Norm Standlee out of the lineup, Frankie Albert kept it on the ground and threw only four passes all day.

Second, the system had plenty of room in it for excellent individual effort, and Pete Kmetovic and Albert both turned in sterling performances. A 39-yard touchdown run by Kmetovic, a fumble recovered by Kmetovic, a 39-yard touchdown run by Hugh Gallarneau, an interception by Kmetovic, and an 18-yard touchdown run by Rod Parker, all in quick succession after halftime, sealed the Stanford win. Albert had punted superbly during the game. He missed one punt, aiming for the coffin corner and getting only 14 yards out of it, but averaged over 58 yards per punt for his other seven attempts.

Third, it seemed clearer than ever that Shaughnessy's promise of a Rose Bowl appearance for Stanford, which had seemed an endearing but empty gesture by an overmatched newcomer only two months before, was about to be fulfilled. The win assured Stanford of at least a tie for the conference championship. "Stanford's invincible Indians nailed their football battle flag on the ramparts of the Rose Bowl today," claimed the Associated Press,[43] and asserted that the vote of conference representatives was a mere formality. The *Oakland Tribune* openly hailed the Indians as the 1941 Rose Bowl team and hinted they were in even if California, their lone remaining opponent, beat them convincingly. But Shaughnessy, true to form, would have none of it. "Rose Bowl?" he scoffed. "Don't know anything about it and could care less. We play California next according to our schedule." Observers wondered how Shaughnessy could keep his emotions so bottled up. A year removed from 85-0 and 61-0 losses at Chicago and humiliation at the hands of Beloit, he now was a seeming certainty to be a coach in the most famous football game in the world. Yet, instead of the slightest hint of celebration in his actions, words, or demeanor, he remained the same old dour Clark Shaughnessy, focusing on one game ahead and no further.[44]

The press pumped away at Shaughnessy and the Stanford players for a comment. The practice of the day was for the team selected to represent the Pacific Coast Conference to then invite its own opponent, and the Stanford players, when pressed, indicated they would like a crack at Texas A&M, if only to put their bruising runner, Norm Standlee, up against the toughest runner in the southwest, John Kimbrough. Shaughnessy politely expressed fondness for Minnesota, his alma mater, and Bernie Bierman, his old teammate and backup at fullback. But he knew the university would not let the Gophers go to a bowl game.[45] The longstanding practice of all the Big Ten schools was to limit each team to eight games, thus precluding any bowl appearances. He turned his attention to the two weeks ahead and the one opponent he knew awaited him, the California Golden Bears.

****

The much-awaited showdown between the two undefeated teams, Boston College and Georgetown, was expected to be the highlight of a busy weekend. It was the most anticipated football game in Boston since 1928, the year the Eagles went undefeated. New England, said one columnist, was "more aroused than at any time since Paul Revere."[46] The winner could be mentioned in the same breath as Cornell as eastern leaders.

The allure of the matchup was diminished only marginally by the fact that each team had built its undefeated record against weak competition. With the exception of the Tulane game, which the Eagles wisely added to their schedule late, there was no team on its docket that seriously challenged them. That it was playing its most difficult schedule in years did little to offset the reality that its perfect record was at the expense of the likes of Centre, Idaho, St. Anselm's, and Manhattan. Further, the Eagles again managed to construct a schedule where each of its games, again with the exception of Tulane, was played in Boston, with the schedule split between Alumni Field and Fenway Park. When put up against the schedules of other top teams vying for national recognition, their easy schedule was a hindrance. When the first Associated Press poll had come out on October 16, the Eagles' accomplishments had been enough to secure them eighth place in the rankings, but writers were aware of the lack of rigor. "Each of the top ten, except for Boston College, matched with Idaho, will have to go all-out Saturday to defend its ranking," said the AP report in an earlier weekly preview.[47] John Kieran, in the *New York Times*, noted sardonically that the Eagles' schedule "wasn't the toughest in the country."[48] Tennessee, also undefeated and coming off an undefeated, untied, and unscored-upon season in 1939, was afforded the same skeptical treatment, and Kieran said of them both, "Sending them against some of their rivals was like getting a steamroller to press a pair of pants."[49]

The Georgetown Hoyas were relative newcomers to the top ranks of competition. The school didn't even have a decent practice field for the team, and the players had to work out on a hard clay lot with a single rusty goal post at one end.[50] Unlike Boston College, they had no glittering seasons of past glory to boast. And unlike Boston College, which during its streak generally bowled over its opposition, the Hoyas seemed to specialize in come-from-behind squeakers. Georgetown was riding a 23-game unbeaten streak dating back to 1937, a streak most seriously threatened when it beat Temple in the 1939 opening game, 3-2, on a field goal by Augie Lio. With less than two minutes left in the game Georgetown moved the ball from its own 20-yard line into field goal range, and then Lio entered the contest and calmly kicked the game winner with 34 seconds remaining. Three weeks later Georgetown tied Syracuse, its only blemish, as Lou Ghekas took a reverse around right end for a 73-yard touchdown run in the final minutes of a game played in rain and snow squalls and near-gale force winds. Two weeks after that, Georgetown also cut it close to the margin in beating George Washington on a blocked punt. On October 11, it had relied on two fourth period touchdowns to overcome stiff resistance from an outmanned Waynesburg team. But aside from these games, it had constructed its three-year winning record over the likes of Roanoke, Virginia Tech, and Randolph-Macon, not considered the top competition of the day. Georgetown coach Jack Hagerty predicted his team would win, but added, "I don't believe we fully realize how good Georgetown is. The boys themselves don't know. I don't know because they haven't been extended."[51]

Neither did the oddsmakers know. In Washington the game was rated a tossup, but in Boston the odds favored the Eagles by as much as 2-1.[52] One national columnist, Eddie Breitz, saw Boston College as 5-7 favorites.[53] Another, Harry Grayson, favored Boston College by a touchdown in a game, he said, "I wouldn't miss for anything."[54] There were only opinions, and no hard facts, to go by. Many felt Georgetown was lucky, but others believed that some degree of luck must surely enter any long streak. Mal Stevens, coach of an NYU team soundly beaten by Georgetown, thought the Hoyas could play with anybody. Ray Flaherty, coach of the Washington Redskins, thought they were better than either Penn or Michigan. Some of the Syracuse players, who had lost to both Georgetown and Cornell in 1940, thought Georgetown the better team.[55] As for the Associated Press poll, it had Boston College rated eighth and Georgetown ninth, but that was little more than a collective guess by the voters.

The lack of a clear indication of how good either team was only added to the intrigue. Both the Eagles and the Hoyas had big physical teams, especially in the line, in the aggregate almost exactly equal in size. It would be the only time all year either team faced an opponent it did not significantly outweigh. Manhattan coach Herb Kopf thought the Eagle players were bigger than those of any pro squad.[56] Yet the Hoyas were seen as the more powerful of the two teams. They were thought to be more capable of grinding out yardage with a punishing running attack led by backs Jules Koshlap, who was also an accomplished ambidextrous passer, a powerful fullback in Jim Castiglia, and the speedy Lou Ghekas. Further, the anticipated wet weather and slippery field were seen to favor their straight-ahead style.

But the Eagles had more explosive ability. Monk Maznicki, blocking back Henry Toczylowski, and speedy outside threat Lou Montgomery made a fine backfield foundation to which were added two future College Football Hall of Famers, Charley O'Rourke and Mike Holovak. With the sophomore Holovak's arrival, Montgomery was relegated to a substitute role, but with his speed he was able to provide a valuable change of pace to the offense. Montgomery still saw plenty of playing time. Many would argue that O'Rourke, a slippery, cunning, deadly accurate passer who may also have been the best punter in the country, would be the best, as well as the smallest, player on the field. O'Rourke, like no other player on either team, had the proven capability to break open a tight game. He hailed from nearby Malden, Massachusetts, and at 6 feet tall and 158 pounds, with a skinny frame, he was an easy caricature for the press. One account called him "a scrawny splinter of a lad with a pasty face and a tuft of straw-colored hair."[57] Another called him a "wisp of straw among massive oaks."[58] A third, somewhat overdone, called him "a wisp of a wraith with an arm as accurate as Bill Tell's bow."[59] But Frank Leahy liked to keep O'Rourke's talents hidden, using only the necessary tools to win a game. Against Idaho he threw no passes, against Manhattan only one, and against Centre he played only sparingly. Unfortunately for O'Rourke, his coach's strategy may have reduced his chances for more national recognition.

Mike Holovak had excellent football bloodlines. His older brother Pete had been a standout halfback at Fordham and was currently playing professionally with the Newark Bears. When his father, a Czech immigrant, died while he was still in high school, Holovak got a job as a church sexton to support his family. He caught the eye of Frank Leahy, who recruited him while he was at Seton Hall Prep School and Leahy was still at Fordham, and when Leahy moved to Boston College the two of them went together. As a sophomore, Holovak became the Eagles' starting fullback in 1940. Before graduating from Boston College, Holovak would be a consensus All-America performer.

The Boston College line was, as Herb Kopf pointed out, beefy. Eagle center Chet Gladchuk, who was officially listed at 232 pounds but largely suspected of weighing at least 250,[60] would as usual be the largest man on the field. Gladchuk, end Gene Goodreault, and guard George Kerr, the team captain and the smallest of the group at 180 pounds, in time would all be inducted into the College Football Hall of Fame. Yet the experts still considered Georgetown to have the stronger of the two lines, largely on the merits of its own two future Hall of Famers, Boston native Augie Lio at guard, and at tackle the most remarkable athlete on the field, Al Blozis. On the football field Blozis's nickname was "Big Bertha" for the holes he could open up for the Hoya running attack. But when he performed for the track team, he was "The Human Howitzer."

Born in Garfield, New Jersey, Alfred C. Blozis was the son of a Lithuanian day laborer. One day while a student at Dickinson High in Jersey City, he was nearly hit by a shot putter's errant toss. Angered, he picked up the shot and heaved it back from where it came, and the astounded track coach immediately recruited him as a member of the team. Blozis decided to attend Georgetown over Notre Dame, and although he was a talented if unpolished shot putter at 6' 6" tall and 245 pounds, his favorite sport was football.

By the time Blozis was eligible for varsity track and field competition in the spring of 1940, as a sophomore at Georgetown, effective mentoring by track coach "Hap" Hardell had molded his raw talent and transformed him into the best shot putter in the world. Championships and records came with regularity. On February 17, at the New York Athletic Club Games at Madison Square Garden, he set a new world indoor record with a heave of the 16-pound shot of 53' 8 ¼". The *New York Times* put the world on notice: "He is a comer who cannot miss,"[61] And it was right. At a time when any throw more than 51 feet was considered a notable event, Blozis was consistently throwing in the 52- and 53-foot range, and speculation rose that he was primed for a monumental heave very soon. It happened only a week later, again at Madison Square Garden, in the National AAU Indoor Championships. With the steeplechasers circling the track around him, Blozis let go with his record heave that was met with a deafening roar from the crowd.[62] His throw was 55' 8 ¾", the third longest in track history. Before the year was out, he broke both the IC4A indoor and outdoor mark, and for good measure shattered the IC4A outdoor discus record by nearly 4 feet. On June 22 at the NCAA Championships, he set a new NCAA and American outdoor record, heaving the shot 56' ½", and finished third in the discus. The winner's discus throw was 5 feet shy of Blozis's IC4A record.

So as Al Blozis lined up at tackle for Georgetown against the Boston College Eagles, he did so as the NCAA outdoor shot put champion and the world record holder in the indoor shot put. If the 1940 Olympics had not been canceled, he would have been a near certainty for a gold medal, having surpassed the Olympic records in the shot put by nearly three feet and in the discus by nearly two feet.

As a football player he was nearly as unpolished, and opposing linemen with more finesse and experience found ways to easily offset his prodigious size and strength. He was not a consistent starter for Georgetown, even in his junior year, but as with his shot putting efforts, he was a fast learner. Wellington Mara, owner of the New York Giants, for whom Blozis would play after graduation, recalled that his coach Steve Owen said of him, "He'll be the best tackle who ever put on a pair of shoes." His linemate with the Giants, legendary center Mel Hein, agreed: "He could have been the greatest tackle who ever played football."[63]

Blozis was not through with his track and field accomplishments. In the spring of 1941 he continued to break his world indoor records with regularity, and finished the season with a new IC4A outdoor record and a defense of his discus title. At the end of the year, Al Blozis, who despite his accomplishments never became a household name, was selected by the United Press as one of the three greatest athletes of 1941. The other two were Ben Hogan and Joe Louis.[64]

In the spring of his senior year he started all over again. A toss of 57' ¾" at the National AAU Championships on February 28, 1942, set yet another new indoor world record and came within a quarter of an inch of the greatest outdoor throw ever. The next week, his throw of 57' 9 ½" in practice, though it didn't count for the record, was at the time the greatest ever made, indoor or outdoor. He finished out his collegiate career with a defense of his IC4A outdoor shot put title, in which he set a new meet record, and discus title, and then won his third consecutive NCAA shot put championship and third consecutive National AAU shot put championship.

****

When the two evenly matched teams squared off at Fenway Park, it was a cold, soggy, overcast day, the same type of weather most of the country had been experiencing for weeks. The Eagles' practices during the week had been moved indoors to the Boston Latin School gymnasium after the rain had turned their practice field into a sodden mess,[65] but when the tarpaulin was taken off the Fenway Park field, it was in good shape. The game was played in a steady cold mist.

Sometimes when teams engage in a highly anticipated game they don't live up to the advance publicity, and sometimes they play a game to be remembered for ages. Allison Danzig called the game, "the nearest thing to an epic that Eastern football has provided in many years."[66] Jack Munhall of the *Washington Post* called it "a football epic to rank with the most exciting ever played."[67] Bob Considine, at year's end, declared it the best game he had seen all season and added, "And there are few college teams in history that either team could not have licked that day."[68] Grantland Rice, who liked superlatives, simply called it the greatest game of football ever played.[69]

It was a game of ebb and flow, as most great games are, and the first quarter broke decidedly Georgetown's way. Augie Lio set the tone for the Hoyas by booting the opening kickoff into the end zone. The Eagles' first attempt to move the ball was hindered by a holding call, forcing a punt from their own goal line, and Lou Ghekas returned it for Georgetown to the Eagle 33-yard line. After the Hoyas mustered nine yards on three plays, Lio kicked a field goal from the 32-yard line, and Georgetown had the first lead, 3-0. But when the Eagles got the ball back with poor field position, they decided on a quick kick. O'Rourke's punt was blocked by a tandem of Lio and Earl Fullilove, rolling out of bounds at the ten yard line. From there it was a matter of a few plays before Jules Koshlap rushed into the end zone for a Georgetown touchdown, and when Lio kicked the extra point, the Hoyas had a 10-0 lead before the game was five minutes old.

The home crowd was hushed. The five-minute span was the first time all year the Eagle line had been outhit and outplayed, on offense and defense, and the first time the Eagles had trailed all year. That the Hoyas' lead had been built with such ease left the Eagle fans with their collective countenance as dark as the leaden sky. The muscle of Blozis and the finesse and experience of Lio on the line were tilting the contest toward the Hoyas.

But then the tide turned. The Eagles took the ball from their own 25 to the Georgetown 22-yard line on six plays, largely on the passing of Charley O'Rourke to Henry Toczylowski, and then it was time to use a play that Leahy had kept tightly under wraps until that moment. Leahy had been fanatic all year about keeping his team's talents and tricks out of the eye of opposing scouts, a tactic made possible by an easy schedule. But now it was time for the great unveiling. O'Rourke lateraled to Lou Montgomery who rolled to his right, and while in the grasp of Augie Lio, crossed up the defense by passing the ball downfield. It grazed the fingertips of Hoya defender Allen Matuza before falling into the arms of Henry Woronicz at the three-yard line, and Woronicz walked in for the first Eagle touchdown. When the extra point was missed, Georgetown's lead had been cut to 10-6 at the end of the first period.

Then the skinny O'Rourke took over. After two exchanges of punts, he found his Eagles in a familiar place—backed up to their own 10-yard line. But this time the Eagle offense chose an aggressive attack. First O'Rourke twisted free off right tackle for a beautiful 30-yard run, then completed a pass to Monk Maznicki for thirty more, taking the ball to the Georgetown 28-yard line. Shirley Povich of the *Washington Post* thought O'Rourke was perhaps the best passer in college football and wrote of him, "Rushing the passer was no defense against O'Rourke today. He calmly sidestepped and turned the ball loose almost at leisure."[70] O'Rourke followed this with a pass to Gene Goodreault at the 17, on a play on which the All-American end was injured and had to leave the game, and a run for a first down at the six. When the Hoya defense stiffened, O'Rourke and the Eagles found themselves at a critical point, fourth and goal at the Georgetown 9-yard line. This is where, according to many observers, the defining break of the game took place. On a hot streak, with everything seemingly going his way, O'Rourke tried to hit Maznicki with a pass at the goal line. Maznicki and a defender went up for the ball (the *New York Times* said it was Jack Doolan; the *Washington Post* claimed it was Bill McLaughlin), neither caught it, and the ball fell to the ground. But an official some 35 yards behind the play called pass interference on the Hoya defender—Povich later termed the call "abysmal"[71] — giving Boston College the ball on the one yard line. From there Holovak scored the touchdown, Maznicki kicked the extra point, (on his second try, awarded on a Georgetown offside), and Boston College led 13-10 at halftime.

As the third quarter began, Georgetown recaptured momentum when Al Blozis's crushing tackle on the burly Mike Holovak caused him to fumble. Blozis recovered, then he and Lio led with power blocking for Jim Castiglia and Jules Koshlap, as the Hoyas moved the ball 65 yards down the field. Then, abandoning power for finesse, Georgetown broke out its own secret play, scoring on a fancy triple reverse from the six-yard line. The extra point was blocked by Maznicki, and Georgetown led again 16-13.

Once again Boston College fought back, once more behind the efforts of O'Rourke. His running and passing "galvanize[d] the depressed stands into a roaring cauldron of unalloyed joy," wrote Danzig.[72] All game long he "passed like a Baugh and ran like a will-o'-the-wisp," said the Associated Press.[73] He passed 18 yards to Toczylowski—Jack Munhall of the *Washington Post* said he was "pegging the leather like a baseball"[74]— and then connected with Maznicki at the ten-yard line. Maznicki carried the ball into the end zone to complete a 43-yard touchdown play, the longest of the day. When the extra point was again missed, the Eagles led 19-16.

Again the momentum shifted, and as the fourth quarter drew near its close, darkness descended on Fenway Park. It was past dusk, the thick wintry clouds weakening the last frail beams of daylight, and it was almost too dark to read the game clock. The more the fans craned their necks to catch every detail of the riveting action on the field, the more they were exposed to assault by the wintry chill and the cold wet mist. Few cared.

Georgetown marched the ball to the Boston College 31-yard line, threatening one last assault on the goal line. At this point, Jack Hagerty made an important strategic decision. He took his stalwart guard Augie Lio, who so emphatically had carried the battle in the early going, out of the game. Two Boston College linemen, George Kerr and Ed Zabilski, as well as Holovak and O'Rourke in the backfield, had played the entire contest, offensively and defensively, in a game where the tackling had been ferocious since the start.

164

Hagerty hoped that fresh blood would make a difference against his exhausted foe. But he had another angle as well. By taking Lio, his best tackle as well as his kicker, out of the game he was sending an unmistakable message to his own team that, trailing by three points, there would be no field goal. Georgetown was going for a touchdown and a win. On the other sideline, Leahy was inclined to risk leaving his exhausted players in rather than put the team's fate in the hands of substitutes. He had ordered O'Rourke to fair catch as many punts as he could during the game, hoping to spare him at least some brutal contact, and he hoped his star had something left for the finish.[75] Like a baseball pitcher taken out in the ninth inning, Lio could only sit on the bench and watch. Confidently the Hoyas pushed the ball closer, reaching the 18-yard line. Three times the Hoyas tried to score by pass, three times their fans peered into the fading light, discerning as much from the cheers from the other side as from what little their eyes could make out in the almost absent light. Jules Koshlap, badly injured in the third period but refusing to leave the game, was described by Shirley Povich as pain-wracked and dog-tired.[76] He tried valiantly to find an open receiver, but could not. Boston College took over on downs, needing only to run out the clock to preserve a sensational victory.

But it was not to be. An aroused Georgetown defense stifled the Eagles, who ran three plays and lost nine yards. They would have to punt from their own end zone. Leahy sent Chet Gladchuk back into the game for the express purpose of assuring a good snap from center, and O'Rourke stepped back into his end zone, from where he had earlier had one punt blocked. Any mistake, any false move would spell disaster. The Hoya fans screamed urgently for one more stout effort as both sides lined up for the play that would, in all probability, settle the game. There was about a minute and five seconds left to play. Gladchuk snapped the ball to O'Rourke.

But O'Rourke did not punt it. At first he just held the ball. The Georgetown defense, perhaps confused by this ploy, seemed not to rush but to hesitate.[77] Then as the Hoyas snapped back to life he began to run back and forth in the end zone, burning up time on the clock. The more desperate the Hoyas became in their pursuit, the more elusive and slippery O'Rourke became, dodging and side-stepping the defenders in a desperate game of keep-away. He was "like a penned-up fox, and just as smart," said the Associated Press.[78] Finally, his purpose achieved, he allowed himself to be tackled in the end zone. Rather than risk a blocked kick, O'Rourke had taken a deliberate safety, giving Georgetown two points, when they needed three to tie, and possession of the ball by free kick. Just as importantly, O'Rourke's caper had taken about thirty-five seconds off the clock. The score was now Boston College 19, Georgetown 18, with 30 seconds to go.

Georgetown fielded the free kick and got the ball back near midfield with perhaps 15 seconds to go, ran two plays in near total darkness, and could not score. The last play was a desperation pass that fell incomplete. For the fans, the most reliable sense was sound, so dark was the field. Most detected the outcome by the joyous shriek from among their fellows below them in the stands, as the last futile pass fell incomplete to the Fenway turf. O'Rourke was carried from the field on the shoulders of the joyous Eagle supporters.

Skeptics might wonder whether, on the key play, Gladchuk's role was merely to snap the ball. Some might suspect he also carried the play in from the sideline to O'Rourke. Years later, Holovak recalled the event. "I still don't know to this day if Leahy had sent in the play or if Charley just did it....Charley was the guy who, in a tough situation when you needed a play, came through so often."[79] But nobody ever questioned the incident, and there is no evidence of anything other than that O'Rourke called his own play.

Opinions of the game were nearly unanimous. It was "one of the few ballyhooed engagements that lived up to advance notices," wrote Harry Grayson.[80] O'Rourke had been the best player on the field and had offered an outstanding performance in victory, and Maznicki had been nearly as good. Koshlap and Lio had been superb in defeat. Each team had advanced its status, erasing any doubts about its toughness or prowess. The game had turned on the pass interference penalty, a bizarre twist of fate that could have gone either way. "There was just about as much difference between the two teams as between two new dimes," said the Associated Press.[81] And the coaching had been superb. Whereas in most high-stakes games the usual strategies had heretofore been to become more conservative, both Georgetown and Boston College had taken risk after risk, time and again pushing their opponent's back to the wall. It had been an epic football game, and the only differences of opinion were of degree.

But as the cold and weary fans filed out of Fenway Park, they could not have known it, but a hundred miles to the north a contest of even longer lasting importance was being played out.

CHAPTER 14
HONOR ON THE LINE

It is not what a lawyer tells me I may do, but what
humanity, reason, and justice tell me I ought to do

--EDMUND BURKE, *TheThirteen Resolutions*

"Gentlemen, next year there is only one game on the schedule. Cornell."[1]
With that single-minded statement at the end of the 1939 season, Earl "Red"
Blaik, Dartmouth football coach, set the priority for his team's 1940 campaign.
His feelings toward Cornell, voiced with Ahab-like intensity, came with, what
were to him, good reasons. And before the game was played, the reasons
would only multiply.

On Thursday, leading up to that weekend, Cornell President Edmund
Ezra Day, a Dartmouth graduate of the Class of 1905 and son-in-law of Dean
Charles F. Emerson of Dartmouth, was scheduled to be the principal speaker
at Dartmouth Day, a traditional fall assembly of Dartmouth students. Day
had a PhD in economics from Harvard, where he had also been chair of the
economics department, and he had served as first dean of the University
of Michigan School of Business Administration. After several years with
the Rockefeller Foundation, he had become President of Cornell University
in 1937. One of the key speakers at his inauguration ceremony had been
President Ernest Martin Hopkins of Dartmouth.[2] Day arrived in Hanover two
days before the football team to deliver his address.

Originally the Cornell-Dartmouth game had been scheduled to be played
in Ithaca, based on the home-and-home agreement between the two teams,
but at Cornell's request, in order to fit Yale back on its schedule, the venue for
this game had been switched to Hanover.

Cornell and Dartmouth first played football against one another in 1900,
and had played annually since 1919, a total of 23 games in all. Cornell had
won ten, Dartmouth twelve, and there had been one tie. One of Dartmouth's
biggest wins, 53-7, and biggest losses, 59-7, had been in games with Cornell.

In 1934, Earl Blaik arrived as Dartmouth's new football coach, and the
Indians' fortunes immediately began to improve. Blaik had played three years
of football at Miami of Ohio, and in his senior year the team went undefeated.

He graduated in 1917, then enrolled at West Point, where he graduated in 1920. He was named to Walter Camp's All-America team in 1919 and was awarded the coveted Army Athletic Association saber as the outstanding athlete in his graduating class. He began his coaching career as an assistant at Wisconsin in 1926 and returned to West Point as backfield coach from 1927 to 1934, before taking the head coaching job at Dartmouth.

In his first three years, Blaik built a 21-6-1 record, and Dartmouth claimed a spot among the Eastern football powers, just behind Pitt and Fordham. In the fall of 1937, when the Indians were deemed too young and inexperienced to continue their dominant play, they surprised the experts by going undefeated. Their record included two ties, 9-9 against Yale, led by the Heisman Trophy winner Clint Frank, and then 6-6 against Cornell. The Associated Press ranked Dartmouth seventh in the nation at year's end.

In the past the fortunes of the two teams had waxed and waned through normal cycles, but by 1938, the friendly rivalry began to take on a new dimension. Both teams were poised to lay claim to top honors in the East. By the sixth week of the season, Cornell was in top form and had been bested only by the heroics of Syracuse's Wilmeth Sidat-Singh three weeks before. The strength of the team was its line, led by All-American end Brud Holland and captain Al Van Ranst at center. But Dartmouth came to Ithaca in even sharper form, on a 22-game undefeated streak and ranked fourth in the nation. Its powerful running game, led by the crushing Bob MacLeod and the swift Joe Cottone, had met little resistance as the Indians plowed through their schedule. The game, said Allison Danzig, was a natural, and though more than 30,000 fans were expected to see the game in Ithaca, he maintained it could have drawn 80,000 had it been played in New York City.[3] Oddsmakers had installed Dartmouth as a solid favorite.

But Cornell dominated the game. Hal McCullough ran for one touchdown and passed for another as the Big Red built a 14-0 lead. By the end of the third quarter, Cornell had made 14 first downs to Dartmouth's one. Only a long touchdown pass by Cottone to Ed Wakefield kept Dartmouth in the game, 14-7. In the fourth quarter, Dartmouth staged a comeback with a series of furious thrusts into Big Red territory, only to have each turned away. Suddenly the jubilant Cornell team was being lauded as the equal of any in the country. Dartmouth's winning streak was broken, its dreams of an undefeated season shattered. "Their line simply dominated us," explained Blaik.[4] The better his team, it seemed to Blaik, the more Cornell frustrated its advance to national glory. The following week, the dispirited Indians would lose as well, to Stanford.

The next year, 1939, Cornell dispatched Dartmouth with ease, 35-6, before the largest crowd ever to see a game at Memorial Field. Cornell presented a vastly superior team, with more speed in both the backfield and the line, and Carl Snavely's polished passing attack was far more than the modestly talented Dartmouth team could fend off. Throughout his career, Blaik had built a reputation as an innovator and an excellent tactical thinker, surrounding himself with people of similar skills. He and his line coach Harry Ellinger tried a variety of line shifts and other schemes to foil the Cornell blockers, but nothing worked. When Dartmouth lined up to stop the run, Cornell simply passed over them or ran reverses around them. Blaik was duly impressed by Cornell's intricate and precise line play: "It was beautiful to see, even if it gave me a sinking feeling,"[5] he said.

By the 1940 rematch, with Cornell only a year more experienced, there was every reason to believe the Indians were in for more of the same. Indeed, the game on the surface looked like a mismatch. Undefeated Cornell was at least a 4-to-1 favorite and had surrendered only two touchdowns all year. Dartmouth, on the other hand, was in the midst of a mediocre season in which it had lost even to weak Yale, for the first time in six years, although it did manage to beat St. Lawrence, Harvard, and Sewanee. "Apparently this is one of the weakest Dartmouth teams in some time," lamented Robert F. Kelley in the *New York Times*.[6] "It's Dartmouth's turn to be run over by the Cornell steamroller," wrote Harry Grayson.[7] But the Indians had shown moments of brilliance and had played well in defeat the week before against Princeton, when their running backs had gained 320 yards rushing. That performance raised hopes for an upset. Only two weeks before, John Kieran of the *New York Times* had written that beating Cornell "looks to be a bigger job than either Yale or Dartmouth can handle."[8] But on November 11, after the Princeton game, having had a change of heart, he thought the "...Hanoverians will have a real chance to haul Cornell out of the unbeaten ranks."[9] The Dartmouth seniors, and Blaik, had a motive of revenge. It had been only two years since the roles had been reversed, with their winning streak on the line. If the script in this rivalry called for long winning streaks by highly-ranked teams to be snapped, they were more than willing to play their part.

By game time, Earl Blaik had other incentives motivating him. Never in his life, as a player or a coach, had he experienced a losing season. Every team he had been associated with, at Miami, Wisconsin, Army, and Dartmouth, had been winners. A loss to the heavily favored Big Red would guarantee five losses in a nine-game schedule. The prospects for Blaik, a proud man, were almost too much to bear. And in his 1939 loss to Cornell, Blaik perceived a degree of celebration by the Big Red players that he thought was excessive. Few others took note of the incident, but to him it sparked emotions that bordered on a grudge. Then, earlier in the season, Cornell had laid upon Army, his beloved alma mater, the worst defeat in its long and proud football history. To Blaik, revenge became an imperative.

The Dartmouth team, under Blaik's determined guidance, practiced hard all week in forbidding weather. The rain and mud in Hanover presented an obstacle so daunting the team finally had to move its practice inside, where it paid special attention to the things it could expect from the Cornell offensive juggernaut. Cornell had statistically the most powerful offense in the nation, averaging over 400 yards per game, well ahead of its nearest competitor, Texas Tech, and was the only one of the leading teams in the country to have accumulated more yards passing than rushing.

Blaik did not have it in his nature to give up, concede, or stop devising new plans of attack, no matter how daunting the challenge seemed. His determination to beat Cornell was unbounded. Always learning, even in defeat, he was never without another idea and the nerve to try it. For this game he devised a special defensive scheme in which the tackles and guards set up a yard and a half back from the line of scrimmage, even with the linebackers, and did not commit until the ball was snapped. Halfback Ed Kast described it this way. "We lined up a yard off the line of scrimmage, and we would slant or loop at a predetermined time. We went with the flow of the play...."[10] Blaik borrowed elements of this plan from the approach Franklin and Marshall had used in defeating Dartmouth earlier in the year.[11] He was hoping this tactic would confuse the Cornell linemen just enough to throw off their blocking schemes. The Cornell player Blaik was most worried about was Mort Landsberg because of his speed, and he assigned one linebacker, Bob Crego, to shadow him throughout the game.

"Blaik was a hard guy to play for. He was demanding, but I have to say he was a fair coach all the way," said Dartmouth team captain Lou Young years later.[12] Young was, from an early age, well familiar with the feel of championships. His father had been head coach of the 1924 Penn team, whose locker room was one of Lou's favorite playgrounds, when the Quakers shared the national championship with Notre Dame and the Four Horsemen.

In Ithaca, the Big Red team held one last spirited scrimmage in the rain, then had its Thursday night dinner at Willard Straight Hall, the student union. The team followed the same itinerary and routine as it had the year before. They took a bus to the East Ithaca train station, where they boarded the 8:30 train to Greenfield, Vermont, planning to work out Friday at Deerfield Academy and to spend Friday night in Newport, New Hampshire.

The Dartmouth players spent the night before the game, as was their custom, at the Bonnie Oaks Inn in Fairlee, Vermont, where Blaik preferred quiet relaxation for his men.[13] The student manager of the Dartmouth team was a sophomore named Charles S. Feeney. Years later, reflecting on the day, Chub Feeney, by then a successful baseball executive with the New York and San Francisco Giants and president of the National League, recalled, "We expected to get murdered." On the Cornell bench, the feelings were equally clear. "We expected a cakewalk," said Big Red halfback Bill Murphy.[14]

When the Cornell team arrived in Hanover the weather was, as expected, abominable. It had been raining and snowing steadily for four days, although by Saturday morning it had begun to taper off. Still, a light snow continued to fall through the pregame warm-ups. The field had been covered with a tarpaulin and appeared at first to be in reasonably good shape, but before long it would turn into a slippery muddy mess.

What followed was one of the most remarkable games in the history of college football. It was not an aesthetic game, to be sure, and for most of the contest it was not particularly exciting. But its outcome is still debated to this day, with awe and admiration. It routinely makes experts' top-ten lists of great moments in sports, and as only a few such moments can do, it profoundly changed the lives of those who were involved in it, as well as those who would be inspired by it over the years.

Although 15,000 fans were originally anticipated, only about 8000 fans showed up at Memorial Field, the weather was so forbidding. The western side of the field was lined with concrete stands, which were nearly full, but the other side, which had wooden stands, was filled only in the middle. Among the fans at the game was a large contingent of Cornell alumni who had chartered a series of special trains to carry them from Boston, where they had been attending a meeting of the newly organized Cornell Alumni Association.[15]

The referee for the game was W.H. "Red" Friesell, Jr, a man with 22 years of experience and no stranger to controversy. Standing just over five feet tall with flaming red hair and weighing less than 140 pounds, the 45-year-old Princeton graduate had been an outstanding athlete in his youth. While playing football for his prep school, Shady Side Academy in Pittsburgh, he had made a spectacular tackle of an opponent named Dave Herron and suffered a broken neck in the process, remaining unconscious for two weeks. In time Friesell recovered, and though his football career was at an end, he became captain of the Princeton swimming team and won the intercollegiate diving championship in 1915 and 1916.[16] Dave Herron also went on to excel in a different sport, winning the U.S. Amateur Golf Championship in 1919 by beating the legendary Bobby Jones in the final at Oakmont, 5 and 4.

Friesell cut a comical figure on the field as he scurried about among the bigger and taller players, his towel hanging low out of his back pocket. But he understood what every lion tamer understood. To be in charge, you have to act as if you are in charge. *Time* said of him, "Born with a flair for showmanship as conspicuous as his red hair, he chases a football like a beagle after a rabbit."[17] He had refereed the Ohio State-Cornell game three weeks earlier and had forcefully dealt with Francis Schmidt's accusations against Carl Snavely. He had been the referee as well in the controversial Harvard-Penn game the week before. The degree of respect afforded him can be measured by his refereeing assignments over the years: Yale-Harvard, Dartmouth-Harvard, Columbia-Stanford, Army-Notre Dame, Army-Navy. He worked all the big games.

As game time approached, it began to snow harder. Cornell won the coin toss and elected to kick off. Ray Wolfe of Dartmouth took Jim Schmuck's kick at the ten-yard line, and while the field was still firm, almost ran the opening kickoff back for a touchdown. He was caught from behind by the last Cornell defender only after he had crossed midfield. Then the slogging began. Throughout the first half both teams were mired in the increasingly slippery field. By all accounts, Dartmouth had far the better of it. The combination of the mud, the play of an inspired underdog, and Blaik's unique defense kept the Big Red at bay. With its passing game at a disadvantage in the mud, Cornell failed to reach midfield at any time in the first half. Dartmouth was able to penetrate Cornell territory three times, once getting to the Cornell 26 before Bob Krieger missed a field goal, and once to the six-yard line on runs by the diminutive Joe Arico. The game was scoreless at halftime. William D. Richardson, writing for the *New York Times*, commented that in the first half, "...the Indians had outplayed Cornell as completely as any team ever had been outplayed."[18] Cornell's vaunted passing attack was sputtering in the snow and mud, while Dartmouth had yet to throw a pass. The Big Red had lost five men to injury in the first quarter, including the entire left side of the line,[19] but it was expected that at halftime they would make the necessary adjustments to get the team back in the game.

On cue, in the third quarter, Cornell mounted a drive to the Dartmouth 17-yard line before Bill Murphy's pass was intercepted in the end zone by Wolfe. The scoreless game of field position continued until, early in the fourth period, Hal McCullough of Cornell had to punt from his own end zone and Arico, who seemed to be one of the few men on the field who could handle the mud, returned it to the Cornell 26. Dartmouth worked the ball down to the eight-yard line before the Big Red defense stiffened and Bob Krieger kicked a field goal that put Dartmouth ahead, 3-0. And the clock continued to wind down.

With about two and a half minutes remaining in the game, Cornell had time to mount one last desperation drive. Again it was Walt Scholl, coming off the bench, who brought the spark of life to the frustrated Cornell offense. Ray Hall punted the ball away for Dartmouth, and the speedy Mort Landsberg fielded it at his own 35-yard line, returning it six yards before he was tackled. Lou Bufalino ran for no gain, then Scholl passed for a first down at the Dartmouth 46-yard line. After an incomplete pass to Ray Jenkins, Scholl completed another pass to Jim Schmuck at the 31 for another first down. In the nick of time, Scholl finally had the team moving as it had been unable to move all day. After Landsberg's run gained two more yards, Cornell tried a different wrinkle with Bufalino passing to Scholl, who was interfered with at the 18. The pass interference by the Dartmouth player probably saved a touchdown. At that point Snavely made a substitution, taking Bufalino out of the game and replacing him with the starter Bill Murphy. The sweeping hands on the big clock at the end of the stadium inched toward zero, racing the Big Red as they marched closer and closer to the goal line. Murphy ran for two yards, then caught another Scholl pass to get the ball to the six-yard line for a first down and goal to go. The crowd, wet and cold but thrilled, suddenly had an epic struggle to observe. Foregoing their protective bundlings, the fans were now poised on the edge of their seats. The game turned out to be, claimed Richardson, "...one of the most thrilling gridiron encounters that has ever been waged."[20]

Then began the much-studied final series of plays. Dartmouth dug in for the goal line stand that would define the season for both teams; with nothing to lose, it was determined to exact its revenge. And Cornell, with everything to lose, was equally determined to keep its unbeaten streak and national championship hopes alive. There were 45 seconds left on the clock. Blaik sent two fresh ends into the game to stiffen his defense. Landsberg ran for three yards, Scholl for one, and then Landsberg dove forward for what many thought was a touchdown. Lou Conti, the Cornell guard, later said that at the end of the play, he was lying in the end zone and Landsberg was lying on top of him. But Friesell, disagreeing, spotted the ball on the one-yard line with but a few precious seconds remaining. Snavely made an attempt to substitute end Alva Kelley into the game, but Cornell had no further time outs. Cornell was penalized five yards for delay of game, and Friesell marched the ball back to the six. The prevailing opinion in the press box was that Snavely had purposely taken a five-yard penalty to stop the clock, a commonly used ploy.[21] But a touchdown from this spot would be immensely more difficult.

At this point it must have occurred to Walt Matuszczak, however briefly, that a field goal would tie the game and keep alive Cornell's unbeaten streak. It would also spell the end to any reasonable hopes for a national championship. And he surely remembered that only the week before, on just such a field, Tom Harmon had slipped in the mud and missed a point-blank extra point that cost Michigan the game against Minnesota. Perhaps he also recalled Army's missed field goal against Notre Dame from even closer range. "After the timeout, we went into our huddle, and I said we're going for a win and not a tie. Everyone agreed," he recalled.[22] Cornell was going for the touchdown, do or die, fourth and goal from the six-yard line. There were ten seconds left to play.

Once again, as it had two years before when the roles had been reversed, the game would go down to the last play. That day, the Indians' Joe Cottone had been swamped by the Big Red defense as he attempted one last desperation pass. In the huddle, Matuszczak called a play he hoped would have a different outcome.

The snap went directly to Scholl, who took the ball and rolled out to his right. A Dartmouth defender was immediately on him, pressuring him to throw the ball before he was ready. Off balance, on the run, his timing interrupted, falling backward and off his feet with a defender in his face, he let it go. It was as much a desperation fling as a pass, and the ball never got to the intended receiver in the end zone. A Dartmouth defender, who was stationed on the goal line and shadowing Scholl's moves, sliding to his left as Scholl rolled right, had a chance to intercept the ball, but ended up knocking it to the ground in the end zone.

The Dartmouth fans were ecstatic, and the sidelines erupted in jubilation. Their shrieks of joy pierced the raw November air while, in the Cornell contingent, hearts sank. The dream, it appeared, had died. The clock showed three seconds left to play. Earl Blaik, pacing the sidelines in a stylish black overcoat, black fedora, and white scarf to ward off the raw chill, had, it appeared, pulled off the upset of the year and appeared to have his retribution. Whatever feelings of satisfaction he may have been harboring were well masked behind a practiced stoic exterior.

Under the rules of the day, an incomplete pass on fourth down in the end zone was a touchback, and the defending team was awarded possession on its twenty-yard line. Friesell put the ball under his arm and started marching purposefully to the twenty when suddenly he stopped and conferred with head linesman Joe McKenney, the same official who was unable to stop the clock in the 1939 Michigan-Penn game. Then he turned, went back to the six-yard line and placed the ball down, emphatically announcing that it was Cornell's ball on fourth down. Friesell appeared to have changed his mind about the down and the ball placement, but he declined to explain why. Again the Dartmouth sideline erupted, but this time it was not in jubilation but in confusion and outrage. "On the sideline, we were certain it was fourth down," recounted Dartmouth end John Kelley.[23] Dartmouth captain Lou Young, Cornell captain Walt Matuszczak, and Friesell engaged in a heated discussion on the field. Young contended that Cornell had run its four downs and demanded that the ball be handed over to Dartmouth. But Matuszczak countered that there had been offsetting offside penalties called on the last play, and that fourth down had to be replayed. If so, whatever outward indication there might have been of a penalty, if any, had certainly not been made evident to all participants. Later, Lou Young related his recollection. "I knew Cornell used four downs and it was our ball. Our entire team knew it. I asked Red what was going on, and he just said Cornell had another down."[24] Other Dartmouth players on the field seemed less sure. "We didn't know they were getting an extra down," said Dartmouth end Joe Crowley.[25] For the second week in a row, it appeared, Friesell's crew was embroiled in a dispute over a mysterious offside call. Signaling such a penalty is the responsibility of the linesman, but as with his counterpart in the Harvard-Penn game the week before, Joe McKenney, a football man experienced as a player, coach, and referee, had only his whistle and vocal chords—and no flag—to signal his action.

Perhaps as confused as the players, but knowing from long experience that decisiveness in such cases is a virtue, Friesell shoved the persistent Young in the face[26] and ordered him to go back to his huddle. Young, for fear of being penalized, did so. The football rulebook stated, "Field captains only may appeal to the referee and then solely on questions of interpretation of the rules. They are not allowed to question the jurisdiction of any official or to argue questions of fact." Friesell might not have been clear about the reason for his decision, but he was emphatic about what it was. It was Cornell's ball and it was fourth down on the six-yard line. There was time for one more play.

The teams lined up again. Again the ball was snapped directly back to Scholl, and again he rolled to his right. This time he had a split second longer to throw and lofted the ball into the corner of the end zone where Bill Murphy caught it on his fingertips just before stepping out of bounds. Friesell's hands shot up, signaling a touchdown. The scoreboard clock showed no time remaining. It was Cornell's turn for jubilation while the Dartmouth sideline stood in stunned disbelief. Nick Drahos kicked the extra point and the game was over. Cornell had won an unexpectedly close contest, 7-3. Whatever confusion there might have been on the field had been resolved by the referee.

But reporters in the press box were perplexed. They referred to their notes and all concluded that Cornell had run five plays. There seemed to be only two possibilities. Either offsetting offside penalties had indeed been called—that plausibly could have been the subject of the brief discussion between Friesell and McKenney—or the officials had simply lost count of the downs. For a brief time a third possibility was discussed, that a penalty had been called against Cornell on third down for offside or illegal motion, thus nullifying that down, and that the 5-yard penalty had been imposed for that infraction and not delay of game on the Kelley substitution. But the Dartmouth captain did not appear to have been given the opportunity to accept or decline such a penalty, and so the detectives in the press corps quickly dismissed that possibility.[27]

The Dartmouth locker room was pandemonium. Chub Feeney offered the following simple account: "Players were yelling and screaming. Nobody knew what the hell had happened."[28] Dartmouth athletic director William H. McCarter said that Friesell had told him there had been only four legal downs, and he thus offered congratulations to his counterpart Jim Lynah on the Cornell victory.[29] According to a Cornell official, later in the evening McCarter commented that Dartmouth's play charts were confused and that he felt the correct score was 7-3 in favor of Cornell.[30]

In his autobiography, *The Red Blaik Story*, Blaik maintained that, after the game, he and Dartmouth President Ernest Martin Hopkins gave Friesell a ride to the train station in White River Junction. During the trip, Blaik said, Friesell admitted to the two that he might have made an error.[31] To all others, Friesell remained mum.

The threads of recollections of the events of that evening are left to be woven into a fabric of a plausible account. All three men who Blaik maintains were in the car were men of impeccable integrity. It appears implausible that they would subject themselves to the appearance of impropriety by having such a discussion without a representative of Cornell present. Further, it is known that Day was Hopkins's guest at the game and that immediately after the game he was not with the rest of the Cornell party, leaving open the question of his whereabouts. It is not plausible that Hopkins would have abandoned his guest and excluded him from a discussion on the game's outcome. Although Blaik makes no mention of it, it is more plausible that Day, too, was in the car on the trip and heard Friesell's comment.

Meanwhile, on the Dartmouth campus, fans and students wildly celebrated what was at the least a great moral victory. Players were hailed as victorious heroes. Indeed, the belief in the Dartmouth camp was that the Indians had won more than a moral victory and had defeated the mighty Big Red, within the framework of the properly applied rules. Upon returning from the train station, Blaik assured the assembled crowd that he had every faith in Friesell, that he was a great referee, and that Dartmouth would abide by the decision of the Eastern Intercollegiate Football Association in the matter, to whom an appeal would be filed. But Blaik was quick to remind the fans that the scoreboard read Cornell 7, Dartmouth 3. Any reversal by appeal would be an action never before taken in the history of college football.

There was as much confusion in the Cornell locker room as anywhere else. Many of the players were unaware of the issue. "I can honestly say that I don't remember anybody saying anything at that time," said Lou Conti about a fifth down. Bud Finneran agreed. "I know that there was a big argument going on about it between our captains and the referees. But you're told to stay out of it. If you weren't the captains, you didn't go over and get into anything. The officials wouldn't allow that anyway. I was not aware, to tell you the truth, that we had five downs at that time," he said.[32]

Matuszczak's later recollections square with them. "When Murphy caught the ball in the end zone we thought we won," he said. "Later, on a train going home, a reporter was checking his charts and mentioned he thought we had five downs. I don't remember his name, but to the best of my knowledge all our guys thought we scored on a fourth-down play."[33] Matuszczak's later recollections made no mention of any offside penalties, regarding which other earlier accounts said he had vociferously argued.

Others in the Cornell camp were aware that an issue had arisen but were confident that Friesell had dealt with the matter on the field satisfactorily. They were confident that offside penalties had been called on the first Scholl pass, that in the heat of the moment the signal had simply been overlooked, and that their victory had been earned by legitimate means.[34] Snavely in particular was insistent that both teams had been called offside on the first fourth-down play, thus nullifying the play, and several members of the press corps were in agreement with him.[35] It was the belief of some of the Cornell players that McKenney had advised Friesell in their short discussion that it was fourth down coming up.[36] This position bolstered the view that McKenney had called an offside penalty.

However, the opposite view would be expressed by some in the days ahead, that is, that Friesell had ignored the advice of McKenney that it was *not* fourth down. In his autobiography, Blaik maintained that two different referees advised Friesell that there had been no offside penalty called.[37] In determining what actually had happened on the field, it is important to establish whether Friesell and McKenney agreed or disagreed about the down count. Years later, McKenney expressed no doubt about the down. He said that he kept track of downs by slipping a rubber band over a finger after each down, and he had four fingers inside the band at the critical moment.[38] If true, then it appears that Friesell had overruled McKenney on the field. Friesell never spoke about that detail of the event, so we will never know exactly what transpired.

Outside of the Cornell locker room, the discussion was more focused. There seemed to have been no serious dispute at the time that five plays had been run. Louis Boochever, Cornell's Director of Public Information, admitting that the ball had been snapped five times, said, "My recollection is that a penalty was called for both teams being offside on the play before we completed the winning pass. In the excitement I may have been wrong."[39]

A note of caution must be sounded about accounts and recollections of this game, or any game. In the heat of the moment it is sometimes difficult for observers to be specific and accurate about what they see. As any courtroom observer knows, accounts of events can vary widely from witness to witness, even when all are under oath and trying earnestly to relate the truth.

There was one particular key play, the pass interference play that set up Cornell's last series, that emphasizes the point. The account of the play in the *Cornell Alumni News* relates that the play was a pass from Scholl to Bufalino.[40] The *New York Times* describes it as a pass from Bufalino to Scholl, on which interference was called on Ed Kast.[41] Earl Blaik, in his memoirs, claims the intended receiver was Mort Landsberg, and the penalty was called on Bob Crego.[42] Additionally, as to Scholl's first fourth-down pass into the end zone, credit for knocking down the pass is variably given to Ray Wolfe, Ray Hall, and Don Norton. In each case at least two of the accounts are wrong. Perhaps after all these years it matters little whose names are attached to these deeds, but the point is that eyewitness accounts, even those by seasoned professional observers, cannot always be relied upon, and that after-the-fact recollections, no matter how prominent the participant, are equally suspect as to detail. And Blaik's autobiography in particular includes minor factual errors on other topics. While these errors do nothing to detract from the major messages and themes of his story, they must be kept in mind when weighing his account of the game. Blaik was quick to discount the accuracy of his own recollections. "Anyone who has been coaching football has reason for trouble with his memory," he once remarked.[43] The widely varying recollections about what happened right after the game, some distorted by failing memories after many years, merely attest to the massive confusion that reigned that evening and the next day.

Jim Lynah and Bob Kane were at the Hanover Inn about 45 minutes after the game, presumably at about the same time that Friesell was being driven to the train station, and were prepared to enjoy a celebratory dinner. There they received word that a tempest was brewing in the Dartmouth locker room.[44] Kane's account of the moment[45] describes a lighthearted and dismissive reaction by the two, grounded in their suspicion that the fuel for the controversy was a simple overreaction by a Dartmouth student manager. Both men had witnessed a confused ending of the game, saw the referee forcefully deal with the matter, and had heard a degree of protest from disgruntled players and fans, none of which was an uncommon occurrence. They had also received congratulations on their victory from their Dartmouth counterparts. There was no reason for the issue to be elevated to a higher level. They did, however, deem it important enough to discuss with President Day. After they phoned Day, Kane left to be with the team, making his own trip to the train station, and departed with the players for Ithaca.

Day and Lynah remained in Hanover to discuss the matter, and within a short period of time their assessment of the issue shifted from a minor disturbance as perceived by Kane to one of the most significant events in the history of Cornell athletics. The most plausible explanation for this shift is that Day had heard with his own ears—on the way to the train station—Friesell's admission that he might have made a mistake. Neither Kane nor Lynah had been privy to that information. It is not plausible that what was done next could have been based merely on the unsubstantiated allegations of an angry crowd.

Cognizant of what was on the line—the unbeaten streak, the undefeated season, the national title—Day and Lynah had to have regarded one more controversy in an already controversy-laden season as the last straw. They were cognizant as well of one more thing on the line, more important than any other—the honor of their university—and that they might have to choose between the two. And so they took a step never before taken in college football, and never taken since. They prepared and released the following joint statement Saturday night: "If the officials in charge of today's Dartmouth-Cornell game rule after investigation that there were five downs in the final series of plays, and that the winning touchdown was scored on an illegal fifth down, the score of the game between Dartmouth and Cornell will be recorded as Dartmouth 3, Cornell 0."[46]

As they began their trip home, the Cornell players, oblivious to the controversy, were in a festive mood. By this time, everyone was aware that some confusion had occurred, but the Big Red players and fans felt justified in assuming that the officials had straightened everything out on the field correctly, and all were aware of what the scoreboard read when the final gun went off. There was no reason for anyone to think that this football game was any different from every other football game ever played. "The official made a mistake, you know, so what?" said one of the players.[47] It happened all the time.

Before boarding the homeward train, the players stopped in White River Junction and most of them bought bright red and green checked hunting caps as trophies to wear in festive celebration. Although Dartmouth fans were throwing rocks at their train,[48] they remained confident in their victory. On the ride home, several of them engaged in quiz sessions to pass the time. Nick Drahos conducted one on Greek and Roman mythology.[49] But Bob Kane had an additional memory. Kane was more aware of the issue than the others, based on his experience at the Hanover Inn, but he was unaware, as was everybody else, of what Day and Lynah had done about it. "I do recall that when we were taking the train back to Ithaca, Nick Drahos, who kicked the extra point, kept saying we had a fifth down. Most of the guys disagreed with him or just said the game was in the hands of the officials."[50] Now Kane was hearing that even some of the Cornell players were expressing doubt.

Later, as twilight faded along the East Coast, fans, hungry for the scores of their favorite teams, huddled around the radio, tuned perhaps to WOR in Boston or WCBS in New York. They would hear the football news of the day, offered by a dispassionate reporter in staccato fashion: Penn State 25, NYU 0; Texas A&M 25, Rice 0; Colgate 7, Syracuse 6; Harvard 14, Brown 0; Cornell 7, Dartmouth 3. They would have no reason to doubt that Cornell had emerged victorious in a surprisingly tight match and had remained undefeated and still in contention for the national title.

Little did the players and fans know what lay in store. Little did anyone know.

The next morning the story began to unfold further. On the front page of the *New York Times*, as was customary, a box containing the major football scores from Saturday was included, and it confirmed Cornell's victory, 7-3. Inside, where the records of the teams were listed, Cornell's name had an asterisk next to it, indicating an undefeated, untied season. The first paragraph of William D. Richardson's story in the *New York Times* gave further confidence, as it related Cornell's desperation pass from Scholl to Murphy with less than three seconds remaining that had netted the victory. But the headline over the story provided an inkling of something different: "Disputed Cornell Play Tops Dartmouth, 7-3, At Finish."[51]

And what a dispute! The football world was in turmoil. Here, in the heart of the race for the national championship, was a critical game involving the second-ranked team in the country, a game that had so far defied all attempts to determine the winner. In the entire history of college football there had never been a dispute like this. As to who had won, the answer, Richardson promised, lay "in a strip of celluloid known as a film...being developed feverishly in a darkroom somewhere."[52]

Much was made, mostly by columnist Bob Considine, of the irony that Carl Snavely, the master of film analysis, now had his fate in the hands of the film analysts.[53] But that was not really the case. By this time it was generally acknowledged that the ball had been snapped five times, which is all the films could confirm. Dartmouth's game films were developed first and, to nobody's surprise, appeared to establish that five plays had indeed been run. But by Sunday that was old news. What really mattered was whether a penalty had been called, and the referees already knew the answer to that. Either they had called an offside or they had not. The delay, ostensibly to review the film, was more valuable as an opportunity for everybody to collect their thoughts on an issue the likes of which had never before come up.

Asa Bushnell, head of the Eastern Intercollegiate Football Association, made it clear that he and his organization had no role in handling the matter. He emphasized that the role of his organization was merely to assign neutral officials to college football games. Indeed, his position was underscored by the former unwieldy title of his organization: The Eastern Association for the Selection of Football Officials. Bushnell had long been concerned with the quality of the officials' work and was committed to assuring the highest standard of performance possible. In 1938, he had monitored the performance of all the game officials under his jurisdiction and had fired 125, winnowing down the number eligible for use in college games to the 150 best.[54] Red Friesell was among the elite of that group.

If Earl Blaik had held any hopes of help from Bushnell, he would be sadly disappointed. "Our association has no authority in the matter nor do the officials have any authority to make any change after their decision has been made," Bushnell said. He further explained that he expected a report from the game officials, as was customary, but if the report showed that an error had occurred, "...we can't do anything." In a colossal understatement, he called the matter a "rather unique case."[55]

The controversy itself would have made it unique. But if Cornell were true to its word, what it was prepared to do about the controversy made the entire affair doubly so. For the first time in the history of college football Cornell was proposing to change the game results after the contest was over, and in so doing, put an end to its own undefeated season and championship hopes.

On Monday morning, Kane and Snavely reviewed Cornell's film of the game. Painfully but inevitably they came to the same conclusion. There had been five downs. The film also showed that on third down Landsberg had made it into the end zone.[56]

As frustrated as anybody, Dartmouth director of athletic publicity Robert P. (Whitey) Fuller said, "The next move appears to be up to the officials or

Cornell."[57] But with the officials out of the picture, that left only Cornell. By mid-day Monday, as everybody waited for a report from the officials, there still was no resolution. There was nothing to do but sit and wait.

CHAPTER 15
TANGLED IN THE WEB

Man is born unto trouble, as the sparks fly upward.

--JOB 5:7

Controversies were nothing new to college football or to sports in general. One of the first football controversies affecting the outcome of a game happened on October 21, 1922, in a game between Columbia and NYU. Like the Cornell-Dartmouth game, this one was expected by the experts to be a one-sided contest, so much so that Buck O'Neill, coach of the heavily favored Columbia team, did not bother to show up for the game, turning over duties to his assistant, Joe Brooks.

The game was played at old South Field in Morningside Heights, where the field was surrounded by a running track. The seating capacity was just under 10,000, but Columbia authorities, faced with a sellout, were prepared to sell an additional 2,000 standing room tickets between the back of the end zone and the track.

Columbia had a potent running attack, fueled by the outside running of team captain Walter Koppisch and Ben Roderick and the inside running of a 210-pound line smasher who would, in a few short years, become much better known to the New York sports media, Lou Gehrig. Early in the game Columbia was bottled up deep in its own territory, frustrated because it couldn't get its running attack going. About five minutes into the game Gehrig was ejected for slugging another player, but Columbia kept running plays at the middle of the NYU line as if Gehrig were still in the game. It didn't work. The Lions, unable to move the ball, were forced to punt from inside their own 10-yard line.

The punt by Ben Roderick was blocked by NYU tackle Al Naggie. The ball bounced off the field of play into the spectators standing behind the end zone and was covered on the track by an NYU player, Toorock. Referee William N. Morice ruled it a touchdown, and when NYU kicked the extra point, the Violets had a 7-0 lead. Thus the score remained into the fourth quarter of a hard fought game, until with three minutes left in the contest, Columbia finally countered with a touchdown of its own. But the extra-point attempt by Roderick was blocked by Berkwit of NYU, and when Columbia could not mount an attack in the remaining time, NYU left the game with what appeared to be a tremendous 7-6 upset victory.[1]

The following Monday more scrutiny was paid to Morice's decision to award NYU a touchdown on the blocked punt. Morice, a graduate of Penn, was a seasoned professional whose experience included, among others, the 1913 Notre Dame-Army game of Dorais-to-Rockne fame. But the rule was clear: "A blocked kick which, after being blocked, crosses the kicker's goal line and goes into the stand or among the spectators shall count as a safety." Nobody questioned that the ball had bounced in some fashion into the spectators, and thus it appeared that Morice had erred. He should have ruled the play a two-point safety and not a six-point touchdown. More importantly, his error compromised the outcome of the game. Oddly, the exact same play occurred in the Springfield-Stevens game that same day and was properly ruled a safety.[2]

Morice finally made a statement on Wednesday and only made matters worse. From Philadelphia he wired, "Some hours after the finish of the New York University-Columbia game on Saturday, October 21, I discovered that I had made a wrong ruling in connection with the touchdown I allowed New York University on a Columbia kick, which was blocked and which went into the grand stand back of the Columbia line....[T]his should have been declared a safety....In justice to Columbia, I feel that I must publicly admit my error and reverse my decision on the play in question, so that the final official score should have been 6 to 2 in favor of Columbia...." Columbia kept its distance from Morice's decision. "Anything he did was on his own initiative," said Graduate Manager R.W. Watt. Morice's statement was "applauded last night by men neutral in the matter," stated the *New York Times*.[3]

It was not applauded at NYU, however. Coach Tom Thorp, a former Columbia assistant coach and a man who, like Morice, had refereed games in the past, and who would be on the crew who refereed the Army-Notre Dame Win-One-For-The-Gipper game in 1928, exploded. "We outfought them and outplayed them in their own backyard, and we don't have to out-talk them.... [N]ow that the game is finished we won't allow anybody to question it. Mr. Morice has made a serious error if he has reversed any decision of the game, and we believe that the true sportsmen will side with us in this matter," he said. Thorp argued that it is not possible to fairly reverse the score of a game based on an occurrence partway through the game. "Had only two points been awarded our style of game would have been entirely different," he explained.[4]

The next day, NYU officials were described as "somewhat agitated." Thorp put to rest any fear of that description being exaggerated when he made this statement: "Never in my life have I heard of such an absurd piece of work as Mr. Morice is trying to foist upon us. It goes without saying that neither I nor my men will accept any such illegal decision. Just where Mr. Morice gets the right to change his decision is beyond my comprehension." Thorp had two good points. First, Morice's authority to take any game-related action ended when the game ended. He simply had no authority to change the outcome of the game four days after it was over. Second, to reverse the score simply replaced one brand of injustice with another. As the *New York University Daily News* pointed out, "We challenge his right to award the game to our opponent after he had made a decision in the first quarter of play that guided the attack of our team the following three quarters."[5]

Regardless of how technically correct Coach Thorp might have been, public opinion was not on his side. It just didn't feel fair for a team to claim a win based on points not rightly earned. The *New York Times,* in a position widely accepted, opined that Morice had done "the right and manly thing" in admitting his error.[6]

With the mounting animosity, there appeared to be no way to settle this issue, and indeed it has never been settled. To this day NYU claims a 7-6 victory in the game, and Columbia a 6-2 victory. The dispute quickly faded into memory as other events overtook it, but the lessons remained. Fairness is an elusive concept. Technical correctness is not enough if one wants to avoid the stigma of unearned victory.

Another notable dispute arose in a game between Notre Dame and Carnegie Tech played in South Bend on October 22, 1938, and it created an even higher level of ill feeling. A glimpse at this game through a modern lens does not do justice to its importance. The rivalry between the two undefeated teams was a heated one, and Notre Dame was hungry to avenge its 9-7 loss to the Tartans the year before. At the time of the game, Notre Dame was ranked 5th in the nation by the Associated Press, and Carnegie 13th.

Carnegie had dominated the game statistically, and with about eleven minutes left in the fourth period and the game still scoreless, Carnegie had the ball on its own 46-yard line with about a yard to go for a first down. Paul Friedlander, the Carnegie substitute quarterback, asked Referee John Getchell to tell him which down was coming up, and Getchell answered, incorrectly as it turns out, that it was third down. It was in fact fourth down. Accordingly Friedlander, instead of punting, called a running play. On the attempt to pick up the first down the Carnegie ball carrier Ray Carnelly fumbled, and although his teammate recovered the ball, Carnegie was still short of first down yardage. To the surprise and chagrin of the Carnegie team the ball went over on downs to Notre Dame. Carnegie coach Bill Kern and his players vigorously protested, but to no avail. The simple truth was that, regardless of what the referee had said, it was fourth down, not third down. The Irish had their third string team on the field at the time, and within three plays they scored the only touchdown of the game against a rattled Carnegie defense. The final score was 7-0.

Kern was livid. "It was the biggest bonehead I ever saw pulled by any official," he said. "It certainly meant defeat for us." Notre Dame was unsympathetic. Irish Coach Elmer Layden responded, "I only want to point out that it is the quarterback's responsibility to know what down it is. The scoreboard and the linesman's marker showed fourth down." Then his tone turned accusatory. "The Tech players knew it was fourth down because they checked signals when Friedlander called for a running play. But he called it again, apparently trying to take a chance with official sanction." As for Getchell, all he could offer as explanation was, "I just said third down instead of fourth down, that's all there is to it."[7]

Layden's reaction is perhaps a little harsh, since the scoreboard and linesman's markers are not official and are frequently wrong. Players should be able to seek reliable information from an official source, and it seems hard to fault the Carnegie quarterback for what he did. But on the other hand, Notre Dame suffered in this matter by having a cloud cast over its rightfully earned win. There was not a thing Notre Dame could or should have done about the matter. It was just a tough break.

For Carnegie, which finished the year ranked 6th by the Associated Press, it was the only regular season loss of the year. After upsetting crosstown rival and defending national champion Pitt in the last week of the season, snapping Pitt's 22-game undefeated streak, the Tartans earned a trip to the Sugar Bowl, where they faced the already crowned national champion Texas Christian and the Heisman Trophy winner Davey O'Brien. By this time, Bill Kern had come to accept the error and graciously extended an invitation to John Getchell to referee in the game. Although the Tartans led 7-6 at halftime, they eventually fell 15-7. The Irish remained undefeated until losing their last game of the year to Southern California, and they shared the 1938 national championship with Texas Christian. Bill Kern was named College Football Coach of the Year. What would have happened had Carnegie been told it was fourth down will never be known, but the incident probably played an immense part in the outcome of the 1938 season.

Other things can be learned about controversies by looking to examples in other sports. One of the most famous controversies of all time happened in major league baseball during the National League pennant race of 1908. Professional baseball had built a fervent support base in the cities where it was played, and fans, both male and female, from every segment of society regularly flocked to the parks to root for their heroes. The fans were both wildly passionate and thoroughly partisan.

On September 23, the Giants and Cubs found themselves in a virtual tie for first place and were scheduled to play that afternoon at the Polo Grounds. The Giants made one change to their usual lineup. Reliable first baseman and leadoff hitter Fred Tenney had to miss his first game of the year with a bad back, and in his place the Giants inserted the 19-year-old Fred Merkle, in his second season with the Giants, batting seventh.

In the bottom of the ninth inning with the score tied 1-1, the Giants had two out and the slow-footed Moose McCormick a runner on first. Up to the plate strode Fred Merkle. The *New York Times'* account of the game the next day said, in as insincere a statement as has ever been made, "If he will only single we will ignore any errors he will make in the rest of his natural life."[8]

Merkle lined a sharp single into right field deep enough to allow the lumbering McCormick to reach third base. The crowd was ecstatic, and the *New York Times* described the fans as "screaming like a batch of Coney barkers on the Mardi Gras occasion."[9] Al Bridwell followed with a single up the middle, hit so sharply that it knocked Bob Emslie, the umpire behind second base, off his feet. Emslie later claimed he did not see the rest of the play. McCormick trotted home with what appeared to be the winning run for the Giants.

Every player at the Polo Grounds in those days knew that, at game's end, an early start on the dash across centerfield to the clubhouse was highly advantageous. In the absence of security, thousands of delirious fans rushed out onto the field, milling and clawing at the fleeing players from both teams, when suddenly, as the *New York Times* reported, "there is a doings around second base."[10] Accounts of what happened next vary wildly, and no recollection by any of the players or eye witnesses completely coincides with another. Yet, some elements are common to most accounts. When the ball was hit by Bridwell, Merkle apparently left first base, ran part of the way down to second base, and then seeing McCormick score, veered off and began the dash across center field, perhaps, as it was later suggested, in a boyish desire to be the first in the clubhouse. He never touched second base, according to most accounts, and thus left open the possibility of a force play. Several players on each team immediately caught on to what was happening. Artie Hofman, the Cubs' centerfielder, tracked the ball down and threw it to Johnny Evers, who was standing near second base. But the throw was off target and Joe McGinnity, Giants pitcher who was coaching either first base or third base (accounts differ) wrestled the ball away from Evers and pitcher Rube Kroh, who was not in the game, and to keep Evers from completing the play, flung the ball into the stands. Evers produced a ball from somewhere (nobody knows whether it was the actual game ball), tagged second base, and demanded that home plate umpire Hank O'Day call Merkle out. Meanwhile, Giants players, including at least Mike Donlin and Christy Mathewson, tried to physically corral Merkle and herd him back to second base.

Players, fans, and umpires were all involved in the skirmish that followed, and there were several injuries. At least one fan suffered a fractured skull when he was hit in the head with a bat swung by another fan. Police were called to the scene and with their guns drawn, it took them a half hour to restore order. O'Day justifiably feared for his life in the milling crowd and confusion, and fled the field. The *New York World* described him as "rattled and evasive."[11] When called upon to rule on the matter he "seemed very uncertain about what he should do and was a long time coming to a decision, and when he did he seemed uncertain as to its justification."[12] Ultimately he sided with the Cubs, ruling that Merkle had not reached second base, that he had been forced out, and that the run did not score.

Based on O'Day's belated ruling, the game went down in the books as a tie. An appeal was made to National League President Harry Pulliam, who was equally reluctant to act, and only the next day confirmed the game a tie. It would have to be replayed. Appeals were immediately filed. Both sides claimed victory, the Giants because they felt they had scored the winning run, and the Cubs because they felt entitled to a forfeit win, the home team Giants having failed to clear the field for further play. Threats, accusations, and insults were hurled back and forth between the players, the team officials, the fans, the umpires, and the press of the two cities. Differing versions of the occurrences on and off the field were bandied about, but it all served merely to stoke the fires rather than to resolve the controversy.

The press was hardly sympathetic to Merkle. The *New York Times* called the play a "blunder" and cited "censurable stupidity on the part of player Merkle."[13] A writer for the *New York Herald*, reflecting on the game, wrote, "[A]ll our boys did rather well if Fred Merkle could gather the idea into his noodle that baseball custom does not permit a runner to take a shower and some light lunch in the clubhouse on the way to second." The next day Giants manager John McGraw was forced to put the pain-wracked Tenney back in the lineup rather than risk playing Merkle again, and Gym Bagley of the *New York Evening Mail* wrote, "A one-legged man with a noodle is better than a bonehead." Two days later Tenney could not make it through both games of a doubleheader, and Merkle had to come in to replace him. Jack Ryder of the *Cincinnati Enquirer* wrote, "No plays came up in which Merkle had to think, so he got by."[14]

Laid aside all this is another fact that, if possible, complicates matters even further. It is undeniable that the custom of the day was for the players to vacate the field as quickly as possible after the game was over, and so what Merkle did was commonplace and accepted practice. Merkle's teammate, Al Bridwell, stood up for him: "I think that under the circumstances any ballplayer on any ballclub would have done the same thing Merkle did. They did it all the time in those days."[15] The *New York Herald* said, "An enormous baseball custom has had it from time immemorial that as soon as the run has crossed the plate everyone adjourns as hastily and yet as nicely as possible to the clubhouse and exits."[16] Bill Klem, who would in time earn a spot as one of the most revered umpires in baseball history, called the ruling "the rottenest decision in the history of baseball,"[17] maintaining that the force rule in baseball was never meant to apply to situations of that type.

On October 2, Pulliam finally issued his decision, confirming that the game was a tie and would have to be replayed. Speculation abounded that he waited as long as possible in hopes the matter would resolve itself on the field, making his decision unnecessary. Again the decision was appealed, this time to the National League Board of Directors. When the regular season ended, the Giants and Cubs were still tied for first place, pending the outcome of the appealed game. On October 6, at noon, the Board reached its decision, and required that the appealed game be replayed on October 8. The winner would be National League champion.

The Cubs won the game, 4-1, and then went on to beat the Tigers in the World Series. The level of animosity felt by the Giants toward the Cubs, the umpires, and the National League was immense. Sam Crane in the *New York Evening Journal* wrote, "The Cubs will be acknowledged as champs, but their title is tainted, and New York lovers of baseball will never acknowledge them as the true winners of the pennant."[18]

Fred Merkle went on to play in the major leagues for 16 years, including eight more with the Giants and four with the Cubs. Despite a fine career, he carried the nickname "Bonehead" to his grave, and the game of September 23 is to this day known as the Merkle Game. Harry Pulliam dealt poorly with the stress of the controversy and went into a deep depression. On July 19, 1909 he committed suicide in New York. Every team in the National League except the Giants sent a delegation to his funeral. Giants Manager John McGraw's comment on hearing of Pulliam's death was, "I didn't think a bullet in the head could hurt him."[19]

Yet one more important sports controversy of the time took place on Thursday, September 22, 1927, when Jack Dempsey and Gene Tunney, fighting for the world heavyweight boxing championship, became embroiled in what has become known in boxing history as the Long Count. A year earlier, in Philadelphia, Tunney had taken Dempsey's heavyweight title in a ten-round decision in which many observers thought he had won all ten rounds.

The rematch was a natural for promoter Tex Rickard. Tunney, who grew up in Hell's Kitchen in New York, learned to box in the Marines, where he had been light-heavyweight champion of the Allied Expeditionary Force in France. He was an avid reader and Shakespearean scholar, and was seen by many as an effete snob. Dempsey, born in Manassa, Colorado, learned his brawling ways by clearing out saloons in the raw western towns and mining camps along the rails where he traveled as a hobo. He built his early professional career under the name Kid Blackie. He became known as the Manassa Mauler, a vicious hammer-handed brute with a keen killer instinct. His fans adored him, not only for his bloodthirsty ring style but also for his larger than life persona. "I'll knock the big bookworm out inside of eight rounds," he bragged.[20] He was loathed by others, however, because he never served in the military, even though the tactics he used to evade service were all legal. Beloved or reviled, Dempsey, unlike his opponent, was an icon of the age.

When Rickard set the rematch for Chicago's Soldier Field, it was one of the biggest events of any type of its time. A crowd of almost 105,000 attended the event, and special trains and their crews from all over the country worked feverishly as throngs of boxing fans converged on Chicago. "The greatest troop movement since the war"[21] was the way one railroad official described it. About 22,000 people were expected to entrain for the fight. Some 14,000 hotel rooms in downtown Chicago, all rented for three-day minimums, had been reserved, as well as 8,000 rooms on the outskirts of the city.[22] More than 6000 Chicago policemen and National Guard troops kept order as the crowd filed in. All leave in the Chicago police department had been canceled. Governors of ten states were present. More than 1200 newspaper men were there to cover the event. The Burns Detective Agency stationed 100 agents at the turnstiles to look for counterfeit tickets. Graham McNamee broadcast the bout to 50 million listeners over 70 stations whose signals carried all over the country and into Mexico and Canada. At that time it was the largest radio audience in history.

For those who could not afford the tickets, the sale of radios was brisk. The *Chicago Tribune* set a weekday circulation record in the days leading up to the contest. For fifty cents, a fan near Times Square in New York could board a bus and just sit in it and listen to the radio broadcast.[23] All the prisoners at Sing Sing in upstate New York were allowed to listen to the broadcast of the bout, and all the inmates at the New Jersey State Prison at Trenton, except for the four on death row, were afforded a similar privilege.[24]

In Melbourne, Australia, reception of the American short-wave signal was poor, but large crowds gathered around newspaper offices, as they did in Tokyo, to read posted bulletins as the fight progressed. In Guayaquil, Ecuador, thousands of fans clogged traffic in front of *El Telegrafo*, a local newspaper, to hear news of the fight. Radio reception was excellent in San Juan, Puerto Rico; thousands of South Africa residents stayed up all night in Capetown to hear a rebroadcast of the fight at 5 AM; in Shanghai news of the fight was enthusiastically received just after noon; and near Winnipeg thousands of trappers listened in to a clear reception link.[25] Passengers aboard the liner *Berengaria* in the middle of the Atlantic huddled around a radio to listen to the contest.[26] The fight was an international event of the first order.

Estimates were that in New York alone over $3 million had been wagered on the fight,[27] and perhaps as much as $10 million worldwide.[28] Writers such as Westbrook Pegler contended that the background of promoter Tex Rickard did not instill confidence for a fair and above-board fight.[29] For both Tunney and Dempsey, as well as referee Dave Barry, rumors abounded of mob tie-ins.[30] The mayor of Jersey City, Frank Hague, a friend of Tunney's, asked the champion directly if the rumor he had heard that Tunney was going to take a dive in the seventh round had any truth to it. Tunney denied it.[31] It was rumored that Nick the Greek had $50,000 on Tunney. Other rumors had Al Capone with $50,000 on Dempsey.[32] Naturally many assumed that if bets of that size had been placed by people of that type, advance arrangements regarding the outcome had been made.

"Ugly rumors were circulating immediately preceding the fight," wrote boxing writer James P. Dawson, "as is characteristic of all such major battles in this era of big business in pugilism." That Tunney arrived for the weigh-in in the back seat of an armored car did nothing to allay those concerns. The fight had a "lingering piscine aroma,"[33] wrote Dr. Ferdie Pacheco, who later spent fifteen years in the corner of Muhammad Ali.

When the fight finally began following a brief rain shower, Tunney again had his way with Dempsey through the first five rounds, winning at least four of them. His superior boxing skills kept the slugging Dempsey at bay until, about fifty seconds into the seventh round, Dempsey caught the champion against the ropes and hit him with a flurry of hard square punches. Jimmy Jones, racehorse trainer of Triple Crown winner Citation, saw it from his ninth row seat. "Dempsey was like a cat...the way he pounced," he said. "After chasing Tunney all night, Dempsey finally got a whack at him. And he whacked him good!"[34] Tunney hit the canvas for the first time in his career and set off worldwide pandemonium. The high society and senators in the front row seats, the fans in the buses in Times Square, the inmates at Sing Sing, and the passengers at sea all simultaneously gasped. For the first time in history, people all over the globe were riveted by exactly the same event at exactly the same moment.

Despite the pandemonium and mass confusion that erupted, there is little disagreement on what happened. The knockdown timekeeper, Paul Beeler, rose to his feet and began the count. Dempsey had retreated to his own corner and was resting against the ropes there, only a few feet from Tunney, who lay stunned on the canvas. Referee Dave Barry directed Dempsey to a neutral corner, but Dempsey refused to budge, unresponsive to Barry's increasingly frantic instructions. Beeler stopped counting.

Finally, Dempsey sensed the significance of what he was being told and went to the corner where Barry was directing him. Possibly as many as five seconds had elapsed. Barry returned to the fallen Tunney and, with timekeeper Beeler, began the count again, not picking up where Beeler had left off but starting over at "one." At Barry's count of nine Tunney was back on his feet. It was agreed by most observers that Tunney was on the canvas for about fourteen seconds, although others later argued that the elapsed time may have been as long as seventeen seconds.

Here a difference of opinion exists. Dawson in the *Times* said of Tunney, "He got to his feet with the assistance of the ring ropes and with visible effort at the count of 'nine.' He was groggy, stung, shaken, his head was whirling...."[35] James O'Donnell Bennett, writing in the *Chicago Tribune*, saw it similarly. He wrote, "Up to the count of seven the champion lay almost flat on the west side of the squared circle."[36] Writing years later, Dr. Ferdie Pacheco concluded, "Looking at the film today, studying it in slow motion, I have to conclude that if the injured Gene Tunney had gotten up at a legitimate eight count, he would clearly have been knocked out. No one could survive Jack Dempsey's fury when he had an opponent in trouble."[37] But others saw it differently. Harvey Woodruff in the *Chicago Tribune* wrote of the moment, "Meantime Champion Gene...rose on one knee and with his senses rapidly recuperating coolly awaited the count of nine before arising to his feet.... Whether the count was long or correct, Tunney could have stepped to his feet before he did."[38] "Gene Tunney could have arisen from the canvas at the count of five had he so elected," agreed Shirley Povich of the *Washington Post*. "By the time the referee had tolled to three on the second count, he had recovered sufficiently to gain his composure."[39] The question for the ages, to which there will never be a definitive answer, is whether Tunney could have gotten up from the canvas in ten seconds clearheaded enough to avoid Dempsey's onslaught. The "long count" may well have saved him. Tunney, graced with a few extra precious seconds, managed to survive the rest of the round, knocked Dempsey down in the eighth round and claimed a unanimous decision in ten rounds, thus retaining his heavyweight title.

Though Tunney had displayed clear superiority, immediately in question was whether he had won an undeserved victory. "Intentionally or otherwise, I was robbed of the championship," said Dempsey. "This is the biggest injustice I have ever seen in a ring,"[40] added Dempsey's manager Leo Flynn.

On an emotional level, Dempsey's argument had great appeal. Dempsey had clearly floored Tunney, and Tunney clearly took advantage of at least fourteen seconds allotted him to gather himself and get up. But Dempsey's emotional argument loses some of its steam when the neutral-corner rule is brought forth. It states, "When a knockdown occurs the timekeeper shall immediately arise and announce the seconds audibly as they elapse. The referee shall first see that the opponent retires to the farthest corner and then, turning to the timekeeper, shall pick up the count in unison with the timekeeper, announcing the seconds to the boxer on the floor. Should the boxer on his feet fail to stay in the corner, the referee and timekeeper shall cease counting until he has so retired." This explains why Beeler stopped counting, but it does not explain why the count, when it resumed, began again at "one." Commissioner Paul Prehn, present at ringside, added that an amended version of this rule, allowing for a restart of the count, had been adopted, explained to both fighters, and agreed to before the bout.[41] Prehn also explained that under Illinois rules "a man is not regarded as 'down'...until the man scoring the knockdown goes to a neutral corner or takes a position an appreciable distance from his fallen foe."[42]

Timekeeper Beeler explained his actions. "As soon as Tunney fell in the seventh round," he said, "I began counting. I had counted four before Dempsey reached a neutral corner. Barry then began to count and I dropped my count and resumed it with him. Tunney got up on the count of nine." Barry also explained. "One of the most emphatic instructions was in regard to knockdowns. I told both fighters that the man who scored a knockdown must retire to the farthest corner before I would start the count. Dempsey did not obey this instruction." Dempsey's reply was lame. "When Tunney fell, I did go into a corner," he said. "In spite of these things the referee made me go into still another corner."[43] To Dan Daniel, cofounder of *Ring* magazine, he said, "I couldn't move. I just couldn't. I wanted him to get up. I wanted to kill the sonofabitch."[44]

Knowledgeable boxing men and average fans debated the issues, each person in his own way. "There is no question that, under the rules, Tunney was entitled to the long count," wrote John Kieran in the *New York Times*.[45] Shirley Povich, writing of Tunney, said, "...a true count would surely have found him on his feet and ready to resume the battle."[46] But the public, the average fans on the streets—the newsboys, the shopkeepers, the barbers and the bricklayers—continued to feel otherwise. Dempsey's fans felt strongly that he had demonstrated himself the better man. They bitterly disputed any claim that Tunney could have arisen on time and felt the champion had defended his title on a technicality. Said one observer, "The conclusion the public draws from this is that Dempsey won the fight whether he won it or not."[47] That heavyweight title fights at the time were almost always settled by knockout and not decision gave Dempsey an additional edge in public opinion.

On Wednesday, Westbrook Pegler wrote another "I told you so" article about corruption in boxing, terming the entire matter "cultural shenanigans."[48] The Long Count controversy would continue to simmer for years. While some reached their judgments based on what seemed in their guts to feel right and fair, others parsed the language in the neutral corner rule, looking for justification for the officials' action. Still others wondered what role, if any, the huge wagers and the characters who made them played in the strange outcome. Dempsey would never fight again, and Tunney would fight only one more bout before retiring. But doubts still linger about whether the right man won that fight in 1927. The entire controversy emphasizes that public opinion does not always gravitate to where the facts would lead. Sometimes it is steered by forces more fundamental than manmade rules, guided by primal instincts as to right and wrong and unpolished emotions as to the nature of earned victory.

CHAPTER 16
RESOLVED

A great nation is like a great man:
When he makes a mistake, he realizes it.
Having realized it, he admits it.
Having admitted it, he corrects it.

--THE TAO TE CHING

On Monday, November 18, two days after the Cornell-Dartmouth game was over, the controversy was finally resolved. In a special report to Asa S. Bushnell, commissioner of the Eastern Intercollegiate Football Association, Red Friesell made this statement:

"Since the conclusion of Saturday's Cornell-Dartmouth football game at Hanover, I have made careful and thorough study of all evidence having to do with the final series of plays which led to Cornell's touchdown and a 7-to-3 victory just as time expired in the fourth quarter.

"On the basis of numerous charts kept by the press and motion pictures taken by both of the competing colleges, I am now convinced beyond shadow of doubt that I was in error in allowing Cornell possession of the ball for the play on which they scored.

"I find that, after a Cornell first down on the 6-yard line, there followed three line plays which gained five yards, then an extra time-out penalty which cost Cornell five yards, then a forward pass into the end zone knocked down by Dartmouth.

"At this point Dartmouth was entitled to take the ball on their 20-yard line, first down, with about six seconds of play remaining. Unfortunately, however, thinking it was Cornell's ball, fourth down, on the 6-yard line, I awarded it to them for what actually was an illegal fifth-down play—a play which produced the winning score.

"This mistake was entirely mine as the game's referee, and not shared in or contributed to by any of the three other officials. I realize, of course, that my jurisdiction ceased at the close of the game and that the football rules give me no authority to change even an incorrect decision such as the one described, but I do want to acknowledge my mistake to you as Commissioner of the Eastern Intercollegiate Football Association, and if you see fit, to the football public as well."

Friesell's report was silent on the matter of the alleged offside penalty. Bushnell also put forth a report from Joe McKenney, the linesman, clarifying that he had not called any offside penalty on the play,[1] which was really the key issue in the entire controversy. It is unclear why that was not immediately obvious on the field of play and why it required two days to clarify the matter. It is clear though that, regardless of their respective roles in the mixup, Friesell accepted the entirety of the blame, allowing none of it to touch McKenney or any other participant.

It all could have ended there, and in most cases would have. The referee had made an error, the game was over, and nothing more could be done. That, at least, is how each of the numerous controversies of 1940 and years past had been handled. To do otherwise would be totally at odds with the tradition and history of conflict resolution in college football. But both James Lynah and Edmund Ezra Day knew the cost of controversy. They had experienced it all year long, and this issue, they knew, would tower over all the others. They knew as well the lessons of history. In the midst of controversy it is almost impossible to come out whole, with honor and reputation intact, no matter what the facts prove to be. Controversy does not treat well those caught in its web, and it often reflects poorly on the integrity of the participants and the sport, whether the facts justify such reflection or not. The humiliation that would hang over Fred Merkle for decades, the despair that would cause Harry Pulliam to take his life, the hard feelings that lingered between NYU and Columbia, the "piscine aroma" of the Long Count, the acrimony that welled up when Notre Dame beat Carnegie Tech, were all indications of the wages of controversy. Victory without honor, they knew, was a valueless thing.

Despite the temptations of the usual course, Cornell had promised something different. Its president and athletic director had stated that they would not accept a win tainted as this one had been tainted. Now it was time to act on that promise.

They acted immediately. Lynah sent to William H. McCarter, Dartmouth Graduate Manager, the following telegram: "In view of the conclusion reached by the officials, that the Cornell touchdown was scored on the fifth down, Cornell relinquishes claim to the victory and extends congratulations to Dartmouth." Carl Snavely followed with a similar telegram to his counterpart, Earl Blaik: "I accept the final conclusions of the officials and without reservation concede the victory to Dartmouth with hearty congratulations to you and a gallant Dartmouth team."

Nothing like it in the history of college football, before or since, had taken place. No game officials or commissioners had any authority over the situation. Only Cornell could undo the error made by others, and with those few words put an end by its own hand to its undefeated streak, its perfect record for 1940, and all hopes of a national title.

But what Cornell gained back was even more significant. McCarter wired back, "Thank you for your wire. Dartmouth accepts the victory and your congratulations, and salutes the Cornell team, the honorable and honored opponent of her longest unbroken football rivalry."

So it was done. Legend has it that President Day, being a Dartmouth man, was of the opinion that Dartmouth would never accept an offer of concession but that Carl Snavely was sure that Earl Blaik would accept it. Blaik, after all, had invested great emotion in the outcome. But that story does not ring true. Day and Lynah's statement was a unilateral position that the score would be changed. It was not an offer of concession. It did not ask Dartmouth to concur.

Cornell was a once-defeated team. Arthur J. Daley in the *New York Times* wrote, "Friesell had the courage to admit that he had been wrong and Cornell had the sportsmanship to yield a success it felt it had not rightly earned." Without there being a chance for the events to sink in, each team was immediately asked by a charity to replay the "conceded" game in New York for the benefit of the Infantile Paralysis Fund. Dartmouth declined.[2]

There was one more telegram. Red Friesell wired to Dartmouth team captain Lou Young the following: "I want to be the first to admit my very grave error on the extra down as proven by the motion pictures of both colleges. I want to apologize to you, your players, Coach Blaik, all assistant coaches, and Mr. McCarter. I assume full responsibility. I want to thank you for the very fair treatment accorded me after the game. Lou, I am so sorry for you were such a grand captain and leader. Give my regards to President Hopkins."[3] In today's world of qualified apologies, minced words, and spin doctors, there can be no question why Red Friesell was so highly regarded in his day.

In Hanover, the Dartmouth campus erupted in celebration—for real this time. The Dartmouth band circulated from dormitory to dormitory, and students, faculty members, and townspeople all gathered in town to sing the praises of the members of the football team, who appeared one by one before the crowd to accept their adulation. Then everybody began to march down the main street, with merchants and townspeople crowding the doorways and hanging out of second-story windows. The Dartmouth band played "*Far Above Cayuga's Water,*" Cornell's alma mater. President Hopkins, in a prepared statement, said, "The whole thing is in accord with the fine spirit of sportsmanship which Cornell has always shown in its long relationship with Dartmouth."[4]

Back in Ithaca on Monday afternoon, President Day personally interrupted the football team's practice to break the news. The freshman team, the lightweight team, and the varsity players all assembled before him, stoically awaiting the words they knew he would speak. He told them they were still the best team he had seen in forty years.

Bob Kane was rightfully concerned about addressing the players. "We, in effect, were losing their first football game for them in over two years on a giveaway. No one had ever given a game away before. One doesn't correct officials' mistakes....It was a thing that had to be done, but it was a melancholy task," he wrote later.[5]

On Tuesday, Norman Thomas, perennial Socialist candidate for President and an avowed isolationist, was scheduled to appear in Barnes Hall on the Cornell campus to discuss his views on the defense of America. Thomas had gathered just fewer than a million votes in the presidential election two weeks before. But that same day the student council scheduled for Bailey Hall, about three blocks away, a massive pep rally for the upcoming Penn game. Pep rallies earlier in the season had been notable for their lack of attendance, but under the circumstances this one promised to be different. Bands and sound trucks were to be deployed throughout the campus to attract students to the rally. By that time, news of the forfeit had been widely circulated, Cornell had dropped to fifth in the Associated Press weekly ratings, and the Penn Quakers loomed on the horizon. Arrangements were made to start Thomas's talk after the conclusion of the rally. Thomas wisely chose to attend the rally before making his talk.

The affair, attended by 2,500 Cornell students, turned out to be not so much a pep rally as an explanation to the student body by President Day and Coach Snavely as to their reasoning behind the Dartmouth forfeit. Also present from the team were Walt Scholl, Captain Walt Matuszczak, Bud Finneran, and Al Kelley.

Snavely, speaking first, tried to employ levity to lighten the moment, commenting that it was the first game he ever lost through arbitration. Day was more to the point in his explanation. Both he and Snavely had been subjected to a long and painful list of tribulations week after week during the season, and he likened his burden to that of Job's in the Bible. Some of the things that had happened had made him deeply resentful, he explained. "That affair at Hanover ought to cap the climax of things hard to take. At Hanover I saw the greatest football finish ever played out by a great team. The score may come off, but the play remains," he said. "If we hadn't made that decision, we'd have been explaining that game for as long as football has a place in intercollegiate athletics—and I want no Long Count in Cornell's athletic history."[6] It had to be particularly irksome to Day that Ohio State, which had a similar situation following the Purdue game and followed the time-honored tradition of doing nothing about it, then turned on Cornell with charges of poor sportsmanship. Day needed to say nothing about the matter. The press did it for him. The affair of the Buckeyes' illegal substitution was dredged back up, not so much to castigate the Buckeyes for their lack of action, but to praise Cornell for its initiative.[7]

Norman Thomas came to the platform and gave a short speech in which he expressed renewed confidence in America after such a fine example of sportsmanship.[8] Then, not missing a beat, he walked the few blocks to Barnes Hall and gave his prepared speech before 500 students and faculty on the importance of staying out of the brewing war.

Earlier that day Edward P. White, the Cornell football manager, had sent the game ball to his counterpart at Dartmouth. It was official.

The Cornell student body was fully supportive of Day and Lynah. In an editorial, the *Daily Sun* stated its position: "Exhibiting the true spirit of sportsmanship for which every Cornellian desires his University to be known, President Day and Athletic Director Lynah have stated that we will not accept a tainted victory. And that is as it should be. Cornell has nothing to be ashamed of in its athletic record, and there is no reason for blemishing ourselves by winning a game on questionable grounds....In this decision every Cornellian will concur, and in concurring will not lose one bit of respect for our team. For its inspired play of the final minutes cannot be cancelled, nor can its record of sportsmanship, and honorable competition....[W]e rest secure in the knowledge that our record of sportsmanship still stands unscarred."[9]

Allison Danzig in the *New York Times* added his piece. He said that the warm response Cornell had received for its actions was "more than compensation for the defeat...."[10]

"Hats off to Cornell," wrote the *Syracuse Herald-Journal*. "The Big Red today looks bigger than ever. It has shown the world that its red is the same as that to be found in *The Red Badge of Courage*....Every once in a while, one of America's universities bobs up with an act that makes the Nation particularly proud of its intercollegiate athletes."[11]

Most of the mail received by the Times on the subject was favorable to both Cornell and Referee Friesell. Only a few dissenters felt that the handling of the matter by Cornell was too noble, that the referee's actions on the field are final, and that each side can "like it or lump it."[12]

Tom Harmon, interviewed in Ann Arbor, said, "There isn't a team in the Big Ten that would have displayed such sportsmanship. In my opinion, Cornell is about tops in any man's football league and their gentlemanly action at Hanover showed them to be good losers—and that's something that's hard to be when an undefeated season is at stake."[13]

Plans were made for the Cornell and Dartmouth glee clubs to combine to sing the "Star Spangled Banner" and "America" at the National Interfraternity Conference at the Hotel Commodore in New York, where Wendell Willkie would be the keynote speaker, on November 29.

Showing that there were no hard feelings anywhere, Snavely sent this wire to Red Friesell: "Perhaps you would be pleased to know that Cornell

197

wholeheartedly approved your acknowledgment of error and retains even higher regard for your competency, integrity as an official. Have requested the central office to assign you to Cornell-Dartmouth 1941 game if possible."[14] Events would work against that happening, but the sentiment was unmistakably gallant.

Nevertheless, it was a tough pill for the Cornell players to swallow, and they were not happy. "They figured they had been victimized many times before by officials' errors and no one had been generous enough to correct the mistakes," said Bob Kane.[15] For some, it took awhile to get over the disappointment. Bill Murphy, who caught the last-second pass in the end zone, said years later, "I was really bitter right afterward. I was only 21 at the time, and it was a big thing to me. But upon reflection, I'd have to say what happened was genuinely good for football."[16] Lou Conti added, "If I had been a grown person with some authority, I never would have offered to give the game away." His stance, too, has softened with the years. "I think they made the right decision—*now*. At the time, I didn't think so. But we did what was right."[17]

Others accepted what happened sooner and more easily. "Winning evaporates in time," said Bud Finneran, "but something like this goes on forever."[18] Walt Matuszczak was emphatic. "We were proud of what we did, prouder of that than the unbeaten season. It was a matter of conscience. It was the right thing to do all around."[19]

Cornell historian Morris Bishop has penned a fitting conclusion: "But today, I suppose, no one really cares very much whether or not we beat Dartmouth in 1940. We do care that Cornell sportsmanship was nobly vindicated, that we were willing to yield our victory for the sake of honor."[20]

CHAPTER 17
INTO HISTORY

And now the matchless deed's achiev'd
Determin'd, dar'd, and done.

--CHRISTOPHER SMART, *A Song to David*

The accolades for the Cornell gesture mounted during the week, but not everybody was made happy by the events. Asa Bushnell, as Commissioner of the Eastern Intercollegiate Football Association, worried that Cornell's actions might set a precedent for reviewing the outcomes of games after their completion based upon perceptions of error or unfairness. He saw that the precedent could be harmful to the sport, its players and its officials. Cornell's actions were disruptive to the accepted pattern of the day, which was to play the game, record the results, and move on to the next game. The pattern gave short shrift to any notion of error correction, no matter the cause and no matter the consequence. And Bushnell was not quick to embrace a new perspective that placed the actions of his referees, generally an imperial and officious lot, under increased scrutiny.

Bushnell's views, though self-serving, were not without merit. His point was well demonstrated by events surrounding the Columbia-NYU game of 1922, in which an error by the referee early in the game changed the outcome, and in which protests of an attempt to reverse the error raised an even larger issue. Bushnell argued, correctly, that a game of football unfolded a play at a time, each play building on the outcome of the play before it. It was manifestly impossible, he argued, to fairly alter a game by later altering a play in the middle of it, no matter the cause.

Further, Bushnell feared that Cornell's actions would prompt a flood of protests with which his office had neither the authority nor the resources to deal. It must have been discomfitting to him to stand by idly while others decided the outcome of a game officiated by one of his referees, and it must have been equally discomfitting to him to picture himself involved in the settlement of a series of such controversies. Bushnell attempted to minimize the impact by noting the unique circumstances of the Cornell-Dartmouth game, that is, that the defining moment occurred on the final play of the game.

Only under such circumstances, he argued, that one case in a million, could a reversal of a game's outcome be condoned.[1]

****

Although the celebration of Thanksgiving in America long predates college football, the two institutions have combined over the years as happily and as naturally as turkey and cranberry sauce. The football games of Thanksgiving week in general and Thanksgiving Day in particular have long served as a rite of autumn unto themselves, a culmination of the season often offering the best games and the longest rivalries. Feast, prayer, foliage, and roaring crowds have always combined to make a unique American tradition.

It should come as no surprise that in 1940 there were complications. The year before, President Roosevelt, at the behest of the National Dry Retail Goods Association, had issued a proclamation establishing Thanksgiving Day as the third Thursday of November, rather than the last, as Abraham Lincoln had initiated, in order to lengthen the traditional Christmas shopping season. Although Roosevelt's proclamation had official effect only in the District of Columbia, 23 states elected to follow it, another 23 states elected to observe the holiday at its traditional spot on the calendar, and two states, Texas and Colorado, observed both days. In 1940, the six states of New England, Thanksgiving's traditional home, as well as ten other states—Pennsylvania, Tennessee, North Carolina, Florida, Arkansas, Oklahoma, Kansas, Iowa, South Dakota and Nevada—adhered to tradition and celebrated Thanksgiving on November 28. The 32 other states followed the president's lead and celebrated on November 21.

****

The Cornell-Penn game of November 23 had been anticipated by football fans since the beginning of the season as one of the premier events on the eastern football schedule. That it would not serve as Cornell's coronation, due to the events in Hanover the week before, seemed only to heighten interest in the game, and Franklin Field officials were looking at the first sellout of the 80,000-seat stadium since the 1930 Penn-Notre Dame game. Tickets that sold for $3 to $3.50 at the box office were being hawked by scalpers for up to $25 a pair.[2] Cornell fans, peeved because all of the tickets reserved for them were in the end zones,[3] were still in a festive and upbeat mood. A victory dinner had been planned and posters printed to celebrate a Big Red triumph. Naturally, one of them fell into the hands of Penn coach George Munger, who duly posted it on the Quakers' locker room wall. It read: "Cornellians—A cheerful mourning party has been arranged for our late opponents, our wicked victories, and for Penn. Everybody invited."[4] The reaction in the Penn locker room was predictable.

200

The Big Red was a bruised team. The Dartmouth game had taken a toll, and ends Jim Schmuck and Kirk Hershey and guard Howie Dunbar would play at half strength, while halfback Mike Ruddy and guard Pete Wolff would not play at all. Determined to offset its weaknesses, Cornell went through a rigorous three-hour practice on Wednesday, and the football team stayed behind after classes let out at 4 pm for the Thanksgiving holiday in New York. The Big Red practiced on Thursday afternoon and again on Friday morning before heading on to Philadelphia, where the team stayed overnight at the Bellevue-Stratford Hotel. Penn, too, practiced through Thursday, then headed out of town for a day to rest before the contest. Meanwhile, on campus, 2,500 Penn students held a rally in support of their team.

The Quakers had lurked a half step behind Cornell all year, losing only to Michigan and stumbling badly in tying Harvard. But while they turned up cold in some contests, they were spectacular in others. Their 48-0 drubbing of Army the week before, exceeding even the 45-0 defeat Cornell had administered, gave warning that the Penn Quakers were not to be underestimated.

The state of mind of the Cornell players was difficult to peg after the events of the prior week, and probably differed from man to man. Surely there was disappointment, anger, chagrin, renewed determination, and perhaps a bit of sadness as the team prepared to take the field for the last time. Some observers recognized that the heavy burden on Cornell's shoulders came not merely from the defeat by Dartmouth but also from an accumulation of slights, insults, and charges that had built up over the season. The *Syracuse Herald-Journal* noted that the accusations by the Harvard student newspaper were as hurtful as the lost football game. "They were just college boys, nothing more," it said of the Big Red team, "and they were bewildered by abuse that they had not expected and which they did not deserve."[5] To Cornell the game may have been an opportunity to redeem itself, to reestablish itself, perhaps to reclaim Eastern football supremacy. For the Quakers, it was an opportunity to correct those who held all year long that Cornell, and not they, were the better team. And for Penn too it was the last game for Francis X. Reagan who, along with O'Rourke of Boston College and very few others, could lay legitimate claim to the title of best football player in the East.

The game was played in good weather, a rarity in the autumn of 1940. Had it not been played in the aftermath of the Fifth Down shocker, it would have been considered a classic on its own, but instead it remains hidden in the shadow of that momentous game. Observers sometimes dare to compare it to the epic Boston College-Georgetown game of the week before. It had many of the same elements—abrupt momentum swings, heroic individual efforts, nerve-wracking near-misses, daring play-calling and nail-biting moments of suspense, albeit not in the same supply. Yet it did not have two undefeated teams, and although it was called "one of the most thrilling see-saw battles in the...history of the rivalry,"[6] there can be no comparing this or any other game to the epic of the week before.

The emotions of the Big Red, whatever they might have been, were expected to play a role in the outcome, and apparently they did. Some thought that, like wounded animals, they would be even more dangerous than before. Some figured their spirit had been broken. Others felt Cornell had shown signs of overconfidence against Dartmouth and might be likely to exhibit the same failing again. Whatever the case, Cornell's usual clearheaded decision-making had a lapse, and that lapse led directly to its downfall.

The game began in a manner familiar to Big Red fans. After Bill Murphy fumbled to start the game and Penn recovered deep in Cornell territory, Mort Landsberg blocked a Quaker field goal attempt and Cornell took the ball back at its own 21-yard line. Netting 55 yards in passes on the next three plays, Cornell's aerial assault was again dominating play. Landsberg finished off the drive with a touchdown run from the 3-yard line and then, a minute later, Murphy scored on another staple of the Cornell attack, a 60-yard run on a sweep around end. Cornell took a 13-0 lead in the first seven minutes of play and appeared to be by far the better and stronger team.

Then, still in the first period, came the sequence of plays that defined the game. Frank Reagan, with one of his many great punts of the day, a 57-yard effort, backed Cornell up to its own 8-yard line. The prevailing game strategy of the era dictated that Cornell punt from its own end zone to gain field position. Conventional strategy further dictated against the taking of risks with such poor field position, especially when the tide of battle was favorable and the game young. There was simply no room in the conservative mindset of the day for what Cornell did next. Thus, when Hal McCullough stood in the end zone in punt formation ready to receive the snap, Penn was so sure he was going to punt that it did not cover Bill Murphy, standing all alone near the sideline.

What happened next could have been called a bold risk, a daring gamble, a brilliant maneuver or, if it had worked, a coup de grace. Instead of punting, McCullough let fly with a long pass to Murphy. Had Murphy caught it, he could have easily run the 92 yards to the end zone, probably putting the game out of reach for Penn. But McCullough's pass sailed over his head, and the opportunity was lost. The following play could not be described so charitably, since gambles are more often described not by their wisdom but by their outcome. Perhaps it was the result of pent-up frustration, the football equivalent of a primal scream. Perhaps it was a futile attempt to compensate for the shortcomings of the week before. Perhaps it was, like the play before it, simply an attempt to put the game out of reach, relying too much on the element of surprise. Or perhaps, as Bill Boni of the Associated Press described it, it was simply "too cocky."[7] The *Syracuse Herald-Journal* called it, "one of the most boyish displays of bad football the gridiron has seen in years."[8]

Had the first play worked, noted Whitney Young of the Associated Press, Walt Matuszczak, the Cornell signal-caller, would have been hailed as a genius. Had the second play worked, which he was about to call, he would still be regarded as a genius. But since both failed, said Young, he was to be dismissed as a lunkhead.[9] Matuszczak, in the huddle, called his own signal. Cornell, on second down, tried to pass again, this time with a disastrous outcome. Murphy threw a pass over the middle, trying to get the ball to Matuszczak. Penn captain Ray Frick, stepping in front of him, intercepted it and ran it back to the 11-yard line.

In fairness to Matuszczak, he did not invent the pass to Murphy out of thin air. The Big Red had run the exact same play earlier in the year against Syracuse for a long gain, although in that case it had been Swifty Borhman, not McCullough, who had thrown the pass. And, against Ohio State, McCullough had successfully run out of punt formation from the end zone. But teams that embrace risk, as Cornell had, must often pay the price for failure. In retrospect, there is no question that the failed gamble was the turning point in the game.

After Reagan carried the ball four times, Penn had not only its first score but also the momentum of the game solidly on its side. When Reagan soon ran for a second touchdown, the score was tied, 13-13, and, as soon as Penn got the ball back, Reagan made a 52-yard run that set up a Penn field goal, and Penn had the lead, 16-13 at halftime.

Weakened by injuries, Cornell began to fight back in the second half, and for long stretches looked like the Big Red of old. The heavily bandaged Hal McCullough passed to Matuszczak for 20 yards, to Kelley for 35, and to Schmuck in the end zone, only to have the referees disallow the touchdown, because McCullough had been within five yards of the line of scrimmage when he threw his pass, violating the passing rules of the day. On the next play, he passed to Schmuck again, but in trying to keep his feet inbounds the injured end dropped the ball. Undeterred, the Big Red got the ball back and launched another assault. This time, McCullough took the team 72 yards, passing twice to Kirk Hershey for 32 yards apiece. But, on the second of the two plays, Hershey, already hurt, had to be taken from the field. When McCullough ran the ball across the goal line, Penn vigorously objected, claiming he had been tackled short of the line, but to no avail. By the end of the third quarter, Cornell had the lead back, 20-16. But midway through the fourth quarter, after Penn captain Ray Frick intercepted his third pass of the day, Frank Reagan once again asserted his dominance. Penn moved the ball 43 yards in three plays, Reagan carrying it the final 16 yards, and Penn recaptured the lead, 22-20. For the final seven minutes of the game Cornell tried, valiantly but ineffectively, to recapture its lost momentum and the lead, and when the game ended, Penn, and not Cornell, wore the Ivy League crown.

Frank Reagan, who played all 60 minutes, was the best player on the field. He set a new Penn season scoring record with 103 points, and in Allison Danzig's words, "hung up his cleats in accepted Hollywood fashion."[10] Meanwhile, back in Ithaca, a major snowstorm was predicted for upstate New York. Forecasters were calling for a foot of snow and high winds. On Wednesday morning, the Cornell students awoke to a new landscape. They found their campus blanketed with snow, hiding all below it, crisp and white and clean.

****

The week leading up to the Ohio State game on November 23 had been a lackluster one for the Michigan players. In September, the schedule makers surely had figured on this game as being a fitting capper to the Big Ten season, but with the Buckeyes foundering and Minnesota already having wrapped up the conference title, the spark was gone. Saturday's game would be the last for Tom Harmon, Forest Evashevski, and the rest of the Michigan seniors, and the last as well for the retiring athletic director, Fielding Yost. Yet Fritz Crisler had trouble all week summoning the fighting spirit the team had shown all year. On Thursday, Crisler put the team through a two-hour workout in intermittent rain, its last before the game, but the team was listless.[11] That same day the United Press announced its All-Big Ten team for 1940. Harmon and end Ed Frutig were picked for the first team, as was Don Scott of the Buckeyes, who just edged out Evashevski. But in the poll of Big Ten coaches, scouts and players, it had been Dave Rankin, Purdue's fine end, who was selected as the conference's outstanding player. It was the second year in a row that Harmon had been snubbed. The weather forecast for Saturday in Columbus called for hard rain, which should have been no surprise, and the Buckeyes were hoping that the weather would, as it had for Minnesota, provide some relief from Harmon's onslaught.

The weather turned out as forbidding as forecast, and more than 73,000 rain-soaked fans watched a one-sided contest play out. Harmon's season and Michigan's had symmetry. The 40-0 pounding he and the Wolverines administered to Ohio State mirrored their 41-0 opening-day defeat of California, and Harmon was equally dominant in each. What the fans saw was not Michigan against Ohio State but Harmon against the legend. Harmon entered the game with 30 career touchdowns, needing only one to tie the career record of Red Grange. When only a few minutes into the game he scored on a run from the 8-yard line, he equaled the record of the Galloping Ghost. After Paul Kromer returned a punt 81 yards for another touchdown, Harmon followed with two touchdown passes, one of 17 yards to Evashevski and one of 16 yards to Ed Frutig. When in the third period he scored on a 17-yard run, the record was his. With 38 seconds remaining in the game he added his 33rd career touchdown on a run from the 7-yard line.

204

Moments later, with 20 seconds to go, he left the game and the field to a standing ovation from the Columbus crowd. Though it didn't see a competitive game, the crowd was witness to history and was delighted with what was served up. Fans clawed at Harmon as he left the field, shredding his jersey, only part of which made it with him to the locker room. There he made his first order of business to praise his blockers. Indeed, Evashevski had played an equally outstanding game. "Each time Capt. Evashevski called on the Gary Gale to carry the mail, he personally conducted him into the open pastures, where he needed no further directing," said one report.[12] But for Harmon the moment was bittersweet. Though awash in personal acclaim, he left the college playing field for the last time with his team never having beaten archrival Minnesota and never having won a Big Ten title.

The praise came rolling in. "Thomas Dudley Harmon became one of football's immortals today," said the United Press.[13] Despite the achievements of many great teams that day, "the football headlines belonged to an individual...Tommy Harmon of Michigan,"[14] said the Associated Press. "The glory that was Red Grange's shifted to the mighty shoulders of Michigan's Tommy Harmon today,"[15] it announced in another article. After the game, Harmon's jersey was retired, and Number 98 took its place alongside Bennie Oosterbaan's 47, never to be worn by a Wolverine again.

Later that week the Heisman Trophy was to be awarded, and the contest was not expected to be close. Of the ballots cast by the nation's sportswriters, Arthur J. Daley, writing earlier in the *New York Times*, said, "Advice is hereby given...not to waste time in counting them. Tommy Harmon of Michigan will win in a complete landslide. How can he miss, and who can challenge him for the distinction?"[16] On Monday, to the surprise of nobody, Harmon was announced as the winner of the Maxwell Trophy, given to the season's outstanding star, and on Wednesday the Downtown Athletic Club named him the Heisman Trophy winner in balloting that, predictably, was not close. John Kimbrough of Texas A&M finished a distant second in the voting, and George Franck of Minnesota came in third.

****

On November 23, two disappointed teams squared off in Evanston. Three weeks earlier, when Notre Dame had been ranked second in the Associated Press poll and Northwestern eighth, this would have been a matchup of irresistible attraction. But three weeks of poor play by Notre Dame coupled with Northwestern's tough run-ins with Minnesota and Michigan put an end to any lofty hopes for either team. The game may have been seen as a consolation match between the two, but Northwestern had been good enough to seriously challenge for the national crown while Notre Dame, though thought to be worthy, was not. The Wildcats convincingly demonstrated the difference as they, and Bill DeCorrevont in particular, took out their frustrations in a

20-0 romp. Decorrevont, finally fully healthy, justified his rave reviews with perhaps his best game as a collegian. He threw a 32-yard touchdown pass for the first Wildcat touchdown, set up the second with a brilliant 27-yard run when he cut back against the Irish defense and reached the 9-yard line, then scored the touchdown on fourth down from the 4-yard line. Notre Dame never seriously challenged in the game.

The game ended Northwestern's season, but the Irish had one more encounter with Southern California. While the Irish were traveling to Los Angeles for the game, 15 members of the Trojan team were hospitalized with the flu. When they got out of their sick beds, they put up a good fight, but the Irish prevailed 10-6, as Milt Piepul scored all their points. The game ended with the Trojans at the Notre Dame goal line but unable to score. Though the season had to be a disappointing one for the Irish, they at least ended in good fashion, scoring a win in a growing intersectional rivalry.

****

There remained for the Minnesota Gophers one last challenge. Dismissed at the beginning of the season by even their most vocal supporters, the Gophers now had only Wisconsin standing between them and an undefeated season, the Big Ten title and in all probability, the national championship. Wisconsin coach Harry Stuhldreher had been an All-American halfback at Notre Dame in 1923 and 1924, where he had been one of the legendary Four Horsemen. He had come to Wisconsin in 1936 after an outstanding career as head coach at Villanova. Stuhldreher, like most of the bevy of college coaches spawned from Notre Dame during those Rockne years, was a strong proponent of Rockne's offensive system, the most notable element of which was the Notre Dame Box. A variation on the single wing, this approach involved a shift of three of the four backfield men just before the snap of the ball into a box to the left or right of the center. Its theory was that by using it the offense could deploy additional blocking power at the point of attack faster than the defense could adjust to it. Often the backs were still in motion at the instant the ball was snapped, giving them an additional advantage. While Rockne's scheme did little to diversify an offense or promote a passing attack, it was highly effective in promoting a power running game.

Knute Rockne did not invent the system. It had been handed down to him by his predecessor Jess Harper, who had picked it up from his mentor at Chicago, Amos Alonzo Stagg.[17] Some thought Minnesota coach Doc Williams, Stagg's old Yale teammate, produced the seminal ideas on the use of the shift, and others thought Williams copied the idea from a Wisconsin high school.[18] Rockne had simply refined the concept, applied it to his team's needs and talents, and taught it to his players more effectively than had any other coach, with startlingly effective results. The Notre Dame system was widely used in college football, each practitioner picking it up from his mentor, adding his own wrinkles and improvements, suiting it to his own particular circumstances, and then passing it along to his charges. Curly Lambeau, a freshman on Rockne's first team, took the same ideas and applied them to the pro game, creating a championship team at Green Bay. This inheritance and adaptation of ideas was then, and is still today, the time-honored method by which change has evolved in the game of football. Stuhldreher, who had the advantage of having flourished as a player under the system and of having learned it first-hand at the knee of the master himself, made Rockne's Notre Dame Box the foundation of Wisconsin football.

Indispensable to the Badger team were two sophomores from the small town of Lancaster, Wisconsin. Dave Schreiner and Hadley Mark Hoskins (known to his close friends as Had but to the rest of the world as Mark) were inseparable as young boys, hanging out and playing football every free moment of the day. When they graduated from high school and went off to college, their coach predicted that one of them would be an All-American and at least one of them would be captain.[19]

At Wisconsin, both matured quickly as football players. In their first varsity game together as sophomores, on October 5, 1940, the Lancaster connection paid its first dividend against Marquette when Hoskins threw a touchdown pass to Schreiner, and then ran 53 yards for another touchdown. The pass play was the subject of particular excitement in Madison, because it included a perfectly executed fake by Hoskins, and when Schreiner caught the ball there was not a defender within 20 yards of him.[20] The course was set for great things. The two instantly, if not imaginatively, became known as the Touchdown Twins. "The Lancaster twins, Hoskins and Schreiner, performed in great fashion....Considering it was the first college game for the two sophomores, they must be given great credit," said the *Capital Times*.[21] The other Madison paper, the *Wisconsin State Journal*, was equally boastful. "Playing in his first college game, Hoskins showed the poise of a veteran, and his running style and passing are distinctly stylish. Another boy you'll be hearing a lot of is Dave Schreiner, another sophomore from Lancaster...he was one whale of a football player in his college debut," it wrote.[22] Hoskins saw plenty of playing time as a sophomore left halfback, the key spot in Stuhldreher's offensive scheme, and in subsequent years would take over the starting role. Schreiner, already a starter as a sophomore, became an All-American performer his junior year. When he repeated as an All-American his senior year and was named the Most Valuable Player in the Big Ten, there was talk that he might be one of the greatest ends ever to play the game. At the end of the 1942 season Hoskins and Schreiner were chosen team co-captains of record. Their high school coach's prophecy had come true.

****

When 40,000 fans gathered in Camp Randall Stadium in Madison on November 23, 1940, to greet the visiting Minnesota football team, the Gophers had already clinched the Big Ten title and were playing with the strong likelihood that a win would mean the national championship. The student newspaper pointed out, "If Minnesota wins in a romp today the Gophers will probably retain the Number 1 position in national polls that they hold today. A Wisconsin win would—well, let's not think about it."[23] While the *Minnesota Daily* might have revised its opinion of the Gophers' prospects— only weeks before it had discounted the likelihood of an undefeated season as improbable—the Minnesota fans were not ready yet to rank their team on par with the recent greats of the Pug Lund era. But undeniably this team had placed a fourth national title within their grasp. The Badgers, with a 4-3 record, were playing for a winning season. Oddsmakers made the Gophers 3-1 favorites.

Two of the most painful moments in George Franck's career had come at the hands of the Badgers' George Paskvan. In the 1939 Wisconsin-Minnesota game, Paskvan had made a vicious tackle of Franck. "That so-and-so hit me harder than I ever was hit in my life," said Franck. "I thought he had broken me in two." Then, in a spring track meet, a discus thrown by Paskvan skidded onto the track and hit Franck in the ankle.[24] It had been an accident, but surely those two incidents were on their minds as the two stars prepared to play their last college contest.

The game began ominously for Minnesota. Early in the game, Franck fumbled a punt deep in Minnesota territory. But when the Gophers held and got the ball back, his great punt regained field position, if only temporarily. Two plays later, Dave Schreiner scored for Wisconsin on a 72-yard pass play, catching the ball at the Minnesota 45-yard line, shaking off two tacklers and running the rest of the way for a touchdown. Then his teammate Tommy Farris intercepted Bruce Smith's pass at midfield and ran it all the way back for a second touchdown. Before the quarter was over the Gophers were down, 13-0. Great teams must be able to win when they are ahead 13-0, which that day Cornell could not do, and when they are behind by that score. Minnesota would be challenged to show whether they had the makings of a champion.

The initial response was largely the work of Bill Daley. When they got the ball back the Gophers put on a long drive sparked by Daley's 27-yard run, and when they pushed the ball to the 12-yard line, Daley ran it in from there. Then he intercepted a pass on a fake punt, and a few plays later Bruce Smith scored the touchdown that tied the game, and it remained that way until halftime. In the final period, with Minnesota ahead by three points, George Franck intercepted Mark Hoskins's pass and ran it back 27 yards for the clinching touchdown. The final score was 22-13.

Schreiner had played brilliantly in the game, so much so that a few days later, when Minnesota named its all-opponent team, it was the sophomore

Schreiner, and not Purdue's Big Ten MVP Dave Rankin, who was chosen on the team.

When the final Associated Press poll of the year came out, it showed Minnesota, as expected, in first place. Maybe at the beginning of the year Bernie Bierman secretly believed they could do it, but not many other people had a clue that the Gophers had a national championship in them. The experts were proven wrong. On November 26, the Minnesota team met and chose Bruce Smith as team captain for 1941. Typically, when Smith was named, his reaction was, "Gee...when my name was called off, I...I just couldn't believe it." His first order of business, after praising his teammates, was to pledge another national championship in 1941.[25]

****

On Thursday, November 28—Thanksgiving had been celebrated the week before in Texas—the Texas A&M Aggies prepared to close the deal. One win away from a second consecutive undefeated season and a probable invitation to the Rose Bowl, they had climbed to second place in the Associated Press poll, trailing only Minnesota, which had completed its season. An impressive victory over Texas, against whom they had never won in Texas Memorial Stadium, might again catapult them to the top. But Longhorns coach Dana X. Bible, who had coached the Aggies from 1917 to 1928, had a plan. Knowing that his team would likely be unable to run against the stiff Aggie defense, he laid out a simple but effective approach. After the Aggies' opening kickoff went out of bounds, Texas threw two passes, one for 34 yards and one for 33 yards, and before the fans were settled in their seats they had the ball on the Aggie one-foot line. On their third play, Pete Layden dove into the end zone. The teams played for 59 more minutes, but the final score was 7-0. Texas A&M's 19-game winning streak and hopes for another national title were in flames.

****

On November 30, the 1940 Army-Navy game was played, as always, before a huge throng. More than 100,000 people crowded into Municipal Stadium in Philadelphia to witness what was, in truth, one of the least exciting games of the great rivalry. Going into the game, Army had won only one of eight games, and the Cadets' 45-0 loss to Cornell had been more than matched a few weeks later when the Penn Quakers flattened them 48-0. Navy had won five games, losing only to Penn and Notre Dame, while playing Columbia to a scoreless tie. The pregame pageantry, an elaborate precision marching drill conducted by 1,800 West Point Cadets and 2,600 Annapolis Midshipmen, was far more exciting in its pomp and color and far more expertly executed than the game itself. Army, which had lost to Navy the year before, 10-0, was a big underdog, and put on an even weaker performance than anticipated. A superior Navy team dominated play throughout the game, and entering the fourth quarter, held a 14-0 edge. Then, as was so often the case in 1940, something happened.

On the first play of the fourth quarter, an Army player fell victim to the restrictive substitution rule: he had been detected entering the game late in the third period after having been taken out earlier that same period. Sentence was about to be imposed—a fifteen-yard penalty and expulsion from the game for the offending player—when it came to light that the player in question was center Bill Gillis, Army team captain. Despite the letter of the rule, the Navy players beseeched the referee to mark off the penalty but to allow their opponents' captain to stay in the game. Such a request put the referee in a difficult position. Surely he could appreciate the special nature of the rivalry and the gesture of sportsmanship being extended, but the rule was explicit. Here, only two weeks after the Fifth Down debacle, any referee familiar with the huge professional embarrassment that befell Red Friesell could be expected to be especially careful not to run afoul of the rulebook or to take any undue risk in its interpretation. So soon afterward, only extreme caution could reasonably be expected of any game official.

But the referee for the game was not someone merely familiar with the Friesell incident. It was Red Friesell himself. Not one to duck and hide from criticism, Friesell was anxious to stay in the arena. The week before, he had refereed the Yale-Harvard game, mercifully without incident. An aggressive enforcer of the rules, he was nonetheless anything but rulebound and anything but risk-averse. When he set his mind on the right course of action he took it and stood behind his decision, even if it meant sticking his neck out to do so. Friesell granted Navy's request and, contrary to the rules, Bill Gillis was allowed to stay in the game.

Navy continued to dominate the game until late in the fourth quarter. With but a few seconds left to play and victory out of reach, the Cadets launched a drive that carried them to the Navy 33-yard line. Running with a lateral from one of his teammates, Gillis accounted for much of the yardage in the drive. Hoping to avert a second consecutive shutout at the hands of Navy, Army tried one last desperation pass into the end zone, only to have it intercepted by a Navy defender as time ran out. Just before, a small group of Midshipmen had made their way onto the field in the far end zone, and in time-honored tradition, began tearing the goalpost down before the final play. With the game clock striking zero, they stopped only to stand at attention while the Army and Navy bands together played the national anthem. As soon as the last note was sounded they finished their demolition work, and the rest of the Midshipmen poured out onto the field and helped carry away the dismantled goalpost.

But Navy had been ruled offside on the last play, and Army was entitled to another play and another chance to score, a situation that caused a huge challenge for Friesell, since order was unlikely to be restored. In a rivalry as intense as Army-Navy any opportunity to score was taken seriously. Friesell appeared to be on the brink of yet one more difficult offside dispute. But the day was saved by Bill Gillis, still in the game, who, seeing Friesell in trouble, repaid his debt to him and to Navy by declining the penalty, graciously accepting defeat and the ignominy of a second consecutive shutout. Among people like Friesell and Gillis, that was the way things were done.

****

The rivalry between the football teams of the University of California and Stanford University dates to before the turn of the century. California began playing football against local clubs as early as 1882, and Stanford, founded in 1885, began fielding a football team by 1891. Originally, the game played on the west coast bore only faint resemblance to the more polished form of the game played by easterners; it more resembled rugby. The first game of football between the two schools took place on March 19, 1892, on San Francisco's Haight Street Grounds, and immediately attracted students of both schools and residents of the area. Accounts differ, but it is likely that the first game attracted between 10,000 and 20,000 spectators, far exceeding expectations and the preparations of the two student managers who arranged the game, Herbert Lang of California and Herbert Hoover of Stanford, one day to become President of the United States. Adding to the troubles, neither manager remembered to bring a ball, and a sporting goods proprietor in attendance was dispatched on horseback to his store and returned an hour later with a makeshift ball. Stanford won the first game, 14-10, and prevailed in the early years of the rivalry, aided by the coaching of Walter Camp in 1894 and 1895 and Fielding Yost in 1900. By the turn of the century, the Ax had become the trophy of the victors, and by 1903 the game had left San Francisco to be played thereafter on one campus or the other.

But Stanford was in for a jolt in 1902 when it invited the powerful Michigan Wolverine team west to play in the first Rose Bowl game. Stanford found that its level of play was not competitive with that found in the Midwest, and the game was terminated by mutual consent in the third quarter as Michigan, coached by Yost, won, 49-0. The Rose Bowl, too, was suspended, not to be played again until 1916. During a time when the University of Washington, under coach Gil Dobie, remained undefeated for 63 games between 1907 and 1917, playing mostly teams from the Pacific Northwest, both California and Stanford suspended football and reverted to rugby, deemed a safer game. California switched back to football in 1915 and Stanford in 1918.[26] The rivalry was suspended for four years due in part to the war and in part to a dispute between the two schools regarding freshman eligibility.[27]

Following the reintroduction of football, California became competitive by 1920 and won the 1921 Rose Bowl game against Ohio State. Stanford followed a similar path to success, and its 1924 team, with the great Ernie Nevers, went to the Rose Bowl but lost to Notre Dame. When the schools renewed their rivalry, California went from 1918 to 1924 without losing, and Stanford went from 1924 to 1930 without a defeat. The 1924 game was a tie. By 1940, the Big Game, as the hotly contested series came to be called, stood with 15 wins for Stanford and 14 for California. There had been seven ties, and California had won the last four games. As with many rivalries, there had been a number of upsets over the years.

Stub Allison's Golden Bears had reason in September to expect better than their 4-4 record, but their last two games had been impressive wins against Southern California and Oregon, and Clark Shaughnessy was not about to sell them short. In some circles the Indians were 2 ½-to-1 favorites, in others 3-to-1, and few people were taking that talk seriously. Among California's losses was a tough 7-6 defeat to Washington, and after their opening-day thrashing at the hands of Tom Harmon and Michigan they had been competitive in every game.

With two weeks to rest and recover, Norm Standlee was expected to be at full strength for Stanford, although Shaughnessy wavered on the issue all week. Stub Allison readied his team for battle and devised three trick plays to help his cause, all three involving his best player, tackle Bob Reinhard, a high school teammate of Frankie Albert. In addition to being an outstanding lineman, Reinhard also did most of the punting for the Bears and, unknown to many, could easily pass the ball 60 yards on the fly. The big trick play had Reinhard lining up to punt but instead passing to the swift and glue-fingered halfback Jim Jurkovich running to the end zone. Allison intended the play to be used in a punting situation near midfield, and the Bears ran the play successfully many times during secret practice during the week. They were confident they could score a touchdown with it.[28] But sometimes the best-laid plans go awry before they have a chance to unfold. Near the end of the week Reinhard came down with the flu, and by Friday morning he was checked in to Cowell Memorial Hospital. A number of players on each team were down with a touch of it, and Pete Kmetovic had spent a night earlier in the week in the hospital as well.[29] California publicity man Walter Frederick denied Reinhard was ill or hospitalized, and school officials had him admitted under the fake name "Johnny Green." But by Friday night, when his temperature spiked at 103.5 degrees, California dropped all secrecy and admitted that their best player would not be available.[30]

The game was played in Memorial Stadium, the same venue in which Tom Harmon had scorched the Bears more than two months before, but this time the crowd was near stadium capacity as 80,000 fans looked on. The game was broadcast around the world by General Electric's powerful shortwave radio station KGEI, as was the Army-Navy game earlier in the day. Before the game was a minute old, Jurkovich, the other half of the trick play combo, suffered a kick to the head and, bruised and bleeding, was forced by doctors to sit out the rest of the game. Jurkovich was so injury-prone that *Oakland Tribune* columnist Art Cohn maintained he should not have been playing football at all.[31] California, already at a disadvantage, would have to give battle without two of their most potent weapons.

Late in the first period Stanford took the ball at its own 22-yard line and, largely on a 22-yard run by Gallarneau, a 12-yard pass by Albert and an 18-yard run by Kmetovic, moved the ball to the 1-yard line as the quarter ended. On the first play of the second quarter Kmetovic ran for the touchdown. Albert kicked the extra point, and Stanford led, 7-0. After Albert missed a long field goal attempt, Stanford got the ball back when a snap by the California center sailed over the punter's head, and a few moments later Gallarneau scored on a short touchdown run. But by halftime Stanford had shown about all the offense it would show, and the second half, dominated by California's offense and Stanford's defense, produced a starkly different type of contest.

The most important five plays of the game occurred in the third quarter. Just past midfield, Albert's pass was intercepted by the Bears' Carl Hoberg, in the game to replace the injured Jurkovich, and Hoberg, with a group of five blockers in front of him, had what appeared to be a clear path to the goal line. Only Albert remained between Hoberg and the end zone, and he somehow fought off the five blockers and tackled Hoberg on the 1-yard line. "How he did it probably no one will ever know," said Prescott Sullivan of the *San Francisco Examiner* of a tackle deemed by football historians to be one of the four best tackles of the decade.[32] "Albert cut across the field, leaped over one potential blocker, shook off a block by another, sidestepped a third, and caught Hoberg by the right arm at the 10," explained James W. Johnson, Stanford football historian.[33] Then, only three feet from the end zone, the Bears launched four running plays at the middle of the Stanford line, and gained only inches. The Bears had been turned away. Later, as time in the game expired, Jack McQuarry of California scored a touchdown, wriggling free from Albert before diving into the end zone.

The play on which the game hinged could have created some controversy, but forthrightness averted the problem. Hoberg, on his long run with the intercepted pass, was grabbed by Albert at the ten-yard line, which slowed them just enough for Jack Francis of Stanford to catch both players at the five-yard line. The three of them tumbled to the ground, rolling into the end zone, and the referee determined that Hoberg had been downed a yard short of the goal line. Many California supporters loudly disagreed, maintaining that Hoberg had scored, but Hoberg himself, after the game, said he thought his knee touched the ground on the one-yard line.[34]

By a final score of 13-7 Stanford had secured an undefeated season, one of the most remarkable turnarounds in the history of college football, and a sure spot in the Rose Bowl. That Stanford found itself in such a position—

"you probably would have been clamped into the nearest asylum for even hinting that the Indians would march unbeaten," said the United Press[35]—was remarkable enough. But that it earned that spot based on a fabulous tackle by its offensive magician and a stirring rock-ribbed goal line stand by a team that specialized in razzle dazzle was almost too much to believe.

Stanford fans streamed onto the field and tore down the goalposts. Amidst the jubilation, the Stanford team was presented with the Ax, the symbol of victory in the rivalry. Only a year before, Clark Shaughnessy was given the ax in a different sort of way at Chicago, and now newspaper photos showed him and a towel-draped Frankie Albert admiring the trophy in the locker room.[36]

****

It seemed that there would be no limit to the notable games of 1940. On Christmas Day, in San Antonio, St. Mary's faced off against the All-Stars of the Southwest in a charity game played for British War Relief. There was little reason to remember the game, except for the All-Stars' lineup, which included Maurice Britt of Arkansas at one end and Jack Lummus of Baylor at the other. The two had played against each another on October 12, when the Razorbacks beat the Bears, 12-6. Each had started at end and had cracked his leather-helmeted head against the other all game long. On this day they were teammates.

Maurice "Footsie" Britt, born in Carlisle, Arkansas, and raised in nearby Lonoke, would go on to play a year of professional football with the Detroit Lions after graduation before entering the army. Between July and November of 1943, while fighting with the Third Infantry Division in Italy, Britt was awarded a Bronze Star, a Silver Star, a Purple Heart, and helped win for his battalion a Presidential Unit Citation.[37] On November 10, at Monte Rotundo, Maurice Britt, in fending off a German counterattack, earned the Congressional Medal of Honor, as well as the Military Cross of the British Empire, the Valore Militare Merit from the Italians, and his second Purple Heart.

Jack Lummus was born on a cotton farm in Ennis, Texas. After college he played professional baseball for the Wichita Falls Spudders before turning to pro football with the New York Giants, for whom he played 10 games in the fall of 1941, including the NFL Championship game. On February 19, 1945, he waded ashore as a lieutenant with the 5th Marine Division on Iwo Jima. On March 8, in intense combat near Kitano Point, he lost both legs while leading his platoon in a charge against an entrenched Japanese position. Thinking at first that he was standing in a hole, some of his men, when they found out he wasn't, considered a mercy shooting. But Lummus inspired his men to charge 300 yards ahead, before he was taken to an aid station, and died during emergency surgery.[38] On Memorial Day, May 30, 1946, he was posthumously awarded the Congressional Medal of Honor.[39]

Maurice Britt and Jack Lummus each caught a touchdown pass in the All Stars' victory. No other football team in history has ever had a starting lineup with a future Medal of Honor winner at each end.

CHAPTER 18
THE CURTAIN COMES DOWN

This has been a season, hasn't it?

--CLARK SHAUGHNESSY, STANFORD COACH

The process of constructing the four major bowl matchups was in full swing. The upset of Texas A&M, thought to be a sure bet for the Rose Bowl, had muddied an already complicated picture. The Sugar Bowl struck first, before the Stanford-California game was even over, securing an attractive match between undefeated Boston College and undefeated Tennessee. As bowl officials sweated, Boston College edged a surprisingly tough Holy Cross team 7-0, and Tennessee prevailed over Vanderbilt, 20-0. It had been speculated all week that the Volunteers might be in line for a Rose Bowl invitation, but they knew that their weak schedule left them without strong support, and they took a good deal when it was offered. The Cotton Bowl secured once-beaten Fordham as one of its participants, but Texas A&M would not commit as an opponent, hoping for a juicier chance in the Rose Bowl. Southern Methodist and Rice were backup choices. The least certain was the Orange Bowl, which leaned toward Mississippi State as one participant and either Georgetown or Lafayette as the other.

Immediately after Stanford's win over California, the Pacific Coast Conference presidents made it official and named the Indians to a spot in the Rose Bowl, a move that had been deemed all but official for three weeks. Stanford Athletic Director Alfred R. Masters indicated it would not pick its opponent until the next day.

Complications abounded, both in the short term and the long term. Rose Bowl officials held out hope that somehow Stanford could persuade Minnesota to play in the game, and the Big Ten to let them. A matchup between those two undefeated teams, and between their coaches, former teammates Bernie Bierman and Clark Shaughnessy, would be the most exciting possible outcome, thought the sportswriters. In the long run, a formal relationship between the Pacific Coast Conference and the Big Ten, whereby the Rose Bowl would have a representative from each conference each year, was also being pursued by many officials. Once steadfastly opposed by the Big Ten, the idea was one that could at least now be discussed. Before the start of the season, Fielding Yost, longtime leader of Michigan athletics, said he was positive the Big Ten would go for the idea, but the influential Arch Ward, sports editor of the *Chicago Tribune,* felt that opposition was growing and insurmountable.[1] By the end of the season, Iowa, it was known, was in favor of such a long-term relationship. Wisconsin, Minnesota, and Purdue were opposed. Northwestern and Illinois appeared to be leaning against it, and Indiana, Michigan, and Ohio State leaning for it. Chicago, still a conference member but a nonparticipant in football, would not vote. Arch Ward was right. The votes were not there.

The Big Ten had a number of concerns about a permanent Rose Bowl relationship, aside from the longstanding concern of infringement upon the academic role, enough alone to dissuade some members. The Rose Bowl was run by outside promoters, and the colleges were mere participants in their promotion, an arrangement that soured many university officials. New Year's Day was seen as too late a date to suit the Big Ten, which concluded its season earlier than most west coast teams. And a regular venue at the Los Angeles Coliseum meant away games and difficult travel every year for Big Ten teams. An alternative version, involving management by a joint committee of the two conferences, a game date of December 1, and a venue alternating between the Los Angeles Coliseum and Soldier Field in Chicago, was seen as more palatable by some and more likely to garner Big Ten support.[2]

But the long-term issue clarified the short term. Minnesota, it was clear, would not play in the 1941 Rose Bowl, even if the Big Ten were to allow it, and appeared to be as negatively inclined to the idea as any school in the conference. The attitude of the administration was shared by the student body. While sportswriters were urging Minnesota to go to the Rose Bowl, Professor Henry Rottschaefer, Minnesota's conference representative, pointed out that the faculty had voted unanimously in October against such a measure, and he was going to cast his vote accordingly with the Conference. Rottschaefer cited conflicts with exam schedules as his reason for personally opposing the measure.[3] The student newspaper, the *Minnesota Daily,* urged sportswriters to "call off their dogs and let the boys get back to their school work." Reasoning that football is an extracurricular activity and that the basic purpose of the university is academics, the newspaper concluded that "we must continue to be opposed to the Rose Bowl agitation and all other proposals which ignore the basic purposes of this University."[4]

Attuned to reality, Stanford, it was rumored, had unofficially offered the Rose Bowl spot to Nebraska as early as Saturday night. Nebraska was a member of the Big Six Conference, which also had a ban on postseason play, but was not as rigid about it as the Big Ten. The rule had been waived in 1938 for Oklahoma and in 1939 for Missouri, and the rumor had it that official approval from the conference was all that was needed and was forthcoming.[5] The rumor was right. The next day Nebraska made it official, Texas A&M

accepted the Cotton Bowl bid, and the Orange Bowl ultimately settled on Mississippi State and Georgetown. Lafayette, undefeated and untied, was left uninvited despite rallies by its entire 1,000-member student body.

****

On December 10, the ten-team National Football League held its annual draft of college football players in Washington, D.C., three weeks before the bowl games were played. The Chicago Bears, fresh off their 73-0 victory in the championship game two days before, had traded for the first-round rights of two other teams, the Steelers and the Eagles, and so George Halas had three first-round draft choices, including the first overall pick. It seemed that Halas always had a leg up on his competition, both on and off the field.

Tom Harmon, uninterested in playing professional football, had asked earlier that his name be withdrawn from the draft, but Chicago, using the Eagles' pick, took Harmon with the first pick anyway. The Chicago Cardinals, picking second, took John Kimbrough of Texas A&M. Then the Bears chose again, using the Steelers' pick, and took Stanford's Norm Standlee third. The Cleveland Rams chose Rudy Mucha, Washington's center, next. The Detroit Lions chose Jim Thomason of Texas A&M, then the New York Giants chose George Franck of Minnesota. Green Bay chose George Paskvan of Wisconsin, and the Brooklyn Dodgers chose Dean McAdams of Washington. The Bears, with their third pick of the first round, chose Don Scott of Ohio State, and the Redskins closed out the first round by taking Forest Evashevski of Michigan, who had also indicated, like Harmon, that he did not want to play pro football.

Many of these men sensed already that the future was not going to unfold in neat fashion. Heightened global tensions promised a different future for them and their families, and in this respect the sports heroes of 1940 were no different from the rest of the Americans of their generation. The nation was on the brink of war. Many of the sport stars of the time did not wait for the other military draft and enlisted in the service right out of school, or even before the end of school.

****

Franklin Roosevelt, now free of electoral pressures, readied the nation for war. On December 17, he outlined his Lend-Lease Plan, in which he proposed making available to Britain whatever materiel it needed to defend itself, with the expectation that the United States would be repaid after the war. In laying out his travel plans for a spring trip to Georgia, he added the ominous qualifier, "if the world survives."[6]

Roosevelt's plan was well received by the majority of the American public. Sen. Burton K. Wheeler of Montana, the nation's arch-isolationist, spoke strongly against it, claiming that the German people wanted peace as much as anybody. Wheeler said it would "plow under every fourth American boy,"[7] and Roosevelt countered by terming Wheeler's comments, which infuriated him, "the most untruthful, the most dastardly, unpatriotic thing that has ever been said."[8] Roosevelt argued in his fireside talk, "No man can tame a tiger into a kitten by stroking it." Three quarters of Americans heard the speech,[9] and they were siding with Roosevelt.

Nearly 70 percent of Americans, according to polls, favored helping the British defend themselves, even if it meant a risk of going to war.[10] Roosevelt had won a resounding victory in the battle for American public opinion, and the rest, it could be argued, was inevitable.

****

On December 3, when Nebraska's acceptance of Stanford's invitation to play in the Rose Bowl became official, the news set off nonstop celebration on the Cornhusker campus. Classes were dismissed and long parades of students marched through campus beating drums and honking their car horns. Nebraska coach Biff Jones would be the tenth coach to try to dismantle Clark Shaughnessy's T-formation.

On December 8, the National Football League Championship game was played between the Chicago Bears and the Washington Redskins. It was a rematch of a game played three weeks before, which the Redskins had won, 7-3. But this game would be different. Fresh from completing an undefeated regular season for Stanford and three weeks before the Rose Bowl, Clark Shaughnessy was on the sidelines as an assistant to George Halas, feeding him ideas on how to run the Bears' T-formation. He had told sportswriters he was going to Chicago to visit his brothers, but he spent his time scouting out the Redskins' defensive strategy and proposing plays to counteract it.[11] He scripted a play to be used as the second in the game, and promised it would go for a touchdown. It did.[12] Due in no small part to Shaughnessy's preparations, the Bears won the game, 73-0, the most lopsided NFL championship game ever played.

The referee for the game was Red Friesell. Stepping out of the college ranks and into the pros did nothing to aid his escape from the difficulties and controversies that seemed to follow him everywhere. Again he was faced with a dilemma—the Bears had kicked so many extra points into the seats that the officials were literally short of footballs—and again he used his best judgment to solve it. After the score reached 66-0, Friesell ordered the Bears not to kick any more extra points, and they complied.[13]

Nebraska's Biff Jones attended the game, hoping to gain a few pointers by watching the Redskins contain the Bears' version of the T-formation offense. It is safe to say he came away empty handed. To escape the snow of Nebraska he took his team to Phoenix to practice before New Year's Day, resigned to the reality that the upcoming game would match Nebraska's brawn against Stanford's speed and trickery. Stanford was the favorite.

The game was one in which the score merely confirmed what was evident by the play on the field. Nebraska was a good team, but Stanford was faster and better. Nebraska started out well when Butch Luther ran the opening kickoff nearly to midfield, and after it ran seven running plays, Vike Francis scored the game's first touchdown. The Cornhusker defense was also impressive in the third quarter when it held Stanford for four downs from inside the one-yard line. But the game belonged to Stanford's Pete Kmetovic. First, his 29-yard run in the first quarter set up Stanford's first touchdown, scored by Hugh Gallarneau. Then he made a brilliant 40-yard runback of a punt for touchdown in the third period, sharply reversing fields, giving up ten yards of ground, and dashing down the right sideline, sealing the Stanford victory, 21-13. Most observers thought the final score was a fair assessment of the relative strength of the two teams.

Biff Jones was gracious in defeat and lavished praise on the Stanford team. When he saw Butch Luther, Nebraska's fastest man, pulled down from behind by Gallarneau, far from Stanford's fastest, he said, "I knew we were in for a tough afternoon." Frankie Albert, whose 40-yard touchdown pass to Gallarneau had provided Stanford's second score, was also lauded by Jones. He was "far and away the best quarterback I have seen in years," he said.[14] Later he added, "Go tell Clark Shaughnessy I'll buy him 120 acres of fine corn land if he'll tell me where I can get a Frankie Albert."[15] Shaughnessy returned the compliments, calling Nebraska a "great club—the toughest we met this year."[16] And Jones added, "I think Stanford played as well against us as Minnesota."[17]

The play of the day, the play that sent everybody home talking, was Kmetovic's punt return. "Just when you think he is going at top speed, he slips the throttle another notch and really slips into high gear," marveled Henry McLemore of the United Press.[18] The downfield blocking for Kmetovic gained equal admiration. On the play, "Huskies were strewn like cornstalks over the turf,"[19] said the Associated Press. "Stanford's blockers smashed the fatigued Husker tacklers, two were knocked unconscious, others sent flying like rag dolls," said another observer.[20] Jones himself remarked that at the end of the play he couldn't see a Nebraska man on his feet.[21]

The Orange Bowl game was not nearly so exciting. Mississippi State, unbeaten but tied once by Auburn (a team Boston College had defeated easily), beat Georgetown, 14-7. The Hoyas outgained the Maroons in the air and on the ground but fell victim to penalties and bad breaks at inopportune times. Most significantly, they had a 59-yard pass play nullified, and later a drive for the potentially tying touchdown died on the six-yard line. Mississippi State scored its first touchdown on a blocked punt. After the game, the Hoyas, feeling that they had outplayed Mississippi State, wished they could play the game again, but it was too late for that.[22] Despite the statistical difference, said the Associated Press, "there wasn't much doubt that the better team won."[23]

A better game was played in the Cotton Bowl, where a tough and competitive Fordham team, losers only to St. Mary's, gave the defending national champion Texas A&M Aggies all they could handle before falling, 13-12. The Associated Press billed the game as a match between "a sly little fellow with a compass in his hips and a giant who simply bullies his way around a football field."[24] The principals in that comparison were Fordham's 165-pound Len Eshmont and the Aggies' 222-pound bruiser, John Kimbrough. But there were others who upstaged the two stars in this contest. "Rams Defeated by Aggies But Not Outplayed," said the headlines over a United Press story. It was a "once-in-a-lifetime, bruising, battering, hell-for-leather affair," said the story,[25] a game in which Fordham, a 9-5 underdog, held the statistical advantage and outplayed the Aggies for most of the contest. In the first half, the Fordham line, in the spirit of their predecessors, the Seven Blocks of Granite, completely bottled up the Aggie running attack led by Kimbrough. When the Rams pulled off a Statue of Liberty play with Steve Filipowicz passing to Jimmy Noble and followed it with a Filipowicz touchdown run, they had a 6-0 halftime lead over the thoroughly outplayed Aggies.

But on the second play of the second half, the Aggies' Marion Pugh threw a 62-yard touchdown pass to third-string halfback Earl "Alabama" Smith, who caught it at the 35-yard line and outraced Ram defender Eshmont to the end zone. Then, the game tied, the breaks started to go the Aggies' way. Fordham's Jim Blumenstock faked a punt from his own end zone and instead passed to Jimmy Noble. Noble lateraled to Jim Lansing, who carried the ball nearly to midfield, but the referees ruled that Noble had made a forward lateral and brought the ball back to the four-yard line. But when Blumenstock punted, for real this time, Fordham was penalized for unnecessary roughness in the end zone, and Texas A&M took possession at the one-yard line. Kimbrough scored the touchdown, the extra point was good, and suddenly Texas A&M had a 13-6 lead. Some observers thought that Fordham had nearly given the score away.[26]

In the fourth quarter, Fordham fought back, and Blumenstock scored a touchdown on a 15-yard run. Steve Hudacek, who had had an extra point attempt blocked earlier, lined up for the tying kick. Again it was partially blocked. The United Press said it was John Kimbrough who blocked it, while the Associated Press claimed it was Martin Ruby. But both agreed the ball, after a hand had been laid on it, floated lamely toward the uprights, hit the crossbar, went straight up in the air, hung there for what seemed forever, and dropped into the end zone, short. That was the game. "We sure were lucky to win," said victorious coach Homer Norton. "That's football," answered Fordham's Jim Crowley.[27]

The best game of the day was the Sugar Bowl, between undefeated rivals Tennessee and Boston College, or at least the Eagles' white players. Lou Montgomery was again forced to sit out. He traveled with the team to New Orleans, but played in what the press called a "colored game" elsewhere in town.[28] The betting line favored Tennessee, and the Volunteers were overwhelming favorites among coaches from around the country. To some experts, the game seemed to hinge on how well the skinny but talented Charley O'Rourke could stand up against the Tennessee pounding he was sure to take. But another predicted that if O'Rourke played as he had against Georgetown, "Tennessee will bow in the Sugar Bowl."[29] Both were right. By game's end it was O'Rourke, as he had against Georgetown, who put the Eagles on his frail shoulders and carried them to victory, 19-13.

The contest was played as if it were composed of two separate events, both spectacular. For the first 57 minutes, the two teams played on even terms. Twice Tennessee scored touchdowns, and each time the Eagles countered with one of their own to tie the score. Neither team had any significant statistical edge. The hitting was hard, and at halftime O'Rourke was battered, bruised, and bloody. He was given salt tablets, which only made him violently ill, and Frank Leahy decided to rest him for the third period. Late in the fourth quarter, with the score tied, Tennessee drove deep into Eagle territory, but a field goal that would have given them the lead was blocked. With three minutes to go and the score till tied, Boston College took the ball at its own twenty-yard line.

Thus began the second part of the contest, and it was all O'Rourke. The rested star, playing in his last college game, drove his team 80 yards in seven plays for the winning touchdown. After three running plays that picked up a first down, he passed to Ed Zabilski for 20 yards, to Zabilski again for 19, and to Monk Maznicki for seven yards. Boston College now had the ball on the Tennessee 24-yard line.

The day before the game, Leahy had cooked up a new play, or rather had borrowed it right out of the Tennessee playbook. He called it "Shift Right— Tennessee Special," and this seemed like a good time for it. O'Rourke took the snap from center, faded back to pass, pulled the ball down, and dashed over left tackle. He sidestepped two linebackers, cut sharply to his right, and found himself in a race to the goal line with three other defenders.[30] Then, according to one account, in "an amazing display of broken field running, [he] zig-zagged his way 24 yards over the goal for the winning touchdown."[31] O'Rourke had beaten the Volunteers using their own play. Fittingly, moments later, O'Rourke's interception of Tennessee's desperation pass ended the game. Tennessee's loss was only its second in nearly three years, and Boston College had an undefeated season that would go down as the finest in the school's history.

On the last afternoon of the football season, in Dallas and Pasadena, in Miami and New Orleans, reporters flooded into locker rooms and flocked around tired football coaches trying to squeeze out one last comment, another line for one last story. But the best line of all that afternoon belonged to Clark Shaughnessy. Exhaling in a combination of relief and euphoria, the downtrodden and suddenly triumphant coach said simply, "This has been a season, hasn't it?"[32]

CHAPTER 19
ON DISTANT FIELDS

And early though the laurel grows
It withers quicker than the rose.

--A.E. HOUSMAN, *To An Athlete Dying Young*

On December 7, 1941, the National Football League had planned its last day of regular season play. The New York Giants, with rookies George Franck, Frank Reagan, and Jack Lummus, were scheduled to face the Brooklyn Dodgers at the Polo Grounds. The bombs began to fall on Pearl Harbor just before kickoff, but it was the third period before rumors rippled through the stands and the public address system began to summon specific military personnel to their stations. At halftime, the Giants' team chaplain told owner Wellington Mara that the Japanese had bombed Pearl Harbor, but no general announcement was made in the stadium.[1] Messages started to come across the ticker tape in the press box, but in the stands there was only a strange suspicion that something might be up. Hours later the nation was at war.[2]

Later, Wisconsin coach Harry Stuhldreher told the *Columbus Citizen*, "I keep picturing the boys who are playing for me as they may be a year from now, battling a Jap or a Nazi with a bayonet....The boys are preparing themselves not only for the games to come, but for their future in the armed services....We coaches don't like to be asked, 'How many boys will you lose to the armed forces?' We don't lose them. We contribute them....Some of my friends feel it seems brutal to be preparing young men for war. It doesn't seem brutal to me. It seems the opposite. We're in it. They'll be in it soon. All of us may be in it before it's over."[3]

The war effort cut across every segment of American society, and the college football stars of the day contributed their fair share, and more. The same competitive fire that drove them to excel on the football field drove then to great feats while serving their nation at war. For some, it meant an early but glorious death.

As late as 1940, only four Negroes had graduated from West Point and none from Annapolis. There was not a single trained Negro military pilot in the United States. But in 1940, the War Department had plans to train 45,000 new pilots, and indicated that among them would be Negroes to be trained in the Civil Aeronautics Authority and to serve in separate Negro outfits.[4]

In August of 1942, Wilmeth Sidat-Singh signed up with the U.S. Army and went off to pilot training. He was assigned to the 332nd Fighter Group, which soon became known as the Tuskegee Airmen, an elite segregated unit that went on to fame and distinction protecting Allied bombers over Germany. He was a member of one of the first graduating classes of the 332nd, and in May of 1943 was assigned to Selfridge Field in Michigan. On May 9, while on a routine training flight over Lake Huron, his single-seat P-40 fighter developed engine trouble. He bailed out, and when he hit the water he became entangled in the parachute lines and drowned. His body was recovered six weeks later, on June 26. He was 25 years old. Wilmeth Sidat-Singh is buried in Arlington National Cemetery.[5] On February 26, 2005, Syracuse University retired the jersey of Wilmeth Sidat-Singh. It hangs in honor from the rafters of the Carrier Dome.

After the 1939 football season was over and Nile Kinnick was awarded the Heisman Trophy, he completed his senior year by being inducted into Phi Beta Kappa and elected senior class president. In the College All-Star Game he passed for two touchdowns and drop-kicked four extra points. Passing up pro football, he entered the University of Iowa Law School, and after his first year ranked third in a class of 103 students. He quit school in September and joined the Naval Air Corps Reserve, and on December 4, 1941, three days before Pearl Harbor, he began active duty. He chose to fly fighters.

On June 2, 1943, the *USS Lexington*, with Kinnick on board, was conducting routine training operations in the Gulf of Paria between the coasts of Venezuela and Trinidad. "The task which lies ahead is adventure as well as duty, and I am anxious to get at it," he wrote.[6] Kinnick took off with a flight of F4F Wildcat fighter planes from the carrier deck when, about 90 minutes into a morning of training, his plane began to leak oil badly. He was close enough to the carrier to return, but the Lexington's deck was crowded with planes and crew waiting to take off. Kinnick decided to ditch his plane in the water rather than endanger crew members on the carrier deck, and was observed to make a perfect landing in the water and emerge from the cockpit. But minutes later, when a rescue crew showed up on the scene, there was no sign of Kinnick or the plane. His body was never found. Nile Kinnick was 24 years old.

Fifteen months later his younger brother Benjamin Kinnick, a B-25 pilot, was shot down and killed on a bombing mission in the Pacific, near New Guinea. A move began immediately to rename Iowa's football stadium in honor of Kinnick and ten other Iowa athletes killed in the war,[7] but Kinnick's family resisted it. In 1972, with his family finally concurring, the University of Iowa retired Nile Kinnick's number 24 jersey and renamed its football venue Kinnick Stadium. The coin tossed at the beginning of each Big Ten game bears the likeness of Nile Kinnick. In 1996, the wreckage of Kinnick's plane was found in 100 feet of water on the floor of the Gulf of Paria, but at the urging of his family it was allowed to remain in its resting place. Subsequent efforts to raise the wreck and possible remains have also been resisted.

Don Scott was the best player on an underperforming Ohio State team, and the All-American did all he could to keep the Buckeyes on a winning path. He enlisted in the Army Air Corps on March 15, 1941, and was commissioned on November 1, 1941. By the autumn of 1943, Don Scott had flown nine combat missions as a bomber pilot over German-occupied Europe. On October 1, 1943, he was flying his B-25 Marauder bomber with two other crew members on a routine training flight. Returning to base in England he encountered heavy weather, and his plane crashed near the base. There were no survivors. Capt. Don F. Scott was 23 years old.

Hurlin' Hal Hursh of Indiana, who led the Big Ten in passing in 1940 and who dueled both Nile Kinnick and Don Scott on the gridiron, befell a similar fate to these two stars. Drafted by the Cleveland Rams of the NFL, he turned instead to baseball and played briefly with the Riverside Reds, Cincinnati's Class C farm team. By June of 1942, he was a sergeant stationed at Compton Field in California where he served as an airplane mechanic. A year later he was in combat in the Pacific. On August 30 and 31, 1943, a massive air raid was launched against a Japanese stronghold on Marcus Island, north of the Marianas and less than a thousand miles from Tokyo. Although the operation was a huge success, one of the airmen lost in the operation was Sergeant Harold Hursh.[8] He was 23 years old.

When Bill Gillis bailed out Red Friesell in the 1940 Army-Navy game, it would not be the last time he would answer a distress call. On August 12, 1944, as Patton's Third Army streaked from Normandy toward Paris, Major Bill Gillis was a battalion commander with the 35th Infantry Division. When elements of the division became trapped and surrounded on Hill 317 near Avranches, Gillis's battalion launched a frontal assault that, after two days of intense fighting, broke through the German lines and rescued more than 300 isolated American troops. Gillis, wounded in the hand, received a Purple Heart and a Silver Star during the action.[9] Six weeks later, on October 1, 1944, Bill Gillis was killed in action in the Gremercy Forest in France. By the time of his death, he had won the Distinguished Service Cross, the Silver Star, the Bronze Star, two Purple Hearts, the Distinguished Service Order (British), the Croix de Guerre, the Silver Gilt, and Vermilion Stars (French).

After he graduated in the spring of 1942, Al Blozis was turned away from military service because of his height. Frustrated, he turned to professional football, where the Giants had selected him in the NFL draft, and he played with them for two years, the second year attaining All-Pro status. After repeated attempts to gain an exemption to military height requirements, he finally succeeded in enlisting in the army on December 9, 1943. He was originally assigned to Walter Reed Hospital as a physical instructor, but soon volunteered for combat infantry duty. While in infantry officer training at Fort Benning, Georgia, he threw a hand grenade over 94 yards, easily the longest throw on record, and about three times the distance expected of an average infantryman.

He was commissioned an infantry officer in the fall of 1944. While on leave from the army, he played the last few games of the season for the Giants, then played with them in the NFL championship game against the Green Bay Packers on December 17, 1944. Two days later, his leave up, he was on his way to France, where he was assigned to a unit heavily involved in the Battle of the Bulge.

On January 21, barely a month after playing in the NFL championship game, Al Blozis died a hero's death. Bogged down in a raging snowstorm in the Huertgen Forest near Colmar, France, Blozis was in charge of a patrol of twelve men scouting enemy positions. An old man from the nearby village told them that they were surrounded by Germans and that the rest of their unit had pulled out. Two of his men became separated from the rest of the patrol in the snowstorm, and when Blozis set out himself to look for them he was hit by enemy machine gun fire and killed.

Al Blozis was 26 years old. He is buried in a military cemetery in St. Avold, France. When reporters descended on his mother's house in North Bergen, New Jersey, she produced for them 130 medals, 12 watches and 14 trophies, all earned by her son in athletic competition.[10]

In February of 1945, Butch Luther, former Nebraska star, was a captain in the U.S. Army and company commander of Co.I, 3rd battalion, 85th regiment of the 10th Mountain Division. His unit was engaged in fierce combat with German forces near Mt. Belvedere on the east coast of Italy. One night, when he and another soldier were in their foxhole, they heard German voices just yards ahead of their position. Looking up, they saw two Germans with a machine gun thirty yards away. They left their foxhole, charged the German position, threw hand grenades, and dove back into their foxhole. In the few seconds before the grenades detonated, the Germans fired back. Luther lay dead on the ground, shot through the head.[11] One of the replacements brought in to the company during the action was Lt. Bob Dole, later Senate Majority Leader from Kansas and, in 1996, the Republican presidential candidate. He confirms Luther's fate. "A day or two after I got there I remember seeing his helmet, with a hole right between the captain's bars," he wrote.[12]

On April 1, 1945, Easter Sunday, American forces launched an amphibious invasion of Okinawa, the last stepping stone before the planned invasion of the Japanese mainland only 400 miles away. *Time* reported, "U.S. troops were advancing in the old-fashioned, inescapable way, one foot at a time, against the savage, rat-in-a-hole defense that only the Japanese can offer."[13] American forces were killing 1,000 Japanese soldiers a day, but little ground was gained in the fray. "This isn't that kind of fighting," explained Lt. Gen. Simon Bolivar Buckner, American Tenth Army commander.[14] Buckner himself would be killed in the fighting.

On May 15, "Irish" George Murphy, the former Notre Dame football captain, led his platoon of 60 men from the 6th Marine Division up Sugar Loaf Hill, a mound of coral and volcanic rock anchoring one end of the Japanese defensive line. With his men running out of ammunition, Murphy ordered them to fix bayonets while he covered their retreat down the hill. When he stopped to help one of his wounded men he was shot and killed by the advancing Japanese.[15] Of the 60 men of the 3d Platoon that Murphy took up Sugar Loaf Hill, 49 were killed or wounded.[16]

On Okinawa, the carnage continued. Two days later, on May 17, Marine Pfc. Ed Van Order,[17] the only junior to start a game for Cornell in 1940, was killed in the continuing action. On June 6, Bob Bauman, a Wisconsin teammate of Dave Schreiner and Mark Hoskins, was shot through the head and killed. The Marine who found his body on the trail was Schreiner.[18] Then, on June 20, Schreiner and his company were securing the Kiyuma Gusuku castle, one of the last strongholds on the island. There are conflicting stories of what happened that day, but Terry Frei, a sports historian who has chronicled the 1942 Wisconsin Badgers, has put forth a theory that Schreiner was shot down while accepting the surrender of Japanese troops under a white flag.[19] What is known for certain is that he was shot in the torso, badly wounded, and taken to an aid station where he died the next day, June 21. It was the last day of hostilities in the battle for Okinawa.

On July 2 the Okinawa campaign was officially over. The cost was immense. Irish George Murphy, Ed Van Order, Bob Bauman, and Dave Schreiner were among more than 12,500 GI's, Marines, and sailors who gave their lives on Okinawa.

EPILOGUE

Not even the gods can undo what has been done.

--PLUTARCH, *Consolatio and Apollonium*

Carl Snavely was an emotionally weary man by the end of the 1940 season. Rumors had been abundant all year that he would soon be on the move. One rumor had him leaving for Maryland. Another insisted that he had been offered and had rejected a ten-year contract to coach the Philadelphia Eagles of the National Football League.[1] Whatever the validity of those rumors, he chose to stay put. While the entire football world around him was busy converting to the T-formation, Snavely was a single wing man to his core and continued to run the offense with great success. By 1944, the Football Writers Association termed him the nation's foremost authority on the single wing.[2]

But just before the beginning of the 1944 season, his son, a Navy Ensign, was lost at sea. On September 21, the Navy announced that Ensign Carl G. Snavely, Jr., a Cornell graduate who had lettered in football in 1941, was missing in action in a plane crash while on active duty. Ensign Snavely had been co-pilot of a bomber that went down while on patrol off the coast of Newfoundland.

By December, Snavely had decided to leave Cornell and return to North Carolina. "He was made an attractive offer, an offer that Cornell couldn't or wouldn't match," said the *Cornell Alumni News*. The opportunities to recruit quality players with fewer restrictions and to take his successful team to a bowl game were open to him at North Carolina. "[H[e could be happy at Cornell no longer. Thus, from the Cornell standpoint as well as his own, it was better to leave...."[3]

He took North Carolina to three major bowl games, twice to the Sugar Bowl and once to the Cotton Bowl. When asked by the press for his reaction to the news that Charlie "Choo Choo" Justice, perhaps the greatest player he would ever coach, had agreed to come to North Carolina, his dry and evasive ways were never more on display. "I hope he comes out for football," he replied.[4]

When Ed McKeever, Snavely's successor at Cornell, was found siphoning alumni money to the players, he was summarily fired.[5]

****

Mort Landsberg, too, suffered the loss of a family member in the war. His brother, Lt. John J. Landsberg, who had also been a student at Cornell and had left school to become a Marine fighter pilot, was shot down and killed in the Ryukyu Islands on June 29, 1945.

Other members of the Big Red served with distinction during the war. Lou Conti, a Marine captain, served 17 months in the South Pacific as a dive bomber pilot and also logged time as an aerial photographer. Conti made a career of the military, and later retired as a major general. On June 21, 1944, Marine Captain Ray Jenkins was leading a reconnaissance patrol on Saipan when a Japanese machine gunner opened up and killed one of his patrol members and wounded another. Jenkins was hit in the left arm, spent two months recuperating in a hospital, received a Purple Heart, and returned to duty with his artillery unit. Lt. Walt Sickles, his fellow backup—and fellow pitcher on the baseball team—spent a year pitching for the minor-league Baltimore Orioles, and then was seriously wounded in the left leg while fighting in Luxembourg. Marine Captain Bud Finneran earned a Bronze Star while leading a rifle company in action on Bougainville in the fall of 1943, and after a promotion to Major, participated in the invasion of Iwo Jima in February, 1945. Army Air Force Lt. Walt Scholl flew 72 missions in the Mediterranean and earned the Silver Star and Distinguished Flying Medal. And Army Sgt. Hal McCullough, who the press said had left the Penn game looking like he had been to war, then went to war and was awarded a Bronze Star in Germany. He wiped out a machine gun nest and single-handedly captured a group of German soldiers. "They made me mad," he explained in a letter home, "and my Irish stubbornness did the rest."[6] Alva Kelley served as an Army officer for five years and returned home after the war to become a football coach. He served as head coach at Brown, Colgate, and Hobart.

****

Nick Drahos played pro football for the New York Americans of the fledgling AFL, and later in life became an expert on bird life on Guam and a freelance wildlife and nature photographer.

****

Jim Lynah never returned to Cornell after the war. In 1944, he was replaced as Athletic Director by Bob Kane, who had been acting Director since Lynah began splitting his time in 1940 with the National Defense Commission. Bob Kane remained as Athletic Director and as Dean of Physical Education and Athletics until 1976. He served as president of the United States Olympic Committee from 1977 to 1980. Edmund Ezra Day continued as Cornell president until his retirement due to health reasons in 1949. While in the stands watching a football game against Columbia later that fall, he suffered a serious heart attack. He died on March 23, 1951. His ashes are interred on campus.

****

In 1945, Cornell and the seven other universities of the loosely organized Ivy League joined in an Ivy Group Agreement that governed participation in football and set forth understandings among them as to academic standards, eligibility, and financial aid. By 1954, the agreement had been extended to cover all sports, and in the 1956 season the Ivy League began football competition among the eight universities sharing the same philosophy, with every school playing each of the others every year. The restrictive provisions of the agreement put the eight schools on even footing and provided a balance to their liking between academics and athletics, but made competition with top-notch opponents outside the Ivy League impractical. Cornell's last win against a major opponent outside the Ivy League came in 1951 when the Big Red defeated defending Rose Bowl champion Michigan at Schoellkopf Field.

****

Immediately after Ohio State's crushing loss to Michigan, the rumors, simmering for weeks, began to heat up that Francis Schmidt was about to be fired as coach. Schmidt called it a "cock-and-bull story" and athletic director L.W. St. John denied it as well. The rumors maintained that not only Schmidt's record but also his propensity to be at the "storm center" of numerous arguments were the cause of his demise.[7] On December 16, after the athletic board had met, Schmidt and four members of the coaching staff submitted their resignations. "The board is dissatisfied," Schmidt said dryly. On March 16, 1941, Francis Schmidt accepted the head coaching position at the University of Idaho.

****

The week after the Fifth Down game, Dartmouth won its final contest of the season against Brown and secured for Earl Blaik another winning season. Over Christmas, Blaik decided to leave Dartmouth and return to his alma mater, Army. Blaik would be the first civilian coach at Army in 40 years, and Dartmouth's victory over Cornell had been a deciding factor in Army's determination to make the change. Blaik was quick to embrace the T-formation ideas of Clark Shaughnessy. In 18 seasons as head coach at Army he compiled a 121-33-10 record, including two national championships in 1944 and 1945, when the West Point ranks swelled due to the war. His most difficult challenge came in 1951 during a widespread cheating scandal at West Point that involved many members of the football team and caused his own son to resign from the Academy. The next year, he suffered his only losing season.

231

****

Elmer Layden was disappointed when the Notre Dame president offered him only a one-year contract renewal at the end of the season. On the advice of Arch Ward, the *Chicago Tribune* sports editor, he refused to sign the contract and instead put his name into the running for the newly created position of commissioner of the National Football League, a post Ward himself had just turned down.[8]

Carl Storck, President of the NFL, was in trouble. He had helped found the league in 1921 and had overseen its original growth spurt, but it had outgrown Storck's capabilities to lead it. More importantly, Storck was an outspoken opponent of the NFL player draft, a system deeply loved by the owners. Storck called the system unfair and dictatorial and vowed to fix it.[9]

On February 3, 1941, Elmer Layden was hired as the first Commissioner of the National Football League with expansive powers and a salary of $20,000, twice what he was paid at Notre Dame and more than twice what Storck had been paid. Officials in South Bend tried to talk Layden out of his decision, but he would not be moved.[10]

Frank Leahy's contract at Boston College was also due to expire, and after adding a Sugar Bowl victory to his undefeated season, he was looking for a substantial raise from his $9,500 annual salary. Boston College, on the other hand, had reached the conclusion that $9,500 was already more than it wanted to pay a football coach.[11] Rumors of Leahy's departure abounded, but finally, on February 4, he signed a new five-year contract to coach Boston College with a substantial pay increase for both him and his assistants.

Rumors were flying in South Bend as well, but speculation about Layden's replacement never wandered outside the circle of Notre Dame alumni. Despite the swirling rumors, Notre Dame never had any interest in any candidate except Frank Leahy, the man who, hours before, had signed a new five-year contract at Boston College. On Saturday, February 15, having secured a release from his contract with Boston College, Leahy signed a contract to return to his alma mater as Notre Dame's football coach and athletic director. Between 1941 and 1953, largely using the T-formation, Frank Leahy had six undefeated seasons, four national championships, and between 1946 and 1949 his Notre Dame teams had a 39-game undefeated streak, punctuated only by two ties.

But back in Boston there were plenty of hard feelings. Different accounts of the story reveal different versions about Boston College's degree of willingness to let Leahy out of his contract. Nearly two decades later, after Leahy's retirement from Notre Dame, the idea was floated of his returning to Boston College, but school officials there would not even consider it.[12]

Boston College replaced Leahy with Denny Myers, the line coach at Brown, and by 1942 Myers, using the T-formation, had the Eagles poised for another run at the national championship. With one game remaining, there stood only a mediocre Holy Cross team between the Eagles and an undefeated season, a certain Associated Press national championship, and a bid to the Sugar Bowl. The Eagles booked the Terrace Room at the Cocoanut Grove, a ritzy Boston night club, for their victory party. But about the game, a writer for the *Boston Globe* said, "This is anything-can-happen-day."[13] It was one of those lines that, years later, can keep a reader awake all night.

Sometimes forces act in ways hard to explain or understand. That Holy Cross upset the nation's top team was almost too much by itself to believe, but that the final score was 55-12 defied any pretense of logic. While Holy Cross played flawless football, Boston College was plagued by untimely penalties, fumble after fumble, interceptions, poor execution, and critical injuries. The Eagles, shell-shocked and disheartened, and shorn of any hopes of a national championship or a Sugar Bowl bid, cancelled their celebration. Surely at least some of the players dwelled on how empty their lives would be without the anticipated national championship.

But when they awoke the next morning the Eagles learned that the Cocoanut Grove, filled beyond capacity with over 800 patrons, had burned to the ground overnight. By the time the final death toll had been counted, 492 people had lost their lives in one of the greatest tragedies ever to hit the city of Boston. Only two members of the Boston College contingent, the equipment manager and his wife, who evidently did not get the word about the cancellation, were present, and both died in the flames.[14] Had the Eagles won as expected that afternoon, there is no telling what would have happened to the national champion football team, nor is there any telling what the players' thoughts were when they heard the news. One thing, however, is for sure. The tragedy offered a new perspective on the importance of winning and the role of a national championship in one's life.

****

In addition to Kinnick Stadium at the University of Iowa, there are numerous other tributes and memorials to the football stars and prominent figures of that era. The week after the death of Don Scott, his widow Leone gave birth to a baby boy in Columbus. She named him Don. A month later the Ohio State board of trustees named the university's new airfield Don Scott Airport. St. John Arena, erected on the Ohio State campus to honor L.W. St. John, served as home to the Buckeye basketball team until 1998, and still hosts a variety of athletic events in other sports. Dave Rankin, the Big Ten's Most Valuable Player in 1940, became the co-holder of the world record in the indoor 60-yard low hurdles. He returned to Purdue after the war and served as Purdue track coach for 35 years. The Rankin Track and Field Facility at Purdue is named in his honor. The University of Wisconsin named Schreiner Hall, on North Orchard Street, close by Camp Randall Stadium, in honor of

Dave Schreiner. It houses facilities for the School of Education. The United States Military Academy dedicated the Gillis Field House at West Point to its fallen hero Bill Gillis, the 1940 football captain. East Avenue on the Cornell campus passes by Edmund Ezra Day Hall, the university administration building. Up the hill to the east on Campus Road, directly across from Schoellkopf Field, is Lynah Rink, home of the Cornell hockey team. Beyond that lies the Robert J. Kane Athletic Complex. Among the deeds for which these men are remembered is the decision to forfeit Cornell's 1940 football game against Dartmouth. Plaques honoring Jack Lummus and Al Blozis were dedicated at the Polo Grounds, where they played for the Giants. When that venue met the demolition ball, the plaques were transferred to Yankee Stadium, but have been lost now for some time. The U.S. Navy Prepositioning Ship *USNS 1ˢᵗ Lt. Jack Lummus (T-AK3011)*, named after the Medal of Honor recipient, was dispatched to Port au Prince, Haiti, in January 2010. There it provided humanitarian relief efforts to Haiti's earthquake victims. His Medal of Honor is on permanent display at Baylor's Floyd Casey Stadium.

****

After being awarded the Medal of Honor, Maurice Britt returned to combat. On January 24, 1944, in fighting at Anzio, Britt lost his arm when hit by a shell from a German tank.[15] His loss did not deter him from attending law school at the University of Arkansas, starting his own business, and being elected lieutenant governor of Arkansas in 1966.[16]

****

On February 11, 1943, Dr. Eddie Anderson left Iowa and joined the U.S. Army Medical Corps, where he served on the staff of veterans' hospitals in Iowa and in England, and in field hospitals in France and Germany. When the war was over, Anderson returned to Iowa to coach the Hawkeyes from 1946 to 1949. In January of 1950, with a year remaining on his contract, Anderson approached university officials with the request that he be granted tenure at the University of Iowa Hospital. His request was not granted, and he left Iowa to return to Holy Cross, where he coached until 1964. When he retired after 38 seasons his career record was 201-125-15. At the time, he was only one of four coaches in college football history to have amassed at least 200 victories.

****

In addition to the loss of the great Kinnick, World War II imposed even more pain on the Iowa Hawkeyes. Erwin Prasse, the team captain of 1939, also played baseball and basketball at Iowa, and although he was drafted by the Detroit Lions of the NFL after graduation, he opted instead to pursue a professional baseball career. He played second base for the Springfield Cardinals and Asheville Tourists of the St. Louis Cardinal organization before entering the service. On January 13, 1945, Erwin Prasse, then an Army captain, received serious shrapnel wounds to his right arm while in charge of a night reconnaissance patrol at the Roer River[17], near the border between Germany and the Netherlands. His dreams of a major league baseball career were over. Mike Enich, the 1940 captain, became a major in the Marines and was wounded in the chest by a sniper on Okinawa. Although he survived, he was hospitalized for an extended period. He later recovered and graduated from the University of Iowa Law School in 1948.[18] Ken Pettit was also badly wounded in the Pacific, struck in the arm by an airplane propeller. Bill Hofer, the freshman team coach, received shrapnel wounds on Okinawa. Both Enich and Pettit, recovering from their wounds, were in attendance at the 1945 Iowa-Indiana game, where they were hailed as returning heroes.[19]

****

On June 27, 1944, Army Lieutenant Mark Hoskins, the former Wisconsin star, set out on his 34th combat mission as a co-pilot flying B-17 Flying Fortresses from the major airfield at Foggia, Italy. The mission to Budapest was flown in cloudy weather that did not allow the pilots to stay in formation, and many of them turned back. German fighter planes cut what was left of the formation to pieces, and Hoskins and the rest of his crew, their plane in flames, parachuted out over the Danube River. He spent the rest of the war in a German POW camp. His younger brother, Pfc. Charles Hoskins, was killed in Luxembourg on January 22, 1945, where he had been a member of Patton's Third Army.[20]

****

Amos Alonzo Stagg continued coaching at the College of the Pacific until 1946, then joined his son as co-coach at Susquehanna University until 1952, completing a 72-year career in college coaching. Stagg lived to the age of 102.

****

The Stanford turnaround directed by Clark Shaughnessy was arguably the greatest in the history of college football. And Shaughnessy's feat was not only a turnaround for his team, but also for himself personally. A year after struggling with the likes of Beloit and Wabash, Shaughnessy achieved the singular status of having coached a Rose Bowl champion and an NFL champion in the same season. In the ranks of college football coaching, there was no hole deeper than the one he climbed out of at Chicago, and no summit higher than the one he scaled.

Shaughnessy's years in Chicago were among the most difficult any coach has ever endured, and he later credited George Halas with helping him get through. "I couldn't have carried on except for Halas," he said. "Believe me, I'll never forget it."[21]

Halas biographer Jeff Davis wrote that after the Rose Bowl game, "everything else in football was obsolete. In the space of three weeks, George Halas...and Clark Shaughnessy...launched a football revolution with their T-formation attack."[22] In 2002, ESPN rated the development of the T-formation the second most important sports innovation of all time, right behind free agency.[23] While the single wing had its undeniable charm, it relied on exceptional athletes like Sammy Baugh or progressive coaches like Carl Snavely to bring the passing attack into the game. But the T-formation, especially when paired with the unlimited substitution rule change of 1941 and a rule change in 1945 that allowed a pass to be initiated from anywhere behind the line of scrimmage, opened the door for the modern game of football.

Faced with the threat that Stanford would drop football during the war, Shaughnessy left Palo Alto after two years to pursue a college coaching career that took him to Maryland, Pitt, and Hawaii. Meanwhile, he maintained his relationship with the Bears and continued to help steer Sid Luckman through his personal and professional issues, for which Luckman was thoroughly grateful.[24] He was succeeded at Stanford by his assistant Marchy Schwartz, and after 1942 Stanford did indeed drop football for the duration of the war.

By 1948, Shaughnessy had left the college ranks. He became the head coach of the Los Angeles Rams, and his innovative ways followed him. He converted Crazylegs Hirsch from halfback to end, and in the process employed three receivers for the first time, a staple of the modern professional offense. Hirsch responded by setting a league record for receiving yards that lasted for 19 years and earned him entry into the Pro Football Hall of Fame. Shaughnessy left after two seasons due to friction with the team owner. He returned to Chicago, where he served once more as an assistant to George Halas until 1962. "The term 'genius' is thrown around a lot among coaches, but Shaughnessy was the only real genius," said Richie Petitbon, who played for him with the Bears and became defensive coordinator and head coach of the Washington Redskins.[25] When Shaughnessy left the Bears for good in 1962, it was due to what he again called friction. He never felt he got the credit he deserved for the T-formation.

Shaughnessy's grandson, Bill Kreutzmann, Jr., was a founding member and drummer for the Grateful Dead and still performs with the band's successor, The Dead.

****

In 1941, Red Friesell planned on officiating in the NFL, but his career was a short one. On September 28, 1941, in a rough game between the Philadelphia Eagles and the Brooklyn Dodgers, Friesell suffered a broken leg. That game would be the last in a career that spanned 575 college and professional contests.

He turned to real estate, where he enjoyed a long and successful career, though he carried the moniker "Fifth Down Friesell" to his grave.[26] Some men would retreat from such opprobrium, but Friesell routinely attended Cornell and Dartmouth reunions, where he was warmly received. He enjoyed the good friendship of Cornell halfback Bill Murphy, the man who caught the negated touchdown pass, for the rest of his life.[27] Ironically, Bob Krieger, who kicked Dartmouth's field goal in that game, also played for the Eagles in the game in which Friesell broke his leg. Twenty five years later, at a reunion, Krieger said, "Someone knocked a player into Red, who fell and broke a leg. I think I smiled for a week." But he had his arm around Red's shoulder when he said it.[28]

****

Frankie Albert finished second to Bruce Smith in the Heisman Trophy balloting in 1941, then served in the Navy for three years, where he was stationed in the Pacific. He played for the San Francisco 49ers for seven years and coached them for three years, with success at each level, but did not enjoy coaching. He felt his emotional disposition did not lend itself to the profession and he retired after the 1958 season.

****

Hugh Gallarneau played two years of pro football with the Chicago Bears before joining the Marines, and finished first in his class at Quantico. He was trained in the field of radar and became a night fighter director. He was the Marines' first "ground ace," a controller whose planes brought down at least five Japanese planes. He saw combat at Tarawa, Roi-Namur, Engebie, Saipan, Tinian, and Guam, and received the Bronze Star during his service. When he returned from the war, he rejoined the Chicago Bears, and by the time his pro career was over he had played on two NFL championship teams. He entered the field of retail and became president of Society Brand Clothes, a division of Hart, Schaffner, and Marx.[29]

****

Mike Holovak joined the Navy in 1943 and was made a PT boat commander in the Pacific, where he was under heavy fire from the first day he arrived. His boat was credited with sinking nine Japanese ships.[30] After the war, he retired from the Navy with the rank of Lieutenant Commander, and returned to football. He played briefly with the Chicago Bears and Los Angeles Rams of the NFL, then returned to Boston College where he became head football coach in 1951. He left to become the first director of player personnel and backfield coach for the Boston Patriots of the fledgling American Football League in 1960. Midway through the 1961 season he became head coach of the Patriots, a post he held through the 1968 season. He also coached and held administrative positions with the San Francisco 49ers, Oakland Raiders, and New York Jets, and served as general manager of the Houston Oilers.

****

A day after the Sugar Bowl, a battered but victorious Charley O'Rourke told the press he had no interest in playing pro football. "You play professional football three or four years, you're through, and what have you?" he pondered. Willing to call his career over, he said he was going to take the advice of his cousin and go into teaching in his home town of Malden.[31] But he changed his mind and played one season with the Chicago Bears as a backup to Sid Luckman, and then entered the service during the war for three years. In 1946, he began a four-year career in the All-America Football Conference with the Los Angeles Dons and the Baltimore Colts. In 1950, he joined Eddie Anderson's staff as an assistant coach at Holy Cross, then served as the head coach at the University of Massachusetts from 1952 to 1959. Later he served as commissioner of the Pop Warner League, a youth football organization.

****

After graduation, Lou Montgomery worked as an insurance agent in Hartford, Connecticut, and later as a travel coordinator for Western Airlines.

****

Like many other graduating seniors, George Kerr, though drafted by the Pittsburgh Steelers, chose to pass up pro football. He graduated from Boston College as class salutatorian, then entered the priesthood, and was ordained in 1945. He embarked on a distinguished career within the church, and was named Monsignor in 1964. He served as assistant director of the Catholic Charitable Bureau, director of the Nocturnal Adoration Society, and chaplain of the children's home, Nazareth, in Jamaica Plains. He also served as pastor of St. Francis de Sales Parish in Roxbury and St. Francis Xavier Parish in Weymouth.[32] He served as chaplain of the Boston Fire Department.

****

Augie Lio was drafted by the Detroit Lions and played for them and three other teams in the NFL until 1947, mostly as a kicker. After he retired as a player, Lio served for 37 years as a sportswriter and editor at the *Passaic Herald and News*.

****

By April of 1943, Tom Harmon was an army pilot stationed in the Caribbean. His celebrity intact, a photo of him posing in front of his B-25 bomber appeared in newspapers across the country. Then, on April 14, his parents received a telegram informing them that their son was missing in action, and that he had not been heard from since April 8. A special mass was said for Harmon and that afternoon, on April 16, word was received in Ann Arbor that he was safe.[33] Soon the details came out. On a training mission over the Caribbean, his plane was hit by lightning and crashed in the remote jungle of Surinam. He was the only one of six crew members to survive. Equipped with only a compass, a bolo knife and a few chocolate bars, he navigated through the jungle for four days until arriving safely in a small native settlement.[34] Rescuers searched for two weeks for the missing members of Harmon's crew, but although they were able to find the plane wreckage, they were unsuccessful in finding any trace of the missing fliers.[35]

Greatly shaken by the loss of his crew, Harmon opted out of flying bombers, and within a few months he was in the Pacific flying single-pilot fighter planes. On August 26, 1943, in an attack on Japanese installations and shipping at Hong Kong, Harmon shot down his first Japanese plane.[36] In letters home Harmon did not mention the feat but promised his family a Zero for Christmas.[37] In another letter to Fritz Crisler, he said, "You can always outguess these Jap pilots because they fly like mechanical men."[38]

On October 30, Harmon was flying one of four P-38 fighters accompanying a flight of bombers over the Yangtze River, 350 miles inside Japanese-occupied China, in an attack on the port of Kiukiang. Harmon was flying in the "grief spot," the tail position in the wing formation,[39] when the flight was attacked by a swarm of Zeroes. Harmon shot down two of them, his second and third kills of the war,[40] before his gas line was punctured by enemy fire. His plane in flames, Harmon bailed out and was rescued from Japanese ground troops by Chinese guerrillas.

Back home, on November 4 and for the second time in seven months, the Harmon family received word that their son was missing in action. In a letter dated November 6, Lt. Gary H. Hammond, a friend of Harmon's in China, wrote to his mother in Ypsilanti, Michigan, "Four men...were missing in a raid. One, we know for sure, is walking back and we have rumors that two more are coming also. We think that Harmon is walking out, too."[41] On these words the Harmon family hung their hopes for a month.

But it was not that simple. The Japanese recognized whom they had shot down, and a dogged search for Harmon followed. For 29 days the guerrillas smuggled the badly wounded Harmon through the hostile territory and thick jungle, dodging the Japanese day and night, until he reached the safety of an American base. On November 30, Harmon's family and friends gathered for a mass of thanksgiving in the same chapel where, seven months before, they had given thanks for his first escape from death. A week later Louis and Rose Harmon received this cablegram from their son: "Arrived safe, sound and healthy. Thinking of you. Everything in perfect shape."[42] For his heroics, Tom Harmon was awarded a Silver Star and Purple Heart.

Harmon married Elyse Knox, an actress from Hartford, Connecticut, and at their wedding, at which Forest Evashevski was best man, she wore a gown made of the material from Harmon's parachute. Beginning in 1946 he played two years with the Los Angeles Rams, but his skills had deteriorated and his war injuries were problematic. He enjoyed a long and successful career in sports broadcasting, including coverage of football, golf, and the Olympics. His son, Mark Harmon, was a star football player at UCLA and became an accomplished actor, most notably in the highly successful television series *NCIS*.

Forest Evashevski, too, decided to pass up pro football, although drafted by the Washington Redskins, and coached football at Hamilton College for one year before joining the Navy. In 1952, he became head coach at Iowa. Like Eddie Anderson before him, he inherited a Hawkeye program in woeful shape. By his second year he had the Hawkeyes ranked ninth in the country after a controversial tie against top-ranked Notre Dame, coached by Frank Leahy, as the Irish scored two touchdowns by faking injuries. By 1956 the Hawkeyes were Big Ten champions for the first time since 1921 and Rose Bowl champions for the first time ever. The Hawkeyes won the Rose Bowl again in 1958, and the Football Writers Association of America voted them the national champion, a title they shared with Louisiana State.

****

George Franck finished third in the Heisman Trophy balloting and was the Most Valuable Player in the 1941 College All-Star Game, catching a touchdown pass from Tom Harmon. He was sworn in to the Naval Air Corps at halftime, along with Dave Rankin of Purdue, Bob Saggau of Notre Dame, and Ed Frutig of Michigan. He played a year of pro football with the NFL's New York Giants before going on active duty.

By September, 1944, Franck was a captain in the Marines and a fighter pilot in the Pacific, involved in heavy fighting in the Marshall Islands. While on a strafing run, his Marine Corsair was hit by enemy antiaircraft fire, and he was forced to ditch in the ocean. He was successfully rescued after repeated attempts while under enemy artillery fire from nearby Wotje Atoll.[43] It was the seventh time Franck had survived a plane crash. "If you're not a very good pilot, you can manage seven crashes very quickly," he later explained.[44]

His pilot days over, Franck later took part as a ground observer in ground-air support. In February, 1945, in his first ground action, he landed on Iwo Jima late in the morning of the first day of that campaign. By fate, he found himself sharing a shell crater with Jack Chevigny, a former Notre Dame football star and former head coach of Texas and the Chicago Cardinals. Under heavy fire, Franck opted to seek better cover, but Chevigny stayed put, arguing that lightning never hits the same place twice.[45] Within fifteen minutes, just as Franck had feared, another shell landed in the hole, and Chevigny was killed.

Iwo Jima was a "nightmare—that's the best way to describe it," he later said.[46] By the time the war was over, George Franck had earned nine battle stars.

****

In 1941, with Bruce Smith as team captain, Minnesota again went undefeated and won the national championship. Bruce Smith became the only player in Minnesota history to win the Heisman Trophy, despite a 1941 season plagued by injuries. Three times that year—against Pitt, Northwestern, and Wisconsin—he was carried off the field on a stretcher. In his NFL career, also marred by injury, he was hurt so badly in a game while playing for the Packers against the Bears that he received the last rites from a Catholic priest. Released by the Packers after his injuries had slowed him, he finished his career with the Los Angeles Rams, where his coach was Clark Shaughnessy.

In 1967, Bruce Smith was diagnosed with colon cancer. While a patient at St. Barnabas Hospital in Minneapolis, he deeply impressed Father William Cantwell, a Catholic priest who administered to the spiritual needs of the dying patients. Instead of concentrating on himself, Smith spent all his time connecting with and comforting the other patients, especially the children, who suffered from the same disease that was killing him. As the disease wasted away his body and his weight dropped below 100 pounds, there was no letup in his efforts to comfort others.[47] Father Cantwell learned of Smith's football glory only when somebody else told him about it. "Bruce was such a humble man, always putting the light on others," he said.[48]

When Bruce Smith finally succumbed to his illness, the priest began the long process of gaining canonization. "You could see it immediately; this man had that certain something that God bestows only on a few men in each generation," said Father Cantwell. "Although he was as sick and uncomfortable as any patient in the hospital, he did not complain or find fault or lose patience. He was a Christian optimist with the guts and courage of an All-American." Upon Father Cantwell's retirement, the cause was picked up by Father Michael Martin, a Paulist priest who thought at first that the effort to gain sainthood for a football player was most unusual. "It was the last place I would look for sanctity," he said.[49]

The process under the current Pope Benedict XVI is more closely scrutinized than under his predecessor, Pope John Paul II.[50] But Father Martin is not daunted by the slim chances of success. "Bruce Smith is a perfect example of how to remain a humble, good person even in the midst of fame," he said. He sees him as a common man of uncommon grace and virtue, and hopes there is a place for him in the calendar of saints.[51]

****

By the 1941 football season, the impending war and the buildup of the armed forces caused manpower shortages on the college football field that made continuation of the game as played in 1940 impossible. Rather than scrap football altogether during the war due to extreme manpower shortages, the rulesmakers agreed to allow unlimited substitutions as a way to keep the game viable. Additionally, substitutes were permitted to immediately communicate with their teammates upon entering the game, thus allowing coaches to call plays. By 1945, Fritz Crisler had a fresh group of players ready to play only offense and another just for defense. Earl Blaik called it two-platoon football. The game would never be the same. It was changed not by desire for a different game but by the exigencies of war.

The move toward two-platoon football was originally seen as an advantage for small schools, but its implementation had the opposite effect. By causing the size of the rosters to expand, it steeply drove up the cost of supporting a college football program, and many small schools could no longer compete. In 1952, football was abandoned by 50 colleges when the cost of supporting a large roster became prohibitive.[52]

Unlimited substitution allowed specialized kickers to enter and exit the game as needed, and the last barrier to the modern kicking game began to crumble in 1961. That year, Cornell's Pete Gogolak stepped onto the field at Princeton, and to the gasps of startled onlookers, kicked a 41-yard field goal using a highly unorthodox soccer-style approach. Gone was the erratic straight-on style—Gogolak kicked an unheard-of 44 straight extra points for Cornell using his new approach—and before long every kicker in the game was copying him.[53] What was once highly unorthodox soon became conventional, and as a result kicking took on an entirely different role in the game of football.

****

Among the many schools that dropped varsity football due to cost was Georgetown. In 1970, the Hoyas reinstated football with a Division III team until the NCAA, because Georgetown fielded an elite Division I basketball team, mandated either a Division I football team or no team.[54] Georgetown has struggled with Division I status, and although football plays an important role on campus, wins have been few.

NYU's football team, too, fell victim to the increased costs of the two-platoon era. After having discontinued the team for two years at the beginning of the war, the Violets began play again in 1944, until the varsity program was permanently discontinued following the 1952 season. Between 1940 and its demise, the team enjoyed only one winning season, in 1946, and when the Violets played Fordham at the Polo Grounds in 1950 the game attracted only 1500 fans.

****

After graduating from NYU, Leonard Bates served in the military and then worked as a guidance counselor in New York City for many years. The cause of his supporters, seemingly so tenuous in 1940, gradually advanced, but the steps were small and painful.

In 1941, Cornell played Navy in Baltimore and ignored protests, mostly by its own alumni, to participation by its black halfback Sam Pierce. The game proceeded without incident, and Pierce became the first black athlete ever to compete against Navy. Later in his life, Samuel R. Pierce would serve for eight years as U.S. Secretary of Housing and Urban Development under President Reagan.[55] In 1946, Penn State chose to stick together and refuse to play against the University of Miami rather than exclude their two black teammates, Dennis Hoggard and Wally Triplett.[56] By 1947, Harvard, with its black tackle Chester Pierce, was able to play in a game at the University of Virginia without incident on the field, although Pierce was denied the same dining arrangements as the rest of the team, and all of the Crimson decided to eat together.[57] On New Year's Day 1948, Penn State became the first integrated team to play in the Cotton Bowl, although the team, which chose to room together, had to stay at Dallas Naval Air Station. They were welcomed without objection by Southern Methodist, and the two teams played to a 13-13 tie.

Matters took an ominous turn on October 20, 1951, in Stillwater, Oklahoma, in a game between Drake and Oklahoma A&M. The undefeated Drake team was led by its star black quarterback, Johnny Bright, the NCAA all-time leader in combined rushing and passing yardage. Early in the first period, Bright was slugged in the face by A&M defender Wilbanks Smith. Bright responded by throwing a 61-yard touchdown pass on the next play, but then had to leave the game with a broken jaw. Both the Oklahoma A&M players and coach J.B. "Ears" Whitworth insisted nothing inappropriate had happened, and that Bright had been inadvertently injured by a clean shoulder hit. But two photographers from the *Des Moines Register*, John Robinson and Don Ultang, captured the play on film. When their photos appeared in the paper and subsequently in *Life* magazine, they clearly showed No. 43, Bright, far removed from the play, and No. 72, Smith, winding up and nearly coming off his feet in punching him. Wilbanks Smith was left without a defense, and the two photographers won a Pulitzer Prize for their work.

The reaction was immediate and thunderous. Smith's actions were "the most flagrant violations of rules, good sportsmanship and decency this writer has ever heard of in football," wrote Gus Schrader in the *Cedar Rapids (IA) Gazette.* "If the Aggies are permitted to get away with that kind of stuff then there is no hope for American sports and games. We might as well chuck them all over board and go to Russia for our recreation," he finished.[58] Sec Taylor of the *Des Moines Register* called for Oklahoma A&M's jersey No. 72 to be retired "so that no other of its athletes will be contaminated by the mockerism [sic] it represents. The jersey bearing that number should be fumigated."[59]

Other incidents flared up across the South. In 1954, Cornell's black player Dick Jackson was denied hotel accommodations at the Shamrock Hotel in Houston where the team was scheduled to play Rice. The entire hotel staff went on strike rather than admit a black man to the facility, and Jackson and a white teammate stayed at the home of a local alumnus.[60]

On January 2, 1956, Bobby Grier became the first black player to participate in a Sugar Bowl game as Georgia Tech beat the Panthers, 7-0. A month before, Rosa Parks had been arrested in Montgomery, Alabama, for refusing to yield her seat on a bus to a white person, and passions in the South had been aroused anew. Pitt defied demands by Governor Marvin Griffin of Georgia that Grier be left home.[61] But it was 1965 before a second black player would participate in a Sugar Bowl game.[62]

Small schools, too, refused to play by the old rules and willingly accepted the consequences. Hillsdale College, its football team undefeated, refused to accept a bid to the 1956 Tangerine Bowl rather than leave its black players home.[63]

The final blow to segregation in college football may well have come in September of 1970 when an all-white Alabama team, coached by Paul "Bear" Bryant, as steadfast an icon of southern football as there has ever been, hosted an integrated Southern California team at Legion Field in Birmingham. When Sam "Bam" Cunningham, the Trojans' black fullback, got through with his team, Bryant had been beaten, 42-21, but more significantly Bryant came to realize that he simply could not compete without black athletes on his team. Some pundits claimed that Cunningham did more to integrate the state of Alabama in 60 minutes than Martin Luther King, Jr. did in 20 years.[64]

****

On April 15, 1947, Jackie Robinson, playing for the Brooklyn Dodgers, broke major league baseball's color barrier. Displaying a mixture of athletic brilliance and steely determination, Robinson paved the way for major advances for civil rights on the field and by extension in society as a whole. In 1962 he was inducted into the Baseball Hall of Fame.

****

For more than two decades the Cornell-Dartmouth Fifth Down game stood as the sole example of a contest whose outcome was confused by official error on the last play. Then, on November 18, 1961, in South Bend, it happened again, this time leaving a distinctly different aftertaste. Syracuse clung to a 15-14 lead with three seconds remaining as Notre Dame lined up for a desperation 56-yard field goal. The kick was missed, but just after the ball left the kicker's foot, a Syracuse defender plowed into both kicker and holder, drawing a penalty flag. Given a second chance from 15 yards closer, Notre Dame made the kick and left the field with a 17-15 victory.

But howls of outrage immediately followed, and Syracuse officials, though they did not file a protest, maintained that Notre Dame had won as a result of the game officials' error. Acknowledging that the game could not end on a penalty against the defense, they cited the rule explaining that after the ball left the kicker's foot Syracuse was no longer on defense. The game should have been over, they argued, after the missed kick.

Immediately following the contest, three officials assigned to the game by the Big Ten agreed and admitted their error. Big Ten Commissioner Bill Reed and Asa Bushnell, now Commissioner of the Eastern College Athletics Conference, issued a joint statement to the effect that the game officials erred. Syracuse Athletic Director Lew Andreas said, "We believe absolutely Syracuse won the game, 15-14."[65] But Rev. Edmund C. Joyce, Notre Dame vice-president, expressed surprise at the commissioners' statement and said, "We felt and still feel that the officials made the proper decision on the field."[66] To Walter Byers, executive director of the NCAA, none of this mattered. "There is no authority anywhere, no redress, once the game ends. The score cannot be changed unless Notre Dame wants to acknowledge that the game belongs to Syracuse,"[67] he said. Thus the battle lines were drawn.

After the NCAA Rules Committee reviewed the matter and confirmed that the game officials had erred, it appeared that Notre Dame might forfeit the game. Rev. Theodore M. Hesburgh, Notre Dame president, said, "Everybody knows Notre Dame doesn't want to win a game it really didn't. If the rules committee determines that we didn't, we'll act accordingly."[68] But then he reversed his position, stating that Notre Dame would never concede the game, and threatened to sever athletic ties with Syracuse. Notre Dame coach Joe Kuharich called the matter closed. "You can't go back and change ball scores," he said. "Why should Notre Dame change the score? There is no redress." He finished by saying that "for anyone to press for a redress of the game is ludicrous."[69]

Then, 29 years later, it happened again. On October 6, 1990, Colorado beat Missouri 33-31, with a touchdown on the last play of the game. It was immediately apparent that the touchdown had been scored on a fifth down when sideline officials failed to update the down markers. Colorado, ranked 12th in the nation and considered by some to have a good chance at the national championship, was disinclined to forfeit the victory.

But it was not that simple. On what he thought waa third down, the Colorado quarterback had spiked the ball to stop the clock, apparently as misled as anybody about the down count. Referees, Big Eight commissioner Carl James, and Colorado officials all initially remained silent on the matter. Colorado coach Bill McCartney, a Missouri graduate, attempted to deflect attention to the slippery artificial surface at Missouri's Faurot Field. "The biggest story is not how the game ended, it's that field. It's a joke to college football," he said.[70] His attempts to change the subject did not work, and he finally admitted, when pushed, that his team had received five downs. "I didn't realize it at the time, but we sure did," he said. But when asked how he would feel about a reversal of the outcome on appeal, he deemed such a possibility unfair "because the field was treacherous. It was not a playable field," he maintained.[71]

Soon the win was labeled by the press as tainted. "Get serious," was sports columnist Arne Green's response to McCartney's comments, and Missouri coach Bob Stull felt that McCartney had exaggerated his description of the field conditions and added, "We slipped too."[72] But McCartney replied, "I have given them (Colorado administrators) my opinion that in no way, shape, or form would we forfeit this game if I have anything to do about it."[73]

Big Eight Commissioner Carl James ruled, "The final score in the Missouri-Colorado football game will remain as posted," and the entire seven-man officiating crew was suspended indefinitely.[74] Colorado won the rest of its games in 1990, and when it defeated Notre Dame in the Orange Bowl, 10-9, was chosen by the Associated Press as national champions. Georgia Tech ended the season rated first in the Coaches' Poll.

Colorado's handling of the incident made analysis of the matter difficult, since people tended to jump to the conclusion that the win was unmerited. But on October 14, an article in the *New York Times*[75] placed the matter in a different perspective. Its author, David M. Nelson, had impeccable football credentials. Dave Nelson had played in the Michigan backfield in 1940 with Tom Harmon, had coached at Delaware, had served as Commissioner of the Yankee Conference, and had served for 30 years as secretary to the NCAA Football Rules Committee. Nelson pointed out that Colorado was as victimized as Missouri in the matter, fooled into an incorrect assumption regarding the downs. No serious person could conclude that Colorado would have intentionally grounded a pass knowing it was fourth down, Nelson argued, and there is no reason to think that, had Colorado run the fifth-down play on fourth down, it would not have scored then too. Nelson had long argued that in football the game is over when the referee says it is over and that no amendment to the score may thereafter take place, even by forfeit. His comments over the years place outcomes such as Cornell-Dartmouth, Notre Dame-Syracuse and Colorado-Missouri in a different light. "The 1940 rule was the same as it is today: the team with the greater number of points at the end of four periods is the winner. Cornell and Dartmouth violated the rule and it has haunted the game and institutions that play by the rules ever since," he wrote. To those who find that harsh, he added, "One of the joys of a college football game is its finality and the lack of an appellate system. Like the rest of football, an official's error is just one more "rub of the green" that is part of a total education."[76]

Over the years, there has been no greater expert on the rules of the game than Dave Nelson. To derive a technical answer to the knotty dilemmas presented by botched endings, nobody has ever set forth a better prescription than Nelson's. His clear thinking, insightful logic, and years of experience brought a fresh perspective to the issue, one missing in the heated and immediate reactions of the fans and the press. But for the thousands of fans who vociferously protested in the stands at Missouri, for the exuberant rowdies who milled about on the infield at the Polo Grounds over a century ago, or for the fans who gathered on the Chicago sidewalks to question the events of that rainy September night in 1927, such answers may seem hollow and unfulfilling. With such answers, the fundamental nature of victory, and indeed the very purpose of athletic competition itself, remains unaddressed.

Cornell's Day, Lynah and Snavely had another idea in mind, one not motivated so much by rules as by honor and integrity. Their answer, though not as technically neat as Nelson's, rings true to the purpose of their institution and to the role of athletic competition. Their action was motivated not so much by an appreciation of the rule of the competition as by its purpose.

On September 10, 2009, Bill Bradley and Ken Dryden, two great college and professional athletes who went on to notable political careers, collaborated in a presentation on the Cornell campus titled "Lives on the Run: Sports, Service, and Leadership." During his remarks, Bradley commented on the importance of integrity, saying, "Integrity, if I were to define it, is going a couple steps beyond what is legal."[77] There was no rule that required Cornell's action. Indeed, it contradicted all rules and all practices of the time. But the gift by the Cornell administration and players to college football and to the reputation of their university far surpasses the value of a national championship or an undefeated season.

On April 27, 1940, Carl Becker, university historian, speaking on the occasion of Cornell's 75th Anniversary, said, "In the process of acquiring a reputation Cornell acquired something better than a reputation, or rather acquired something that is the better part of its reputation. It acquired a character...."[78] Though motivated by something broader than a football game, Professor Becker's comments perhaps still rang in Day and Lynah's ears seven months later.

Over the years Cornell continued to attract accolades for its action. "Cornell's response was...demonstrative of their character," wrote Steve Riach, founder of the nonprofit organization Heart of a Champion.[79] ESPN called it an "unprecedented act of sportsmanship."[80] Rick Reilly of *Sports Illustrated* rated Cornell's decision the Classiest Act in sports.[81] Other commentators have said Cornell "gallantly forfeited the game,"[82] that the act will be "remembered and honored across the decades,"[83] and that it was a "magnanimous act of sportsmanship,"[84] and "one of the finest acts of sportsmanship in college football history."[85] Beano Cook, writing for ESPN, said, "Today, if anybody followed Snavely and Day's honorable lead...it's likely they'd be hung, not in effigy, but in person." Cook rated the Fifth Down game as tied for first with the Win-One-For-The-Gipper speech on his personal list of greatest moments in college football history.[86] The 1940 Cornell football team is one of four teams in the Institute for International Sport Scholar-Athlete Hall of Fame. "The honesty of 'Red' Friesell and the sportsmanship of Cornell will forever make the 'Fifth Down' game an afternoon of college football to remember," said the Institute.[87]

The final word on Cornell's forfeit to Dartmouth that day belongs to its All-American tackle, Nick Drahos. "We figured if they win it, they win it," he said, "and that's the way it should be."[88]

NOTES

Chapter 1

1   *Cornell Alumni News*, Vol. 43, No. 1, September 26, 1940, 4.
2   George Kirksey, "Football Forecast," *Look*, October 8, 1940, 34.
3   Bob MacFarland, "Veteran Squad Greets Snavely For Grid Season," *Cornell Daily Sun*, September 23, 1940, 1.
4   John Kieran, "Delayed Passes," *New York Times*, October 30, 1940, 30.
5   Henry McLemore, "Today's Sports Parade," *Ogden (UT) Standard*, October 21, 1940, 7.
6   Allison Danzig, "Achievements of Cornell, Yale, and Iowa Through Year Exceeded Expectations," *New York Times*, November 27, 1939, 22.
7   Dan Daly, "This Mostly Irishman Banking on New Coach," *Washington Times*, January 4, 2002.
8   James P. Quirk, Minnesota Football: The Golden Years, 1932-1941 (Grantsburg, WI: Mr. Print, 1984), 43.
9   Jerry Brondfield, "Critics Calling Cornell Greatest Team in Eastern Football History," *Dunkirk (NY) Evening Observer*, October 11, 1940, 17.
10 Eddie Dooley (ed.), *Illustrated Football Annual, 1940*, 26.
11 Dillon Graham, "Cornell Has All Any Good Team Has—Plus a Crop of Instinctive Performers," *Gallup (NM) Independent*, November 7, 1940.
12 "The Talk of the Town," *New Yorker*, November 30, 1940, 10-11.
13 Tom Brokaw, The Greatest Generation (New York: Random House, 1998), 277.
14 Garry Schumacher, "Cornell Players Jig to Swing Music in Clubhouse," *San Antonio Light*, December 1, 1940, part 6, 5.
15 Snavely Has Veteran Team," *Burlington (NC) Times-News*, September 14, 1940, 6.
16 John Lardner, "Lardner Says," *Montana Standard*, September 8, 1940.
17 "The Perennial Dirge," *Reno (NV) Evening Gazette*, September 7, 1940, 4.
18 Romeyn Berry, "Now, In My Time!" *Cornell Alumni News*, Vol. 43, No. 5, October 24, 1940, 68.
19 "Sport: Midwestern Front," *Time*, November 6, 1939, 35-38.
20 Ibid.
21 Michael Bradley, Big Games (Washington, D.C.: Potomac Books, Inc., 2006), 225.
22 "Sport: Midwestern Front," *Time*, November 6, 1939, 35-38.

23   Richard Rainbolt, Gold Glory (Wayzata, MN: Ralph Turtinen Publishing Co., 1972), 26.

24   Gerald Holland, "The Man Who Changed Football," *Sports Illustrated*, February 3, 1964.

25   Harry Grayson, NEA Service Sports Editor, "Star Players Prove Big Three of Football Isn't Exactly Soft," *Sandusky (OH) Register*, November 23, 1940, 6.

26   "Pitt Planes Arrive in Seattle," *New York Times*, September 29, 1939, 27.

27   Bill Pennington, The Heisman (Regan Books, 2004), 39.

28   "Michigan Team Continues Flight," *San Mateo (CA) Times and Daily News Leader*, September 26, 1940, 13.

29   Bernie McCarty, "Tom Harmon—Michigan 41, California 0, September 28, 1940," *College Football Historical Society Newsletter*, Vol. XIII, No. 1, November, 1999, 17.

30   "Michigan Blanks California, 41-0, Harmon Getting Four Touchdowns," *New York Times*, September 29, 1940, S1.

31   Bernie McCarty, "Tom Harmon—Michigan 41, California 0, September 28, 1940," *College Football Historical Society Newsletter*, Vol. XIII, No. 1, November, 1999, 17.

32   Jeff Faraudo, "One Day, Two Bay Area Events Make College Football History," *Oakland Tribune*, March 25, 2004.

33   "Fan Tackles Michigan's Harmon On Touchdown Run," *Life*, October 14, 1940, 47.

34   Art Cohn, "Cohn-ing Tower," *Oakland Tribune*, September 30, 1940, 9.

35   Pennington, The Heisman, 130.

36   Coles Phinizy, "Rock of Ages," in Ron Fleder (ed.), The College Football Book (New York: Sports Illustrated Books, Time, Inc., 2008), 96.

37   "Interview: John Druze," *College Football Historical Society Newsletter*, Vol. XIV, No. 3, May, 2001, 1-3.

38   Allen Barra, "Is the Gridiron Game Still the Same?" *Wall Street Journal*, September 10, 2009, D7.

39   Douglas S. Looney, "One Is More Like It," *Sports Illustrated*, September 3, 1990.

40   "Marquette Is Beaten, 45-41, By Manhattan," *College Football Historical Society Newsletter*, Vol. IX, No. 1, November, 1995, 5. See also: "Touchdowns In Quantity," letter to the editor by Edmund Arthur, *New York Times*, November 16, 1940, 10.

41   Darren Everson and Reed Albergotti, "What's So Great About Punting?" *Wall Street Journal*, November 17, 2009, D10.

42   Sam Jackson, "More Than 40 Games Ending 7-6 Show Need For Kick Specialists," *Cumberland (MD) Sunday Times*, November 24, 1940, 16.

43   Richard Whittingham, Rites of Autumn—The Story of College Football (New York: The Free Press, 2001), 37.

44   Stewart Mandel, "Behind the Wildcat," *Sports Illustrated*, October 12, 2009, 74.

45 "N.U. Footballers Wear New Transparent 'Hats,'" *The Minnesota Daily*, October 31, 1940, 11.

46 "Around the Big Ten," *The Minnesota Daily*, October 12, 1940, 7.

Chapter 2

1. University of Chicago Physical Education and Athletics, History, http:// athletics.uchicago.edu/history/history-stagg.htm, accessed June 12, 2009.
2. Robin Lester, "Legends of the Fall." *The University of Chicago Magazine*, October, 1995.
3. William D. Richardson, "On College Gridirons," *New York Times*, October 25, 1940, 26.
4. "Stanford Too Fast and Wise for Nebraska," *Jefferson City (MO) Post-Tribune*, January 2, 1941, 9.
5. Charles Bartlett, "University of Chicago Gives Up Football," *Chicago Daily Tribune*, December 22, 1939, 27.
6. Ibid.
7. Arnold Derlitski, "U. of Chicago Abandons Intercollegiate Football," *Hagerstown (MD) Daily Mail*, December 22, 1939, 9.
8. James W. Johnson, The Wow Boys (Lincoln and London: The University of Nebraska Press, 2006), 13.
9. Arnold Derlitski, "U. of Chicago Abandons Intercollegiate Football," *Hagerstown (MD) Daily Mail*, December 22, 1939, 9.
10. "What U. of Chicago Students Think About Loss of Football," *Chicago Daily Tribune*, December 23, 1939, 15.
11. John Sayle Watterson, College Football (Baltimore, MD: Johns Hopkins University Press, 2000), 195.
12. Arnold Derlitski, "U. of Chicago Abandons Intercollegiate Football," *Hagerstown (MD) Daily Mail*, December 22, 1939, 9.
13. Watterson, College Football, 197.
14. Al Warden, "Patrolling the Sports Highway," *Ogden (UT) Standard-Examiner*, December 22, 1939, 9.
15. Johnson, Wow Boys, 23.
16. "Vote Ouster of Thornhill at Stanford," *Chicago Daily Tribune*, December 16, 1939, 17.
17. "Mentioned at Stanford," *Chicago Daily Tribune*, December 22, 1939, 28.
18. "Coach Shaughnessy, Victory-Starved at Chicago, Leads Hungry Stanford Toward the Rose Bowl Table," *Newsweek*, November 4, 1940, 44.
19. Quirk, Minnesota Football, 21.
20. Johnson, Wow Boys, 16-17.
21. Dick Hyland, "Shaughnessy Believed in Line for Stanford Job," *Los Angeles Times*, January 7, 1940, A12.
22. "In Waltz Time," *Time*, November 18, 1940, 61.

23. "Shaughnessy Appointed Head Grid Coach at Stanford," *Los Angeles Times*, January 12, 1940, 19.
24. Dick Hyland, "Shaughnessy Believed in Line for Stanford Job," *Los Angeles Times*, January 7, 1940, A12.
25. Ron Fimrite, "A Melding of Men All Suited to a T," *Sports Illustrated*, September 5, 1977.
26. Ibid.
27. Johnson, Wow Boys, 22.
28. Ibid., 24.
29. Ron Fimrite, "A Melding of Men All Suited to a T," *Sports Illustrated*, September 5, 1977.
30. "Shaughnessy Will Use Own System, He Tells Stanford," *Chicago Daily Tribune*, March 8, 1940, 33.
31. Ibid.
32. Red Smith, "Glenn Scobey Warner," in To Absent Friends (New York: Atheneum, 1982), 74; (originally published in *New York Herald Tribune*, September 9, 1954).
33. "Wow Boys Dazzle the Coast," *Sports Illustrated*, September 19, 1966.
34. Ron Fimrite, "A Melding of Men All Suited to a T," *Sports Illustrated*, September 5, 1977.
35. Jeff Faraudo, "One Day, Two Bay Area Events Make College Football History," *Oakland Tribune*, March 25, 2004.
36. Ron Fimrite, "A Melding of Men All Suited to a T," *Sports Illustrated*, September 5, 1977.
37. Johnson, Wow Boys, 53.
38. "Stanford Stock Goes Up With 27-0 Win Over Dons," *Oakland Tribune*, September 29, 1940, 14-A.
39. Bill Tobitt, "Stanford Preps for Oregonians," *Oakland Tribune*, September 30, 1940, 9.
40. Vinny DiTrani, "Skins View It Beyond 3-D," *Bergen County (NJ) Record*, January 23, 1992.
41. "Stanford Stock Goes Up With 27-0 Win Over Dons," *Oakland Tribune*, September 29, 1940, 14-A.
42. "35 Huskies Move on Minneapolis," *Minnesota Daily*, September 25, 1940, 17.
43. "Phelan Hopes This Will Be Huskies' Year," *Minnesota Daily*, September 25, 1940, 17.
44. Dooley, *Illustrated Football Annual*, 94.
45. "Phelan Hopes This Will Be Huskies' Year," *Minnesota Daily*, September 25, 1940, 17.
46. Dooley, *Illustrated Football Annual*, 76.
47. "Best Bet for Top Ten Teams," *Look*, October 8, 1940, 34.
48. William Oscar Johnson, "New Deal in Gopherland," *Sports Illustrated*, November 5, 1984.

49. Sherm Langley, "Across the Sports Desk," *Minnesota Daily*, September 25, 1940, 18.
50. Dooley, *Illustrated Football Annual*, 43.
51. Quirk, Minnesota Football, 218.
52. "Bernie Says Gophers 'May Win,'" *Minnesota Daily*, September 25, 1940, 17.
53. "Coming Fast," *Minnesota Daily*, October 10, 1940, 13.
54. Quirk, Minnesota Football, 20, 34, 60, 215.
55. Rainbolt, Gold Glory, 62.
56. Quirk, Minnesota Football, 15.
57. Ibid., 35.
58. Lefty Farnsworth, "Four Historic Tackles of the Forties," *College Football Historical Society Newsletter*," Vol. III, No. 1, November, 1989, 16-18.

Chapter 3

1. Felix R. McKnight, "Conscription Bill Would Wreck Southeastern Conference—McKnight," *San Antonio Light*, August 14, 1940, 11-A.
2. "Roosevelt Offers A Defense Program Against Rising Menace of Dictators," *New York Times*, January 5, 1939, 1.
3. "$552,000,000 For Defense Is Asked By Roosevelt," *New York Times*, January 13, 1939, 1.
4. Richard Snow, A Measureless Peril (New York: Scribner, 2010), 81.
5. John Lukacs, The Last European War (New Haven, CT: Yale University Press, 1976), 56n.
6. Philip Sieb, Broadcasts from the Blitz (Washington, D.C.: Potomac Books, Inc., 2006), 7.
7. Quoted in Sieb, Broadcasts From the Blitz, 25.
8. H.W. Brands, Traitor to His Class (New York: Doubleday, 2008), 531-2.
9. Ibid., 530.
10. George Soule, "If Germany Wins," *The New Republic*, April 22, 1940, 525-6.
11. "If Hitler Writes the Peace," *The New Republic*, May 20, 1940, 660.
12. Sieb, Broadcasts From the Blitz, 152.
13. Oswald Garrison Villard, "Will Hitler Strike At England?" *The Nation*, March 16, 1940, 366.
14. Freda Kirchwey, "Can We Stay Neutral?" *The Nation*, April 20, 1940, 503-4.
15. "Everything For Defense," *Time*, July 1, 1940, 18.
16. Ian Kershaw, Fateful Choices (New York: The Penguin Press, 2007), 207-8.
17. Quoted in Sieb, Broadcasts From the Blitz, 26.
18. "Everything For Defense," *Time*, July 1, 1940, 18.
19. "If Hitler Writes the Peace," *The New Republic*, May 20, 1940, 660.
20. "Reaction," *Time*, May 27, 1940, 17.

21. Nicholson Baker, Human Smoke: The Beginnings of World War II, The End of Civilization (New York: Simon and Schuster Paperbacks, 2008), 190.
22. Lukacs, The Last European War, 100-101.
23. Kershaw, Fateful Choices, 211. See also: Brands, Traitor to His Class, 547-8.
24. "The Shape of Things," *The Nation*, June 15, 1940, 721.
25. "Non-Belligerency," *The New Republic*, June 17, 1940, 807.
26. "Aid to the Allies," *Time*, June 17, 1940, 14.
27. Sieb, Broadcasts Fron the Blitz, 41.
28. Freda Kirchwey, "Supposing Hitler Wins," *The Nation*, May 25, 1940, 640.
29. George Soule, "If Germany Wins," *The New Republic*, April 22, 1940, 525-6.
30. "If Hitler Writes the Peace, *The New Republic*, May 20, 1940, 660.
31. Drew Pearson and Robert S. Allen, "Can We Keep Hitler Out of the Americas?" *Look*, July 16, 1940, 20.
32. Walter Lippmann, "The Economic Consequences of a German Victory," *Life*, July 22, 1940, 64.
33. Vincent Sheean, "What a Hitler Victory Means to the United States," *Look*, August 13, 1940, 13.
34. Philip Kaplan and Richard Collier, Their Finest Hour—The Battle of Britain Remembered (New York: Abbeville Press, 1989), 42.
35. Simon Schama, A History of Britain, Vol. III: The Fate of Empire, 1776-2000 (New York: Hyperion, 2002), 552.
36. Hanson W. Baldwin, "The Battle of Britain: How It Will Be Fought," *New York Times*, June 23, 1940, 4E.
37. Winston S. Churchill, Memoirs of the Second World War (New York: Bonanza Books, 1978), 307.
38. "100 Planes Clash In Battle Over a Convoy In Channel," *New York Times*, July 11, 1940, 1.
39. Kaplan and Collier, Their Finest Hour, 44.
40. George Axelsson, "Berlin Sees Drive on Britain Matter of Days, If Not Hours," *New York Times*, July 29, 1940.
41. Schama, A History of Britain, 522.
42. Robert M. Leckie, Delivered From Evil (New York: Harper and Row, 1987), 189-90.
43. Kaplan and Collier, Their Finest Hour, 189.
44. Sieb, Broadcasts from the Blitz, 77.
45. Leckie, Delivered From Evil, 199.
46. Sieb, Broadcasts from the Blitz, 77.

Chapter 4

1. "Football Receipts Stolen as Kansas and Nebraska Play," *New York Times*, November 4, 1928, Sec. 11, 1.

2. Rachel Bachman, "When Football Is an Economic Strategy," *Wall Street Journal*, January 6, 2012, D10.
3. "Yale Football had a $1,000,000 Year," *New York Times*, November 2, 1928, 23.
4. "For the Glory of Cornell," *Cornell Daily Sun*, October 31, 1940, 4.
5. "Colgate Reports Deficit," *New York Times*, November 8, 1940, 32.
6. "Football Pays For All Sports, Report Reveals," *Cornell Daily Sun*, October 31, 1939, 1.
7. "Cornell Shows Profit," *New York Times*, October 19, 1940, 12.
8. Henry McLemore, "McLemore's All-America Team is...The University of Chicago," *Look*, June 4, 1940, 24.
9. Francis Wallace, "Football's Civil War," *Look*, October 22, 1940, 20.
10. Watterson, College Football, 184.
11. John H. Whoric, "Sportorials," *Connellsville (PA) Daily Courier*, December 18, 1939, 7.
12. Henry McLemore, "Big Ten Headed For Rose Bowl," *Waterloo (IA) Daily Courier*, October 30, 1940, 14.
13. Watterson, College Football, 180.
14. Ibid.
15. Francis Wallace, "Test Case at Pitt," *Saturday Evening Post*, October 28, 1940, 14-15.
16. Michael Oriard, King Football, (Chapel Hill and London: University of North Carolina Press), 114.
17. "Jock Out," *Time*, March 20, 1939, 34.
18. Watterson, College Football, 188.
19. "Jock Out," *Time*, March 20, 1939, 34.
20. "Ohio State to Open With Pitt in 1940," *New York Times*, November 22, 1939, 25.
21. "Jock Out," *Time*, March 20, 1939, 34.
22. "Joe Sephus' Cullings, *Cumberland (MD) Sunday Times*, November 24, 1940, 16.
23. Whitney Martin, "Galloping Down the Sports Trail," *Titusville (PA) Herald*, October 23, 1939, 6.
24. Oriard, King Football, 41.
25. Gary R. Edgerton, The Columbia History of American Television (New York: Columbia University Press, 2007), 10-15.
26. Edgar M. Jones, "How About Television?" *The Nation*, April 6, 1940, 447.
27. "The Age of Television," *The New Yorker*, July 27, 1940, 22.
28. Edgar M. Jones, "How About Television?" *The Nation*, April 6, 1940, 447.
29. L. Gordon Crovitz, "Technology Predictions Are Mostly Bunk," *Wall Street Journal*, December 28, 2009, A15.
30. Sieb, Broadcasts from the Blitz, 7.
31. Stan Grosshandler, MD, "TV's First Game," *College Football Historical Society Newsletter*, Vol. VI, No. 4, August, 1993, 4-5.

32. Zachary Kent, The Story of Television (Chicago: The Children's Press, 1990), 14.
33. Ibid., 16.
34. James L. Baughman, Same Time, Same Station (Baltimore, MD: The Johns Hopkins University Press, 2007), 1.
35. Whittingham, Rites of Autumn, 44.
36. Baughman, Same Time, Same Station, 2.
37. Tom Farrey, "NCAA Might Face Damages in Hundreds of Millions," *ESPN.com* (http://sports.espn.go.com/espn/print?id=2337810&type=story), February 20, 2006.
38. Hannah Karp, "Texas Football Boosters Think Big," *Wall Street Journal*, December 17, 2009, D7.
39. Steve Weiberg, Jodi Upton, A.J. Perez, and Steve Berkowitz, "Pay Booms in Hard Times," *USA Today*, November 10, 2009, 1A.
40. Steve Berkowitz, "Riches Await Saturday's Winner," *USA Today*, December 1, 2010, 1A.
41. Steve Weiberg, Jodi Upton, A.J. Perez, and Steve Berkowitz, "Pay Booms in Hard Times," *USA Today*, November 10, 2009, 1A.
42. Steve Berkowitz, "Salaries Spike for College Football Assistants," *USA Today*, March 10, 2010, 1C.
43. http://ncaafootball.fanhouse.com/2009/06/15/as-notre-dames-tv-money-dwindles-so-too-should-its-independence/).
44. "CBS, ESPN See Record Numbers For College Football Coverage," *Street and Smith's Sports Business Daily*, December 16, 2009.
45. Paul Banks, "Despite Outdated Postseason Structure, College Football Shows Superb Ratings," *Washington Times*, March 2, 2010.
46. Alan Scher Zagier, "Seeking Prime Seats? Take Out a Mortgage," *Virginian-Pilot*, March 31, 2010, S3.
47. Watterson, College Football, 198.
48. Taylor Branch, "The Shame of College Sports," *Atlantic*, October 2011, 102.

Chapter 5

1. "Don Scott to Read Papers After Grid Season's Over," *Mansfield (OH) News-Journal*, October 3, 1940, 15.
2. "Ohio State Victory by Error is Bared," *New York Times*, October 18, 1940, 27.
3. Ibid.
4. "Ohio State's Victory Was Illegal, But It Will Stand," *Mansfield (OH) News-Journal*, October 18, 1940, 15.
5. "Ohio State Victory by Error is Bared," *New York Times*, October 18, 1940, 27.

6. Bob MacFarlane, "Harvard and Ohio State," *Cornell Daily Sun*, October 18, 1940, 8.
7. "Ohio State's Victory Was Illegal, But It Will Stand," *Mansfield (OH) News-Journal*, October 18, 1940, 15.
8. "Hank Says," *Capital (WI) Times*, October 16, 1940, 14.
9. John Kieran, "One More for the Book," *New York Times*, October 18, 1940, 29.
10. "On the Campus and Down the Hill," *Cornell Alumni News*, Vol. 43, No. 4, October 17, 1940, 55.

Chapter 6

1. Fredric Alan Maxwell, "The Late Great 98," *Michigan Today* (http://michigantoday.umich.edu/2008/09/harmon.php), accessed November 17, 2008.
2. Pat Zacharias, "The Wolverines' Legendary Tom Harmon," *Detroit News*, February 19, 1995.
3. Pennington, The Heisman, 39.
4. Mark Purcell, "Tom Harmon, 1920-1990," *College Football Historical Society Newsletter*, Vol.III, No. 3, May, 1990, 17-18.
5. *Time*, November 6, 1939.
6. Ibid.
7. Elizabeth McGarr, "Conquering Hero," *Sports Illustrated*, August 20, 2008.
8. John Lardner, "This Here Now Harmon," *Newsweek*, October 21, 1940, 44.
9. "East Squad Bickering is Denied by Coaches," *Arizona Republic*, December 30, 1940, Sec. 2, 2.
10. "Harmon Back at the Books," *Lowell (MA) Sun*, January 8, 1941.
11. "44 Seniors Meet in East-West Contest," *Mason City (IA) Globe-Gazette*, January 1, 1941.
12. "Evashevski Elected to Class Presidency," *Minnesota Daily*, November 27, 1940, 7.
13. John Lardner, "This Here Now Harmon," *Newsweek*, October 21, 1940, 44.
14. "Footballer Harmon Sports 'B' Average," *Minnesota Daily*, October 15, 1940, 6.
15. William D. Richardson, "Harmon is First by Wide Margin in Heisman," *New York Times*, November 28, 1940, 30.
16. James B. Lane, City of the Century: A History of Gary, Indiana (Bloomington: Indiana University Press, 1978), 216, 220.
17. "Backs," *Time*, October 23, 1939, 59-60.
18. W.C. Heinz, "Ghost of the Gridiron," in David Halberstam (ed.), The Best American Sportswriting of the Century (Boston: Houghton Mifflin Company, 1990), 260.
19. James Crusinberry, "Grange Thrills Huge Crowd by Racing to 5 Touchdowns," *Chicago Daily Tribune*, October 19, 1924, A1.

20. "67,000 See Illinois Beat Michigan, 39-14," *New York Times*, October 19, 1924, Sec. 10, 2.
21. Lawrence Perry, "Grange Must Face Iowa U. as Big Test," *Oakland Tribune*, October 20, 1924, 12.
22. Henry Farrell, "Michigan is Defeated, 39 to14, Before Illinois' Immortal Redhead Grange," *Charlestown (WV) Daily Mail*, October 19, 1924, 14.
23. Henry L. Farrell, "Illinois is Picked to Win Big Ten Championship Race; Grange New Football Marvel," *Sheboygan (WI) Press-Telegram*, October 21, 1924, 8.
24. Heinz, "Ghost of the Gridiron," 253.
25. Henry L. Farrell, "Stagg, Rockne and Others Agree That Red Grange of Illinois Has No Equal," *Waterloo (IA) Evening Courier*, November 8, 1924, 12.
26. John M. Carroll, "Red Storms East," *College Football Historical Society Journal*, Vol. XII, No. 2, February 1999, 7-9.
27. Heinz, "Ghost of the Gridiron," 253.
28. Lars Anderson, The First Star (New York: Random House, 2009), 202.
29. Walter Eckersall, "Does Red Grange Outrank Grid Heroes of Other Years?" *Chicago Tribune*, October 22, 1924, 25.
30. "Around the Big Ten," *Minnesota Daily*, October 15, 1940, 7.
31. Pat Zacharias, "The Wolverines' Legendary Tom Harmon," *Detroit News*, February 19, 1995.
32. Robert F. Kelley, "On College Gridirons," *New York Times*, October 23, 1940, 30.
33. Anderson, The First Star, 149 and 219.
34. Heinz, "Ghost of the Gridiron," 264.
35. John Lardner, "This Here Now Harmon," *Newsweek*, October 21, 1940, 44.
36. William D. Richardson, "On College Gridirons," *New York Times*, November 1, 1939, 30.
37. Herb Graffis and Ralph Cannon, "The Army-Navy 1926 Football Game" in Esquire's First Sports Reader (A.S. Barnes and Co., 1971), 195-6.
38. Henry McLemore, "McLemore Says Harmon is All-American Backfield by Himself," *Jefferson City (MO) Post-Tribune*, October 28, 1940, 5.
39. Whitney Martin, "Galloping Down the Sports Trail," *Titusville (PA) Herald*, November 2, 1940, 8.
40. Lee Dunbar, "California Works on Tackling," *Oakland Tribune*, September 30, 1940, 9.
41. Henry L. Farrell, "Stagg, Rockne and Others Agree That Red Grange of Illinois Has No Equal," *Waterloo (IA) Evening Courier*, November 8, 1924, 12.
42. Lawrence Perry, "Grange Must Face Iowa U. as Big Test," *Oakland Tribune*, October 20, 1924, 12.
43. Jim Scott, "Around the Big Ten," *Minnesota Daily*, October 24, 1940, 11.
44. Alfred Wright, "The Best College Player of All Time," *Sports Illustrated*, September 24, 1962.

45. See, for example, Kevin Hynes, "Musings on Red Grange," *College Football Historical Society Newsletter*," Vol. XIX, No. III, May, 2006, 1-3.
46. Fred Jaqua, "Famous Cornell '24 Quarterback Lauds Snavely for Game Precision," *Cornell Daily Sun*, October 28, 1940, 1.
47. Alfred Wright, "The Best College Player of All Time," *Sports Illustrated*, September 24, 1962.
48. Mark Purcell, "Tom Harmon, 1920-1990," *College Football Historical Society Newsletter*, Vol.III, No. 3, May, 1990, 17-18.
49. "65,438 See Michigan Gain 21-14 Triumph," *New York Times*, October 6, 1940, S4.
50. William D. Richardson, "Michigan Topples Harvard by 26-0," *New York Times*, October 13, 1940, S1.
51. Allison Danzig, "Penn and Cornell Uphold Ivy Prestige Despite Toppling of Big Three," *New York Times*, October 14, 1940, 27.
52. "Fifth Official to Control Electric Clock Urged in Aftermath of Penn-Michigan Game," *New York Times*, November 21, 1939, 29.
53. Lefty Farnsworth, "The Flying Irishman," *College Football Historical Society Newsletter*," Vol.V, No. III, May, 1992, 12.
54. "Football," *Time*, November 4, 1940, 46-47.
55. Allison Danzig, "Football Fever Rises Over Ivy League Games," *New York Times*, October 22, 1940, 28.
56. "Michigan, Penn Top Nation's Grid Slate," *Minnesota Daily*, October 24, 1940, 10.
57. Eddie Breitz, "Sports Roundup," *Lowell (MA) Sun*, October 24, 1940, 15.
58. Harry Newman, "Harmon-Reagan Duel is Headliner of Week," *Lima (OH) News*, October 23, 1940, 13.
59. Robert F. Kelley, "Harmon the Star," *New York Times*, October 27, 1940, S1.
60. Graffis and Cannon, "The Army-Navy 1926 Football Game", 196.
61. Wilfrid Smith, "Three Big Nine Leaders Will Fight It Out in Round Robin," *Chicago Daily Tribune*, October 28, 1940, 19.
62. Grantland Rice, "The Sportlight," *Syracuse Herald-Journal*, November 18, 1940, 20.
63. Henry McLemore, "McLemore Says Harmon is All-American Backfield by Himself," *Jefferson City (MO) Post-Tribune*, October 28, 1940, 5.
64. Robert F. Kelley, "On College Gridirons," *New York Times*, October 30, 1940, 30.
65. Henry McLemore, "McLemore Says Harmon is All-American Backfield by Himself," *Jefferson City (MO) Post-Tribune*, October 28, 1940, 5.
66. Allison Danzig, "Cornell, Notre Dame, Minnesota, Michigan Rated Big Four of College Football," *New York Times*, October 28, 1940, 24.

Chapter 7

1. Henry McLemore, "Purple Will Have to Stop George Franck If 'Jinx' Over Gophers is to Hold," *Valparaiso (IN) Vidette Messenger*, November 2, 1940, 10.
2. Harry Grayson, "Harmon's Duel With Franck Should Feature Big Game," *Lowell (MA) Sun*, November 8, 1940, 10.
3. Joel Rippel, Game of My Life—Minnesota (Champaign, IL: Sports Publishing, LLC, 2007), 4.
4. Ibid., 8.
5. Quirk, Minnesota Football, 214.
6. Pennington, The Heisman, 50-51.
7. Joel Rippel, "Dick Wildung Cleared Path for a Heisman," *Minneapolis Star Tribune*, March 23, 2006.
8. Jay Vessels, "Minnesota's Mr. Bruce Smith is Hard to Find—On Or Off the Football Field," *Galveston Daily News*, October 12, 1941, 10.
9. Tom Akers and Sam Akers, The Game Breaker (Ralph Turtinen Publishing Co., 1977), 35.
10. Quirk, Minnesota Football, 259-60.
11. Rainbolt, Gold Glory, 99.
12. Ibid., 118.
13. Quirk, Minnesota Football, 219.
14. "Tackle Thinks He Played Best Game Against Huskers," *Minnesota Daily*, October 22, 1940, 6.
15. Allison Danzig, "Minnesota is Ranked as Top Team with Gridiron Campaign in Full Swing," *New York Times*, October 7, 1940, 24.
16. William D. Richardson, "On College Gridirons," *New York Times*, October 11, 1940, 28.
17. Ibid.
18. "Catching Up with Hall of Famer George 'Sonny' Franck," College Football Hall of Fame, (http://www.collegefootball.org/news.php?id=851), accessed November 18, 2008.
19. Arch Ward, "Gopher Running Attack Beats Ohio State, 13-7, Before 63,199," *Chicago Daily Tribune*, October 20, 1940, B1.
20. "36 Gophers Spend Night in Bayport," *Minnesota Daily*, October 2, 1940, 6.
21. Ray Schmidt, "George 'Sonny' Franck," *College Football Historical Society Newsletter*, Vol. XI, No. I, November, 1997, 1-4.
22. Rippel, Game of My Life, 7.
23. "Gophers Lose Smith, Almost, For Hawkeyes," *Chicago Daily Tribune*, October 23, 1940, 27.
24. Art Cohn, "Cohn-ing Tower," *Oakland Tribune*, September 26, 1940, 65.
25. Bernie McCarthy, "They Overlooked Pete Kmetovic," *College Football Historical Society Newsletter*, Vol. I, No. 5, August, 1988, 16-17.

26. Henry McLemore, "Big Gridiron Problem of '41—Find Suitable Foe for Indians," *Jefferson City (MO) Post-Tribune*, January 2, 1941, 9.
27. "Hugh Gallarneau," *College Football Historical Society Newsletter*, Vol. XII, No. IV, August, 1999, 22-24.
28. Bob Blake, "Phelan Rates Minnesota Over Stanford," *Oakland Tribune*, November 10, 1940, 16A.
29. "Stanford's Tricks Down Oregon, 13-0," *New York Times*, October 6, 1940, 7.
30. "Stanford Dazzles to Beat Oregon U.," *Lincoln (NE) Sunday Journal and Star*, October 6, 1940, 4.
31. Russell Newland, "Shaughnessy's Stanford Team Hailed as Hottest in West," *Los Angeles Times*, October 14, 1940, 17.
32. Russell Newland, "Indian Grids Top Surprise in Conference," *Los Angeles Times*, October 7, 1940, 19.
33. Art Cohn, "Stanford Upsets Broncs, 7-6," *Oakland Tribune*, October 13, 1940, 11-A.
34. Russell Newland, "Shaughnessy's Stanford Team Hailed as Hottest in West," *Los Angeles Times*, October 14, 1940, 17.
35. Bill Tobitt, "Tribe Amazes Shaughnessy," *Oakland Tribune*, October 13, 1940, 11-A.
36. "Stanford Overcomes Washington State," *New York Times*, October 20, 1940, S7.
37. Johnson, The Wow Boys, 80.
38. Allison Danzig, "Sectional Football Leaders Bolster Claims, But Notre Dame Prestige Wanes," *New York Times*, November 4, 1940, 26.
39. Russell Newland, "High Flying Stanford Team Eyes Rose Bowl Bid," *Los Angeles Times*, October 21, 1940, A10.
40. Henry McLemore, "Today's Sports Parade," *Ogden (UT) Standard-Examiner*, October 21, 1940, 7.
41. James A. Sullivan, "Clark Shaughnessy Jumps to Fame in Coast Grid League," *Ogden (UT) Standard-Examiner,* October 21, 1940, 7.
42. "Warner Gives Shaughnessy a Big Hand," *Chicago Daily Tribune*, October 31, 1940, 24.
43. Dick Hyland, "Shaughnessy's Daring, Stanford Pass Defense Chiefly Responsible for Win," *Los Angeles Times*, October 27, 1940, A14.
44. Ibid.
45. "Coach Shaughnessy, Victory-Starved at Chicago, Leads Hungry Stanford Toward the Rose Bowl Table," *Newsweek*, November 4, 1940, 44.
46. Russell Newland, "Shaughnessy, Stanford, Amaze Gridiron World," *Los Angeles Times*, October 28, 1940, A9.

Chapter 8

1. Ron Fimrite, "Nile Kinnick," *Sports Illustrated*, August 31, 1987.

2. "N.Y.U. May Cancel Grid Meeting With Georgia Eleven," *Syracuse Herald*, October 23, 1929.
3. "Benching of Negro Player Brings Protest," *Salt Lake City Tribune*, October 24, 1929, 17.
4. "Who's Boss—The President or the Coach?" *Capital Times (Madison, WI)*, November 4, 1929.
5. "Negro Star on Bench When Violets Engage Georgia University, Decided," *Uniontown (PA) Daily News Standard*, October 24, 1929, 7.
6. "Meehan Will Not Use Myers Against Georgia," *Carnegie Report*, October 24, 1929, 35.
7. "Follow Ups by Chiixx," *Greeley (CO) Tribune-Republican*, October 28, 1929, 8.
8. "New York Students Protest to Officials," *Burlington (NC) Daily Times*, October 31, 1929.
9. Rollie E. Bernhart, "Grid Leaks," *Valparaiso (IN) Vidette-Messenger*, November 6, 1929, 10.
10. "Who's Boss—The President or the Coach?" *Capital Times (Madison, WI)*, November 4, 1929.
11. "N.Y.U. Shows Dash in 2-Hour Session," *New York Times*, November 5, 1929, 37.
12. "Dave Myers Will Play," *Lowell (MA) Sun*, November 7, 1929, 16.
13. "N.Y.U. Tests Ends at Marshall's Post," *New York Times*, November 6, 1929, 33.
14. "Negro Injured May Not Face Georgians," *Cumberland (MD) Evening News*, November 8, 1929, 19.
15. "Says Myers Will Play If Condition Permits," *New York Times*, November 7, 1929, 30.
16. William D. Richardson, "N.Y.U. And Georgia Hold Final Drills," *New York Times*, November 9, 1929, 14.
17. Hugh A. Query, "Grid Gossip," *Gastonia (NC) Daily Gazette*, October 16, 1936, 2.
18. Donald Spivey, "End Jim Crow in Sports: The Protest at New York University, 1940-1941," *Journal of Sports History*, Vol. 15, No. 3 (Winter, 1988), 291-2.
19. "Williams at Full in NYU Practice," *New York Times*, October 21, 1936, 37.
20. "In the Fifteenth Round," *Time*, October 14, 1940, 68-70.
21. Ed Gilleran, "The Battle of the Bronx," *College Football Historical Society Newsletter*, Vol. VI, No. II, February, 1993, 1-5.
22. Arthur J. Daley, "Coach Puzzled by NYU Failure to Make Its Aerial Attacks Click," *New York Times,* October 4, 1940, 32.
23. Ibid.
24. Dooley, *Illustrated Football Annual*, 34.
25. "Violets in Poor Shape For Tigers," *St. Louis Post-Dispatch*, October 31, 1940.

26. Allison Danzig, "Kicks Accounted For Three of College Football's Major Surprises Saturday," *New York Times*, November 13, 1939, 24.
27. "Stevens Goes Rival One Better in Worry Over N.Y.U. Reserves," *New York Times*, October 19, 1940, 13.
28. "Violet Negro Star to Miss Missouri Tilt," *Charleston (WVA) Gazette*, October 19, 1940, 7.
29. "N.Y.U. Wins Fight With Injury Jinx," *New York Times*, October 22, 1940, 29.
30. Spivey, "End Jim Crow in Sports," 285.
31. Edward Wong, "N.Y.U. Honors Protestors it Punished in '41," *New York Times*, May 4, 2001, A1.
32. "It Can Happen Here," letter to the editor by Edgar Lassally, Jr., *New York Times*, October 26, 1940, 24.
33. "The Hands of the North Dirty Too," letter to the editor by Samuel A. Reed, *Minnesota Daily,* October 30, 1940, 8.
34. "Bar Against Bates in Missouri is Hit by NYU Graduate," letter to the editor by Bernard E. Gerstner, *New York Times*, November 2, 1940, 23.
35. "Stand of CCNY Varsity Club," letter to the editor by Sidney Herman, *New York Times*, November 2, 1940, 23.
36. "N.Y.U. Hopes Rest on Feil and Frank," *New York Times*, October 29, 1940, 35.
37. "Violets Will Rely on Aerial Attack," *New York Times*, October 31, 1940, 33.
38. "Bates Left Behind as N.Y.U. Entrains," *New York Times*, November 1, 1940, 34.
39. "NYU Negro Player Now Wants to Play," *San Antonio Light*, October 30, 1940.
40. "One Meet: Eight Records,*" Time,* March 25, 1940, 43.
41. "N.Y.U. Group Rebuked by Mrs. Roosevelt," *New York Times*, April 4, 1941, 23.
42. John Kenneth Galbraith, "Eleanor the Good," *Esquire*, December, 1983, 544-6.
43. Alex Ross, "Voice of the Century," *New Yorker*, April 13, 2009, 78-81.
44. "New Youth Group Upholds the 'Isms,'" *New York Times*, March 31, 1941, 13.
45. John Kieran, "Notes On Recent Operations," *New York Times*, October 17, 1938, 21.
46. Louis Effrat, "Three 4th Period Scores Top Cornell for Syracuse," *New York Times*, October 16, 1938, Sec. 5, 1.
47. Lake Cyphers, "The Lost Hero," *New York Daily News*, February 25, 2001.
48. Ibid.
49. Harry Grayson, "Wolves Set up Early Howl," *Lowell (MA) Sun*, October 23, 1937, 34.
50. Bob Snyder, "Sidat-Singh: SU's Saga of Shame," *Syracuse (NY) Post-Standard*, February 26, 2005, D2.

263

51. Dave McKenna, "The Syracuse Walking Dream," *Washington City Paper*, Vol. 28, No. 21, May 23-29, 2008.
52. "Syracuse Grid Team Pressed," *Canandaigua (NY) Daily Messenger*, October 2, 1937, 8.
53. *Hammond (IN) Times*, January 13, 1937, 18.
54. "Jewish Star Chief Problem of Old Liners," *Frederick (MD) News-Post*, October 20, 1937, 3.
55. Harry Grayson, "Wolves Set Up Early Howl," *Lowell (MA) Sun*, October 23, 1937, 34.
56. Photo caption, "Hindoo Magic," *Lowell (MA) Sun*, October 23, 1937, 34.
57. Photo caption, "Hindu Half..." *Billings (MT) Gazette*, October 24, 1937, 8.
58. Dave McKenna, "The Syracuse Walking Dream," *Washington City Paper*, Vol. 28, No. 21, May 23-29, 2008.
59. "Syracuse Team in Good Form," *Canandaigua (NY) Daily Messenger*, October 20, 1937, 7.
60. "Ossie Solem Builds Orange Defense to Halt Penn State Speed," *Syracuse Herald*, October 27, 1937, 18.
61. Donald H. Harrison, "Jewish Athlete Still Bitter About Ruined Shot at Gold Medal," *San Diego Jewish Press-Heritage*, July 2, 1999.
62. Bob Snyder, "Sidat-Singh: SU's Saga of Shame," *Syracuse (NY) Post-Standard*, February 26, 2005, D2.
63. Al Gould, "Speaking of Sports," *Cornell Daily Sun*, October 21, 1940, 7.
64. Charles Seymour, "War's Impact on the Campus," *New York Times Magazine*, September 29, 1940, 3.
65. "Notes On Draft Registration," *Chicago Daily Tribune*, October 17, 1940, 4.
66. "Millions Register In City and Nation," *New York Times*, October 17, 1940, 1.
67. "Notes On Draft Registration," *Chicago Daily Tribune*, October 17, 1940, 4.
68. "Nation's Notables Answer Call; Three Rockefellers Are Included," *New York Times*, October 17, 1940, 13.
69. "Women Hysterical As Troops Depart," *New York Times*, October 24, 1940, 28.

Chapter 9

1. Gene Schoor, 100 Years of Notre Dame Football (New York: Avon Books, 1987), 1-6.
2. Red Smith, "Gus Dorais and the Forward Pass," in Smith, To Absent Friends, 105 (originally published in *New York Herald Tribune*, January 5, 1954).
3. "Catholics Down Army Squad, 35-13," *Chicago Daily Tribune*, November 2, 1913, B1.
4. "Notre Dame's Open Play Amazes Army," *New York Times*, November 2, 1913, Part 4, 1.

5. "Catholics Down Army Squad, 35-13," *Chicago Daily Tribune*, November 2, 1913, B1.
6. Kevin Carroll, Dr. Eddie Anderson (Jefferson, NC: McFarland and Co., Inc., 2007), 14.
7. "Notre Dame's Open Play Amazes Army," *New York Times*, November 2, 1913, Part 4, 1.
8. John Kieran, "Practice Scrimmage," *New York Times*, November 3, 1939, 26.
9. Earl "Red" Blaik, The Red Blaik Story (New Rochelle, NY: Arlington House Publishers, 1960), 235
10. Carroll, Dr. Eddie Anderson, 20-29.
11. Ibid., 27-28.
12. "Notre Dame Rally Topples Indiana in 13-10 Contest," *Chicago Daily Tribune*, November 14, 1920, A1.
13. Schoor, 100 Years of Notre Dame Football, 42.
14. Carroll, Dr. Eddie Anderson, 30.
15. Schoor, 100 Years of Notre Dame Football, 43.
16. "Physicians See Slim Hope for Gipp's Recovery," *Chicago Daily Tribune*, December 2, 1920, 18.
17. "Gipp Buried on Bleak Hill Near Lake Superior," *Chicago Daily Tribune*, December 19, 1920, A1.
18. Walter Eckersall, "Running Attack of Rockne Crew Trims Army, 13-7," *Chicago Daily Tribune*, October 19, 1924, A2.
19. "Army Is Outplayed by Fighting Irish," *Charleston (WV) Daily Mail*, October 19, 1924, 14.
20. Walter Camp, "Speed Feature of Notre Dame Army Victory," *Oakland Tribune*, October 20, 1924, 12.
21. Beano Cook, "Beano Cook's Top Ten Moments in College Football," in Michael MacCambridge (ed.), ESPN College Football Encyclopedia (ESPN, 2005).
22. ttp://www.americanrhetoric.com/MovieSpeeches/ moviespeechknuterockneallamerican.html, accessed November 10, 2011. See also: Bosley Crowther, "'Knute Rockne—All-American', a Thrilling Biography of the Great Coach, at the Strand," *New York Times*, October 19, 1940, 21.
23. Quin Ryan, "Inside the Loudspeaker," *Chicago Daily Tribune*, November 11, 1928, J6.
24. Whittingham, Rites of August, 16.
25. Dooley, *Illustrated Football Annual*, 43.
26. John Kieran, "Notes on Recent Operations," *New York Times*, October 21, 1940, 24.
27. Robert F. Kelley, "On College Gridirons," *New York Times*, October 23, 1940, 30.
28. Allison Danzig, "On College Gridirons," *New York Times*, October 24, 1940, 35.

29. Steve Snider, "Five Midwest Giants Still Unbeaten, Untied," *Oshkosh (WI) Daily Northwestern*, October 15, 1940, 13.
30. Earl Hilligan, "Irish Appear Headed For Unbeaten Year," *Jefferson City (MO) Daily Capital News*, October 22, 1940, 7.
31. "Notre Dame Downs Georgia Tech, 26-20," *New York Times*, October 13, 1940, S1.
32. Dooley, *Illustrated Football Annual*, 43.
33. Schoor, <u>100 Years of Notre Dame Football</u>, 119.
34. Allison Danzig, "76,000 At Stadium," *New York Times*, November 3, 1940, S1.
35. Allison Danzig, "Evidence Mounts of Cornell Skill," *New York Times*, November 4, 1940, 26.
36. "Sukup Misses First Game in 7 Years," *Minnesota Daily*, November 16, 1940, 7.

Chapter 10

1. Arthur J. Daley, "Thriller to Lions," *New York Times*, October 20, 1940, S1.
2. "Saturday's Football Stars," *Ogden (UT) Standard-Examiner*, October 21, 1940, 7.
3. "Lions' Victory Disputed," *New York Times*, October 23, 1940, 29.
4. Bob MacFarland, "Deliberate Clipping?" *Cornell Daily Sun*, October 22, 1940, 15.
5. Bill Snypp, "Snypp's Sports Snacks," *Lima (OH) News*, November 3, 1940, 14.
6. Robert F. Kelley, "Rout by Penn Not to Sway Yale from Football De-emphasis, Says Spokesman," *New York Times*, October 15, 1940, 30.
7. John Kieran, "Much Ado About Nothing," *New York Times*, October 16, 1940, 32.
8. Joseph P. Lyford, "Yale Will Shun Steam-Roller Gridiron Machine; to Abandon Big-Time Football," *Harvard Crimson*, October 15, 1940.
9. "Simian Pure," *Harvard Crimson*, October 16, 1940.
10. Bob MacFarlane, "Harvard and Ohio State," *Cornell Daily Sun*, October 18, 1940, 8.
11. "Harvard Paper, Athletic Director Charge Cornell Subsidizes Grid," *Cornell Daily Sun*, October 17, 1940, 1.
12. http://www.ivysports.com/history.php, accessed April 21, 2010.
13. "Paper Hits Snavely in New Muck-Raking Charges Against Cornell," *Cornell Daily Sun*, October 25, 1940, 1.
14. Robert McShane, "Speaking of Sports," *Soda Springs (ID) Sun*, November 14, 1940, 7.
15. Harry Grayson, "Answer to Blast at Snavely Is That Harvard Should Join Chicago in Six-Man Circuit," *Capital (WI) Times*, November 7, 1940, 21.

16. Robert J. Kane, Good Sports: A History of Cornell Athletics (Ithaca, NY: Cornell, 1992), 397.
17. Whitney Martin, "The Sports Trail," *San Antonio Express*, October 28, 1940, 2A.
18. Bill Boni, "Careful Carl Snavely—The Man Behind Cornell's Grid Machine," *Marion (OH) Star*, November 7, 1940, 17.
19. Eddie Breitz, "Breitz Sports Roundup," *Burlington Daily Times-News*, October 26, 1940, 6.
20. Harry Grayson, "Answer to Blast at Snavely Is That Harvard Should Join Chicago in Six-Man Circuit," *Capital (WI) Times*, November 7, 1940, 21.
21. Robert McShane, "Speaking of Sports," *Soda Springs (ID) Sun*, November 14, 1940, 7.
22. Allison Danzig, "On College Gridirons," *New York Times*, November 21, 1940, 44.
23. Ibid.
24. Reid Oslin, Tales From the Boston College Sidelines (Sports Publishing, LLC, 2004) 35-47.
25. Anderson, The First Star, 80.
26. Kane, Good Sports, 26-27.
27. Ibid., 27.
28. "About Athletics," *Cornell Alumni News*, Vol. 38, No. 1, September 26, 1935, 5.
29. Kane, Good Sports, 312-13.
30. "Carl G. Snavely New Football Coach," *Cornell Alumni News*, March 19, 1936, 357.
31. Morris Bishop, A History of Cornell (Ithaca: Cornell University Press, 1962), 507.
32. "Undefeated Big Red Tangles With Strong Ohio State Eleven Today," *Cornell Daily Sun*, October 26, 1940, 1.
33. "Ohioans to Plant Tree Here Today," *Cornell Daily Sun*, October 25, 1940, 3.
34. Kane, Good Sports, 316.
35. "Mayo at Quarterback for Navy in Engagement With Notre Dame," *New York Times*, October 21, 1939, 9.
36. Molly O'Toole, "Glory Days," *Cornell Alumni Magazine*, Vol. 112, No.2, September/October, 2009.
37. "Football Hasn't Taken Over," *Cornell Daily Sun*, October 12, 1940, 4.
38. Walter Bingham, "Nostalgia," *Sports Illustrated*, November 22, 1982.
39. Allison Danzig, "Heavy Ohio State Team Favored to Overpower Cornell's Eleven," *New York*, October 28, 1939, 18.
40. Allison Danzig, "Ithacans in Upset," *New York Times*, October 29, 1939, S1.
41. Casey Holmes, "Wild Cornell Mascot Wreaks Havoc," *Cornell Daily Sun*, April 30, 2006.
42. "Errant Mascot Heads for Wilds," *Cornell Daily Sun*, October 31, 1939, 1.

43. Allison Danzig, "Memory of Defeat Spurs Ohio State," *New York Times*, October 26, 1940, 21.
44. "Cornell Rates Scott As 'Superman' Sub," *Minnesota Daily*, October 31, 1940, 8.
45. Al Gould, "The Vanquished Speak," *Cornell Daily Sun,* October 21, 1940, 7.
46. Robert F. Kelley, "On College Gridirons," *New York Times*, October 23, 1940, 30.
47. Arthur J. Daley, "Michigan and Cornell Are Favored," *New York Times*, October 26, 1940, 21.
48. Allison Danzig, "On College Gridirons," *New York Times*, October 24, 1940, 35.
49. John Lardner, "Cornell Joins the Big Ten," *New Yorker*, November 2, 1940, 50-51.
50. "Ex-Referee Baiter Now Strict Official," *Minnesota Daily*, November 13, 1940, 7.
51. Cory Bennett, "Part I: Return to Glory Under Snavely," *Cornell Daily Sun*, November 8, 2007.
52. John Lardner, "Cornell Joins the Big Ten," *New Yorker*, November 2, 1940, 50-51.
53. Al Gould, "Coach Schmidt's Angle," *Cornell Daily Sun*, October 28, 1940, 6.
54. "About Athletics," *Cornell Alumni News*, Vol. 43, No. 6, October 31, 1940, 78.
55. Allison Danzig, "Six Major Elevens of East Unbeaten," *New York Times*, October 28, 1940, 24.
56. Wilfrid Smith, "Cornell Takes Lead In East As Two Rivals Fall," *Chicago Daily Tribune*, October 29, 1940, 19.
57. Grantland Rice, "The Sportlight," *Syracuse Herald-Journal*, November 18, 1940, 20.
58. "Snavely Is Criticized," *New York Times*, October 27, 1940, S6.
59. "Snavely Makes Denial," *New York Times*, October 28, 1940, 24.
60. "Snavely Refutes Schmidt Charges of Illegal Coaching From Sidelines," *Cornell Daily Sun*, October 28, 1940, 1.
61. "W.H. Friesell Saw No Signaling from Coach During Play," *Cornell Daily Sun*, October 29, 1940, 1.
62. John Bentley, "I May Be Wrong," *Nebraska State Journal*, November 9, 1940.
63. Harry Grayson, "Grayson's Scoreboard," *Laredo Times*, November 4, 1940, 4.
64. "Made Pre-Game Protest Says L.W. St. John," *Times Recorder*, October 30, 1940, 10.
65. "Red Friesell Denies Bucks Made Protest," *Charleston Gazette*, October 30, 1940, 8.

66. "St. John Claims Early Protest on Snavely," *San Antonio Light*, October 30, 1940.
67. Donald Peddle, "Grid Dilemma May Be Solved By Forming of New Ivy League," *Harvard Crimson*, November 1, 1940.
68. "1935 Duke Game," *Harvard Crimson*, November 2, 1940.
69. "Football Men Brand Ohio State Signal Calling Charge Absurd," *Lowell (MA) Sun*, November 5, 1940, 10.
70. Robert McShane, "Speaking of Sports," *Soda Springs (ID) Sun*, November 14, 1940, 7.
71. "Sports World Ramblings," *New Castle (PA) News*, October 29, 1940, 12.
72. "Skidding the Sport Field With Skid," *Syracuse Herald-Journal*, October 29, 1940, 21.
73. Ernest Poten, "Sports Variety," *Alton (IL) Evening Telegram*, November 1, 1940, 16.
74. Grantland Rice, "The Sportlight," *Syracuse Herald-Journal*, November 2, 1940, 10.
75. Joe Williams, "Sports Roundup," *Syracuse Herald-Journal*, November 8, 1940, 32.
76. Harry Grayson, "Grayson's Scoreboard," *Laredo Times*, November 4, 1940, 4.
77. William D. Richardson, "On College Gridirons," *New York Times*, November 8, 1940, 29.
78. "An Ohio State Oversight," letter to the editor from "H.B.," *New York Times*, November 2, 1940, 23.
79. Wilfrid Smith, "Cornell Takes Lead In East As Two Rivals Fall," *Chicago Daily Tribune*, October 29, 1940, 19.
80. John Kieran, "Delayed Passes," *New York Times*, October 30, 1940, 30.
81. Dillon Graham, "Cornell Has All Any Good Grid Team Has—Plus a Crop Of Instinctive Performers," *Gallup (NM) Independent*, November 7, 1940.
82. John Lardner, "Study in Semaphore," *Newsweek*, November 25, 1940, 23-24.
83. "The Big Red," *Time*, November 11, 1940, 57-58.
84. "Bushnell Finds Ohio Charges Lack Evidence," *Cornell Daily Sun*, November 2, 1940, 1.
85. "Skidding the Sport Field With Skid," *Syracuse Herald-Journal*, November 15, 1940, 33.
86. "Columbia On Deck," *Cornell Daily Sun*, October 28, 1940, 4.
87. Quirk, <u>Minnesota Football</u>, 6.
88. Art Cohn, "Cohn-ing Tower," *Oakland Tribune*, October 29, 1940, 22.
89. Whitney Martin, "Galloping Down the Sports Trail," *Titusville (PA) Herald*, October 31, 1940, 10.
90. "Interesting Comment," *Burlington (NC) Daily Times-News*, November 8, 1940, 4.
91. Whitney Martin, "Quarterbacks' Errors Prove Football is Still Boys' Game," *Nebraska State Journal*, November 27, 1940, 11.

92. Eddie Breitz, "Sports Roundup," *Laredo Times*, November 4, 1940, 4.
93. Sherm Langley, "Across the Sports Desk," *Minnesota Daily*, October 15, 1940, 7.
94. Quirk, Minnesota Football, 203.
95. Henry McLemore, "Today's Sports Parade," *Ogden (UT) Standard*, October 21, 1940, 7.
96. "Made Pre-Games Protest, Says L.W. St. John," *Times-Recorder*, October 30, 1940, 10.
97. Larry Newman, "Don Scott Brilliant In Defeat; Says 11 Men Needed To Make Team," *Lima (OH) News*, October 23, 1940, 13.
98. Dillon Graham, "Cornell Has All Any Good Grid Team Has—Plus a Crop Of Instinctive Performers," *Gallup (NM) Independent*, November 7, 1940.
99. "Hank Casserly Says," *Capital Times*, December 1, 1940.

Chapter 11

1. Allison Danzig, "Sturdy Squad at Boston College Fails to Curb Dobie's Pessimism," *New York Times*, September 23, 1937, 39.
2. Bill King, "Leahy Plans Hocus-Pocus," *Lowell (MA) Sun*, February 2, 1939, 16.
3. "Sports Chatter," *Fitchburg (MA) Sentinel*, October 9, 1939, 10.
4. "Negro Out of Bowl Game," *New York Times*, December 17, 1939, S5.
5. *Brownsville (TX) Herald*, December 26, 1939, 3.
6. "Boston College Negro Back Given Award," *Galveston (TX) Daily News*, December 24, 1939, 10.
7. Albert Reese, "Here's The Dope," *Galveston (TX) Daily News*, December 30, 1939, 6.
8. Jack Craig, "Some Students of Sports May Need History Lesson," *Boston Globe*, September 22, 1991.
9. Bill Woodside, "Today's Fare for the Fans," *Paris (TX) News*, December 28, 1939, 10.
10. "Sun Promised At Bowl Tilt," *Arizona Republic*, December 30, 1940, Sec. 2, 2.
11. Allison Danzig, "Tulane Game Saturday to Test Strength of Boston College," *New York Times*, September 25, 1940, 38.
12. "Tulane Bows, 27-7, to Boston College," *New York Times*, September 29, 1940, S1.
13. "Parents of Gridman Killed in Auto Accident," *Cornell Daily Sun*, October 11, 1940, 11.

Chapter 12

1. Felix R. McKnight, "Presenting: Sectional Grid Forecasts For 1940," *Montana Standard*, September 8, 1940.

2. Wilfrid Smith, "Three Big Nine Leaders Will Fight It Out In Round Robin," *Chicago Daily Tribune*, October 28, 1940, 19.

3. Walter L. Johns, "National Football Ratings," *Hammond (LA) Times*, October 30, 1940, 20.

4. Tom Siler, "Minnesota Beginning To Show Great Strength," *Oshkosh Daily Northwestern*, October 22, 1940, 13.

5. Bill Boni, "Blonde Bomb!" *Capital Times*, October 6, 1940.

6. Al Gould, "The Vanquished Speak," *Cornell Daily Sun*, October 21, 1940, 7.

7. Bill Kastelz, "Beise Predicts Trouble With Wildcats," *Minnesota Daily*, October 29, 1940, 6.

8. "Minnesota Topples Northwestern, 13-12, On Mernik's Kick and Leads In Conference," *New York Times*, November 3, 1940, S1.

9. Wilfrid Smith, "Northwestern Loses to Minnesota, 13-12," *Chicago Daily Tribune*, November 3, 1940, B1.

10. Ibid.

11. "Minnesota Topples Northwestern, 13-12, On Mernik's Kick and Leads In Conference," *New York Times*, November 3, 1940, S1.

12. Johnson, The Wow Boys, 110.

13. Ibid., 112.

14. Bill Tobitt, "'Toughest All Year', Says Shaughnessy" *Oakland Tribune*, November 10, 1940, 12-A.

15. Sam Jackson, "Stanford Fireball Keeps Fans Either Happy Or Hopping Mad," *Gallup (NM) Independent*, November 25, 1940.

16. Art Cohn, "Kmetovic Scores Two Touchdowns," *Oakland Tribune*, November 10, 1940, 12-A.

17. Johnson, The Wow Boys, 117.

18. Bill Tobitt, "'Toughest All Year', Says Shaughnessy" *Oakland Tribune*, November 10, 1940, 12-A.

19. Allison Danzig, "Passes Halt Lions," *New York Times*, November 3, 1940, 1S.

20. Allison Danzig, "Sectional Football Leaders Bolster Claims, But Notre Dame Prestige Wanes," *New York Times*, November 4, 1940, 26.

21. Robert McShane, "Speaking of Sports," *Soda Springs (ID) Sun*, November 14, 1940, 7.

22. Jerry Brondfield, "Critics Calling Cornell Greatest Team in Eastern Football History," *Dunkirk (NY) Evening Observer*, October 11, 1940, 17.

23. "Cornell Appears Cinch to Have Unbeaten Season," *Waterloo (IA) Daily Courier*, October 30, 1940, 14.

24. Whitney Martin, "Down the Sports Trail," *Jefferson City (MO) Daily Capital News*, October 22, 1940, 7.

25. "Bulldogs Without a Muzzle," *Mansfield (OH) News-Journal*, October 18, 1940, 15.

26. John Kieran, "Stuffing the Ballot Box," *New York Times*, November 9, 1940, 13.

27. Herb Barker, "Herb Barker Keeps Coin Busy Trying to Keep Grid Winners," *Lowell (MA) Evening Sun,* November 8, 1940, 17.

28. John Kieran, "Notes On Recent Operations," *New York Times*, November 4, 1940, 27.

29. Arthur J. Daley, "Cornell's Power Downs Yale, 21-0," *New York Times*, November 10, 1940, S1.

30. "About Athletics," *Cornell Alumni News*, Vol. 43, No. 8, November 14, 1940, 106.

31. Whitney Martin, "Didn't Know Little Brown Jug Was Loaded," *Nebraska State Journal*, November 13, 1940, 34.

32. Quirk, Minnesota Football, 26. See also: Akers and Akers, The Game Breaker, 81.

33. "Sukup Lost to Michigan," *New York Times*, November 8, 1940, 32.

34. Pennington, The Heisman, 41.

35. "63,894 See Minnesota Beat Michigan After 80-Yard Run," *New York Times*, November 10, 1940, S1.

36. "Catching Up With Hall of Famer George 'Sonny' Franck, College Football Hall of Fame, (http://www.collegefootball.org/news.php?id=851), accessed November 19, 2008. See also: Akers and Akers, The Game Breaker, 87; and Quirk, Minnesota Football, 228.

37. "63,894 Take Bath En Masse As Bruce Smith Soaks Wolves," *Minnesota Daily*, November 13, 1940, 6.

38. Tim Brady, "Who Was Bruce Smith?" University of Minnesota Alumni Association (http://www.alumni.umn.edu/Who_Was_Bruce_Smith.html), accessed November 19, 2008.

39. Arch Ward, "Smith's 80-Yard Dash, Mernik's Kick Give Gophers Big Nine Lead," *Chicago Daily Tribune*, November 10, 1940, B1.

40. Akers and Akers, The Game Breaker, 89.

41. Ibid., 106.

42. MinnesotaAlumni.org, http://www.minnesotaalumni.org/s/1118/content.aspx?sid=1118&gid=1&pgid=605&sparam=BruceSmith&scontid=0, accessed April 2, 2012.

43. Akers and Akers, The Game Breaker, 90.

44. Quirk, Minnesota Football, 233.

45. Ibid.

46. "Typhoon at Guam," *Newsweek*, November 11, 1940, 23.

47. "Typhoon," *Time*, November 11, 1940, 20.

48. "Galloping Gertie," *Newsweek,* November 18, 1940, 24-25.

49. "Narrows Nightmare," *Time*, November 18, 1940, 21.

50. "Rumanian Quake Kills 1,000, Sets Oil Afire, Cuts Railways," *New York Times*, November 11, 1940, 1.

51. "West, South Swept By Raging Storms," *New York Times*, November 12, 1940, 1; See also: "Hunters' Storm," *Time,* November 25, 1940, 14-15; and Mark Steil, "The Winds of Hell," Minnesota Public Radio, November 10,

2000 (http://minnesota.publicradio.org/display/web/200011/10_steilm_
blizzard-m/), accessed November 20, 2008.

52. Bill Caldwell, "Classes 'Officially' Open as Blizzard Strikes City,"
    Minnesota Daily, November 13, 1940, 1.
53. William McGurn, "College Football Goes Down the Hatch," *Wall Street
    Journal*, July 7, 2009, A-13.
54. Henry McLemore, "McLemore Issues A Rating of Football Teams But
    Cancels It," *Wisconsin State Journal*, November 15, 1940, 20.
55. Allison Danzig, "Tennessee, Texas A&M, So. California, Cornell, Tulane
    Bunched For Top Post," *New York Times*, November 20, 1939, 24.
56. Sherm Langley, "Across the Sports Desk," *Minnesota Daily*, November 13,
    1940, 7.
57. Bob MacFarland, "Ratings," *Cornell Daily Sun*, November 13, 1940, 6.

Chapter 13

1. Allison Danzig, "Harvard Battles Penn to 10-10 Tie," *New York Times*,
    November 10, 1940, S1.
2. Rob Fleder (ed.), The College Football Book (New York: Sports Illustrated
    Books, 2008), 45.
3. Phil Allen, "The Penalty Flag," *College Football Historical Society
    Newsletter*, Vol. VI, No. I, November, 1992, 1-3.
4. Raymond Daniell, "When Total War Blasts A City," *New York Times
    Magazine*, September 22, 1940.
5. *Life*, October 7, 1940, 90.
6. "U.S. Navy Moves to Strengthen Far East Fleet," *Cornell Daily Sun*,
    October 10, 1940, 2.
7. Brands, Traitor to His Class, 574.
8. Kershaw, Fateful Choices, 184.
9. "The News of the Week in Review," *New York Times*, October 27, 1940, E1.
10. Arthur J. Daley, "Gridiron Leaders Near Titles Today," *New York Times*,
    November 16, 1940, 8.
11. Raymond Daniell, "Coventry Wrecked in Worst Raid on England," *New
    York Times*, November 16, 1940, 1.
12. Churchill, Memoirs, 378.
13. "Harmon Says He'll Play, Discounting Leg Injury," *New York Times*,
    November 13, 1940, 31.
14. Carroll, Dr. Eddie Anderson, 58,63,80,107,138.
15. Pennington, The Heisman, 25.
16. Mike Finn and Chad Leistikow, Hawkeye Legends, Lists, and Lore (Sports
    Publishing, LLC, 1998), 70.
17. Pennington, The Heisman, 21.
18. Ibid., 27.
19. Finn and Leistikow, Hawkeye Legends, 73.

20. Bert McGrane, "Eddie Anderson, Oskaloosa, 1962," *Des Moines Register*, April 1, 1962.
21. Pennington, The Heisman, 28.
22. Ron Fimrite, "Nile Kinnick," *Sports Illustrated*, August 31, 1987.
23. Pennington, The Heisman, 29.
24. Finn and Leistikow, Hawkeye Legends, 75.
25. "Last-Period Drives of 80 and 79 Yards Enable Iowa to Turn Back Minnesota," *New York Times*, November 19, 1939, S7.
26. Quirk, Minnesota Football, 211.
27. Finn and Leistikow, Hawkeye Legends, 73.
28. Allison Danzig, "Tennessee, Texas A&M, So. California, Cornell, Tulane Bunched For Top Post," *New York Times*, November 20, 1939, 24.
29. Allison Danzig, "Predictions Upset By Blue's Showing," *New York Times*, November 27, 1939, 22.
30. Oslin, Tales From the Boston College Sidelines, 47.
31. Pennington, The Heisman, 26.
32. Ron Fimrite, "Nile Kinnick," *Sports Illustrated*, August 31, 1987.
33. Gay Flood (ed,), "Letters," *Sports Illustrated*, September 21, 1987.
34. Carroll, Dr. Eddie Anderson, 169.
35. Ron Flatter, "Everybody's All-American," ESPN.com (http://espn.go.com/classic/000802nilekinnick.html), accessed November 15, 2008.
36. Pennington, The Heisman, 32.
37. Rob Newell, From Playing Field to Battlefield: Great Athletes Who Served in World War II (U.S. Naval Institute Press, 2006), 75.
38. Pennington, The Heisman, 20.
39. "Hawks Are 'Iron Men,'" *Minnesota Daily*, November 28, 1940, 6.
40. Steve Snider, "Iowa Shocks Irish Again, 7-0," *Wisconsin State Journal*, November 17, 1940, 17.
41. Finn and Leistikow, Hawkeye Legends, 72.
42. "Oregon State Tops Stanford, 12-0," *New York Times*, October 1, 1939, S4.
43. "Stanford Tops Oregon State," *New York Times*, November 17. 1940, S7.
44. Bob Blake, "'41 Rose Bowl Team Back to Fundamentals," *Oakland Tribune*, November 17, 1940, A-13.
45. "Stanford Men Favor Aggies For Bowl Bid," *Arizona Republic*, November 19, 1940, Sec. 2, 2.
46. Arthur J. Daley, "Gridiron Leaders Near Titles Today," *New York Times*, November 16, 1940, 8.
47. "Sports Editors Vote Big Red Nation's Best," *Cornell Daily Sun*, October 16, 1940, 1.
48. John Kieran, "Heard in a Huddle," *New York Times*, November 26, 1940, 32.
49. John Kieran, "Passing in Review," *New York Times*, December 1, 1940, 29.
50. Eddie Breitz, "Roundup of Gossip In World of Sport," *Freeport, (IL) Journal-Standard*, November 26, 1940, 9.

51. "Georgetown's Squad Departs for Boston," *New York Times*, November 15, 1940, 27.
52. "Odds Vary on Hoya, B.C. Battle," *Washington Post*, November 13, 1940, 24.
53. Eddie Breitz, "Sports Roundup," *Lowell (MA) Sun*, November 14, 1940, 10.
54. Harry Grayson, "BC Picked to Stop Georgetown in 'Battle of the Bruisers,'" *Lowell (MA) Sun*, November 14, 1940, 10.
55. Jack Munhall, "Hoyas Could Lick Cornell, Says Orange," *Washington Post*, November 4, 1940, 21.
56. Bob Considine, "Peak Moments of 1940," *San Antonio Light*, December 26, 1940.
57. "O'Rourke, Eagle Back Stars in Sugar Bowl Tilt," *Jefferson City (MO) Post-Tribune*, January 2, 1941, 9.
58. Whitney Martin, "Mighty Mite Paces BC to Triumph," *Salt Lake Tribune*, January 2, 1941, 16.
59. "Boston College Bowl Team Is '39 Outfit—Plus Plenty," *Big Spring (TX) Daily Herald*, December 27, 1940, 3.
60. Mark Purcell, "1940 Boston vs. Georgetown," *College Football Historical Society Journal*, Vol. VIII, No. 4, August 1995, 10.
61. Arthur J. Daley, "Fenske Takes Mile at NYAC Games," *New York Times*, February 18, 1940, S1.
62. Arthur J. Daley, "Fenske Captures U.S. Mile in 4:08.8," *New York Times*, February 25, 1940, S1.
63. Robert McG. Thomas, "Two Giants Were Heroes Far From Playing Field," *New York Times*, January 26, 1991, 45.
64. "Georgetown Football History—Chapter 6: The Greatest Hoya of Them All," (http://www.hoyasaxa.com/sports/hist06.htm), accessed January 5, 2009.
65. "Georgetown's Squad Departs for Boston," *New York Times*, November 15, 1940, 70.
66. Allison Danzig, "Eagles Boost National Standing By Triumphing Over Georgetown," *New York Times*, November 18, 1940, 26.
67. Jack Munhall, "Georgetown's Streak Ends," *Washington Post*, November 17, 1940, SP1.
68. Bob Considine, "Peak Moments of 1940," *San Antonio Light*, December 26, 1940.
69. Oslin, Tales From the Boston College Sidelines, 58.
70. Shirley Povich, "This Morning," *Washington Post*, November 17, 1940, SP1.
71. Shirley Povich, "A Sporting Life," *Washington Post*, October 29, 1989, W22.
72. Allison Danzig, "Georgetown Streak Ended By Boston College, 19 to 18," *New York Times*, November 17, 1940, S1.
73. Bill Boni, "Boston College Removes Hoyas From Unbeaten Ranks," *Cumberland (MD) Sunday Times*, November 17, 1940, 17.

74. Jack Munhall, "Georgetown's Streak Ends," *Washington Post*, November 17, 1940, SP1.
75. "Six Survive As Upsets Trim Title Contenders," *Arizona Republic*, November 18, 1940, Sec.2, 2.
76. Shirley Povich, "This Morning," *Washington Post*, November 117, 1940, SP1.
77. Mark Purcell, "1940 Boston vs. Georgetown," *College Football Historical Society Journal*, Vol. VIII, No. 4, August 1995, 10.
78. "Georgetown Is Beaten, 19-18, By Boston College," *Chicago Daily Tribune*, November 17, 1940, B6.
79. Oslin, Tales from the Boston College Sidelines, 59.
80. Harry Grayson, "Grayson's Scoreboard," *Panama City (FL) News-Herald*, November 22, 1940, 2.
81. "Boston College Bowl Team Is '39 Outfit—Plus Plenty," *Big Spring (TX) Daily Herald*, December 27, 1940, 3.

Chapter 14

1. Bob Duffy, "Men of Honor," *Boston Globe*, December 29, 2001.
2. Morris Bishop, A History of Cornell (Ithaca, NY: Cornell University Press, 1962), 523.
3. Allison Danzig, "Dartmouth, Notre Dame, Yale, and Navy Favored in Big Football Games Today," *New York Times*, November 12, 1938, 19.
4. Blaik, The Red Blaik Story, 158.
5. Allison Danzig, "On College Gridirons," *New York Times*, November 22, 1939, 25.
6. Robert F. Kelley, "On College Gridirons," *New York Times*, October 23, 1940, 30.
7. Harry Grayson, "BC Picked to Stop Georgetown in 'Battle of the Bruisers,'" *Lowell (MA) Sun*, November 14, 1940, 10.
8. John Kieran, "Notes On Recent Operations," *New York Times*, November 4, 1940, 27.
9. John Kieran, "Notes On Recent Operations," *New York Times*, November 11, 1940, 25.
10. Bob Monahan, "The Colorado-Missouri Snafu Wasn't Unique," *Boston Globe*, October 10, 1990.
11. "Fifth Down and a Red Face," in Harold Claasen (ed.), Football's Unforgettable Games (New York: Ronald Press, 1963), http://www.archive.org/stream/footballsunforge007568mbp_djvu.txt).
12. Bob Monahan, "The Colorado-Missouri Snafu Wasn't Unique," *Boston Globe*, October 10, 1990.
13. Jeffrey Hart, "Fifth Down and Goal to Go; Dartmouth Spoils Cornell's Title Hopes," *The Dartmouth Review*, July 16, 2007.
14. Ron Fimrite, "Nowhere to Hide," *Sports Illustrated*, October 15, 1990.

15. "Van Order Listed On First Eleven as Red Entrains," *Cornell Daily Sun*, November 15, 1940, 1.
16. "The Red Badge of Courage," *New Yorker*, December 4, 1937, 90-92.
17. "Sport: Time Out for Red," *Time*, October 27, 1941, 61-62.
18. William D. Richardson, "Pass Halts Green," *New York Times*, November 17, 1940, S1.
19. Claasen, Football's Unforgettable Games.
20. William D. Richardson, "Pass Halts Green," *New York Times*, November 17, 1940, S1.
21. "Skidding the Sport Field With Skid," *Syracuse Herald-Journal*, November 18, 1940, 20.
22. Bob Monahan, "The Colorado-Missouri Snafu Wasn't Unique," *Boston Globe*, October 10, 1990.
23. Bob Duffy, "Men of Honor," *Boston Globe*, December 29, 2001.
24. Bob Monahan, "The Colorado-Missouri Snafu Wasn't Unique," *Boston Globe*, October 10, 1990.
25. Bob Duffy, "Men of Honor," *Boston Globe*, December 29, 2001.
26. Bob McFarland, "Friesell Statement on Game Awaited, Bushnell Says Action Up To CUAA," *Cornell Daily Sun*, November 18, 1940, 1.
27. "Skidding the Sport Field With Skid," *Syracuse Herald-Journal*, November 18, 1940, 20.
28. Ron Fimrite, "Nowhere to Hide," *Sports Illustrated*, October 15, 1990.
29. Bob McFarland, "Friesell Statement on Game Awaited, Bushnell Says Action Up To CUAA," *Cornell Daily Sun*, November 18, 1940, 1.
30. "Big Red Will Change Score, If Justified," *Syracuse Herald-Journal*, November 18, 1940, 20.
31. Blaik, The Red Blaik Story, 163.
32. Cory Bennett, "Part II: The Fifth Down Game," *Cornell Daily Sun*, November 8, 2007.
33. Bob Monahan, "The Colorado-Missouri Snafu Wasn't Unique," *Boston Globe*, October 10, 1990.
34. "Unless Cornell Relents, It's 7-3 Against Indians," *Chicago Daily Tribune*, November 18, 1940, 21.
35. "Skidding the Sport Field With Skid," *Syracuse Herald-Journal*, November 18, 1940, 20.
36. William D. Richardson, "Legitimacy of Play Against Dartmouth Rests On Whether Friesell Signaled Double Offside," *New York Times*, November 18, 1940, 26.
37. Blaik, The Red Blaik Story, 163.
38. Bob Monahan, "The Colorado-Missouri Snafu Wasn't Unique," *Boston Globe*, October 10, 1990.
39. "Big Red Will Change Score, If Justified," *Syracuse Herald-Journal*, November 18, 1940, 20.
40. "Concede to Dartmouth," *Cornell Alumni News*, Vol. 43, No. 9, November 21, 1940, 122-3.

41. William D. Richardson, "Legitimacy of Play Against Dartmouth Rests On Whether Friesell Signaled Double Offside," *New York Times*, November 18, 1940, 26.
42. Blaik, The Red Blaik Story, 162.
43. Earl H. Blaik, recorded interview by Charles T. Morrissey, December 2, 1964 (page 1), John F. Kennedy Library Oral History Program.
44. Bishop, A History of Cornell, 534.
45. Kane, Good Sports, 41.
46. "Concede to Dartmouth," *Cornell Alumni News*, Vol. 43, No. 9, November 21, 1940, 122-3.
47. Cory Bennett, "Part II: The Fifth Down Game," *Cornell Daily Sun*, November 8, 2007.
48. Ron Fimrite, "Nowhere to Hide," *Sports Illustrated*, October 15, 1990.
49. "Concede to Dartmouth," *Cornell Alumni News*, Vol. 43, No. 9, November 21, 1940, 122-3.
50. Bob Monahan, "The Colorado-Missouri Snafu Wasn't Unique," *Boston Globe*, October 10, 1990.
51. William D. Richardson, "Pass Halts Green," *New York Times*, November 17, 1940, S1.
52. William D. Richardson, "Legitimacy of Play Against Dartmouth Rests On Whether Friesell Signaled Double Offside," *New York Times*, November 18, 1940, 26.
53. Bob Considine, "Strange Fate Shunts Snavely, Lombardi, Griffith from Spot Atop Sports Pinnacle," *Waterloo (IA) Daily Courier*, November 21, 1940, 15.
54. Robert F. Kelley, "On College Gridirons," *New York Times*, November 3, 1938, 29.
55. "Bushnell Says Only Cornell-Dartmouth Authorities Can Act on 'Fifth Down,'" *New York Times*, November 18, 1940, 26.
56. Kane, Good Sports, 41.
57. "Bushnell Says Only Cornell-Dartmouth Authorities Can Act on 'Fifth Down,'" *New York Times*, November 18, 1940, 26.

Chapter 15

1. Bob Royce, "The Great Mix-up of 1922," *College Football Historical Society Newsletter*, Vol. III, No. 1, November, 1989, 13-15.
2. "Point Disputed At Columbia Also Came up In Springfield," *New York Times*, October 25, 1922, 15.
3. "Referee Reverses Columbia Contest," *New York Times*, October 25, 1922, 15.
4. Ibid.
5. "N.Y.U. Questions Morice's Authority," *New York Times*, October 26, 1922, 15.

6. "Football Officials Side With Morice," *New York Times*, October 27, 1922, 21.
7. "Carnegie Coach Assails 'Bonehead' Ruling," *New York Times*, October 25, 1938, 26.
8. "Classy and Thrilling Ball," *New York Times*, September 24, 1908, 7.
9. Ibid.
10. Ibid.
11. G.H. Fleming, The Unforgettable Season (Lincoln, NE: University of Nebraska Press, 1981), 248.
12. Ibid., 245.
13. "Blunder Costs Giants Victory," *New York Times*, September 23, 1908, 7.
14. Fleming, The Unforgettable Season, 247, 255, 257.
15. Lawrence S. Ritter, The Glory of Their Times (New York: The MacMillan Company, 1966), 128.
16. Fleming, The Unforgettable Season, 247.
17. Cait Murphy, Crazy '08 (New York: Smithsonian Books, 2007), 194.
18. Fleming, The Unforgettable Season, 316.
19. Murphy, Crazy '08, 295.
20. Jack E. Steele, "Was Jack Dempsey Robbed By The 'Long Count'?" *Sports Illustrated*, September 28, 1987.
21. "Fight Crowds Come By Air, Road, Rail," *New York Times*, September 23, 1927, 20.
22. Mel Heimer, The Long Count (New York: Atheneum, 1969), 222.
23. Bill Dwyre, "'Long Count' Owns This Date," *Los Angeles Times*, September 22, 2007.
24. "Convicts Listen to Fight," *New York Times*, September 23, 1927, 20.
25. "Fans World Over Listened to Fight," *New York Times*, September 24, 1927, 10.
26. Heimer, The Long Count, 274.
27. "Chicago Wagering Even At Ringtime," *New York Times*, September 23, 1927, 19.
28. Heimer, The Long Count, 222.
29. Westbrook Pegler, "Fair Fight Or Otherwise, Fans Will Never Know," *Chicago Daily Tribune*, September 22, 1927, 23.
30. Dr. Ferdie Pacheco, The 12 Greatest Rounds of Boxing (Toronto: Sport Media Publishing, Inc., 2003), 30-31. See also: R.R. Bearden, "The Time Tunnel: 75th Anniversary of 'The Long Count,'" (http://www. eastsideboxing.com/news/DempseyvsTunney.php), accessed November 30, 2008.
31. Jack E. Steele, "Was Jack Dempsey Robbed By The 'Long Count'?" *Sports Illustrated*, September 28, 1987.
32. "Chicago Wagering Even At Ringtime," *New York Times*, September 23, 1927, 19.
33. Pacheco, 12 Greatest Rounds, 31.
34. William Nack, "The Long Count," *Sports Illustrated*, September 22, 1997.

35. James P. Dawson, "Championship Fight Brings Spectacle to Chicago Unprecedented in Ring History," *New York Times*, September 23, 1927, 18.
36. James O'Donnell Bennett, "Crowd Screams At Tense Drama As Gene Rises," *Chicago Daily Tribune*, September 23, 1927, 1.
37. Pacheco, 12 Greatest Rounds, 34.
38. Harvey Woodruff, "Tunney Wins By Decision," *Chicago Daily Tribune*, September 23, 1927, 1.
39. Shirley Povich, All Those Mornings (New York: Public Affairs, 2005), 23.
40. "Dempsey To Appeal Decision On Fight," *New York Times*, September 23, 1927, 1.
41. Ibid.
42. James P. Dawson, "Tunney Is Ready For Dempsey Again," *New York Times*, September 24, 1927, 1.
43. Don Maxwell, "Dempsey Tells His Story," *Chicago Daily Tribune*, September 24, 1927, 1.
44. Jack E. Steele, "Was Jack Dempsey Robbed By The 'Long Count'?" *Sports Illustrated*, September 28, 1987.
45. John Kieran, "Sports of the Times," *New York Times*, September 25, 1927, S2.
46. Povich, All Those Mornings, 24.
47. "Dempsey Is the Hero Despite His Defeat," *New York Times*, September 24, 1927, 10.
48. Westbrook Pegler, "Pegler Finds the Cry 'Crooked' Always Follows in Wake of Title Prize Fights," *Chicago Daily Tribune*, September 28, 1927, 23.

Chapter 16

1. "Cornell Concedes 3-0 Gridiron Victory To Dartmouth," *Arizona Republic*, November 19, 1940, Sec. 2, 2.
2. Arthur J. Daley, "Dartmouth 3, Cornell 0 Official Score As Ithacans Refuse Victory," *New York Times*, November 19, 1940, 31.
3. Michael Stroup, "The Spell of Dartmouth Football," *Dartmouth Review*, January 31, 2005.
4. "News of Belated Victory Starts Parade through Hanover Streets." *New York Times*, November 19, 1940, 31.
5. Kane, Good Sports, 42.
6. "Cornell Wants No 'Long Count,' President Tells Students," *New York Times*, November 20, 1940, 29.
7. "Skidding The Sport Field With Skid," *Syracuse Herald-Journal*, November 19, 1940, 21.
8. Bob MacFarland, "Day Explains Cornell Stand on Indian Game," *Cornell Daily Sun*, November 20, 1940, 1.
9. "It's Up To 'Red' Friesell," *Cornell Daily Sun*, November 18, 1940, 1.

10. Allison Danzig, "On College Gridirons," *New York Times*, November 21, 1940, 44.
11. "Skidding the Sport Field With Skid," *Syracuse Herald-Journal*, November 19, 1940, 21.
12. John Kieran, "Fun In Time and Space," *New York Times*, November 21, 1940, 45.
13. Bob Graham, "Michigan's Harmon Rates Big Red First in Sportsmanship, Ability," *Cornell Daily Sun*, November 25, 1940, 1.
14. "Cornell Seeks Friesell As Referee Next Year," *New York Times*, November 21, 1940, 44.
15. Bishop, A History of Cornell, 534.
16. Ron Fimrite, "Nowhere to Hide," *Sports Illustrated*, October 15, 1990.
17. Jerry Crowe, "Cornell's Sportsmanship Didn't Feel That Good to Everybody," *Los Angeles Times*, November 7, 2010.
18. Ibid.
19. Bob Duffy, "Men of Honor," *Boston Globe*, December 29, 2001.
20. Bishop, A History of Cornell, 534.

Chapter 17

1. "Policy On Changes Cited by Bushnell," *New York Times*, November 21, 1940, 44.
2. Allison Danzig, "Fifth-Down Aftermath Heightens Appeal of Cornell-Penn 'Natural,'" *New York Times,* November 23, 1940, 30.
3. "An Open Letter to Mr. Kane," *Cornell Daily Sun*, November 12, 1940, 4.
4. "Cornell To Send 4 Teams To Game," *New York Times*, November 21, 1940, 44.
5. "Skidding the Sport Field With Skid," *Syracuse Herald-Journal*, November 25, 1940, 16.
6. Allison Danzig, "Big Red Team Upset," *New York Times*, November 24, 1940, S1.
7. Bill Boni, "Cocky Cornell Is Taken To Cleaners By Penn Grid Team," *Ogden (UT) Standard-Examiner*, November 24, 1940, 9-A.
8. "Skidding the Sport Field With Skid," *Syracuse Herald-Journal*, November 25, 1940, 16.
9. Whitney Martin, "Quarterbacks' Errors Prove Football Still Is Boys' Game," *Nebraska State Journal*, November 27, 1940, 11.
10. Allison Danzig, "Big Red Team Upset," *New York Times*, November 24, 1940, S1.
11. "Wolves Lack Usual Spirit," *Benton Harbor (MI) News-Palladium*, November 22, 1940, 8.
12. "Michigan Runs Rough Shod Over OSU, 40-0," *Charleston Gazette*, November 24, 1940, 12.

13. "Harmon's Three Touchdowns Help Beat Ohio State, 40-0," *Oakland Tribune*, November 24, 1940, 10-A.
14. Herb Barker, "Tom Harmon Ends Play In College," *Valley (TX) Star-Monitor-Herald*, November 24, 1940, 11.
15. "Michigan Batters Ohio State, 40-0," *New York Times*, November 24, 1940, S1
16. Arthur J. Daley, "On College Gridirons," *New York Times*, November 12, 1940, 31.
17. Carroll, Dr. Eddie Anderson, 43.
18. Quirk, Minnesota Football, 4.
19. Roy L. Matson, "Grant County Seat Takes Its Favorite Sons to Its Heart," *Wisconsin State Journal*, November 28, 1942, 7.
20. "'Perfect Play' Scores For Badgers," *Wisconsin State Journal*, October 6, 1940, 1.
21. Hank Casserly, "Badgers Crush Marquette, 33-19," *Capital Times*, October 6, 1940.
22. Henry J. McCormick, "Sophs Pace Badgers 33-19 Triumph," *Wisconsin State Journal*, October 6, 1940, 13.
23. Sherman Langley, "Wisconsin Game Will Determine National Rank," *Minnesota Daily*, November 23, 1940, 1.
24. Henry J. McCormick, "Henry J. McCormick Means No Foolin'," *Wisconsin State Journal*, May 17, 1940, 19.
25. "Captain-Elect Smith Couldn't Believe It," *Minnesota Daily*, November 27, 1940, 6.
26. Bradley, Big Games, 225.
27. John Sullivan, The Big Game (West Point, NY: Leisure Press, 1982), 123.
28. Lee Dunbar, "Bears Secret Pass Play Ruined By Reinhard's Flu," *Oakland Tribune*, December 1, 1940, A-11.
29. Johnson, The Wow Boys, 138.
30. Art Cohn, "Jurkovich Plays Only 60 Seconds," *Oakland Tribune*, December 1, 1940, 10-A.
31. Ibid.
32. Lefty Farnsworth, "Four Historic Tackles of the Forties," *College Football Historical Society Newsletter*, Vol. III, No. 1, November, 1989, 16-18.
33. Johnson, The Wow Boys, 142.
34. Lee Dunbar, "Bears Secret Pass Play Ruined By Reinhard's Flu," *Oakland Tribune*, December 1, 1940, A-11.
35. Stanford Downs California By 13-7," *New York Times*, December 1, 1940, S1.
36. "Portrait of A Football Coach Getting The Ax—And Liking It," *Oakland Tribune*, December 1, 1940, 10-A.
37. Lt. Col. Jack C. Mason, "My Favorite Lion," *Army*, May, 2008, 71-76.
38. W. Thomas Smith, Jr., "The New York Giant Who Died on Iwo Jima," *New York Times*, February 26, 2007.

39. Robert McG. Thomas, Jr., "Two Giants Were Heroes Far from Playing Field," *New York Times*, January 26, 1991, 45.

Chapter 18

1. Art Cohn, "Cohn-ing Tower," *Oakland Tribune*, September 26, 1940, 65.
2. Henry J. McCormick, "Henry J. McCormick Means No Foolin'," *Wisconsin State Journal*, December 1, 1940, 23.
3. "Gophers' Rose Bowl Chances Slight," *Minnesota Daily*, November 26, 1940, 6.
4. "Stadium Is Still Part of the University," *Minnesota Daily*, November 26, 1940, 8.
5. "Cornhuskers Wait Formal OK," *Oakland Tribune*, December 1, 1940, 10-A.
6. Frank L. Kluckhohn, "Roosevelt Hints of Crisis in Saying 'If World Survives,'" *New York Times*, December 16, 1940, 1.
7. Leckie, Delivered from Evil, 189.
8. Kershaw, Fateful Choices, 232.
9. Ibid, 230.
10. Ibid.
11. Johnson, The Wow Boys, 149-50.
12. Red Smith, "Clark Daniel Shaughnessy," in Smith, To Absent Friends, 120 (originally published May 26, 1970 in *Women's Wear Daily*).
13. Ira Berkow, "Footballs Just Kept Disappearing," *New York Times*, December 8, 1990.
14. "Stanford Too Fast And Wise For Nebraska," Jefferson City (MO) Post-Tribune, January 2, 1941, 9.
15. Johnson, The Wow Boys, 172.
16. "Husker Century Part I: Every Rose Has Its Thorns," (http://www.netnebraska.org/extras/husker_century/hc_events/hc_events_1940.html).
17. Art Green, "Kmetovic Beat Us, Says Jones," *Oakland Tribune*, January 2, 1941, 22.
18. Henry McLemore, "Big Grid Problem of '41—Find Suitable Foe For Indians," *Jefferson City (MO) Post-Tribune*, January 2, 1941, 9.
19. Robert Myers, "Mighty Stanford Crew Humbles Nebraska in Rose Bowl, 21-13," *Salt Lake Tribune*, January 2, 1941, 16.
20. "Husker Century Part I: Every Rose Has Its Thorns," (http://www.netnebraska.org/extras/husker_century/hc_events/hc_events_1940.html), accessed February 11, 2010.
21. "Rose Rivals Praise Opponents," *Salt Lake Tribune*, January 2, 1941, 16.
22. "Hoyas Desires Another Crack At Miss. State," *Jefferson City (MO) Post-Tribune*, January 2, 1941, 9.
23. Larry Rollins, "Maroons Win Over Hoyas; Score, 14 to 7," *Salt Lake Tribune*, January 2, 1941, 16.

24. "Stellar Backs To Wage Duel In Cotton Bowl," *Arizona Republic*, December 30, 1940, Sec. 2, 2.
25. "Rams Defeated By Aggies But Not Outplayed," *Jefferson City (MO) Post-Tribune*, January 2, 1941, 9.
26. Felix R. McKnight, "Texas Aggies Turn Back Fordham Eleven, 13-12, *Salt Lake Tribune*, January 2, 1941, 16.
27. "Rams Defeated By Aggies But Not Outplayed," *Jefferson City (MO) Post-Tribune*, January 2, 1941, 9.
28. Eddie Breitz, "Sports Roundup," *Lowell (MA) Sun*, January 8, 1941.
29. Harry Grayson, "Tempe, Stanford, Aggies Get Nod In Holiday Tilts," *El Paso Herald-Post*, December 25, 1940, 14.
30. Oslin, Tales From the Boston College Sidelines, 60-61.
31. Whitney Martin, "Mighty Mite Paces B.C. To Triumph," *Salt Lake Tribune*, January 2, 1941, 16.
32. "Rose Rivals Praise Opponents," *Salt Lake Tribune*, January 2, 1941, 16.

Chapter 19

1. "Battle Cry: 'Infamy' A Day to Remember," (http://seahawks.com/news/aspx?id=16946), accessed November 29, 2010.
2. Frank Graham, Jr., "The Day the War Came to the Polo Grounds," *Sports Illustrated*, October 24, 1966.
3. Terry Frei, Third Down and a War to Go (Madison, WI: Wisconsin Historical Society Press, 2005), 99.
4. "National Defense: Army," *Time*, October 28, 1940, 19.
5. Lake Cyphers, "The Lost Hero," *New York Daily News*, February 25, 2001.
6. Newell, From Playing Field to Battlefield, 77.
7. Gus Schrader, "Gassin' With Gus," *Iowa City Iowan*, October 20, 1945.
8. Robert F. Dorr, B-24 Liberator Units of the Pacific War (Osprey Publishing, 1999), 37.
9. Bill Yenne, Operation Cobra and the Great Offensive (New York: Pocket Books, 2004), 117-18.
10. "Blozis Was Killed Jan. 21 in France," *New York Times*, April 9, 1945, 14.
11. James F. McIntosh, MD, Wisconsin at War (Wisconsin Veterans Museum Foundation, 2002).
12. Oliver North with Joe Musser, War Stories III (Lanham, MD: National Book Network, 2005), 132.
13. "World Battlefronts: To the Death," *Time*, May 21, 1945, 29.
14. "Okinawa: Roll-Back," *Newsweek*, May 21, 1945, 66-67.
15. James H. Hallas, Killing Ground on Okinawa—The Battle for Sugar Loaf Hill (Annapolis, MD: The Naval Institute Press , 1996), 104.
16. Ibid., 105. See also: George Feifer, Tennozan (New York: Ticknor and Fields, 1992), 309n.; Terry Frei , "Remembering the Fallen Heroes," *ESPN.com*, November 11, 2004 (http://sports.espn.go.com/espn/

print?id=1920697&type=story); Major General Lemuel C. Shepard, Jr., "The Okinawa Campaign," in Pictorial History of World War II, Vol. II (Veterans' Historical Book Service, Inc., 1951), 315-16; and William Manchester, Goodbye, Darkness—A Memoir of the Pacific War (Boston: Little, Brown and Company, 1979), 364.

17. "Mosquito Bowl," *Pacific Stars and Stripes*, August 31, 1986, B8.
18. Frei, Third Down and a War to Go, 146-54.
19. Ibid., 194-97. See also: Ellen D. Goldlust-Gingrich and Kurt Gingrich, "The Letters of Dave Schreiner," *Wisconsin Magazine of History*, Autumn 2003, 41.

Epilogue

1. "Joe Sephus' Cullings, *Cumberland (MD) Sunday Times*, November 24, 1940, 16. See also: Eddie Breitz, "Short Shots," *The Daily Mail*, December 20, 1940.
2. "Coaches Discuss Play," *Cornell Alumni News*, Vol. 47, No. 10, November 15, 1944, 190.
3. "Snavely to Leave," *Cornell Alumni News*, Vol. 47, No. 13, January 1, 1945, 256-7.
4. Rick Brewer, "Justice Was the Major Star, But Snavely Ran the Show," *Car-O-Lines*, October 12, 2006 (http://tarheelblue.cstv.com/sports/m-footbl/spec-rel/101206aa.html).
5. Kane, Good Sports, 321-25.
6. *Cornell Alumni News*, Vol. 48, No. 2, August, 1945, 46.
7. "Schmidt Thru With Bucks Says Paper," *Nebraska State Journal*, November 27, 1940, 11.
8. "Elmer Layden Becomes Pro Football Ruler," *Waterloo (IA) Daily Courier*, February 4, 1941.
9. "National Loop Head Would Alter Pros' 'Unfair' Draft Plan," *Syracuse Herald-American*, December 8, 1940.
10. Schoor, 100 Years of Notre Dame Football, 111.
11. "Skidding the Sport Field With Skid," *Syracuse Herald-Journal*, November 15, 1940, 33.
12. Oslin, Tales From the Boston College Sidelines, 63-69.
13. Jack Thomas, "The Cocoanut Grove Inferno," *Boston Globe*, November 2, 1992.
14. Oslin, Tales From the Boston College Sidelines, 88.
15. Gary Bloomfield, Duty, Honor, Victory, America's Athletes in World War II (Guilford, CT: The Lyons Press), 247.
16. Wolfgang Saxon, "Maurice Britt, 76; Helped Shift Arkansas Politics, *New York Times*, November 29, 1995, D19.
17. Carroll, Dr. Eddie Anderson, 184.
18. Finn and Liestikow, Hawkeye Legends, 74.

19. Gus Schrader, "Gassin' With Gus," *Iowa City Iowan*, October 20, 1945.
20. "Charles Hoskins Killed in Action," *Wisconsin State Journal*, February 23, 1945, 2.
21. "Coach of Bears Forces His Way In Hall of Fame," *Cumberland (MD) Sunday Times*, January 5, 1941, 17.
22. Johnson, The Wow Boys, 177.
23. Jeff Faraudo, "One Day, Two Bay Area Events Make College Football History," *Oakland Tribune,* March 25, 2004.
24. "Luckman Sends Note of Thanks to Shaughnessy," *Wisconsin State Journal*, November 22, 1945, 30.
25. Vinny DiTrani, "Skins View It Beyond 3-D," *Bergen County (NJ) Record*, January 23, 1992.
26. Cullen Murphy, "Fine Points," *The Atlantic*, March 2001.
27. Ron Fimrite, "Nowhere To Hide," *Sports Illustrated*, October 15, 1990.
28. Bill Monahan, "The Colorado-Missouri Snafu Wasn't Unique," *Boston Globe*, October 10, 1990.
29. "Hugh Gallarneau," *College Football Historical Society Newsletter*, Vol. XII, No. IV, August, 1999, 22-24.
30. "Rams Sign Lt. Holovak," *Ironwood (MI) Daily Globe*, December 30, 1944, 8.
31. "Charley O'Rourke Discloses He Will Pass Up Pro Grid," *Miami (OK) Daily News-Record*, January 3, 1941, 4.
32. Rev. Charles F. Donovan, S.J., "Boston College's Boston Priests: An Account of Boston College Men Who Became Priests of the Archdiocese of Boston, 1877-1993," September, 1993, 27.
33. "Tommy Harmon Safe After Crash," *New York Times*, April 18, 1943, 3.
34. "Harmon Describes His Jungle Escape," *New York Times*, April 22, 1943, 10. See also: Pennington, The Heisman, 44.
35. "Search Proves Vain for Harmon's Crew," *New York Times*, May 4, 1943, 5.
36. "Harmon Gets First Zero in a Raid on Hong Kong," *New York Times*, August 29, 1943, 17.
37. "Lt. Tommy Harmon Missing in China," *New York Times*, November 5, 1943, 1.
38. James B. Lane, "Harmon Was Only No. 2 Hero Here," *Gary (IN) Post-Tribune*, January 22, 1998.
39. "Chinese Guerillas Saved Lieut. Harmon," *New York Times*, December 3, 1940, 9.
40. Fredric Alan Maxwell, "The Late Great 98," *Michigan Today* (http://michigantoday.umich.edu/2008/09/harmon.php), accessed November 17, 2008.
41. "Harmon's Parents Give Thanks Twice," *New York Times*, December 1, 1943, 4.
42. "Harmon Cables Parents," *New York Times*, December 8, 1943, 8.
43. Stan Carlson, "Football Players and the War," *College Football Historical Society Newsletter*, Vol. V, No. 4, August 1992, 4. See also: Bloomfield,

Duty, Honor, Victory, 278; and "Capt. Franck Is Saved," *New York Times*, September 8, 1944, 14.

44. Maury White, "George 'Sonny' Franck, Davenport, 1997," *Des Moines Register*, July 6, 1997.
45. Gene "Bear" Carrington, "Who Is John Gunn?" (http://jarheadjocks.com/john_gunn_8.html), accessed February 20, 2010, 4. See also: Richard Goldstein, "A Football Giant Was a Hero at Iwo Jima," *New York Times*, February 19, 2005, D6.
46. "Iwo Jima Still a Vivid Nightmare For Many Iowans," *Des Moines Sunday Register*, February 14, 1965.
47. Author interview with Father William Cantwell, November 22, 2010.
48. Rachel Blount, "Mr. Smith Goes to…Sainthood?" *Minneapolis Star-Tribune*, September 12, 2006.
49. Ibid.
50. Author interview with Father Michael Martin, October 22, 2009.
51. Rachel Blount, "Mr. Smith Goes to…Sainthood?" *Minneapolis Star-Tribune*, September 12, 2006.
52. Gerald Holland, "The Man Who Changed Football," *Sports Illustrated*, February 3, 1964.
53. Dave Shea, "Gogolak Returns to Kicking Roots," *Watertown Daily Times*, August 3, 2010.
54. Bill Pennington, "Georgetown Gets Serious About Football…Seriously," *New York Times*, October 13, 2007.
55. Kane, Good Sports, 51.
56. Michael Weinreb, "Men Among Lions," *Penn Stater*, November/December 2009, 45-51.
57. Whittingham, Rites of Autumn, 199.
58. Gus Schrader, "Red Peppers," *Cedar Rapids (IA) Gazette*, October 22, 1951, 13.
59. Dave Hanson, "Bright Not Bitter: Blow Helped Clean Up Sports," *Des Moines Tribune*, November 13, 1980.
60. Kane, Good Sports, 96-97.
61. Pete Thamel, "For Black Stars, Bittersweet Memories of Sugar Bowl," *New York Times*, January 1, 2006.
62. Michael Oriard, "Pigskin Pioneers," *The Village Voice*, October 10, 2000.
63. William McGurn, "How Hillsdale Beats Harvard," *Wall Street Journal*, June 2, 2009, A19.
64. Darren Everson, "The Game That Changed Alabama," *Wall Street Journal*, December 4, 2009, W6.
65. Joe Mooshil, "Irish Reject Ruling," *Carroll (IA) Times Herald*, November 22, 1961.
66. "Rules Appear to Uphold Claim of League Bosses," *Winnipeg Free Press*, November 22, 1961.
67. Bill Reddy, "Andreas Has No Comment on Notre Dame's Action," *Syracuse Post-Standard*, November 29, 1961, 17.

68. "Notre Dame Source Hints Break In Grid Series With Syracuse," *Morgantown (WVA) Post*, November 24, 1961.
69. "Kuharich Says Irish Consider Book Closed on Syracuse Tilt," *European Stars and Stripes*, December 6, 1961, 19.
70. Ed Crawford, "Buffs Take the Fifth, Beat MU," *Chillicothe (MO) Constitution-Tribune*, October 8, 1990, 10.
71. "Colorado Isn't Ready To Give Up Tainted Victory," *Alton (IL) Telegraph*, October 8, 1990.
72. Arne Green, "Big Eight's Ruling Unfair, But Correct," *Hutchinson News*, October 9, 1990, 7.
73. "Big Eight Officials Suspended, But Colorado's Victory Stands," *Chicago Daily Herald*, October 9, 1990, Sec. 3, 7.
74. "Big Eight Rules Colorado Victory Will Stand," *Hutchinson News*, October 9, 1990, 7.
75. David M. Nelson, "Fifth Down Or Not, It's Over When It's Over," *New York Times*, October 14, 1990.
76. David M. Nelson, The Anatomy of a Game: Football, the Rules, and the Men Who Made the Game (University of Delaware Press, 1994), 214.
77. Mitchell Drucker, "Bradley and Dryden '69 Talk Sports, Politics at C.U.," *Cornell Daily Sun*, September 11, 2009.
78. Carol Kammen, Cornell: Glorious to View (Ithaca, N.Y.: Cornell University Library, 2003.), 125-6.
79. Steve Riach, "Heart of the Matter," *Vype*, October 6, 2008.
80. http://espn.go.com/sportscentury/moments98/nov.html, accessed January 26, 2009.
81. Rick Reilly, "The List to End All Lists," *Sports Illustrated*, October 5, 1999.
82. "Too Deep Zone: 5ᵗʰ-and-40," *Football Outsiders* (http://footballoutsiders.com/walkthrough/2005/too-dep-zone-5th-and-40), accessed January 26, 2009.
83. "1940 Dartmouth v. Cornell-The Five Down Game," (http://collectableivy.wordpress.com/category/cornell/), accessed January 26, 2009.
84. "The Fifth-Down Game," (http://www.baseball-statistics.com/Greats/Century/football-coll.htm), accessed January 26, 2009.
85. Jack Park, The Official Ohio State Football Encyclopedia (Sports Publishing, LLC, 2003), 178-9.
86. Beano Cook, "Beano Cook's Top Ten Moments in College Football," in Michael MacCambridge (ed.), ESPN College Football Encyclopedia (ESPN, 2005).
87. http://www.internationalsport.com/sa_hof/hof_inductees.cfm, accessed January 26, 2009.
88. John Powers, "Sports Debate: When to Cry Foul," *Boston Globe*, September 15, 2007.

INDEX

Roi-Namur 237
Roosevelt, Eleanor 82, 83
Roosevelt, Franklin 30, 31, 33, 35,
     36, 89, 200, 218
Roper, Bill 92
Rose Bowl 1, 6, 7, 18, 19, 21, 23, 24,
     26, 39, 40, 69, 70, 96, 108, 123,
     129, 133, 134, 148, 157, 209,
     211, 213, 216, 217, 219, 231,
     235, 240
Ross, Barney 75, 76
Rottschaefer, Prof. Henry 217
Royal Air Force 35, 36
Ruby, Martin 221
Ruddy, Mike 4, 87, 103, 135, 201
Runyan, Damon 54
Rutgers 74, 79
Ruth, Babe 52, 53
Ryder, Jack 187

S

Sagarin rating system 1
Saggau, Bob 99, 101, 156, 240
Saipan 230, 237
Sanford, Curtis 125
Sanford, Dr. S.V. 72
San Francisco 49ers 237, 238
San Francisco Examiner 20, 213
San Francisco, University of 15, 22,
     23, 65
San Jose State 19
Santa Clara University 15, 19, 22, 23,
     68, 97, 123, 128
Sarnoff, David 41
Sarron, Petey 75
Saturday Evening Post 34, 40, 45
Schmidt, Francis 19, 46, 47, 111, 113,
     115, 116, 119, 120, 121, 129,
     130, 171, 231
Schmuck, Jim 4, 48, 87, 106, 114,
     171, 172, 201, 203
Schoellkopf Field 110, 111, 112, 136,
     231, 234
Schoenfeld, Robert 82
Scholl, Walt 4, 5, 13, 48, 49, 87, 112,

114, 115, 172, 173, 175, 176,
     177, 179, 196, 230
Schrader, Gus 243
Schreiner, Dave 207, 208, 228, 234
Schreiner Hall 233
Schwartz, Marchy 67, 96, 97, 236
Scott, Don 45, 57, 63, 64, 112, 113,
     114, 115, 121, 204, 218, 226,
     233
Sevareid, Eric 34
Seven Blocks of Granite 11, 123, 221
Sewanee 169
Sewell, Bill 69
Seymour, Charles 88
Shaughnessy, Clark 16, 17, 18, 19,
     21, 23, 25, 26, 61, 65, 66, 67,
     68, 69, 70, 88, 119, 133, 134,
     135, 157, 158, 212, 214, 216,
     219, 220, 223, 231, 235, 241
Shaw, Artie 89
Shaw, Buck 19, 20, 23, 68, 97
Sheean, Vincent 31, 34
Sickles, Walt 4, 230
Sidat-Singh, Wilmeth 84, 85, 87, 168,
     225
Silver Gilt 226
Silver Star 140, 214, 226, 230, 239
single wing 12, 13, 21, 229, 236
Sing Sing prison 189
Sinkwich, Frank 102
Sitko, Steve 153
Smith, Bruce 26, 27, 43, 52, 56, 60,
     61, 62, 64, 65, 121, 130, 131,
     139, 140, 142, 149, 208, 209,
     237, 241
Smith, Clipper 19, 97
Smith, Earl "Alabama" 221
Smith, Red 22
Smith, Wilbanks 243
Smith, Wilfrid 59, 115, 118
Snavely, Carl 1, 2, 3, 5, 6, 48, 87,
     105, 106, 109, 110, 113, 114,
     115, 117, 118, 120, 124, 136,
     168, 171, 173, 180, 194, 195,
     196, 197, 229, 236, 247

Wildcat Offense 13
Wildung, Dick 26, 61, 62, 63
Wilkinson, Bud 25, 67
Willey, Dean Malcolm 142
Williams College 100
Williams, Doc 206
Williams, Ed 75
Willkie, Wendell 89, 147, 197
Will, Len 102
Wilson, Woodrow 30
Wisconsin State Journal 207
Wisconsin, University of 97, 153,
 168, 206, 208, 217, 218, 228,
 233, 241
Wojciechowicz, Alex 11, 123
Wolfe, Ray 171, 172, 177
Wolff, Pete 201
Woodruff, Harvey 191
Woodward, Stanley 2
Wooster, College of 120
World Series 5, 45, 188
World's Fair 41
World War I 26, 88
Woronicz, Henry 163
Wow Boys 69
Wright, Alfred 56
Wynne, Chet 97

Y

Yale University 15, 38, 88, 104, 128,
 136, 145, 167, 168, 171, 206,
 210
Yankee Conference 246
Yankee Stadium 71, 95, 100, 234
Yawkey, Tom 104
Yost, Fielding "Hurry Up" 7, 57, 204,
 211, 217
Young, Lou 170, 174, 195
Younglove, Earl 133
Youngstown College 146
Young, Whitney 203
Yourman, Dr. Julius 81

Z

Zabilski, Ed 164, 222
Zanuck, Darryl F. 42
Zivic, Fritzie 75, 76
Zuppke, Bob 21, 54, 55